Detroit Studies in Music Bibliography, No. 77

Editors
J. Bunker and Marilyn S. Clark
University of Kansas

American Organ Music

of the

Twentieth Century

AN ANNOTATED BIBLIOGRAPHY OF COMPOSERS

by

Sharon L. Hettinger

HARMONIE PARK PRESS • MICHIGAN • 1997

Frontispiece:

Hellmuth Wolff organ, op. 40, Bales Recital Hall, University of Kansas, dedicated in a series of recitals, October 1996, including the premiere of two new works. "On James Higdon's recital, the second movement of Stephen Paulus's *Three Temperaments*, commissioned for the dedication, provided an opportunity to enjoy some of the organ's quiet voices. . . . Michael Bauer premiered Charles Hoag's *Oread Concerto* [with the KU Symphony Orchestra], commissioned for the event. The work utilized a wide palette of organ sonorities and avoided the temptation to rely too heavily on the organ's fortissimo capabilities. There were some hauntingly beautiful moments in the second movement, a set of variations on 'The church's one foundation.'" Marilou Kratzenstein, *American Organist* 31/4 (April 1997): 44-45.

Photograph by Doug Koch. Courtesy The University of Kansas, Office of University Relations.

Copyright 1997 by Harmonie Park Press

Printed and bound in the United States of America
Published by
Harmonie Park Press
23630 Pinewood
Warren, Michigan 48091

Editor, J. Bunker Clark
Book Design, Elaine Gorzelski
Typographer, Colleen McRorie

Library of Congress Cataloging-in-Publication Data

Hettinger, Sharon L., 1955-
    American organ music of the twentieth century : an annotated
bibliography of composers / by Sharon L. Hettinger.
        p.   cm. — (Detroit studies in music bibliography ; no. 77)
    Includes bibliographical references and index.
    ISBN 0-89990-076-3
    1. Organ music—United States—20th century—Bio-bibliography-
-Dictionaries. 2. Composers—United States—20th century-
-Biography—Dictionaries.   I. Title.   II. Series.
ML106.U3H47   1997
016.7865'0973—dc21   97-2602

CONTENTS

ACKNOWLEDGMENTS

I could not have written this book without the help and encouragement of my friends and colleagues.

I should like to express my gratitude for the kind assistance of the staff at the University of Kansas libraries, especially Beth Fleming, for her willingness to "go the extra mile" in locating source material.

My thanks also go to J. Bunker Clark, Charles Hoag, Jim Higdon, and Michael Bauer, whose idea it was that I turn my initial research into a book.

My thanks again to J. Bunker Clark for his enthusiasm for this book and keen eye in editing. To my parents Richard and Joyce Simons, my aunt Lois Lamb, and brothers Eric and Rob Simons, who provided encouragement along the way, I render my thanks. My debt is greatest, though, to my husband Lyle, who read the complete manuscript several times, performed household chores, gave encouragement, and provided me the time I needed to finish this book. Without him, it never would have been.

SHARON L. HETTINGER

Lawrence, Kansas
March 1997

INTRODUCTION

Until now, there has been no compilation of bibliographical material specifically collected about American organ composers and their works. This book deals with those born after 1900. Generally, this information is located in numerous sources, making research particularly time-consuming. Corliss R. Arnold's book *Organ Literature: A Comprehensive Survey* (1973; 2nd ed., 1984) includes an overview of American organ composers in its historical section, and alphabetically lists numerous international composers and their works. *Music Index* (1949-) provides bibliographical citations about composers, but it is not annotated.

This book extends beyond both of these and other similar sources, and fills a bibliographical need for organists and scholars of organ music. It provides the reader with a short biography, sources of biographical data, and annotated bibliographical information about the composers and their organ works. If no specific information could be located about a composer's organ music output, then articles discussing overall compositional style or approach to composition are included. (An * in the bibliography indicates that I did not personally see the article.) This book does not include a listing of the composer's organ works; instead it provides commentary on literature written about the composer, the composer's works, or the composer's style of composition. Although some include no specific references to their compositions, titles may be found in the recent book by Arnold.

The following references provided stepping stones to many other fruitful sources: Arnold's *Organ Literature*, *Music Index*, *New Grove Dictionary of American Music* (1986), Storm Bull's *Index to Biographies of Contemporary Composers* (1964-87), Aaron Cohen's *International Encyclopedia of Women Composers* (1981), and recent issues of organ journals, especially *Diapason* and *American Organist*.

To be included in this book, the composer's name was generally located in one of the sources listed above. A 1993 cut-off date (with a few exceptions) was used because *Music Index* was incomplete after that year when I finished this book. The term "American" here refers to anyone born in the United States, to those of American parentage born elsewhere, or to those who have become naturalized citizens of the United States. "Organ composers" refers to those who have written works for solo organ, organ in chamber ensembles, or who have composed works with "organ" in the title, e.g., *Symphony for Organ*.

Although well-known composers have a wealth of information written about their works, lesser-known composers are not as fortunate. Some lesser-known composers, and indeed their music, may be familiar to organists; authors, however, have not written about them or their works. In several instances, no bibliographical information at all could be located. Instead of dismissing them as insignificant, their names are retained here as suggestions for future investigation.

As many of the composers listed in this bibliography are still living, opportunities to discuss their works abound. To discover additional composers and new organ works composed after 1990, literature may be located by using *Music Index* (CD-ROM is now available for 1979-95; updates appear annually), *Dissertation Abstracts* (also on CD-ROM), current organ, church music, theory, and music education journals, as well as catalogs of new music.

Several broad themes about the nature of American organ composition emerge from this bibliography. First, historians on twentieth-century music appear to be reluctant (or reticent) to discuss organ works of Americans. Why? Perhaps the organ looms as too forbidding. This lack of discussion and analysis of organ compositions has essentially relegated to relative oblivion numerous composers who otherwise might have gained greater recognition among their colleagues and organists. When little or nothing is written about a work, other than its premiere, there is little or no interest on the part of other performers. On the other hand, the more information known about new organ pieces, including formal analyses, background, and other information, the greater the motivation for individuals to consider these new works for programming. Providing this data encourages more performances of those pieces by organists.

Second, six main American institutions of composition seem to dominate the field of composers herein. The Eastman School of Music is represented by 46 individuals, Union Theological Seminary (closed in 1973) by 43, the University of Michigan by 32, Yale University by 19, and Curtis Institute of Music by 13. Professors of composition at these six institutions who have significantly influenced contemporary organ composers are Howard Hanson, Bernard Rogers, Roger Sessions, Harold Friedell, Normand Lockwood, Seth Bingham, Searle Wright, Roy Harris, Joseph Goodman, Ross Lee Finney, Leslie Bassett, Leo Sowerby, Quincy Porter, Paul Hindemith, and Rosario Scalero. The following list gives names of teachers (with dates of teaching), and their students who have composed music for organ.

Not an American institution, but nonetheless a major influence keenly felt on the pens of many American composers, is Nadia Boulanger. More than a tenth of all the composers represented (33 of 324) studied with her in France. Additional French composers also influenced American writers: Dupré, Widor, Langlais, and Honegger. Other American composers studied abroad with their mentors in Germany, Belgium, and the former Czechoslovakia, to name a few countries.

Teachers/Students

CURTIS INSTITUTE OF MUSIC

Vittorio Giannini, 1956-65
Luigi Zaninelli

Joseph Lhevinne, n.d.
Richard Purvis

Bohuslav Martinů, 1955-56
Luigi Zaninelli

Gian Carlo Menotti, 1941-45
Luigi Zaninelli

Rosario Scalero, 1924-33, 1935-46
Samuel Barber
Gian-Carlo Menotti

Lucas Foss
Ned Rorem

unknown
Charles E. Callahan, Jr.
David N. Johnson
Rudolph Kremer
Vincent Persichetti
Gordon Young

other teachers
Isadore Freed, 1924-25
Ned Rorem, 1980-86
John Weaver, 1971
Luigi Zaninelli, 1952-58

EASTMAN SCHOOL OF MUSIC

Samuel Adler, since 1966
Thomas C. Crawford
Karen Griebling-Long
David Isele
Paul Thomas (at North Texas State University)
Walter Watson (at North Texas State University)

Warren Benson, since 1967
Karen Griebling-Long

Aaron Copland, n.d.
Samuel Adler
Edmund Haines
Robert Ward

Henry Cowell, n.d.
Gerald Kemner

Herbert Elwell, summers before 1945
Rosemary Clarke-Naus

Howard Hanson, 1924-64
Wayne Barlow
Thomas Canning
Robert Crane
Leon Dallin
Emma Lou Diemer
John Diercks
Anthony Donato
Paul Earls
Edmund Haines
Thomas S. Huston
Herbert Inch
Dorothy James
Ulysses S. Kay
Homer Keller

Gerald Kemner
Kent Kennan
John LaMontaine
Gardner Read
Margaret Sandresky
Robert Ward
Richard Wienhorst

Alan Hovhaness, n.d.
John Diercks
Mary Jeanne Van Appledorn

John LaMontaine, 1964-65
Robert Morris

Fred Lehrdahl, n.d.
Thomas Crawford

Burrill Phillips, 1933-49, 1965-66
Thomas S. Huston
Lloyd Pfautsch

Bernard Rogers, 1929-67
Wayne Barlow
Thomas Canning
Rosemary Clarke-Naus
Robert Crane
Leon Dallin
David Diamond
Emma Lou Diemer
John Diercks
Anthony Donato
Paul Earls
Edmund Haines
Thomas S. Huston
Ulysses S. Kay
Homer Keller
Gerald Kemner
Kent Kennan
Gail Kubik
John LaMontaine
Robert Morris

Kevin Norris
Gardner Read
Margaret Sandresky
Mary Jeanne Van Appledorn
Robert Ward
Norma Wendelburg
Richard Wienhorst

Edward Royce, 1923-47
Anthony Donato
Herbert Inch
Gail Kubik
Robert Ward

Joseph Schwanter, since 1970
Thomas C. Crawford
Karen Griebling-Long

Francis Tursi, n.d.
Karen Griebling-Long

Paul Whiter, 1935-73
Gardner Read

unknown
John Boda
Paul Bunjes
Edward Diemente
Richard Gore
Dan Locklair
Orpha Ochse
Alma Oncley
Russell Peck
Carl Schalk
Brian Schober
Robert Swift
Richard Warner

other teachers
Wayne Barlow, 1937-78
Thomas Canning, before 1963
Herbert Inch, unknown

JUILLIARD SCHOOL OF MUSIC

William Bergsma, 1946-63
Pozzi Escot
Marga Richter
Conrad Susa

Luciano Berio, 1965-66, 1967-71
Carman Moore

Ernest Bloch, n.d.
Dianne Goolkasian-Rahbee

Elliott Carter, since 1967
Ellen Zwilich

David Diamond, since 1973
Clare Shore

Arnold Fish, n.d.
Dianne Goolkasian-Rahbee

Vittorio Giannini, 1939-56
Dianne Goolkasian-Rahbee
Robert Hebble

Rubin Goldmark, 1924-36
Henry Dreyfus Brant
Vittorio Giannini
Julia Smith

Frederick Jacobi, 1936-50
Julia Smith

Alton Jones, 1921-71
Dianne Goolkasian-Rahbee

Otto Luening, 1971-73
Judith Shatin
Searle Wright

Peter Mennin, 1947-58
Robert Parris

Hall Overton, 1960-71
Judith Shatin

Vincent Persichetti, 1947-87
Carman Moore
Alice Parker
Marga Richter
McNeil Robinson
Clare Shore
Conrad Susa

Roger Sessions, 1965-85
Robert Hebble
Myron Roberts
Clare Shore
Ellen Zwilich

Robert Starer, 1949-74
Dianne Goolkasian-Rahbee

Albert Stoessel, 1927-43
Isa McIlwraith

Bernard Wagenaar, 1925-68
Harold Friedell
John LaMontaine
Ned Rorem
Julia Smith

Hugo Weisgall, 1957-70
Dianne Goolkasian-Rahbee

unknown
Norman Dello Joio
Ellis Kohs
Mathilde McKinney
Harold Stover

other teachers
Esther Ballou, ca. 1943-59
Henry Dreyfus Brant, 1947-54
Harold Friedell, n.d.

Gerre Hancock, since 1971
Anthony Newman, 1967-74
Julia Smith, 1940-42
Robert Ward, 1946-56

UNION THEOLOGICAL SEMINARY
(closed in 1973)

Robert Baker, 1946-73
George Brandon
James Tallis
John Weaver

Seth Bingham, 1920-65
Robert Anderson
Corliss Arnold
James Boeringer
David Gehrenbeck
Everett Jay Hilty
Isa McIlwraith
Robert Powell
Ralph Schultz
Morgan Simmons
Samuel Walter

Frank Bohnhorst, n.d.
Robert Anderson

Clarence Dickinson, 1912-45
Roberta Bitgood

Harold Friedell, n.d.
Robert Anderson
George Brandon
William B. Cooper
Adel Heinrich
John Huston
Jack Ossewaarde
Richard Peek
Lloyd Pfautsch

Robert Powell
Morgan Simmons
Gwyneth Walker

Joseph Goodman, 1959-73
Larry King
Dan Locklair
Richard Stewart
John Weaver

Normand Lockwood, 1945-53
Corliss Arnold
Frank Bohnhorst
Wilbur Held
Everett Hilty
Eunice Kettering
Jack Ossewaarde
Richard Peek
Searle Wright

Hugh Porter, 1931-60
Gerre Hancock
Adel Heinrich

Wallingford Riegger, n.d.
Wilbur Held

Edwin Stringham, 1930-38
Robert Crandell
Eunice Kettering
Myron Roberts

David McK. Williams, n.d.
Roberta Bitgood
Harold Friedell
Jack Ossewaarde

M. Searle Wright, n.d.
George Brandon
David Gehrenbeck
Gwyneth Walker

unknown
Philip Baker
W. Lawrence Curry
Eugene Hancock

Alice Jordan
Austin Lovelace
Donald McAfee
Alma Oncley

other teachers
Robert Crandell, 1962-71
David Gehrenbeck, 1965-71
John Huston, ca. 1942-73
Austin Lovelace, 1963
Samuel Walter, 1957-65
Louie White, 1964-72
Henry Woodward, summer sessions
Alec Wyton, 1956-73

UNIVERSITY OF MICHIGAN

Gerald Bales, n.d.
Gerald Near

Leslie Bassett, since 1952
William Albright
Thomas Janson
Peter Klausmeyer
Robert Morris
Gerald Near
Russell Peck
Richard Toensing

George Cacioppo, 1968-73
Peter Klausmeyer

Ross Lee Finney, 1949-73
William Albright
Leslie Bassett
Edith Borroff
George Cacioppo
George Crumb
Thomas Janson

Peter Klausmeyer
Robert Morris
Alice Parker (at Smith College)
Russell Peck
Ralph Schultz
Richard Toensing
Norma Wendelburg

Hunter Johnson, 1929-33
Robert Crandell
Everett Jay Hilty
Kent Kennan

Eugene Kurtz, 1967-68, 1970-71, 1973-74
Robert Morris

Guy Maier, 1924-31
Elizabeth Gould

George Balch Wilson, since 1961
Peter Klausmeyer
Richard Toensing

unknown
Paul Bunjes
Donald Busarow
Thomas Gieschen
Raymond Haan
Eugene Hancock
Normand Lockwood
Madra Oliver
Jack Ossewaarde

other teachers
William Albright, since 1970
Wallace Berry, 1957-77
William Bolcom, since 1973
Paul Cooper, 1955-67
Robert Crandell, 1932-34
Edmund Haines, 1941-47
Homer Keller, 1947-54
David Raksin, n.d.

YALE UNIVERSITY

Leroy Baumgartner, n.d.
Paul Thomas

Richard F. Donovan, 1947-60
James Beale
Emma Lou Diemer
Carl Staplin
Yehudi Wyner

Paul Hindemith, 1940-53
Kenton Coe
Norman Dello Joio
Emma Lou Diemer
Alvin Etler
Paul Fetler
Lukas Foss
Joseph Goodman
Robert Noehren
Ruth Schonthal-Seckel
Yehudi Wyner

Quincy Porter, 1946-65
Kenton Coe
Paul Fetler
Robert Hebble
Gerald Kemner
Paul Thomas

other teachers
Alvin Etler, 1942-46
Gerre Hancock, since 1974
David Hurd, Jr. (Institute of Sacred Music),
    n.d.
Robert Morris, since 1969
Alice Parker, 1958-73
Gunther Schuller, 1946-47
Peter P. Stearns, 1964-65
Yehudi Wyner, 1964-77

FRENCH INFLUENCE

Nadia Boulanger
Corliss Arnold
Leslie Bassett
Herman Berlinski
Wallace Berry

Kenton Coe
David Joseph Conte
Paul Cooper
Aaron Copland
Robert Crandell

Robert Crane
David Diamond
Cecil Effinger
Donald Erb
Ross Lee Finney
Irwin Fischer
Gerre Hancock
Robert Hebble
Karel Husa
Robert Karlén
Homer Keller
Gail Kubik
John LaMontaine
Normand Lockwood
Donald McAfee
Robert Moevs
Daniel Pinkham
Stanley Saxton
Norma Strandberg
Louise Talma
Samuel Walter
Richard Wienhorst
Henry Woodward

Joseph Bonnet
Searle Wright

Charles Courboin (Belgian; in U.S. from 1920)
Frederick Tulan

Jeanne Demessieux
Frederick Tulan

Marcel Dupré
Charles DeWitt Coleman
Wilbur Held
Clarence Watters

Noël Gallon
Lukas Foss

Hugh Giles
Frederick Tulan

Arthur Honegger
Karel Husa
Homer Keller
Robert Parris
Daniel Pinkham

Vincent d'Indy
Isadore Freed

Jean Langlais
Corliss Arnold
Gerre Hancock
Adel Heinrich
Robert Scoggin

Henri Libert
Alexander Schreiner

Olivier Messiaen
William Albright
Brian Schober

Darius Milhaud
Walter Watson

Louis Vierne
Isadore Freed
Alexander Schreiner

Charles-Marie Widor
Alexander Schreiner

American Conservatory-Fontainebleau
Carl Parrish

École Normale de Musique
Anthony Newman

Introduction

Guilmant Organ School—New York
Roberta Bitgood
Harold Friedell

Paris Conservatory
William Bolcom
Richard Felciano

Longtime resident of France
Ned Rorem

other teacher
Louise Talma—five summers at the American
Conservatory, Paris

Third, throughout the course of this century, a visibly-reduced interest in the arts and humanities is evidenced by the declining number of composers for the organ. Of the 324 composers listed in this bibliography, 262 were born between 1900 and 1939. Composers born after 1940 number only 62. The number of women composing for organ has increased only 5%. The ratio of men to women was 5:1 before 1940, and after 1940 the ratio is 4:1. Colette S. Ripley, author of *Organ Music of Women Composers*, stated to me that women spend more time out of the house working, transporting children, caring for aging parents, tending to household business, than composing. Composing sometimes appears to be overwhelmed by numerous other activities—certainly true for the male population, too.

What is the reason for the decline in the overall number of composers for organ? This problem is not just a composition problem, but also societal and cultural. We no longer have "organ composers" but instead have composers who write for all media, and if they are interested they write for the organ. What, then, holds the composer back from writing for organ? Is it the complexity of the instrument? a lack of interest? a lack of instruction on timbres and pitch of the stops? Is it still perceived as only a "church" instrument and not a recital instrument? Have organists made church organ music and organ recital music synonymous? Are job descriptions for organists more complex and more comprehensive—positions that include a ministry other than music, such as youth director, seniors' advisor, or some other area of ministry—thereby not allowing the musician to function totally as musician? The answer may be one or all of these possibilities. Composers may be waiting for organists to commission them. (Organists should follow Marilyn Mason's fine example of commissioning a new work each year.) Perhaps organists need to make themselves available to theory and composition professors and students to demonstrate the wide array of possibilities available to composers, and thereby encourage more works to be written. And maybe organists should consider taking pen to paper and creating their own works, or recording some improvisations for transcription into notation.

In France, the Roman Catholic church's musical tradition is extremely vital to organ composition. The long history of organ improvisation is deeply embedded in the French tradition, and training for organists always includes comprehensive work in improvising. In America, students are generally taught to adhere to the notes on the page, but very little about improvisation is taught, tried, or discussed. In fact, students who "fool around" are discouraged to do so by their teachers; nonetheless, this should be encouraged and cultivated in our students from an early age.

If, however, new works are unnoticed or unheard, perhaps marketing, publicity, and sales strategies need to be altered. Too many times one can seek "new" music, only to find that the "new" music is a new edition or a re-publication of an old work, music that has been recently imported, or the copyright date ten years old! Some stores will not order new music because they "haven't heard of the composer before," and therefore the music will not be "saleable." This, of course, relates to the scarcity of articles on new music, but organists can also demand that their retailer stock new works. Retailers of organ music can keep up to date through trade journals (*American Organist* and *Diapason*) and order new publications based on information gleaned from these journals. Additionally, a number of retailers are subscribers to new issues of organ music. Their subscription membership guarantees publishers a certain quantity of new music sales. Currently, nearly 3500 retailers subscribe to new issues, guaranteeing that when new works are published, the first run printed will be a minimum of 3500. Some scores, too, may be available only through a rental agency: these agencies need to have a more highly visible advertising campaign (in organ journals). Other scores may be available only in manuscript. The cost of renting scores may be fairly prohibitive and may prevent organists from using them. These, too, however, must be made known to organists so that they may request them for perusal.

Publishers of new organ works look for various elements. Elkan-Vogel, a subsidiary of Theodore Presser, indicated to me that several factors are weighed in the evaluation of a piece: is it a strong piece? will people buy it? will it be profitable? is the composer known? Concordia Publishing House, on the other hand, indicated that 85-90% of the music published there is hymn- or scripture-based. Although some works are recital pieces, most are for worship settings. Concordia looks for original and creative writing within traditional bounds. Morning Star Music, a fairly new publisher, is publishing work accessible to the church musician, both hymn- and non-hymn-based, shorter (2-3 minutes), and functional, with the level of difficulty not as demanding, because "the level of playing is decreasing." Should organists be satisfied with these options? Organists need to encourage composers to write for the instrument and to submit to numerous publishers. Additionally, with computer software available today, composers can typeset and publish their own music and provide it at a lower cost.

Supplemental to all of these factors, the organist must be willing to perform new music. Some get "stuck" with the tried and true, and just "get by" with the "oldies" for recitals. Some don't want to be stretched in their own thinking and playing. These individuals need to be encouraged to perform the latest printed works in their field. Many new works for organ are exciting and of excellent quality. Although a cursory glance can often yield the composer's means of composition, sometimes a deeper study of the work is required to determine the composer's method of composition for the best interpretation. If organists are not willing to perform new works created for them, then there is no reason to decry the lack of new repertory.

ASCAP Membership of Organ Composers
Included in This Bibliography

from ASCAP List of Members (1994), *which includes those both living and deceased*

Samuel Adler
William Albright
Ronald Arnatt
Franklin D. Ashdown
Philip E. Baker
Samuel Barber
Wayne Barlow
Herman Berlinski
Herbert Bielawa
Roberta Bitgood
Harriet Bolz
Radie Britain
Stephen Douglas Burton
Ann Hampton Callaway
Augusta N. Cecconi-Bates
Paul Cooper
William Benjamin Cooper
Aaron Copland
R. Evan Copley
Robert V. Crane
Paul Creston
Robert M. Cundick
W. Lawrence Curry
Curtis Otto B. Curtis-Smith
Noel Da Costa
Leon Dallin
Norman Dello Joio
Stefania B. Denbow
Edward Diemente
Emma Lou Diemer
John H. Diercks, Jr.
Richard W. Dirksen
Paul H. Earls
Cecil Effinger
Merrill Ellis
Robert Elmore
Richard Felciano
William Ferris
Paul Fetler
Ross Lee Finney
Isadore Freed
Harold W. Friedell

Herbert Fromm
Vittorio Giannini
Noel Goemanne
Joseph Goodman
Jack Gottlieb
Elizabeth D. Gould
Raymond H. Haan
Edmund Haines
Paul R. Hamill
Eugene Hancock
Jackson Hill
Charles K. Hoag
Thomas Janson
Donald C. Johns
Robert W. Jones
Alice Yost Jordan
Robert A. Karlén
Gerald E. Kemner
Kent Kennan
Ann S. Ker
Barbara A. Kolb
Gerhard W. Krapf
Gail Kubik
John LaMontaine
Elizabeth (Libby) Larsen
Mary Weldon Leahy
Dan Steven Locklair
Page C. Long
Austin C. Lovelace
Charles R. McHugh
August Maekelberghe
Ada Belle Gross Marcus
Thomas Matthews
Robert Moevs
Carman Moore
Shirley Munger
Gerald Near
Vaclav Nelhybel
Anthony Newman
James F. Niblock
Jack H. Ossewaarde
Alice Parker

Russell J. Peck
C. Alexander Peloquin
Ronald C. Perera
Vincent Persichetti
Lloyd Pfautsch
Boris Pillin
Robert J. Powell
Richard Purvis
Gardner Read
Marga Richter
Ned Rorem
Stanley Saxton
William J. Schmidt, Jr.
Ruth Schonthal Seckel
Alexander Schreiner
Rudy Shackelford
Clare Shore
Paul J. Sifler
Julia Smith
Lani Smith
Harold M. Stover
Newton D. Strandberg
Conrad Susa
William Sydeman
Louise Talma
Paul Lindsley Thomas
Mary Jeanne Van Appledorn
Gwyneth V. Walker
Walter R. Watson
David A. Wehr
Norma Wendelburg
Robert P. Wetzler
Gary C. White
Maurice C. Whitney
David H. Williams
Betty R. Wishart
Dale Wood
M. Searle Wright
Alec Wyton
Gordon Young
Luigi Zaninelli
Marilyn Ziffrin

CHRONOLOGICAL LIST OF COMPOSERS BY BIRTH

Unknown birth years
Marion Dunn
Thomas Richner

b. 1900
Aaron Copland (d. 1990)
Isadore Freed (d. 1960)
Henry J. Markworth (d. 1953)

b. 1901
Dorothy E. James (d. 1982)
Alexander Schreiner (d. 1987)

b. 1902
Clarence Watters (d. 1986)

b. 1903
Radie Britain (d. 1994)
Irwin Fischer (d. 1977)
Beatrice Fisk
Vittorio Giannini (d. 1966)

b. 1904
Guy H. Eldridge, Jr. (d. 1976)
Elizabeth Davies Gould (Hochman)
Herbert Reynolds Inch (d. 1988)
Mathilde McKinney
Clarence V. Mader (d. 1971)
Alma Oncley
Carl Parrish (d. 1965)
Stanley Saxton

b. 1905
Harold Friedell (d. 1958)
Herbert Fromm
Madra Emogene Oliver
Oliver Nelson Russell (d. 1989)

b. 1906
Glenn Winston Cassler
Paul Creston (d. 1985)
W. Lawrence Curry (d. 1966)
Ross Lee Finney (d. 1997)
Eunice Lea Kettering
Normand Lockwood
Louise Juliette Talma (d. 1996)

b. 1908
Roberta Bitgood
Myron D. Casner (d. 1992)
Richard T. Gore (d. 1994)
Halsey Stevens (d. 1989)
John Verrall
Richard Warner
Henry Lynde Woodward

b. 1909
Robert Leech Bedell (d. 1974)
Jan Oskar Bender (d. 1994)
Anthony Donato
Isa Roberta McIlwraith
August Maekelberghe (d. 1975)
Maurice C. Whitney (d. 1984)

b. 1910
Samuel Barber (d. 1981)
Herman Berlinski
Robert Crandell (d. 1976)
Everett Jay Hilty
Robert Noehren
Joseph Roff (d. 1993)

b. 1911
Yuri Arbatsky (d. 1963)
Thomas Canning
Alan Hovhaness
Robert McBridge
Gian-Carlo Menotti
Paul J. Sifler
Julia Frances Smith (d. 1989)

b. 1912
Aksel Andersen (d. 1977)
Wayne Barlow
Harriet Hallock Bolz
Rayner Brown
John Cage (d. 1992)
Heinrich Fleischer
Hugo Gehrke (d. 1992)
Lindsay Arthur Lafford
Claude Means
David Raksin
Myron J. Roberts

b. 1913
Henry Dreyfus Brant
Norman Dello Joio
Robert Hall Elmore (d. 1985)
Alvin Derald Etler (d. 1973)
Kent Wheeler Kennan
Gardner Read
Leland B. Sateren

b. 1914
Paul J. Bunjes
Cecil Effinger (d. 1990)

Nancy Plummer Faxon
Edmund Thomas Haines (d. 1974)
Wilbur Held
William Kroeger
Gail Kubik (d. 1984)
Ludwig Lenel
Zenobia Powell Perry
Martin Stellhorn

b. 1915
Esther Ballou (d. 1973)
David Diamond
John Huston (d. 1975)
Homer Keller
Thomas Matthews
Vincent Persichetti (d. 1987)

b. 1916
Stefania Bjørnson Denbow
Merrill Ellis (d. 1981)
Thomas Scott Huston, Jr. (d. 1991)
Alice Yost Jordan
Ellis Bonoff Kohs
Samuel Walter (d. 1987)

b. 1917
Victor Hildner
Ulysses Simpson Kay (d. 1995)
James Niblock
Vivian Daphne Phillips
Richard Purvis (d. 1994)
Robert Eugene Ward

b. 1918
Paul Bouman
John Cook (d. 1984)
Leon Dallin
Joseph Goodman
Jack Herman Ossewaarde
Alexander Peloquin
Norma Ruth Wendelburg
Searle Wright

b. 1919
Robert Crane
Austin Lovelace
Paul O. Manz
Vaclav Nelhybel (d. 1996)
Newman Powell
David H. Williams
Gordon Young

b. 1920
William Benjamin Cooper (d. 1993)
Paul Fetler
John LaMontaine
Robert W. Moevs
Richard Wienhorst

b. 1921
Rosemary Clarke-Naus
Richard Dirksen
Jack C. Goode
Karel Husa
Lloyd Pfautsch
Margaret Vardell Sandresky
Newton D. Strandberg
Louis L. White (d. 1979)
Alec Wyton

b. 1922
John Boda
Gerhard Brand
Lukas Foss
David N. Johnson (d. 1987)

b. 1923
Leslie Bassett
Frank R. Bohnhorst (d. 1956)
Lee Hastings Bristol, Jr. (d. 1979)
Edward Diemente
Richard Hillert
Robert A. Karlén
Marian McLaughlin (d. 1982)

Dika Newlin
Daniel Rogers Pinkham
Ned Rorem

b. 1924
James Beale
Arthur Alfred Birkby
George Brandon
Richard Albert Hudson
Gerhard Krapf
Gladys Nordenstrom
Robert Parris
Peter Sandloff
Ruth Esther Schonthal-Seckel

b. 1925
Edith Borroff
James Engel (d. 1989)
Philip Gehring
Shirley Munger
Orpha Ochse
Alice Parker
Gunther Schuller

b. 1926
Corliss R. Arnold
Charles DeWitt Coleman (d. 1991)
Paul Cooper (d. 1996)
Robert Milton Cundick
Noel Goemanne
Adel Verna Heinrich
Donald Charles Johns
Mary Weldon Leahy
Daniel Moe
Walter L. Pelz
Vera Nicolaevena Preobrajenska
Marga Richter
Harald Rohlig
William Schmidt, Jr.
Marilyn Jane Ziffrin

Chronological List of Composers by Birth

b. 1927
George Cacioppo (d. 1984)
Emma Lou Diemer
John H. Diercks
Donald Erb
Jacob Frederic Goossen
Rudolph Joseph Kremer
Richard Peek
David William Smart
Mary Jeanne Van Appledorn
Alan D. Walker
Tikey A. Zes

b. 1928
Samuel Adler
Wallace Berry (d. 1991)
Sam Batt Owens
William T. Sydeman

b. 1929
Theodore Beck
George Crumb
Noel George DaCosta
Lester H. Groom
Eugene Hancock (d. 1994)
Ada Belle Gross Marcus
Carl Schalk
Morgan F. Simmons
Paul Lindsley Thomas
Yehudi Wyner

b. 1930
Ronald K. Arnatt
Herbert W. Bielawa
James Boeringer
Evan Copley
Richard Felciano
Jack S. Gottlieb
Paul Robert Hamill
Ruth Lomon
Robert E. Scoggin

b. 1931
David Maulsby Gehrenbeck
Thomas Gieschen
Charles Kelso Hoag
Peter Pindar Stearns
Christopher Uehlein
Harold Vetter

b. 1932
Kenton Coe
Milton Gill (d. 1968)
Robert W. Jones
Gerald Kemner
Larry Peyton King (d. 1990)
Robert Jennings Powell
Ralph C. Schultz
Alan B. Stout
James H. Tallis (d. 1969)
Wilmer Hayden Welsh
Robert Paul Wetzler
Scott S. Withrow (d. 1993)
Luigi J. Zaninelli

b. 1933
Augusta Cecconi-Bates
Pozzi Escot
Page Long
Walter Robert Watson

b. 1934
Robert T. Anderson
Philip E. Baker
Donald A. Busarow
Paul Earls
Gerre Hancock
Robert Christian Hebble
Lani Smith
Carl Bayard Staplin
Frederick Thomas Tulan
David August Wehr
Dale Wood

b. 1935
Donald McAfee
Conrad Susa

b. 1936
Carman LeRoy Moore
Charles William Ore
Elliot Shelling Schwartz
Darwin Wolford

b. 1937
William Ferris
Ann S. Ker
Richard Proulx
John B. Weaver
Gary C. White

b. 1938
William Bolcom
Dianne Goolkasian-Rahbee
Raymond H. Haan
George Calvin Hampton (d. 1984)
Jere Hutcheson
Charles Wuorinen

b. 1939
Fred Bock
Barbara Kolb
Kenneth D. Lowenberg
Kevin Edward Norris
Michael E. Young [OL 95, b. 1942]
Ellen Taaffe Zwilich

b. 1940
Charles R. McHugh
Boris William Pillin
Robert F. Swift
Richard Toensing

b. 1941
Curtis Otto Curtis-Smith

Jackson Hill
Gilbert Martin
Anthony Newman
Ronald Christopher Perrera

b. 1942
Franklin D. Ashdown
Robert Cuckson
Peter Ballard Klausmeyer
Gerald Near
Richard Stewart

b. 1943
Wayne Burcham
Stephen Douglas Burton
Robert Daniel Morris
McNeil Robinson
Joseph Schwantner

b. 1944
William Hugh Albright
Rudy Shackelford
Randall Snyder

b. 1945
David H. Hegarty
Russell James Peck

b. 1946
David Clark Isele
Marilyn Shrude
Harold M. Stover

b. 1947
John Anthony Celona
Thomas Janson
Dennis Michael Lovinfosse
James Melby
David A. Schack
Gwyneth van Anden Walker
Betty Rose Wishart

b. 1948
Stuart S. Smith

b. 1949
Ann Callaway
Clay Christiansen
Mary Jane Leach
Dan S. Locklair
Stephen Paulus
William John Schneider
Judith Allen Shatin

b. 1950
Raymond Hulet Chenault
David Hurd, Jr.
Libby Larsen

b. 1951
Charles E. Callahan, Jr.

Brian Schober
Deborah Teason

b. 1952
George W. Drumwright, Jr.

b. 1954
Clare Shore

b. 1955
David Joseph Conte
Pamela Decker

b. 1956
Thomas C. Crawford
Ellen Harrison

b. 1957
David Mark Cherwien
Karen Jean Griebling-Long

ABBREVIATIONS OF SOURCES

AA73   Kyle, Marguerite Kelly, comp. "The Composer Amer-Allegro." *Pan Pipes of Sigma Alpha Iota* 65/2 (January 1973): 38-80.

ABD   Anderson, E. Ruth. *Contemporary American Composers: A Biographical Dictionary*. Boston: G. K. Hall, 1976.

ABDad   Addendum to ABD.

ACA   *American Composers Alliance Bulletin*. New York, from 1951. Listed as ACA plus volume and number.

AFR   Southern, Eileen. *Biographical Dictionary of Afro-American and African Musicians*. Westport: Greenwood, 1982.

AMH   Pavlakis, Christopher. *The American Music Handbook*. New York: Free Press, 1974.

AS66   *The ASCAP Biographical Dictionary of Composers, Authors and Publishers.* Comp. and ed. by the Lynn Farnol Group. New York: American Society of Composers, Authors and Publishers, 1966.

ASC   *The ASCAP Biographical Dictionary of Composers, Authors, and Publishers.* 2nd ed. Ed. Daniel McNamara. New York: Thomas Y. Crowell, 1952.

ASUC   *American Society of University Composers*. New York: Columbia University, 1966-69.

BB58   *Baker's Biographical Dictionary of Musicians.* 5th ed. Ed. Nicolas Slonimsky. New York: G. Schirmer, 1958.

BB65   Baker, Theodore. *Baker's Biographical Dictionary of Musicians.* 1965 supplement to 5th ed. Rev. and enl. Nicolas Slonimsky. New York: G. Schirmer, 1965.

BB71   _____. *Baker's Biographical Dictionary of Musicians.* 1971 supplement to 5th ed. New York: G. Schirmer, 1971.

BB71ad   _____. Addenda and corrigenda to BB71, above. May 1972.

BB78   _____. *Baker's Biographical Dictionary of Musicians.* 6th ed. Ed. Nicolas Slonimsky. New York: Schirmer Books, 1978.

BB92   _____. *Baker's Biographical Dictionary of Musicians.* 8th ed. Ed. Nicolas Slonimsky. New York: Schirmer Books, 1992.

BBCch   BBC Music Library. *Chamber Music Catalogue.* London: British Broadcasting Corporation, 1965.

BBCpo   BBC Music Library. *Piano and Organ Catalogue.* London: British Broadcasting Corporation, 1965.

BCL   *Avant-Garde.* Ontario: Don Mills, 1968.

BCS   *The Black Composer Speaks.* Ed. David N. Baker, Linda M. Belt, and Herman C. Hudson. Metuchen, N.J.: Scarecrow, 1978.

BDA   Claghorn, Charles Eugene. *Biographical Dictionary of American Music.* West Nyack, N.Y.: Parker, 1973.

BMI   *Broadcast Music Inc.* New York: Broadcast Music, various dates of publication.

BS72   *Biographical Sketches of Winners of 1972 BMI Awards to Student Composers.* New York: Broadcast Music, 1973.

CA   *Composers of the Americas.* Washington, D.C.: Pan American Union, from 1959. Listed by volume number, i.e., CA5, CA12.

CACA   Anderson, E. Ruth. *Contemporary American Composers.* Boston: G. K. Hall, 1982.

CACJ   Jacobi, Hugh William. *Contemporary American Composers Based at American Colleges or Universities.* Paradise, Calif.: Paradise Arts, 1975.

CACJsp   Supplement to the above.

CAP   *Composer.* Ed. David H. Cope. Redondo Beach, Calif: Composers' Autograph Publications, 1969.

CC92   *Contemporary Composers.* Ed. Brian Morton and Pamela Collins. Chicago and London: St. James Press, 1992.

CCC   *Catalogue of Canadian Composers.* Rev. ed. Ed. Helmut Kallmann. Canadian Broadcasting Co., ca. 1952.

CCM   *Catalogue of Chamber Music, 1966.* Toronto: Canadian Music Centre, 1966.

CDC   Young, Percy M. *A Critical Dictionary of Composers and Their Music.* London: Dennis Dobson, 1954.

CLA   *Canadian Music Library Association.* Compiled by a committee chaired by Melva J. Dwyer, of the CMLA. Ottawa: Canadian Library Association, 1960-61.

CME   *Contemporary Music in Europe: A Comprehensive Survey.* Ed. Paul Henry Lang and Nathan Broder. New York: G. Schirmer, 1965.

CPM   *Contemporary Piano Music.* Ed. Isadore Freed. Bryn Mawr: Theodore Presser, ca. 1959.

CR   Ripley, Colette S. *Organ Music of Women Composers.* New York: American Guild of Organists, 1994. Based on D.M.A. diss. with the same title, University of Kansas, 1992.

CRI   *Composers Recording Inc.* New York: Composers Recording Inc., various dates. Listed as CRI, plus record number.

DAS   *Directory of American Scholars.* 5th ed. Managing ed., Dorothy Hancock. New York: Jacques Cattell Press/Bowker Co., 1969.

DCM   *Dictionary of Contemporary Music.* Ed. John Vinton. New York: E. P. Dutton, 1974.

DDM   *Dictionnaire de la musique.* Ed. Marc Honegger. Paris: Bordas, 1970.

DN70   *Directory of New Music.* Los Angeles: Crystal Record Co., 1970.

DN72   *Directory of New Music.* Los Angeles: Crystal Record Co., 1972.

DN73   Cunning, Carol. *Composium Directory of New Music.* Los Angeles: Crystal Record Co., 1973.

DN74   Same, 1974.

DN75   Same, 1975.

DN76   Same, 1976.

DN77   Same, 1977.

DN78   Same, 1978.

EDM   *Encyclopédie de la musique.* 3 vols. Ed. François Michel. Paris: Fasquelle, 1958-61.

EJM   Nulman, Macy. *Concise Encyclopedia of Jewish Music.* New York: McGraw-Hill, 1975.

EMC   *Contemporary Music.* Munich: Edition Modern, Musikverlag Hans Wewerka, ca. 1962.

EMS   *Entziklopedichesky Muzükalnüi Slovar.* Ed. B. S. Sheinpress and I. M. Tampolsky. Moscow: Izdatelstvo, 1966.

EVM   *Encyclopedie van de Muziek.* 2 vols. Ed. L. M. G. Arnitzenius, H. H. Badings, J. B. Broeksz, Flor Peeters, E. W. Schallenberg, and Joseph Smits van Waesberghe. Amsterdam: Elsevier, 1956-57.

GD54   *Grove's Dictionary of Music and Musicians.* 5th ed. 9 vols. Ed. Eric Blom. London: Macmillan, 1954.

GD54s   *Grove's Dictionary of Music and Musicians.* Supplementary volume to the 5th ed. Ed. Eric Blom; Denis Stevens, associate editor. New York: St. Martin's Press, 1961.

HHH   *Musikkens Hvem Hvad Hvor.* Ed. Nelly Backhausen and Axel Kjerulf. Copenhagen: Politikens, 1950.

HLM   Herzfeld, Friedrich. *Lexikon der Musik.* Berlin: Allstein, 1961.

IMD   *Katalog der Abteilung Noten.* Darmstadt: Das Institut, 1966.

IMD2   *Noten-Katalog Nachdrag, 1967.* Darmstadt: Das Institut, 1967.

IWC   Cohen, Aaron I. *International Encyclopedia of Women Composers.* 2nd ed. 2 vols. New York: Books and Music, 1987.

IWW92   *International Who's Who in Music and Musicians' Directory.* 13th ed. (1992-93).
Ed. David M. Cummings. Cambridge: International Who's Who in
Music, 1992.

IWW94   *International Who's Who in Music and Musicians' Directory.* 14th ed. (1994-95).
Ed. David M. Cummings. Cambridge: International Who's Who in
Music, 1994.

JCN   Cage, John. *Notations.* New York: Something Else Press, 1969.

KDK   *Kürschners deutscher Musiker-Kalender 1954.* Ed. Hedwig and E. H. Mueller
von Asow. Berlin: Walter de Gruyter, 1954.

KTL   Altmann, Frank. *Kurzgefasstes Tonkunstler-Lexikon.* Ed. Burchard Bulling,
Florian Noetzel, and Helmut Rosner. 2 vols. Wilhelmshaven:
Heinrichshofen Verlag, 1974-78.

LCI   *A Catalogue of Representative Works by Resident Living Composers of Illinois.*
Carbondale: Southern Illinois University, 1960.

LMD   *La musica.* Parte seconda dizionario. Ed. Guido M. Gatti. 2 vols. Turin:
Unione Tipografico-Editrice Torinese, 1968-71.

LMU   Collaer, Paul. *La Musique moderne,* 1905-55. Brussels: Elsevier, 1955.
Transl. Sally Abeles as *History of Modern Music.* New York: World
Publishing Co., 1961.

MEH   *Malá Encyklopédia Hudby.* Ed. Marián Jurik; Ladislav Mokry, chief editor.
Bratislava: Obzor, 1969.

MGG   *Die Musik in Geschichte und Gegenwart.* Ed. Friedrich Blume. Kassel:
Bärenreiter, various dates from 1949.

MGGs   *Die Musik in Geschichte und Gegenwart.* Ed. Friedrich Blume. Kassel:
Bärenreiter, vol. 15 supplement (Aachen-Dyson), 1973; vol. 16 supplement (Earsden-Zweibrücken), 1979.

MHHH   *Musikkens Hved Hvad Hvor.* Ed. Ludvig Ernst Bramsen, Jr. Copenhagen:
Politikens, 1961.

MIC   *Encyclopedia of Music in Canada.* Ed. Helmut Kallmann, Gilles Potvin, and
Kenneth Winters. Toronto: University of Toronto Press, 1981.

MJM   Soltes, Aavraham. *Off the Willows: The Rebirth of Modern Jewish Music.* New York: Bloch, 1970.

MLA   *Index to Music Necrology.* Comp. Janet Roads Pinkowitz and Dale Good, 1977; Barbara Henry, 1979; Patsy Flech Monokowski, 1981; and Karen Nagy, 1982; annually in the June issue of *Notes.*

MLSR   Schwarz, Boris. *Music and Musical Life in Soviet Russia, 1917-1981.* Bloomington: Indiana University Press, 1983.

MNG   *Musik der neuen Generation.* Vienna: Universal Edition, 1968.

NCE   *The New College Encyclopedia of Music.* Ed. J. A. Westrup and F. Ll. Harrison. New York: Norton, 1960.

NG   *The New Grove Dictionary of Music and Musicians.* 20 vols. Ed. Stanley Sadie. London: Macmillan, 1980.

NGA   *The New Grove Dictionary of American Music.* Ed. H. Wiley Hitchcock and Stanley Sadie. 4 vols. London: Macmillan, 1986.

OCM   Scholes, Percy A. *The Oxford Companion to Music.* 10th ed., rev. Ed. John Owen Ward. London: Oxford University Press, 1970.

OL   Arnold, Corliss Richard. *Organ Literature: A Comprehensive Survey.* 2nd ed. 2 vols. Metuchen, N.J.: Scarecrow, 1984.

OL95   _____. *Organ Literature: A Comprehensive Survey.* 3rd ed. 2 vols. Metuchen, N.J.: Scarecrow, 1995.

PAP   *Anadromi. 50 Ekdiloeis.* Athens: Germaniko Institouto Goethe Athinon Ergastiri Sighronis Mousikis, ca. 1971.

PCM   Eagon, Angelo. *Catalog of Published Concert Music by American Composers.* 2nd ed. Metuchen, N.J.: Scarecrow, 1969.

PC71   _____. *Catalog of Published Concert Music by American Composers: Supplement to the Second Edition.* Metuchen, N.J.: Scarecrow, 1971.

PET   *Orchestra Music and Chorus with Orchestra.* New York: C. F. Peters, ca. 1963.

REM   *Enciclopedia della musica.* 4 vols. Claudio Sartori, editor-in-chief. Milan: G. Ricordi, 1963-64.

SCL   *Southeastern Composers League Catalogue.* Hattiesburg, Miss.: Tritone Press, 1962.

SML   Seeger, Horst. *Musiklexikon.* 2 vols. Leipzig, VEB Deutscher Verlag für Musik, 1966.

TCAC   Edmunds, John, and Gordon Boelzner. *Some Twentieth Century American Composers: A Selective Bibliography.* 2 vols. New York: New York Public Library, 1959-60.

TCH   Bedford, Frances, and Robert Conant. *Twentieth Century Harpsichord Music.* Hackensack, N.J.: Joseph Boonin, 1974.

TSC   Carlson, Effie B. *Twelve Tone and Serial Composers.* Metuchen, N.J.: Scarecrow, 1970.

VER   *Musikkens Verden.* Ed. S. Hagerup Bull. Oslo: Musikkens Verden, 1951. 2nd ed., rev. and enl., 1962.

WCH   Stern, Susan. *Women Composers: A Handbook.* Metuchen, N.J.: Scarecrow, 1978.

WHP   *Wilhelm Hansen Pamphlets.* Copenhagen: Hansen Musik-Forlag, various dates up to 1962.

WI62   *Who's Who in Music and Musicians' International Directory.* 4th ed. Ed. Peter Townend and David Simmons. New York: Hafner, 1962.

WI69   *Who's Who in Music and Musicians' International Directory.* 5th ed. W. J. Potterton, editorial director. New York: Hafner, 1969.

WTM   Ewen, David. *The World of Twentieth-Century Music.* Englewood Cliffs: Prentice-Hall, 1968.

WWAM-Cl   *Who's Who in American Music—Classical.* 2nd ed. Edited by the Jacques Cattell Press. New York and London: Bowker, 1985.

X50-90   *The Music Index.* Annual cumulation, 1949-. Founding editor, Florence Kretzschmar. Detroit: Information Coordinators, 1949-.

American Organ Music

of the

Twentieth Century

AN ANNOTATED BIBLIOGRAPHY OF COMPOSERS

Samuel Adler

B. Mannheim, Germany, 4 March 1928. In 1939, moved to Worcester, Mass. Lessons with Herbert Fromm, Boston, 1941-46; attended Boston University, 1946-48, B.M., 1948; studied with Hugo Norden, Karl Geiringer, Paul Pisk, Harvard University, 1948-50; M.M., 1950, classes with Walter Piston, Randall Thompson, Irving Fine. Summer courses at Berkshire Music Center, Tanglewood: composition with Aaron Copland and conducting with Serge Koussevitzky. Professor of composition at Eastman School of Music since 1966; chairman, department of composition, 1973; professor emeritus, 1995. Many honors and awards, including grants from National Endowment for the Arts, the ASCAP-Deems Taylor Award, 1983, for his book *The Study of Orchestration*, and a Guggenheim fellowship, 1984-85. Books: *Sightsinging: Pitch, Interval, Rhythm* (New York: Norton, 1979); ed. *Choral Conducting: An Anthology* (New York: Holt, Rinehart & Winston, 1971; 2nd ed., 1985); *The Study of Orchestration* (New York: Norton, 1982; 2nd ed., 1989).

AA73, ABDad, AMH, AS66, ASUC, BB58, BB78, BB92, BDA, CACA, CACJ (b. 1929), DCM, DN73, DN75, DN77, IWW92, JCN, KTL, NG, NGA, OL95, PC71, PCM, TCH, X50, X60, X62, X64, X65, X66, X67, X68, X69, X70, X71, X74, X75.

"Awards and Honors." *American Organist* 25 (October 1991): 53.

> Adler is honored at a festival of his music at the University of Kansas, Lawrence, 27 February-3 March 1991. The organ students commissioned him to write a work for the festival, *Epistrophe*, which was published by Augsburg Fortress in 1992.

Drone, Jeannette. "American Composer Update." *Pan Pipes* 75/2 (1983): 19.

> Premiere of Adler's *Toccatina for Two Trumpets and Organ*.

"Here and There." *Diapason* 72 (January 1981): 6.

> Premiere of *Fantasy on the Name Craighead* by J. Melvin Butler, on the occasion of David Craighead's 25th year at the Eastman School of Music.

Kyle, Marguerite Kelly. "AmerAllegro." *Pan Pipes* 51 (January 1959): 47.

> Publication of Adler's *Pastorale* is announced.

52/2 (1960): 33-34.

Premieres of *Toccata for Organ* by organist Herman Berlinski, New York, and *Sonata for Organ* by organist Ralph Kneareem. Adler received the first Lazare Saminsky Memorial Commission and was a 1959 MacDowell Colony fellow.

53/2 (1961): 39.

Premiere of *Toccata for Organ,* by Robert Baker, Evanston, Ill.

54/2 (1962): 34.

Publication of Adler's *Toccata, Recitation, and Postlude* is announced.

55/2 (1963): 37.

Announcement of two premieres: *The Feast of Week* and *The Lord of All.*

56/2 (1964): 41-42.

Music for Worship, an organ anthology edited by Adler, includes two of his works; published by Lawson-Gould.

58/2 (1966): 48-49.

Publication of Adler's *Two Meditations* is announced.

60/2 (1968): 57.

Toccata, Recitation and Postlude for Organ is recorded by Robert Noehren on Lyrichord Records.

63/2 (1971): 47.

Adler is commissioned to write a concerto for organ and orchestra to celebrate Eastman's 50th anniversary.

64/2 (1972): 41-42.

Premiere of *Concerto for Organ and Orchestra* is announced.

65/2 (1973): 39.

Premiere of Adler's *Xenia* is performed by Wilma Jensen in Houston, Tex.

66/2 (1974): 39.

Adler's *Concerto for Organ and Orchestra* is published by Carl Fischer; Adler is appointed chairman of Composition Department at Eastman.

69/2 (1977): 29-30.

Adler's *Xenia* for organ and percussion is recorded on Crystal Records by David Craighead and Gordon Stout.

McCray, James. "An Interview with Samuel Adler." *Choral Journal* 18/9 (1978): 16-18.

This interview discussed Adler's approach to composition, presenting contemporary music, and the influence of his Jewish background on his music.

Myers, M. C. **"A Study and Interpretive Analysis of Selected Aleatory Compositions for Orchestra by American Composers."** *Dissertation Abstracts* 33 (September 1972): 904A-05A. *

Includes Adler's *Concerto for Organ.*

"A New Work by Samuel Adler." *Diapason* 63 (December 1971): 1.

Announcement of premiere of Adler's *Concerto for Organ and Orchestra* by organist David Craighead.

"News and Honors." *ASCAP* 5/3 (1972): 30.

Concerto for Organ receives its premiere by David Craighead, organ, and the Eastman Philharmonic, 12 November 1971.

Rozier, Clair. **"The Organ Compositions of Samuel Adler."** *American Organist* 25 (June 1991): 42-44.

Adler's compositional style is described, and an overview of his eight works for solo organ and six for organ and other instruments is presented.

Rudd, Robert Michael. **"Stylistic Features and Compositional Activities in Organ Literature Since World War II."** *Diapason* 59 (June 1968): 12.

An overview of compositional devices in use after World War II, with a brief description of Adler's *Toccata, Recitation, and Postlude*, 1959. A more thorough discussion is presented by Rudd in his dissertation "Stylistic Trends in Contemporary Organ Music" (Ph.D., Louisiana State University, 1967).

"Samuel Adler, 1986 MTNA Composer of the Year." *American Music Teacher* 36/5 (1987): 9.

This half-page article includes biographical information about Adler, including commissions, grants, and awards he has received.

William Hugh Albright

B. Gary, Ind., 20 October 1944. Piano study with Rosetta Goodkind and music theory with Hugh Aitken at Juilliard Preparatory Dept., in New York, 1959-62; courses in composition with Ross Lee Finney and Leslie Bassett, organ with Marilyn Mason, at the University of Michigan, 1963-70. Studied in France with Olivier Messiaen at Paris Conservatory and private lessons with Max Deutsch, 1968. Joined the faculty of University of Michigan in 1970, to

teach composition and serve as associate director of the Electronic Music Studio. Guggenheim fellowship, 1976; composer-in-residence at the American Academy in Rome, 1979.
ABDad, BB78, BB92, CACA, CACJ, CC92, DCM, DN72, IWW92, NG, NGA, OL, OL95, TCH, X69, X71, X74.

Albright, William. "New Music at the University of Michigan." *New Music of the West* Series 2/1 (1975): 45-46.

A letter to the journal discussing groups that support concert presentations devoted to recently-composed music; many composers listed in this bibliography are involved in those groups, notably George Cacioppo, William Bolcom, and Wallace Berry.

"Albright Wins Queen Award." *Billboard* 80 (30 November 1968): 44.

Announcement that Albright's *Organbook* (1967) wins the Queen Marie José Award.

Belt, Byron. "Music in the Churches." *Music* (AGO) 7 (July 1973): 20-23.

A review of a workshop entitled "Music in the Church . . . a Long View." Composers-in-residence espouse quality compositions, and the relationship between music, the church, and the congregation. Albright gives his opinions on good hymn accompaniments and how to use the works from *Organbook* within the church setting.

Bullat, G. Nicholas, Jerome Butera, Timothy Wissler, and Rudolf Zuiderveld. "AGO '86." *Diapason* 77 (October 1986): 11-15.

A brief overview of Albright's *Chasm*, commissioned by Ann Arbor's AGO chapter, and performed by Marilyn Mason.

Cordes, Joan. K. "A New American Development in Music: Some Characteristic Features Extending from the Legacy of Charles Ives." Ph.D., Louisiana State University, 1976. *Dissertation Abstracts* 37 (December 1976): 3253A. *

"Cuyler, Albright Honored at University of Michigan." *Diapason* 65 (December 1973): 7.

Louise Cuyler and Albright, both professors of music, receive honors for distinguished service.

Fried, Adrienne G. "New York Premieres of Two Works on Albright Program." *Music* (AGO) 6 (March 1972): 30-31.

Very brief mention of Albright's prizes for composition and his position as coordinator of Contemporary Directions Studio, in addition to *Organbook II* having its premiere.

Haller, William. "Organ Works of the Avante-Garde [*sic*]**."** *Clavier* 13/4 (1974): 33-36.

A presentation of the major influences upon contemporary composers: dissonance, off-beat humor, and tape music, among others. Includes a look at *Juba, Pneuma, Organbook I, Organbook II, Stipendium Peccati* (for organ, piano, and percussion), and *Gothic Suite for Organ, Strings, and Percussion.*

Hantz, Edwin. **"An Introduction to the Organ Music of William Albright."** *Diapason* 64 (May 1973): 1, 4-5.

Hantz presents a scholarly look at four major organ works by Albright: *Juba, Pneuma, Organbook I,* and *Organbook II.* A student at the University of Michigan, Hantz offers the composer's own assessments of his works—both in description and analysis, in addition to his own perspectives.

"Here and There." *Diapason* 69 (September 1978): 16.

Premiere of Albright's latest work, *Organbook III.*

"Here and There." *Diapason* 77 (October 1986): 4.

Announcement of the world premiere of Albright's *Symphony for Organ* by organist Douglas Reed. Includes commissioning information.

"KU: Albright Works." *High Fidelity/Musical America* 29 (September 1979): MA27-28.

A discussion at the University of Kansas on the influences in Albright's music, with an overview of *The King of Instruments* and *Organbook III.*

Kehl, Roy. **"The Syracuse AGO Regional Convention."** *Diapason* 64 (August 1973): 8-9.

An overview of Albright's *Gothic Suite for Organ, Strings, and Percussion* and information on the commission.

Kratzenstein, Marilou. **"AGO Cleveland '74: Pressure Brings New Music."** *Diapason* 65 (August 1974): 1, 4-5.

The "Troika" of contemporary music, Gerd Zacher, Jean Guillou, and William Albright, are introduced. Albright discusses "the use of color as structural function, the pitting of one element against another, and the organic growth of music from a single germ," and provides his own musical compositions as examples in this article, which compares and contrasts the three composers.

Lawrence, Arthur. **"The Organ and the Concert Hall: Perspectives on the Use of Organ with Other Instruments."** *Diapason* 73 (March 1982): 18.

A thumbnail sketch of Albright's *Bacchanal for Organ and Orchestra,* noting its requirements for a large orchestra, and an especially large battery of percussion.

Little, Jeanie R. **"Serial, Aleatoric and Electronic Techniques in American Organ Music Published between 1960 and 1972."** Ph.D., University of Iowa, 1976. *Dissertation Abstracts* 36 (June 1976): 7722A.

This in-depth, scholarly work dissects Albright's *Juba, Pneuma, Organbook I,* and *Organbook II,* among other composers' works, in detailed analyses.

Mariat, Madeleine-J. "The Queen Marie José Prize." *American Music Digest* 1 (October 1969): 11.

Albright performed his prize-winning *Organbook* not once, but twice, at a concert 20 March 1969, at Saint-Pierre Cathedral, Geneva; the reviewer disliked the work.

"Music Journal's Gallery of Living Composers." *Music Journal* 31 (annual, 1973): 91-95.

General biography, including awards and prizes. Major works listed and current position held.

Palmer, Larry. "New Music in the Old World." *Diapason* 76 (October 1985): 8-10.

The history of Albright's program sonata for organ, *1732*, is given, with notes about the seven sections.

Parks, Anne. "William Albright's Organbook I—A Master Lesson." *Diapason* 69 (May 1978): 1, 10, 12-13.

A pedagogue's approach to dealing with the technical problems presented in *Organbook I*. The four movements are taught and analyzed in detail, section by section.

"Partitions." *Jeunesse* 49 (1982): 35.

An overview of Albright's *Suite Gothique* is presented, with information about various influences on the work.

Perone, James E. "Pluralistic Strategies in Musical Analysis: A Study of Selected Works of William Albright." Ph.D., State University of New York-Buffalo, 1988. *Dissertation Abstracts* 49 (June 1989): 3546A.

Discusses the problems in analyzing Albright's music, and three main approaches are broached. Included in the discussion are *Organbook* and *Symphony for Organ*.

"Premieres." *American Organist* 20 (May 1986): 13.

The premiere of *De spiritum* is performed by Marilyn Mason, 31 January 1986, commissioned by the Marilyn Mason Commissioning Fund.

"Premieres." *American Organist* 21 (May 1987): 52.

Douglas Reed, organist, and Ted Rubright, percussionist, premiere *Symphony for Organ*, 4 November 1986. Commission information is given.

"Premieres." *American Organist* 27 (March 1993): 49.

Organist Donald Joyce will perform the premiere of Albright's *Chasm* in the 18th Internationale Studienwoche in Cologne and Sinzig.

Raver, Leonard. **"Organist."** *Music Journal* 34 (February 1976): 22-23, 50-51.

A discussion of several new works for organ, liberating the pipe organ from the church and placing it in the concert hall. New effects are found in Albright's *Organbook I* and *Organbook II*, and these are discussed, in addition to other composers' works.

————. **"William Albright's *Organbook III*."** *American Organist* 15 (October 1981): 48.

A journey through Albright's latest work, a set of 12 etudes that not only are "technical studies for the organist," but "compositional studies for the author and resource studies for the organ itself." Raver vividly describes the etudes.

"Recital, Cleveland." *Diapason* 63 (March 1972): 17.

Review of Albright's recital; reviewer noted his program "must have seemed like a visit to another planet." Program included. Reprint from the *Plain Dealer* (Cleveland), 29 January 1972.

Reed, Robert D. **"The Organ Works of William Albright: 1965-1975."** D.M.A., University of Rochester, Eastman School of Music, 1977. *Dissertation Abstracts* 37 (May 1977): 6832A-33A. *

Shenk, Calvert, and Richard De Vinney. **"AGO National Convention Detroit."** *American Organist* 20 (August 1986): 38-42.

A minute mention of *Chasm* as an "intriguing, sonic experience."

Schwartz, Elliott. **"The Gamut of American Music."** *Music & Musicians* 21 (November 1972): 20-22 + . *

"USA Organist Awarded Big Composition Prize." *Diapason* 60 (March 1969): 3.

Albright receives Queen Marie José prize for *Organbook* (1967); lists other prizes, awards.

"William Albright Plays World Premiere." *Diapason* 63 (February 1972): 25.

Premiere of Albright's *Organbook II*, for organ and electronic tape, at the Cathedral of St. John the Divine, New York, 14 January 1972.

Aksel Andersen

B. Ruskin, Neb., 1 March 1912; d. 18 November 1977. Moved to Denmark and served as organist in Vatov, 1932; organist at St. Jacobi, Varde, 1933-48; organist at St. Paul's

Church, Aarhus, 1948-55; organist, Eliaskirken 1956-59; appointed professor at the Conservatory of Copenhagen, 1955; organist at Christianborg Castle, 1959-77. Authored *Improvisation I* (Egtved, Denmark: Edition Egtved, n.d.).

OL, OL95.

"First Performances 1974." *Musical Denmark* 26 (1974-75): 19.

Andersen's *Suite 1974*, for organ, received its premiere on 20 August 1974, at the Frederik's Church.

Hesford, Bryan. "Organ Music of Scandinavia." *Musical Opinion* 98 (September 1975): 643-46.

A look at the influences on Scandinavian organ music: the German *vis-à-vis* the German chorale, and the French through its reputation for skill and dexterity of the performer. Norwegian and Danish composers are mentioned in generational time periods. Andersen's fantasia on the chorale *Christ ist erstanden* is mentioned, with a thumbnail sketch of the work.

[Obituary.] *Musical Denmark* 28 (1976-77): 28.

Obituary notice is given, listing Andersen as professor and organist.

Robert T. Anderson

B. Chicago, 5 October 1934. B.S.M., 1955, from Illinois Wesleyan; M.S.M., 1957, S.M.D., 1961, from Union Theological Seminary, New York. Organ student of Robert Baker, Helmut Walcha; composition student of Frank Bohnhorst, Harold Friedell, Seth Bingham. Held several church positions; since 1960, professor of organ and sacred music, 1981 named Meadows Distinguished Teaching Professor, Southern Methodist University, Dallas, Tex. Fulbright recipient to study in Germany, 1957-59.

IWW92, OL, OL95, X70, X71.

Howell, Richard D. "Recitals and Concerts." *American Organist* 46 (July 1963): 8.

Review of Anderson's organ recital at Temple Emanuel, Dallas, 11 March 1963, in which he performed recent compositions of Langlais and Berlinski.

"News." *Sacred Music* 97/3 (1970): 35.

Premiere of *Hoolaulea* (for two organs) by the composer and Jerald Hamilton, 25 September 1970, at National Shrine of the Immaculate Conception, Washington, D.C.

"Recital." *American Organist* 49 (July 1966): 12.

> A review of Robert Anderson's recital at St. John's Church, Chevy Chase, Md., 27 May 1966. Anderson performed his own *Canticle of Praise* as an encore.

"Recital." *American Organist* 50 (May 1967): 14.

> Anderson's recital at St. Paul's United Church of Christ, Chicago, 4 April 1967, is reviewed. Program included his work *Te Deum*.

"Recitals and Concerts." *American Organist* 40 (April 1957): 126.

> Anderson and soprano Janet Frank perform a duo recital at St. Bartholomew's Church, New York, 20 February 1957. Included on the program was Johann Nepomuk David's *Prelude and Fugue in A Minor* (1931). "Robert Anderson's use of great power dynamically in the prelude was telling—his playing of the fugue made the episodic type of fugal delineation lucid."

"Recitals and Concerts." *American Organist* 43 (November 1960): 28.

> A rave review of Anderson's organ recital at the Interchurch Center Chapel, New York, 21 June 1960; he performed the Final from Langlais's recent *Première Symphonie*.

"Robert Anderson." *American Organist* 43 (November 1960): 31.

> Anderson is appointed instructor in theory and sacred music at Southern Methodist University, Dallas. Includes some biographical information.

"Robert Anderson." *American Organist* 45 (May 1962): 27.

> Colbert-LaBerge Concert Management signs Robert Anderson; some biographical data given.

"Robert Anderson." *Diapason* 53 (May 1962): 45.

> Announces Anderson's new management, Colbert-LaBerge Concert Management; some biographical information.

Spies, Donald. "Recital, Rochester, MN." *Diapason* 62 (June 1971): 26.

> Anderson plays dedicatory recital of new Aeolian-Skinner mechanical action organ at Zumbro Lutheran Church.

Tufts, William O. "AGO Midwinter Conclave." *American Organist* 49 (February 1966): 11-12.

> Lists recital program and brief review of Anderson's concert, which included his own *Canticle of Praise*, *Te Deum*, and Dello Joio's *Laudation*.

Yuri Arbatsky

B. Moscow, Russia, 15 April 1911; d. New Hartford, N.Y., 3 September 1963. Studied piano with Rachmaninov and Lopatnikov in Berlin after his family left Russia in 1919. Later, Hermann Grabner instructed him in Leipzig. Graduated from Leipzig Conservatory, 1932. Appointed conductor in Yugoslavia, while pursuing folklore research inspired by Russian musicologist Kastalski; appointment to Slavonic Institute in Prague, 1942. Received his doctorate from Charles University, Prague, 1944. Emigrated to U.S., 1949, and became church organist in Chicago, 1950-53; served as consultant to the Newberry Library.

ABDad, BB58, BB71, BB78, CACA, DDM, EDM, EVM, GD54s, KDK, KTL, LMD, MGG, OL, OL95, REM, TCH, X51, X57, X58, X59, X64.

"Arbatsky Appointed to Salem Lutheran." *Music News* 42 (November 1950): 12. *

"Arbatsky Leaves Position at Salem Church, Chicago." *Diapason* 43 (January 1952): 37.

Notice of his resignation after only 15 months on the job.

"Arbatsky Opus Premiered by Fleischer." *Music News* 43 (February 1951): 19. *

Includes information on *Saga of Salem*.

Fleischer, Heinrich. "Zur Besprechung von Orgelwerken Yuri Arbatskys." *Musik und Kirche* 29 (May/June 1959): 158.

A discussion of Arbatsky's organ music provides the foundation for succeeding conversations on the American's approach to new music of the 20th century versus the German approach.

"Sursum corda, for Organ or Harpsichord." *Music Review* 19 (August 1958): 250-51.

This work is composed of seven short chorale preludes, and, according to the unnamed reviewer, is "puerile rubbish!"

"Uraufführung neuer Kirchenmusik." *Musik und Kirche* 28 (May/June 1958): 140.

Arbatsky's *Passacaglia* is premiered on 15 January 1958, by organist Herbert Schulze at the Epiphanien-Kirche, Berlin-Charlottenburg. The reviewer, Paul Indra, was highly impressed with this new work, and describes it in length.

"Uraufführung neuer Kirchenmusik." *Musik und Kirche* 31/1 (1961): 42-43.

Herbert Schulze premieres three new Arbatsky works on 12 October 1960, at the Matthäus-Kirche in Berlin-Steglitz: *Konzert in byzantinischer Form* (1959), *Sonata "Nun bitten wir den Heiligen Geist"* (1951), and *Vorspiele zu amerikanischen Hymnen* (1960).

"Yuri Arbatsky Director at Salem Church, Chicago." *Diapason* 42 (December 1950): 26.

> Arbatsky assumes the position of director of music in Salem Lutheran Church, Chicago, 1 October 1950. Provides biographical information.

Ronald K. Arnatt

B. London, England, 16 January 1930. Studied at Trent College and Trinity College of Music, and Durham University, where he received his B.M.; private study in organ with Harold Darke, Paul Callaway, and Conrad Bernier. He came to America in 1947 and served at New York Avenue Presbyterian Church in Washington, D.C. Organist, First Congregational Church, 1948; in 1949-54, Church of the Ascension and St. Agnes, and 1954-83, organist-choirmaster of Christ Church Cathedral, St. Louis. Joined Westminster Choir College faculty, 1987.

ABDad, CACA, OL, OL95, X50, X54, X55, X67, X68.

"A.G.O." *Musical Opinion* 109 (September-October 1986): 338.

> The AGO elects Arnatt, who received an honorary Doctor of Music degree from Westminster Choir College in 1970, as its president.

"AGO Regional Convention Reports 1989." *American Organist* 23 (October 1989): 74.

> Premiere announced of Arnatt's *Pièce de Résistance*; commission information given.

"AGO Regional Convention Reports 1989." *American Organist* 23 (October 1989): 79.

> Premiere of Arnatt's *Two Pieces for Organ Duet*.

"Appointments." *American Organist* 14 (July 1980): 28.

> Notice of Arnatt's appointment to Trinity Church, Boston, as Director of Music and the Arts.

"Convention of A.G.O. Is Notable Success." *Diapason* 45 (August 1954): 1.

> Premiere of Arnatt's *Four Plainsong Preludes*.

"Convention Personalities." *American Organist* 18 (April 1984): 111.

> Arnatt is judge for Holtkamp/AGO composition competition; cites previous positions held by him.

Glass, Henry, Jr. "**Recital, St. Louis.**" *American Organist* 51 (May 1968): 11.

Program and review of Arnatt's recital at St. Louis Priory Chapel. The review is favorable.

Heaton, Charles Huddleston. "**Contemporary Composers: Ronald Arnatt.**" *Journal of Church Music* 15 (June 1973): 10-12.

Biography of Arnatt, comments about his compositions in general with some pieces in particular noted, and a list of compositions are provided.

"**Here and There.**" *Diapason* 80 (July 1989): 3.

Premiere of Arnatt's *Two Pieces for Organ Duet* announced.

"**An Interview with the Candidates for AGO President.**" *American Organist* 20 (April 1986): 200-01.

A discussion with Arnatt as a concerned advocate for education, church music, and pedagogy.

"**New Scores and Instruments Shown at 22nd Convention of Organists.**" *Musical America* 74 (August 1954): 31.

Arnatt performs the premiere of his *Four Plainsong Preludes*, 11 July 1954; written for the 22nd National AGO Convention, he performed the work at the Church of St. John the Evangelist, St. Paul, Minn. "[They] breathed the idiom of today," said the reviewer.

"**Pipings.**" *American Organist* 24 (January 1990): 50.

Arnatt receives a 1989-90 ASCAP award.

"**Pipings.**" *American Organist* 25 (July 1991): 36.

Arnatt receives the 1990 Avis H. Blewett Award for outstanding contributions to the musical life of the community by the St. Louis AGO Chapter.

"**Premieres.**" *American Organist* 23 (August 1989): 37.

Announces premieres of two works by Arnatt: *Octopus Music* and *Sarabande with Variations, for Organ Duo*, commissioned by Elizabeth and Raymond Chenault.

"**Recitals and Concerts.**" *American Organist* 43 (March 1960): 25.

Arnatt, in recital at St. Thomas Church, New York, 16 November 1959, performs two of his works: *Prelude on the Antiphon to the Benedictus for Good Friday Tenebrae* and *Procession*. The review of Arnatt's playing and compositions is favorable.

"**Ronald Arnatt.**" *Diapason* 45 (October 1954): 26.

Appointment to Christ Church Episcopal Cathedral in St. Louis is cited. Includes biographical information.

"Ronald Arnatt." *Diapason* 58 (September 1967): 22.

  Arnatt to tour England September through November; current position listed.

"Ronald Arnatt Is Named Westminster Church Music Department Head." *Journal of Church Music* 29 (November 1987): 28-29.

  Announces Arnatt's new position and lists previous posts.

"Ronald Arnatt of Massachusetts Re-Elected President of AGO." *Journal of Church Music* 29 (January 1987): 29.

  Announces election results; lists previous positions.

Stitt, Mrs. J. Herbert. "Composers Conduct Commissioned Works at Wheeling Festival." *Diapason* 58 (January 1967): 22.

  Arnatt conducts his *Organ Suite with Brass Quartet and Timpani* in its premiere, 25 October 1966, in Wheeling; it is well received.

Widdicombe, Gillian. "Westminster Abbey." *Musical Times* 108 (November 1967): 1040.

  A bland review of Arnatt's performance, 27 September 1967.

Corliss R. Arnold

B. Monticello, Ark., 7 November 1926. Studied at Hendrix College, B.M., 1947; University of Michigan, M.M., 1948; and Union Theological Seminary, S.M.D., 1954. Teachers of composition include Normand Lockwood, Seth Bingham, Leo Sowerby, Nadia Boulanger, and Jean Langlais. Fulbright grant to study in France, 1956. Served at various churches and colleges in Arkansas, New Jersey, New York, Illinois, and Michigan. Music professor, Michigan State University, from 1959; retired in 1991. Authored *Organ Literature: A Comprehensive Survey* (Metuchen, N.J.: Scarecrow, 1973; 2nd ed., 2 vols., 1984; 3rd ed., 2 vols., 1995).

ABD, CACA, OL, OL95.

Arnatt, Ronald. "Concerts and Recitals." *American Organist* 43 (January 1960): 28.

  A review of Arnold's recital in Little Rock, Ark., at Ashbury Methodist Church. Playing from memory caused several lapses in his performance.

"Corliss Arnold Succeeds Francis Moore in Oak Park." *Diapason* 45 (October 1954): 27.

Appointment of Arnold to Illinois Methodist Church as organist and director. Provides some biographical information, positions held, and composition and organ instructors.

"Corliss R. Arnold." *Diapason* 40 (September 1949): 31.

Announces appointment to First Methodist Church, El Dorado, Ark., as organist-director of music.

"Corliss R. Arnold." *Diapason* 50 (September 1959): 5.

Appointment to Michigan State faculty is announced; and as director of music at the Peoples Church, East Lansing.

Franklin D. Ashdown

B. 1942. Internal-diagnostic physician, Alamagordo, New Mexico.

OL, OL95.

"Here and There." *Diapason* 78 (August 1987): 3.

Premiered by British conductor-organist Alistair Jones at the Church of St. Lawrence, London, England, 25 April 1987, the work, *Pavanne on Arthur Bliss*, is based on the tune "Pen Selwood," and is dedicated to Lady Bliss.

"Here and There." *Diapason* 80 (May 1989): 3.

The premiere of *Sunday Scherzo* by Ashdown is performed by organist Joyce Jones, university organist at Baylor University, on 2 February 1989. Dedicatory information is provided.

"Here and There." *Diapason* 81 (October 1990): 3.

Leonard Raver performs the premiere of Ashdown's *Concert Aria* on 9 July 1990, at San Diego's Spreckels Organ Pavilion.

"Here and There." *Diapason* 82 (August 1991): 3.

Ashdown's *Ceremonial Piece* for organ and optional percussion received its world premiere in a performance by Leonard Raver at St. Peter's Church, New York City, on 4 May 1991.

"Here and There." *Diapason* 82 (October 1991): 4.

Organist James Welch premieres *Capriccio and Dialogue on Two Hymn Tunes*, 24 June 1991, in Portola Valley, Calif.

"Here and There." *Diapason* 84 (September 1993): 3.

Preambolo maestoso, for solo organ, was premiered by James Welch at Santa Clara University on May 5.

"Premieres." *American Organist* 18 (May 1984): 41.

Premiere of Ashdown's *Passacaglia in B Minor* is given by organist Leonard Raver, 26 January 1984, in Alamogordo, New Mexico, at Grace United Methodist Church.

"Premieres." *American Organist* 21 (September 1987): 54-55.

Concerns *Pavanne on Arthur Bliss*; see the first "Here and There" article, above.

"Premieres." *American Organist* 22 (June 1988): 44.

Organist Fred Tulan gives the premiere of Ashdown's *Pedal Variations and Toccata*, 16 March 1988, at Central United Methodist Church in Stockton, Calif. The work is dedicated to Tulan.

"Premieres." *American Organist* 23 (July 1989): 40.

The premiere of *Sunday Scherzo* by Ashdown is performed by organist Joyce Jones, university organist at Baylor University, on 2 February 1989. Dedicatory information is provided.

"Premieres." *American Organist* 24 (March 1990): 49-50.

Two premieres of Ashdown works are cited: *Ballade for Flute and Organ*, presented by organist David Aeschliman and flutist Angela Kom at Sunnyside Adventist Church in Portland, Ore., November 1989, and *Festival Entrada on Diadem*, premiered by organist Michele Johns and by brass and percussion students from the University of New Mexico, 20 October 1989, at Redeemer Lutheran Church, Albuquerque. Both works are dedicated to the performer.

"Premieres." *American Organist* 24 (October 1990): 62.

Leonard Raver presents the premiere of Ashdown's *Concert Aria* on 9 July 1990, at San Diego's Spreckels Organ Pavilion.

"Premieres." *American Organist* 25 (August 1991): 36.

Leonard Raver performs the premiere of *Ceremonial Piece* for organ and optional percussion at St. Peter's Lutheran Church, New York City, 4 May 1991.

"Premieres." *American Organist* 25 (October 1991): 55.

Organist James Welch premieres *Capriccio and Dialogue on Two Hymn Tunes* by Ashdown, 24 June 1991, in Portola Valley, Calif. The work juxtaposes "Coronation" and "Old Hundredth."

"Premieres." *American Organist* 29 (January 1995): 54.

> Organist James M. Drake, university organist for Utah State University, premieres *Chorale and Recessional*, 11 October 1994. *Chorale* is based on "Aberystwyth" while *Recessional* is built upon an original theme. The work is dedicated to Drake and is published by H. W. Gray/CPP-Belwin.

Philip E. Baker

B. Burkburnett, Texas, 27 November 1934. He received a B.A., 1957, from Midwestern University, Wichita Falls, Tex.; organ study with Nita Akin, Leonard Raver, and David Lumsden; M.M., 1966, Southern Methodist University; further study at Union Theological Seminary. Organ instructor, S.M.U., 1960-65; associate director of music, 1959-65, and director of music, since 1965, at Highland Park United Methodist Church, Dallas, Tex. OL, OL95.

"Philip Baker." *American Organist* 48 (October 1965): 29.

> Baker is appointed organist and director of music of the Highland Park Methodist Church, Dallas, Tex., effective 1 September 1965. Lists previous positions.

"Philip Baker." *Diapason* 56 (October 1965): 46.

> Appointment of Baker as organist-director of music to Highland Park Methodist Church, Dallas, where he had previously served as organist and associate director.

Esther Williamson Ballou

B. Elmira, N.Y., 17 July 1915; d. Chichester, England, 12 March 1973. Studied at Bennington College and Mills College; graduate degree in composition from Juilliard, student of Bernard Wagenaar. Private lessons with Otto Luening and Wallingford Riegger. Awards: MacDowell Fellowship; honorary doctorate at Hood College; ASCAP award, 1969. Taught at Juilliard and Catholic University; professor of music, American University, 1959-73. AA73, ABD, AMH, BB65, BB71, BB92, CA9, CACA, IWC, KTL, LMD, NG, NGA, OL95, TCAC, TCH, WCH, X56, X61, X62, X64, X65, X66, X67, X68, X69, X71, X75.

Daniel, Oliver. "The New Festival." *American Composers Alliance Bulletin* 5/1 (1955): 3-4.

A few comments from Ballou on her compositional approach; this article primarily serves as notice of a new LP being released.

"Esther Ballou." *Composers of the Americas* 9 (1963): 13-18.

A brief biography in Spanish and English is followed by a chronological catalog of works by Ballou, with duration, notes, and editorial information provided.

"Esther Williamson Ballou." *Pan Pipes* 52/2 (1960): 24.

Gives biographical information on Ballou, some recent premieres and publications, and a list of works-in-progress.

Heintze, James R. *Esther Williamson Ballou: A Bio-Bibliography.* New York: Greenwood, 1987.

Includes biography, works and performance premieres, correspondence, discography, interviews, and alphabetical and chronological listings of compositions.

_____, and Don Hixon. "Communications to the Editor." *Notes* 46/1 (1989): 265.

A response by Marion Gushee to the critical review of Heintze's book, *Esther Williamson Ballou.*

Kyle, Marguerite K. "AmerAllegro." *Pan Pipes* 56/2 (1964): 44.

The premiere of Ballou's *Passacaglia and Toccata* occurred on 15 March 1963, by organist Harlan Laufman at St. Thomas Church, Washington, D.C.

64/2 (1972): 43.

Ballou's *Creative Music Theory* is to be published in 1973 by Holt, Rinehart & Winston.

"Notes for Notes." *Notes* 30/1 (1973): 39.

A request for publications, scores, recordings, manuscripts is issued for the Ballou collection to be housed at American University, Washington, D.C.

[Obituary.] *Music Clubs Magazine* 52/5 (1973): 55.

Notice of Ballou's death in London, England. Gives education information, awards received, and indicates a scholarship fund in her name was begun at American University, Washington, D.C.

"People." *Symphony News* 24/3 (1973): 23.

Ballou's passing, 12 March 1973, is announced.

"A Salute to Women Composers." *Pan Pipes* 67/2 (1975): 5.

Announcement that American University of Washington, D.C., is soliciting scores, recordings, and tapes for a special collection devoted to Ballou.

Samuel Barber

B. West Chester, Penn., 9 March 1910; d. New York, 23 January 1981. At age 14, entered Curtis Institute of Music: piano with Isabelle Vengerova, composition with Rosario Scalero, conducting with Fritz Reiner. Won the American Rome Prize, 1935. Winner of two Pulitzer Prizes in music; three Guggenheim fellowships: 1945, 1947, 1949. Harvard conferred upon him an honorary degree of Doctor of Fine Arts, 1959. Elected to the American Academy of Arts and Letters.

ABD, AMH, AS66, ASC, BB58, BB65, BB71, BB78, BB92, BBCh, BBCpo, BDA, CA5, CACA, CDC, DCM, DDM, DN70, EDM, EMC, EMS, EVM, GD54, HHH, HLM, IMD, KTL, LMD, MEH, MGG, MHHH, NG, NGA, OL, OL95, PAP, PC71, PCM, REM, SML, TCAC, WTM, X50, X53, X54, X55, X56, X57, X58, X59, X60, X61, X62, X64, X65, X66, X67, X68, X69, X70, X71, X74.

"Adagio for Strings, by Samuel Barber, Arranged for Organ." *Diapason* 40 (November 1949): 28.

> Barber's work is arranged for organ by William Strickland and published by G. Schirmer, New York. "Well reset for the organ. . . ."

"Adagio for Strings." *Musical Courier* 142 (November 1950): 29.

> G. Schirmer publishes an arrangement of Barber's *Adagio* by William Strickland. Registrations are provided for pipe organs and Hammond organs.

"American Composers: Samuel Barber." *Musical Courier* 159 (February 1959): 41.

> Brief biography cites Nathan Broder's biography of Barber as a good source.

Ardoin, John. "Samuel Barber at Capricorn." *Musical America* 80 (March 1950): 4-5, 46.

> An intimate look at Barber in his home, Capricorn. His *Toccata Festiva*, for organ and orchestra, lies on a table, awaiting final touches.

"Barber's 'Toccata Festiva' at Organ Unveiling, Ormandy's 25th Anniversary Opener, Philadelphia." *Pan Pipes* 54/2 (1962): 2, 5.

> Barber's *Toccata Festiva*, for organ and orchestra, receives its premiere 30 September 1960; the Philadelphia Orchestra, with Ormandy conducting, performed the inaugural recital for the new Aeolian-Skinner with organist Paul Callaway. Commission information is provided.

Broder, Nathan. *Samuel Barber.* New York: G. Schirmer, 1954; reprint, Westport, Conn.: Greenwood, 1985.

> Composed of artiles about Barber, a discography, and a list of published works.

Day, Wesley A. "New Organ Dedication at Philadelphia Academy of Music." *Diapason* 51 (November 1960): 3.

A brief description of Barber's *Toccata Festiva*, description of the new Aeolian-Skinner organ, and donor/commission data given.

Friedewald, R. E. "A Formal and Stylistic Analysis of the Published Music of Samuel Barber." *Dissertation Abstracts* 17 (December 1957): 3037. *

Henessee, Don A. *Samuel Barber: A Bio-Bibliography.* Westport, Conn.: Greenwood, 1985.

Includes biography, bibliography, discography, works and performances, and an alphabetical and opus listing of works.

Heyman, Barbara B. *Samuel Barber: The Composer and His Music.* Oxford: Oxford University Press, 1992.

Discusses numerous works. Includes an extensive bibliography, thorough notes, and a works list that includes non-published works.

Kirkpatrick, John. *The New Grove Twentieth-Century American Masters.* New York: Norton, 1988.

This book includes Samuel Barber among other important and well-known composers.

McCandless, William E. "Cantus Firmus Techniques in Selected Instrumental Composers, 1910-60." Ph.D., Indiana University, 1974. *Dissertation Abstracts* 35 (January 1975): 4593A.

Discusses traditional cantus firmus sources and techniques. Analyzes the textural, rhythmic, and tonal treatments of pre-existent melodies in ten 20th-century compositions, including Barber's *Wondrous Love*, for organ.

[Obituary.] *American Organist* 15 (May 1981): 37.

Barber's death notice, 23 January 1981; memorial service held at St. Bartholomew's Church, New York, 9 February 1981.

[Obituary.] *Clavier* 20/3 (1981): 16.

Barber's death notice, 24 [sic] January 1981; overview of his life provided.

[Obituary.] *Diapason* 72 (April 1981): 3.

Gives biographical information and lists a chorale prelude on "Silent Night" (from *Die Natali*), for organ.

RePass, R. "American Composers of Today." *London Music* 8 (December 1953): 28-29. *

Rhoades, Larry Lynn. "Theme and Variation in Twentieth-century Organ Literature: Analyses of Variations by Alain, Barber, Distler, Dupré, Duruflé, and Sowerby." Ph.D. diss., Music Theory, Ohio State University, 1973.

Includes illustrations, music examples, and bibliography, in addition to the analyses.

"Samuel Barber." *Composers of the Americas* 5 (1959): 14-21.

A brief biography in Spanish and English is followed by a chronological list of his works. Exclusive publisher to date is G. Schirmer.

Schauensee, Max de. "Barber Premiere." *Musical America* 80 (November 1960): 23.

Paul Callaway performs the premiere of Barber's *Toccata Festiva*, for organ and orchestra, at the inaugural recital of the new Aeolian-Skinner organ at Philadelphia Orchestra's 61st season opener. Commission information is provided.

Singer, Samuel L. "Philadelphia Dedicates New $150,000 Organ." *Musical Courier* 162 (November 1960): 20.

Toccata Festiva for organ and orchestra receives its premiere 30 September 1960. Eugene Ormandy conducts the Philadelphia Orchestra and organist Paul Callaway for the inaugural recital on the new Aeolian-Skinner organ.

Smith, Rollin. "American Organ Composers." *Music* (AGO) 10 (August 1976): 18.

Thumbnail sketches of ten organ composers include Barber; briefly indicates their style of composition and presents an overview of their important organ works.

Sneerson, Grigorij. *Portrety amerikanskyh kompozitorov* (Portraits of American Composers). Moskva: Muzyka, 1977.

Biographical portraits of nine American composers and discussions of their music and its place in contemporary music history include information about Barber.

Stambler, Bernard. "Four American Composers." *Juilliard Review* 2 (winter 1955): 7-16.

A brief look at Ives, Barber, Copland, and Schuman; how the composer was trained and expanded his vista is a part of finding himself compositionally.

"Stoplists." *American Organist* 43 (December 1960): 19.

A review of the Philadelphia Orchestra program, with conductor Ormandy and organist Paul Callaway premiering his *Toccata Festiva for Organ and Orchestra*. Information is provided about the commission and the work in general.

"Toccata Festiva." *Philadelphia Orchestra Program Notes* (5 October 1962): 15, 17.

Edwin H. Schloss's program notes describe Barber's latest work, *Toccata Festiva*, for organ and orchestra. Commission and dedicatory information is provided.

Wayne Barlow

B. Elyria, Ohio, 6 September 1912. At the Eastman School of Music he studied with Bernard Rogers and Howard Hanson: B.M., 1934; M.M., 1935; Ph.D., 1937; courses under Schoenberg at University of Southern California in Los Angeles, 1935. Joined the faculty of Eastman in 1937; he became chair of the composition department and director of its electronic music studio, 1968. Retired in 1973 from the former post, and held the latter until his retirement in 1978. Published *Foundations of Music* (New York, 1963).

ABD, AS66, BB58, BB71, BB92, CACA, DCM, EDM, EVM, GD54, HHH, IWW92, KTL, LMD, MHHH, NG, NGA, OL, OL95, PCM, REM, TCAC, X52, X65, X67, X68, X69, X71.

"Dr. Wayne Barlow." *Pan Pipes* 45 (January 1953): 40. *

"Eastman Installs Electronic Music Studio." *High Fidelity/Musical America* 17 (April 1967): MA2.

Wayne Barlow, a Fulbright recipient to study electronic music studios in Europe, will direct the new electronic music studio at Eastman.

Gay, Harry W. "Music for Organ." *American Organist* 43 (November 1960): 28.

A brief review of Barlow's *Three Christmas Tunes*.

Kyle, Marguerite K. "AmerAllegro." *Pan Pipes* 52/2 (1960): 36.

Three Christmas Tunes for Organ is published by Concordia.

53/2 (1961): 41.

Concordia Publishing House asks Barlow to compose a series of fifty-two hymn voluntaries for organ on Lutheran chorales.

55/2 (1963): 39.

Announces the release of *Hymn Preludes* by Concordia.

57/2 (1965): 46-47.

Hymn Voluntaries for the Church Year is premiered in Buffalo, N.Y., by organist Hans Vigeland.

60/2 (1968): 59.

Publication of *Hymn of the Week* by Concordia is announced; Barlow is appointed chairman of the composition department and director of the Electronic Music Studio at Eastman.

63/2 (1971): 49.

Announces that three voluntaries are included in *The Parish Organist* series (Concordia).

71/2 (1979): 26.

Barlow is named emeritus professor of composition at the Eastman School of Music, 30 June 1978.

"Wayne Barlow." *American Music Teacher* 25/2 (1975): 34.

Article honors Barlow's tenure at Eastman (1937-78). The MTNA will perform a program of his works, 28 March-1 April 1976, in Dallas, for the Festival of American Musical Heritage.

Leslie Bassett

B. Hanford, Calif., 22 January 1923. B.A., Fresno State College, 1947; composition under Ross Lee Finney, University of Michigan; M.M., 1949; doctor of music degree, 1956; private lessons under Arthur Honegger and Nadia Boulanger in Paris, 1950. Appointed to University of Michigan faculty, 1952; full professor in 1965; chairman of composition department, 1970; Albert A. Stanley Distinguished University Professor of Music, 1977. Emeritus, 1991. American Prix de Rome, 1961-63; National Institute of Arts and Letters Award, 1956; in 1966, received the Pulitzer Prize for music for *Variations for Orchestra*; Guggenheim fellowships, 1973-74 and 1980-81; Rockefeller Foundation grant for a stay at Villa Serbelloni in Bellagio, Italy, 1988. Authored *Manual of 16th-Century Counterpoint* (New York: Appleton-Century-Crofts, 1967).

AA73, ABD, AMH, ASUC, BB71, BB78, BB92, BDA, CACA, CACJ, CC92, CRI 148, DCM, DN78, IWW92, KTL, NGA, OL, OL95, PC71, PCM, WTM, X50, X55, X58, X60, X61, X62, X64, X65, X66, X67, X68, X69, X70, X71, X74, X75.

Finney, Ross Lee. "Leslie Bassett." *BMI: The Many Worlds of Music*, July 1966, 16.

Briefly traces Bassett's compositional growth to 1962 via his works, yet only mentions his 1964 *Four Statements for Organ* in passing, with a minute description of the work: "High clusters, low, short double-pedal staccatos, cymbelstern and numerous color changes. . . ."

Johnson, Ellen S. *Leslie Bassett: A Bio-Bibliography.* Westport, Conn.: Greenwood, 1994.

Kyle, Marguerite K. "AmerAllegro." *Pan Pipes* 46 (January 1954): 29-30.

Bassett completed his *Toccata* for organ in the past year.

48 (January 1956): 36.

Marilyn Mason introduces Bassett's *Toccata* for organ, 14 July 1955 at St. Paul's Chapel, Columbia University, New York.

51 (January 1959): 50.

Bassett is named assistant professor of composition and theory at University of Michigan School of Music.

52/2 (1960): 36-37.

Premiere of Bassett's *Organ Voluntaries*, 2 November 1958, by Mary McCall Stubbins, organist, First United Methodist Church, Ann Arbor.

54/2 (1962): 36-37.

Bassett's *Organ Toccata* is premiered by Marguerite Long at the AGO Convention, Toledo, Ohio, 21 June 1961; *Organ Voluntaries* receives its premiere by Gordon Wilson on 8 August 1961, Ann Arbor. Bassett is recipient of Prix de Rome, and is in residence at the American Academy in Rome.

55/2 (1963): 39-40.

Bassett's Prix de Rome was renewed for a second year.

58/2 (1966): 51.

Four Statements for Organ by Bassett is premiered by Marilyn Mason, 13 February 1965, Ann Arbor.

59/2 (1967): 64.

Bassett wins Pulitzer Prize (1966) for *Variations for Orchestra*.

66/2 (1974): 42.

Bassett is named a Guggenheim Fellow for 1973-74.

67/2 (1975): 45-46.

Bassett receives the Naumburg Award for *Sextet for Piano and Strings*.

71/2 (1979): 26-27.

Bassett is named the Albert A. Stanley Distinguished University Professor at University of Michigan, and is the 1978 Distinguished Alumnus from California State University at Fresno.

"Leslie Bassett—A Biographical Profile." *International Trombone Association Notes* 6/3 (1979): 2. *

"Leslie Bassett Retires." *International Trumpet Association Journal* 19/4 (1991): 13.
Announcement indicates Bassett retires from the University of Michigan.

"Liturgies: Organ." *Notes* 42/4 (1986): 856-57.
Bassett's *Liturgies*, commissioned by Marilyn Mason, who also played the premiere, is described in detail.

Parks, Anne. **"Featured Concerts at the Ann Arbor Organ Conference."** *Diapason* 72 (April 1981): 26-27.

> Marilyn Mason, who commissioned Bassett's *Liturgies*, performed the world premiere at the Ann Arbor Organ Conference. The work is well described; Mason also performed other works she commissioned, including Persichetti's *Dryden Liturgical Suite*, and Albright's *Organbook II* and *King of Instruments*.

James Beale

B. Wellesley Hills, Mass., 20 January 1924. A.B., Harvard 1945; further studies at Berkshire Music Center, 1946; B.M., 1946 and M.M., 1947, from Yale. Pupil of Walter Piston, Irving Fine, Aaron Copland, and Richard Donovan. University of Louisville faculty, 1947-48; University of Washington faculty member, since 1948, and full professor, from 1968. Guggenheim grant recipient, 1958-59. Organ music listed in CACA.

ABD, CACA, CACJ, OL, OL95, X62.

No bibliographical information located.

Theodore Beck

B. Oak Park, Ill., 17 April 1929. Pupil of Anthony Donato and Ewald Nolte at Northwestern University. Professor of music, Concordia Teachers College, Seward, Neb. Authored *Forty-Seven Hymn Intonations* (St. Louis: Concordia, 1971).

OL, OL95.

No bibliographical information located.

Robert Leech Bedell

B. Jersey City, N.J., 13 February 1909; d. Syosset, Long Island, N.Y., 22 May 1974. Studied organ, choral conducting, and composition in Brooklyn with Carl F. Schmidt and George Westerfield. Three honorary degrees accorded Bedell: Ph.D. from Temple Bar College;

Doctor of Music, Southwestern College; Doctor of Literature, Findlay College. Director of music and assistant organist in several New York churches including Grace Presbyterian in Brooklyn, 1924-26, Central Presbyterian, Brooklyn, 1927-30, and St. Anne's Episcopal, New York, 1927-45; organist, Brooklyn Museum of Art, from 1932, Brooklyn Institute of Arts and Sciences, from 1934, and St. Anne's Episcopal Church, New York (Morrisania), from 1950—all to 1951 and beyond. Composer-in-residence, Passeonest Monastery, n.d. ABD, CACA, OL, OL95.

"Organ Masterpieces." *American Organist* 32 (March 1949): 78.

Bedell is named editor of *Organ Masterpieces*, recently compiled with Hammond settings added. Pieces by Guilmant, Reger, Commette, Rheinberger, Bach, and Liszt are included.

"Prière à Notre Dame." *Diapason* 41 (May 1950): 37.

Publication of Bedell's *Prière à Notre Dame* by Edwin Ashdown, London, is announced; the work is described as easy.

"Prière à Notre Dame." *Musical Times* 91 (July 1950): 275. *

"Robert Leech Bedell." *Diapason* 42 (May 1951): 34.

A biography of Bedell; recently returned from Germany, he composed a work based on "Adoro te," which is dedicated to his mentor, Dr. Conrad Adenauer.

"Robert Leech Bedell." *Diapason* 47 (March 1956): 31.

Bedell is appointed to Covenant Lutheran Church, Ridgewood, Brooklyn, N.Y. Biographical data included.

Jan Oskar Bender

B. Haarlem, Netherlands, 3 February 1909; d. Hanerau, Germany, 29 December 1994. The only pupil of Hugo Distler; additional studies with Karl Straube and Kurt Thomas at Kirchenmusickalische Institut, Landeskirche, Sachsen, Leipzig. Professor of composition and composer-in-residence at Wittenberg University, Springfield, Ohio, 1965-76; retired to Germany; received the L.L.D., Concordia College, Seward, Nebr., 1974; taught at Valparaiso University, 1977-78; composer-in-residence and visiting professor of organ, Gustavus Adolphus College, St. Peter, Minn., 1979; 1981-91, visiting professor at Lutheran Theological Southern Seminary, Columbia, S.C. Returned to Germany, 1992.

ABD, CACA, CACJ, DN72, DN77, KTL, OL, OL95, X50, X53, X55, X59, X69, X74.

Bender, Jan. "A Processional for the Small Organ." *Church Music*, St. Louis 1 (1974): 7-9.

A score of the music is provided, with a note that the work is intended for a wedding processional.

Folkerts, Davis Lowell. "A Comprehensive Performance Project in Organ Literature with a Catalog of Jan Bender's Published Organ Works." D.M.A., University of Iowa, Organ Performance and Pedagogy, 1973. *RILM Abstracts of Music Literature.*

Provides a complete list of the published organ works by Bender according to typological categories: simple chorale compositions or free organ compositions. Annotations provide practical performance information and suggestions for pedagogical use. Transcribed tape-recorded interviews provide biographical information. Hymnological, source, and liturgical indices included.

Herman, H. David. *Jan Bender.* Minneapolis: Chantry Music Press, 1979.

A biography that includes a discussion of Hindemith's and Distler's influence on Bender's works, and an analysis of Bender's organ works. Contains a complete list of the organ works and an index to the chorales used in his chorale preludes.

————. "Jan Bender and His Organ Music." D.M.A., University of Kansas, 1974.

Myles, Wilfrid. "Jan Bender geehrt." *Musik und Kirche* 58/5 (1988): 283.

Jan Bender is made honorary member of the Association of Lutheran Church Musicians in the U.S.A. A brief biography is provided.

[Obituary.] *American Organist* 29 (April 1995): 53.

The obituary provides biographical details.

[Obituary.] *Diapason* 86 (March 1995): 4.

Highlights of Bender's career are listed in the obituary.

Herman Berlinski

B. Leipzig, Germany, 18 August 1910. Leipzig Conservatory, 1927-32: piano, theory, conducting; harmony with Karg-Elert; composition with Boulanger and piano with Cortot at Paris École Normale de Musique, 1934-38. Emigrated to the U.S. in 1941; became naturalized citizen in 1947. M.S.M., 1935, and D.S.M., 1960, from the Jewish Theological

Seminary of America, New York; organist at New York's Temple Emanu-El, 1954-63; minister of music, Hebrew Congregation, Washington, D.C., 1963-77.

ABD, ACA viii 3, AS66, BB65, BB71, BB78, BB92, BMI, CACA, DCM, IWC, KTL, LMD, NGA, OL, OL95, PC71, PCM, X57, X62, X64, X67, X68, X69, X70, X74.

"AGO Chapter News." *American Organist* 24 (June 1990): 33.

The world premiere of Berlinski's *Sinfonia No. 6: "Prayers for the Night"* for organ, strings, and timpani occurred 19 February 1990 at Westmoreland Congregational Church of Christ, Potomac, Md.

Barrett, Gavin. "London Organ Recitals." *Musical Opinion* 94 (December 1970): 156.

The reviewer considered *The Burning Bush* to have no artistic merit whatsoever; the piece "appalled me by its total lack of direction. . . ."

Berlinski, Herman. "Kol Nidre." *American Organist* 45 (November 1962): 8-12.

A detailed look at the background of the melody, and the text, which is a recitation of seven legalistic terms used for the rescinding of vows; and an in-depth discussion of Berlinski's work.

Bingham, Seth. "Organ Personalities." *American Organist* 46 (November 1963): 10.

Berlinski's biography is brief, but several of his important works for organ are mentioned; announcement of his new position as director of music at the Washington, D.C., Hebrew Congregation.

"Concert Hall: Music for a Seminar." *American Composers Alliance Bulletin* 10/3 (1962): 28.

Three recitals feature Berlinski's works, including *Sinfonia No. 1*, *Prelude to the Festival of Shabuoth*, *From the World of My Father*, and *The Burning Bush*. Comments from reviews are included.

"Herman Berlinski." *Diapason* 55 (January 1964): 38.

Berlinski is appointed director of music and organist for the Washington, D.C., Hebrew Congregation.

"Herman Berlinski." *Diapason* 56 (February 1965): 1.

Berlinski was commissioned to write *Processional*, which was premiered on November 29 at New York's Temple Emanu-El, by organist John Huston.

Kratzenstein, Marilou. "The Organ Works of Herman Berlinski." *American Organist* 23 (April 1989): 52-53.

A thorough examination of Berlinski's kaleidoscope of compositional techniques.

Mervine, Kenrick. "Herman Berlinski after 'The Burning Bush.'" *American Organist* 16 (May 1982): 46-47.

An interview with Berlinski reveals influences on his compositions, elements that make his work "Jewish," programmatic writing, and his use of serial technique. A list of his works and recordings accompanies the interview.

Miller, Malcolm. "Clifford's Tower: A Commemoration at York." *Musical Times* 131 (May 1990): 278.

Berlinski is present to introduce his work entitled *Litanies for the Persecuted*, a nine-section setting for organ, narrator, and alto, of Psalms, poems by the 11th-century poet Ibn Gabirol, and the 17th-century litany "Eleh Eskereh," a kind of Jewish "Passion."

"Prayer at Midnight and Air, from *From the World of My Father*, **for Organ."** *Notes* 14 (September 1957): 610-11.

Berlinski's works are reviewed as highly effective pieces.

"Recitals and Concerts." *American Organist* 43 (April 1960): 24-25.

Berlinski performs his five preludes for the Festivals and Holy Days at Temple Emanu-El, New York, 9 December 1959. The reviewer was impressed with the power of the compositions.

Vinton, John. "Neue Musik in der Synagoge." *Musik und Kirche* 39/3 (1969): 121-23.

Biographical data and Berlinski's compositional style are addressed as a writer of choral and organ music for the Jewish services. The concept of Jewish tradition is considered.

Wallace Berry

B. La Crosse, Wisc., 10 January 1928; d. Vancouver, 16 November 1991. University of Southern California: B.M., 1949; Ph.D., 1956; studied with Halsey Stevens; with Nadia Boulanger, Paris Conservatory, 1953-54. Taught at University of Southern California, 1956-57; University of Michigan, 1957-77, and 1978-91 at the University of British Columbia—where he was head of the music department, 1978-84. President, Society for Music Theory, 1982-85. Authored *Form in Music* (Englewood Cliffs, N.J.: Prentice-Hall, 1966; 2nd ed., rev., 1985); *Eighteenth-Century Imitative Counterpoint: Music for Analysis*, with Edward Chudacoff (New York: Appleton-Century-Crofts, 1969); *Structural Functions in*

Music (Englewood Cliffs, N.J.: Prentice-Hall, 1975; 2nd ed., 1987); and *Musical Structure and Performance* (New Haven: Yale University Press, 1989).

AA73, ABD, ASUC, BB92, CACA, IWW92, NG, NGA, OL, OL95, PC71, X53, X62, X65, X66, X67, X68, X69, X70, X71.

"Alchin Chair of Music." *Music of the West* 7 (March 1952): 4.

Wallace Berry and George Hyde, doctoral composition students of Halsey Stevens at the University of Southern California, will attend the Sixth Annual Symposium of the International Federation of Music Students at the Juilliard School and the Mid-West Symposium for Student Composers at the College of Music of Cincinnati.

Barkin, Elaine. "For Wallace T. Berry (1928-1991)." *Perspectives of New Music* 29/2 (1991): 506.

Includes brief eulogy.

"Here and There." *Diapason* 67 (June 1976): 3.

Marilyn Mason premieres Berry's *Variations for Organ*, 23 April 1976, at the National Shrine of the Immaculate Conception in Washington, D.C.

Kyle, Marguerite K. "AmerAllegro." *Pan Pipes* 52/2 (1960): 38.

Omitted from last year's update: Berry's *Organ Voluntaries* is premiered by organist Mary McCall Stubbins at First Methodist Church, Ann Arbor, 2 November 1958.

56/2 (1964): 45.

Berry is promoted to associate professor at University of Michigan; 30 September 1963, Berry received the University of Michigan's Distinguished Service Award for outstanding faculty. achievement and service.

57/2 (1965): 47.

Fantasy for Organ on "Vom Himmel Hoch" is completed.

58/2 (1966): 52.

Form in Music is released by Prentice-Hall in December; Berry elected to membership in ASCAP.

59/2 (1967): 65.

Berry's *Form in Music* receives its 2nd printing. He is promoted to professor at University of Michigan and wins an ASCAP award.

Rahn, John. "In Memoriam Wallace Berry." *Perspectives of New Music* 29/2 (1991): 507.

In his eulogy, Rahn lists Berry as president of the Society for Music Theory, former chairman of the theory department at the University of Michigan, and head of the School of Music at the University of British Columbia.

Herbert W. Bielawa

B. Chicago, Ill., 3 February 1930. Studied music at home; served in U.S. Army in Germany, 1954-56, and studied conducting there with Bruno Vondenhoff. Returning to U.S., took piano courses with Soulima Stravinsky at University of Illinois, B.M., 1954; enrolled at University Southern California, Los Angeles, and studied composition with Ingolf Dahl, Halsey Stevens, and Ellis Kohs; studied music for cinema with Miklós Rosza and David Raskin. Taught at Bethany College, Kansas. Appointed in 1966 to the faculty of San Francisco State University; established the Electronic Music Studio in 1967.

ABD, BB92, CACA, CACJ, OL, OL95, X62, X68, X69.

Drone, Jeanette, comp. "American Composer Update." *Pan Pipes* 73/2 (1981): 23-24.

Monophones for Organ is premiered May 1980 at Grace Cathedral in San Francisco by Sandra Soderlund.

74/2 (1983): 21.

In fall 1982, Bielawa was composer-in-residence at Briarcombe Foundation Artist Colony, Bolinas, Calif., and in spring 1983 he was at the MacDowell Colony.

"Here and There." *Diapason* 84 (September 1993): 3.

Bielawa is commissioned to write a piece for the rebuilt "mighty" Kimball at the Minneapolis Convention Center, to be premiered in 1994.

"Pipings." *American Organist* 27 (September 1993): 49.

Bielawa is commissioned to write a piece for the rebuilt Kimball pipe organ in the Minneapolis Convention Center, to be premiered 1-2 January 1994.

Torres-Santos, Raymond. "A Comparative Study of the Formal Structure in Music for an Ensemble and Tape." Ph.D., Music, University of California, Los Angeles, 1986. *RILM Abstracts of Music Literature.*

Bielawa's *Spectrum* is analyzed.

"Who's Who at the Convention." *National Association of Teachers of Singing* 19/2 (1962): 4.

Very brief biography; announcement that his one-act opera *A Bird in the Bush* will be performed at the convention.

Arthur Alfred Birkby

B. Collingswood, N.J., 15 December 1924. Received his B.S. in Music Education, Temple University, 1948; associate, Trinity College, London; M.M. and doctor of music degree in organ, Philadelphia Conservatory. Studied with Harry Alexander Matthews, Robert Elmore, and coached with Virgil Fox. Instructor at Westminster College, New Wilmington, Penn., 1952-56; associate professor of music, Western Michigan College, Kalamazoo, Mich., 1956-61; since 1961, professor of music at the University of Wyoming, Laramie. CACA, OL, OL95.

"Arthur Alfred Birkby." *Diapason* 43 (September 1952): 7.

> Birkby assumes position of organist at Westminster College, New Wilmington, Penn.; brief biography.

"Arthur Birkby." *American Organist* 38 (November 1955): 351.

> Birkby is appointed to the faculty of Westminster College, New Wilmington, Penn., official organist of the Youngstown Philharmonic, and organist-choirmaster of First Christian Church, New Castle, Penn.

"Arthur Birkby." *Diapason* 47 (July 1956): 19.

> Birkby is appointed associate professor of organ at Western Michigan College, Kalamazoo, Mich.

"Arthur Birkby." *Diapason* 52 (August 1961): 26.

> Birkby is appointed head of the organ and theory department at University of Wyoming, effective September 1, and also will serve as organist-choirmaster at St. Matthew's Cathedral, Laramie, Wy.

"On Arthur Birkby." *Clavier* 7/1 (1968): 43.

> Birkby joins the staff of *Clavier* as contributing editor. Gives biographical information and previous appointments.

Roberta Bitgood

B. New London, Conn., 15 January 1908. Graduate of Connecticut College for Women, Guilmant Organ School, Columbia University, and Union Theological Seminary. Student of J. L. Erb, William C. Carl, David McK. Williams, and Clarence Dickinson. Served as the first woman president of the American Guild of Organists, 1975-81. Organist-choir director at various churches including Trinity Lutheran Church, Buffalo, N.Y., First Presbyterian Church, Riverside, Calif., Redford Presbyterian Church, Detroit, Mich., First Presbyterian Church, Bay City, Mich.; minister of music, First Congregational Church, Battle Creek, Mich., 1969-76; since 1977, organist-director at St. Mark's Episcopal Church, Mystic, Conn. CACA, IWC, NGA, OL, OL95.

"Appointments." *American Organist* 52 (January 1969): 24.

Bitgood accepts position as organist and director of music at First Congregational Church, Battle Creek, Michigan. Brief résumé.

"Choral and Organ 'Who's Who.'" *Choral Guide* 8 (January 1956): 28. *

"Dr. Roberta Bitgood, Organist and Composer." *Diapason* 46 (April 1955): 9.

Bitgood makes eight-day tour in the United States as organ recitalist and director of children's choir festivals.

Kyle, Marguerite K. "AmerAllegro." *Pan Pipes* 51 (January 1959): 51-52.

Publication of Bitgood's *Chorale Prelude on "Covenanters Tune"* is announced by Flammer.

59/2 (1967): 66.

Bitgood is elected to the AGO National Council.

60/2 (1968): 62.

ASCAP award presented to Bitgood for 1966-67.

61/2 (1969): 46.

Bitgood receives ASCAP award; becomes organist-director at First Congregational Church, Battle Creek, 1 January 1969.

64/2 (1972): 47.

Hope publishes Bitgood's *Rejoice, Give Thanks*, for organ and brass quartet.

69/2 (1977): 34.

Commissioned for an organ dedication at First Presbyterian Church, Lafayette, La., Bitgood's *Meditation on "Kingsfold"* is published by Hinshaw.

"Roberta Bitgood." *Choir Guide* 4 (October 1951): 53.

Photo only.

"Roberta Bitgood." *American Organist* 43 (October 1960): 33.

Bitgood assumes new position as organist and director of music in Redford Presbyterian Church, Detroit. Lists previous positions and some biographical information.

"Roberta Bitgood." *Diapason* 51 (October 1960): 3.

Bitgood assumes duties 1 October 1960 as organist-director of music, Redford Presbyterian Church, Detroit; gives biographical information.

"Roberta Bitgood." *Diapason* 60 (January 1969): 2.

Announces Bitgood's appointment as organist-director of music to First Congregational Church, Battle Creek, Mich.

"Roberta Bitgood Elected President of AGO." *Pan Pipes* 68/4 (1976): 19.

> Bitgood is the first woman and the first non-resident of the New York City area to be elected president of the AGO; she served as first woman vice president in the AGO, and was also the first woman to earn a D.S.M. from Union Theological Seminary; educational history is cited.

"Roberta Bitgood Elected AGO President." *Diapason* 66 (July 1975): 3.

> Same information as in the previous item.

"Roberta Bitgood: New AGO President." *Music* (AGO) 9 (August 1975): 10.

> Same information as in the previous item.

"Season of Great Activity Ends for Roberta Bitgood." *Diapason*, August 1951, 4.

> Bitgood's numerous activities are specified.

Fred Bock

B. New York, 30 March 1939. Studied with Warren Benson, Ithaca College, B.S., 1960; studied with Halsey Stevens and Robert Linn, University of Southern California, M.M., 1962, and began doctoral work. Organist/choir director, Bel Air Presbyterian Church, Los Angeles, 1964-80; Hollywood Presbyterian, since 1980. Founder and director of the music publishing division of Word, 1963-70; started Gentry Publications, 1970, and later Fred Bock Music Co. Honorary doctor of music degree conferred by Taylor University (Upland, Ind.), 1986.

ABD, CACA, OL95.

"Convention Personalities." *American Organist* 18 (April 1984): 111.

> Bock is director of music at Hollywood Presbyterian Church. He received his B.A. from Ithaca College and worked towards a D.M.A. from the University of Southern California. Composition study was with Halsey Stevens. Bock served as general editor of *Hymns for the Family of God* (Paragon Assoc.).

"The Hymnal Companion." *Hymn* 31/4 (1980): 298. *

> Bock's book *The Hymnal Companion*, co-edited by B. J. Leach, is reviewed.

Wasson, D. DeWitt. "Books." *American Organist* 24 (August 1990): 27.

> Fred and Lois Bock's book *Creating Four-Part Harmony: Effective Ideas for Ministers of Music* is reviewed favorably. The title of the book refers to harmony with God, harmony in the church, harmony with the choir, and harmony in your own family.

John Boda

B. Boycesville, Wisc., 2 August 1922. Studied at the Eastman School of Music; joined faculty of Florida State University, Tallahassee, 1946. In 1956, Boda won a national competition to be an apprentice to conductor George Szell and the Cleveland Orchestra.

ABD, AMH, BB65, BB71, BB78, BB92, CACA, CRI 155, OL, OL95, PC71, PCM, TCH, X61, X62, X64.

"Composer Profile: John Boda." *National Association of College Wind and Percussion Instructors* 37/2 (1988-89): 42-44.

> A selected list of Boda's compositions featuring wind and percussion instruments follows highlights of his life.

"John Boda." *Pan Pipes* 47 (January 1955): 32-33.

> Boda, on the music faculty at Florida State University at Tallahassee, is working on his doctorate in composition at the Eastman School of Music.

James L. Boeringer

B. Pittsburgh, Penn., 4 March 1930. B.M., College of Wooster (Ohio), 1952; M.A., Columbia University, New York, 1954; D.S.M., Union Theological Seminary, New York, 1964. Musicology study with Paul Henry Lang and Gustave Reese; organ student of Richard Gore, Claire Coci, and Alec Wyton; composition with Seth Bingham and Douglas Moore. General music studies with Julius Herford; conducting with Rudolf Thomas, Elaine Brown, and Robert Fountain. Instructor of music, University of South Dakota, Vermillion, 1959-62; Oklahoma Baptist University, Shawnee, 1962-64; associate professor, 1964, professor, 1977, chairman of the music department, 1978-80, Susquehanna University, Selinsgrove, Penn.; director of the Moravian Music Foundation, Winston-Salem, N.C., 1980-84. Edited Christian Gregor's *Choral-Buch: A Facsimile of the First Edition of 1784* (Cranbury, N.H.: Moravian Music Foundation, 1984); authored *The Works of Richard T. Gore* (Springfield, Ohio: Chantry Music, 1974) and *Morning Star: The Life and Works of Francis Florentine Hagen* (Winston-Salem: Moravian Music Foundation Press, 1985).

ABD, CACA, OL, OL95, PC71, X62, X65, X66, X67, X69, X71, X74, X75.

"Appointments." *Diapason* 71 (July 1980): 6.

> Boeringer is appointed director of the Moravian Music Foundation and will direct the Foundation's History of Moravian Music in American project.

"Boeringer Is Appointed to New Jersey Church Position." *Diapason* 50 (January 1959): 3.

> Boeringer assumes post as organist-choir director at Calvary Lutheran Church, Leonia, N.J., while studying for his Doctor of Sacred Music degree at Union Theological Seminary.

"Boeringer to Susquehanna Faculty." *American Organist* 47 (July 1964): 24.

> Boeringer is appointed associate professor of music and university organist at Susquehanna University, Selinsgrove, Penn., effective fall 1964. Lists previous positions and memberships to professional organizations.

"Contributing Editors Named." *Journal of Church Music* 21 (January 1979): 17.

> Boeringer, chairman of the music department at Susquehanna University, is named a contributing editor to *Journal of Church Music*; educational history included.

"Director Resigns." *Moravian Music* 29/3 (1984): 59.

> Boeringer resigns as director of the Moravian Music Foundation after serving four years. A biography is included.

"Dr. James Boeringer." *Diapason* 55 (July 1964): 28.

> Boeringer is appointed university organist and assistant professor of music, Susquehanna University; condensed biography included.

"James Boeringer." *Diapason* 53 (October 1962): 35.

> Boeringer is appointed assistant professor of organ at Oklahoma Baptist University.

"James Boeringer to Direct the Foundation." *Moravian Music* 25/1 (1980): 1.

> The appointment of James Boeringer to direct the Moravian Music Foundation is announced. A detailed biography accompanies the announcement.

Frank R. Bohnhorst

B. 1923; d. 20 May 1956. Received B.M. at Illinois Wesleyan University; M.S.M. from Union Theological School of Sacred Music, New York. Composition studies with Grant Fletcher and Normand Lockwood; organ with George Scott and Robert Baker; choral conducting with Alfred Greenfield and Lowell Beveridge. Taught at Westminster College (Penn.) and Hanover College (Ind.); composer-in-residence, Illinois Wesleyan University, 1951-56.
OL, OL95.

"Composer-in-Residence, Illinois Wesleyan." *Pan Pipes* 47 (November 1954): 8, 33.

Composer-in-residence since fall 1951, Bohnhorst is founder of the Illinois Wesleyan Symposium of Contemporary American Music.

"Frank R. Bohnhorst." *Diapason* 41 (November 1950): 34.

Bohnhorst is appointed to the faculty of University of Missouri (Columbia) to teach organ and music theory; also organist-choir director at Missouri Methodist Church. Biographical information provided.

Kyle, Marguerite K. **"AmerAllegro."** *Pan Pipes* 40 (January 1957): 38.

Obituary notice indicates date of death as 20 May 1956; information about a recent commission is included.

William Elden Bolcom

B. Seattle, 26 May 1938. B.A., 1958, from University of Washington, Seattle, studied under John Verrall; composition with Darius Milhaud at Mills College, Oakland, Calif., M.A., 1961; Stanford University, D.M.A., 1964; advanced composition with Leland Smith. Study also at Paris Conservatory, 2nd prize in composition, 1965; Guggenheim fellowship for 1964-65 and 1968-69. Taught at the University of Washington-Seattle, 1965-66; Queens College of the City University of New York, 1966-68; New York University School of the Arts, 1969-70; University of Michigan from 1973, full professor since 1983. Composer-in-residence of the Detroit Symphony Orchestra, from 1987. Pulitzer Prize in Music, 1988, for *12 New Etudes* for piano. Authored *Reminiscing with Sissle and Blake* (New York: Viking Press, 1973); edited the collected essays of George Rochberg, *The Aesthetics of Survival: A Composer's View of 20th Century Music* (Ann Arbor: University of Michigan Press, 1984); and with Paul Oliver and Max Harrison, *The New Grove Gospel, Blues and Jazz with Spirituals and Ragtime* (New York: Norton, 1986).

ABD, BB65, BB71, BB78, BB92, CACJsp, DCM, DN72, IWW92, KTL, NG, NGA, OL, OL95, PC71, X65, X67, X68, X69, X70, X71, X74.

Arnold, Corliss R. **"AGO Colleague Examination Update: Bolcom and Dupré."** *American Organist* 21 (December 1987): 64-65.

A measure-by-measure approach to the performance of "Just as I Am," from *Three Gospel Preludes*.

"Banner Year for Composer Bolcom." *Billboard* 92 (19 January 1980): 48.

Among the many works Bolcom introduced over the past year is his *Three Gospel Preludes*, which he presented in Dallas.

Bullat, G. Nicholas. "AGO '86 Detroit June 30-July 4." *Diapason* 77 (October 1986): 13.

Marilyn Mason premieres the Bolcom work she commissioned, *Gospel Preludes, Book 4*, at the AGO convention. A description of the work is included.

Carl, Robert. "Six Case Studies in New American Music: A Postmodern Portrait Gallery." *College Music Symposium* 30 (1990): 59-63.

An overview of Bolcom's music indicates it is full of virtuosity, tunefulness, facility, and sincerity; Carl also notes Bolcom's apparent love for and mastery of popular music.

Covington, Kate. "Music Reviews." *Notes* 48/3 (1992): 1002-04.

William Albright edits Bolcom's *Hydraulis for Organ*. Covington indicates Bolcom's preference for a variety of textures and colors. Other techniques include clusters, technically demanding pedal trills, double pedal sections, and pedal glissandos. The work's title refers to the earliest of organs, and the primitive sounds convey how the early organ may have sounded.

Drone, Jeanette, comp. "American Composer Update." *Pan Pipes* 75/2 (1983): 22.

Bolcom's *Gospel Preludes, Book 3* is premiered in January 1982 by organist Marilyn Keiser at Emory University; Marilyn Mason gave its first performance in June 1982 at the AGO convention; *Three Gospel Preludes, Book 1* is published by Marks.

Ferré, Susan. "Dallas Premiere of Three Bolcom Works." *Diapason* 70 (September 1979): 17.

Commissioned by the Educational Projects Committee for the 60th anniversary of the Dallas AGO Chapter, Bolcom's *Three Gospel Preludes* were performed twice to let the audience hear and better appreciate the works; a detailed presentation on the *Preludes* included.

Fried, Adrienne G. "New York Premieres on 2 Works on Albright Program." *Music* (AGO) 6 (March 1972): 30-31.

James Ogden, percussionist, and William Albright, organist, perform Bolcom's *Black Host*.

Haglund, Rolf. "William Bolcom—gränsöverskridare." *Musikrevy* 33/3 (1978): 99-102.

In Swedish. A discussion of his style of compositions, primarily his organ works. Some contemporary opinions are given on his compositional style. The author suggests that Bolcom has been long overlooked as a composer of note in the Americas and abroad.

Haller, William. "Organ Works of the Avante-Garde [sic]." *Clavier* 13/4 (1974): 33-36.

A discussion of influential American composers on avant-garde works; includes an analysis of *Black Host* by Bolcom.

"Here and There." *Diapason* 70 (December 1979): 19.

Bolcom's *Humoresk* for organ and orchestra was premiered at New York's Alice Tully Hall on 3 December 1979; Dennis Russell Davies conducted the American Composers Orchestra with Anthony Newman at the organ.

Hiemenz, Jack. "Musician of the Month: William Bolcom." *High Fidelity/Musical America* 26 (September 1976): MA4-5, MA39.

A discussion of William Bolcom's ability to be successful as a crossover composer, and influences on his writing.

"Honors." *American Organist* 27 (June 1993): 43.

Bolcom is elected to the American Academy of Arts and Letters, along with Dizzy Gillespie.

Kyle, Marguerite K. "AmerAllegro." *Pan Pipes* 61/2 (1969): 46.

Bolcom's *Black Host* is premiered 20 July 1968, Ann Arbor; written for organ, chimes, drums and tape, the composer performed the organ part with Sidney Hodkinson, percussion. Bolcom receives a Guggenheim prize, 1968-69.

62/2 (1970): 52.

Bolcom is appointed Composer-in-Residence at New York University, through a Rockefeller Foundation grant.

Mazzatenta, Michael Lawrence. "William Bolcom's *Gospel Preludes* for Organ." D.M.A., Arizona State University, 1991. *Dissertation Abstracts* 53 (July 1992): 14A-15A.

Bolcom's twelve gospel preludes are analyzed with respect to pitch, rhythm, and form. The works include a juxtaposition of jazz, baroque, atonal, and gospel styles.

"Music Journal's Gallery of Living Composers." *Music Journal* 31 (January 1973): 20-24.

A biography, including awards received, major works, and address.

Orledge, Robert. "Liverpool." *Musical Times* 117 (April 1976): 335.

In the "2002" Series, Gillian Weir played Bolcom's *Black Host*, 11 February 1976, with David Corkhill, percussion; reviewer thought it was unsuccessfully performed.

Shenk, Calvert, and Richard De Vinney. "AGO National Convention Detroit, Mich., June 30-July 4." *American Organist* 20 (August 1986): 38-42.

Bolcom's *Gospel Preludes* are performed by Marilyn Mason. "A more ingratiating, jazz-influenced style," this set made a strong impression on the two authors.

Harriet Hallock Bolz

(Mrs. Harold A.) B. Cleveland, Ohio, ca. 1912. Studied with Leo Sowerby (ca. 1945) and Paul Creston. Member of International League of Women Composers, American Women Composers, Inc., National Association of Composers, music editor of *The Pen Women*. B.A. from Case Western Reserve, 1933; M.A. from Ohio State University, 1958. Awards: National Federation of Music Clubs, 1965; Phi Beta Fraternity, 1968, first prize; National League of Pen Women, 1970, 1972, 1976, 1978; grants from New York Arts Council, Meet the Composer, 1978. Private teacher of piano and composition; lectures and writes about contemporary music.
CR.

Bolz, Harriet. **"Meter, Mode and Mood in Modern Music."** *Pen Women* 46/4 (January 1971): 10, 14.

> Bolz describes the challenge given to composers of contemporary music: to make the sounds of new music meaningful to their audiences.

Edith Borroff

B. New York, 2 August 1925. Studied with Irwin Fischer, American University, Chicago: B.M., 1946; M.M., 1948, in composition; Ph.D. in musicology, 1959, composition with Ross Lee Finney at University of Michigan. Won Andrew Mellon post-doctoral award, 1960-61; Faculty posts at Milwaukee-Downer College, 1950-54; Hillsdale College, 1958-62; University of Wisconsin-Milwaukee, 1962-66; Eastern Michigan University, 1966-73; visiting professor at University of North Carolina, 1972-73; from 1973, professor at State University of New York, Binghamton, retired 1992. Authored *Music of the Baroque* (Dubuque, Iowa: Wm. C. Brown, 1970); *Music in Perspective* (New York: Harcourt Brace Jovanovich, 1976); *Music in Europe and the United States: A History* (Englewood Cliffs, N.J.: Prentice-Hall, 1971; 2nd ed., New York: Ardsley House, 1990); *Music in Europe and the United States: Anthology of Musical Examples* (New York: Ardsley House, 1990); *American Operas: A Checklist* (this publisher, 1992); *Music Melting Round: A History of Music in the United States* (New York: Ardsley House, 1995). Organ music listed in CR.
BB92, NGA.

"Premieres." *American Organist* 25 (August 1991): 36.

> Borroff's *Meditation and Toccata* is premiered at the symposium, American Organ Music Since 1970: A Retrospective, at Carleton College, 25-26 April 1991. The piece was written for and performed by organist Mary Ann Dodd.

Regier, Janet E. "The Organ Works of Edith Borroff: An Introduction." D.M.A., University of Oklahoma, 1993. *ProQuest Dissertation Abstracts.*

> An introduction to Borroff's solo organ works that are not well known. Includes biographical information, detailed information about the nine solo organ compositions, and Borroff's own words about her approach to composition.

Paul Bouman

B. Hamburg, Minn., 26 August 1918. B.S., Concordia Teachers College, River Forest, Ill.; M.M., Northwestern University; study at Westfalian Church Music School, Hereford, Germany; teacher-director of music, Ebenezer Lutheran Church, Milwaukee, 1939-45; teacher-director of music, St. Paul Lutheran Church, Melrose Park, Ill., 1945-53; teacher-director of music, Grace Lutheran Church, River Forest, Ill., 1953-83; guest instructor at Valparaiso University and Concordia Teachers College; co-founder, 1971, of the Bach Vesper Cantata Series, Grace Lutheran Church, River Forest. Organ music and biography listed in Arnold's book.

OL, OL95.

No bibliographical information located.

Gerhard Brand

B. Lübeck, Germany, 1922. Served in the U.S. armed forces, World War II, in Russia; received his M.D. Appointed professor of microbiology (oncology) at the University of Minnesota, 1957. Organ music and biography listed in Arnold's book.

OL, OL95.

No bibliographical information located.

George Brandon

B. Stockton, Calif., 4 February 1924. Received A.B. in history from College of the Pacific; M.S.M., 1952, and M.R.E., 1957, from Union Theological Seminary. Pupil of Searle Wright, Robert Baker, and Harold Friedell. On faculty at Eureka College (Ill.), 1957-59;

William Penn College (Iowa), 1959-62; then free-lance composer, organist at First Christian Church of Stockton.

ABD, CACA, OL, OL95.

Heaton, Charles Huddleton. **"Contemporary Composers: George Brandon."** *Journal of Church Music* 15 (September 1973): 12-14.

Brandon's music is useful to churches with small instruments and choirs as well as those with more generous resources; selected list of compositions follows.

Henry Dreyfus Brant

B. Montréal, Québec, 15 September 1913, of American parents. Studied at McGill Conservatory, Montréal, 1926-29. Moved to New York in 1929 where he studied music theory with Leonard Mannes, Institute of Musical Arts, 1929-34; studied at Juilliard Graduate School, 1932-34, with Rubin Goldmark; private theory lessons with Wallingford Riegger and George Antheil, and private composition with Aaron Copland. Conducting lessons with Fritz Mahler, Gustave Mahler's nephew. Taught composition and conducting at Columbia, 1945-52; teacher and student at Juilliard, 1947-54; and Bennington College (Vermont), 1957-80, where he is now professor emeritus. Received two Guggenheim awards, 1947 and 1956. First American to win the Prix Italia, 1955; elected to American Academy and Institute of Arts and Letters, 1979.

ABD, AMH, BB78, BB92, BDA, CACA, CACJ, DCM, JCN, KTL, NG, TCH, X53, X54, X55, X56, X57, X59, X60, X61, X62, X69, X71.

Belt, Byron. **"AGO National Convention, San Francisco 1984."** *American Organist* 18 (August 1984): 28-33.

Brant's *Lombard Street: Spatial Promenades for Organ Solo and Four Percussionists* is performed during the convention. Organist for the work was Fred Tulan.

Gagne, Cole, and Tracy Caras. *Soundpieces: Interviews with American Composers.* Metuchen, N.J.: Scarecrow, 1982.

Furnishes a survey of current trends in American music; offers interviews with numerous composers, including Brant.

Gustafson, Bruce. **"AGO San Francisco: Some Perspectives."** *Diapason* 75 (October 1984): 6, 8-9.

Brant's *Lombard Street* is pronounced effective; his *Orbits* received boos at the end of the performance.

Lee Hastings Bristol, Jr.

B. Brooklyn, N.Y., 9 April 1923; d. Syracuse, N.Y., 11 August 1979. Graduate of Hamilton College, 1947; graduate work at University of Geneva, Switzerland; degree in organ from Trinity College, London. Organist at All Saints Church, Bay Head, N.J., 1947-68; served on Joint Commission on Church Music (Episcopal), 1969-73; president, Westminster Choir College, 1962-69; director of public relations for Bristol-Myers, products division. Authored *Seed for a Song*, biography of Bishop Robert Nelson Spencer (n.p., n.d.); ed., *More Hymns & Spiritual Songs: A Hymnal Supplement Containing Material from Old and New Sources* (rev. enl. ed., New York: Walton, 1977); compiled by Bristol and C. S. Smith, *Six Centuries of Musical Table Graces* (Atlanta: Knox, 1979).

CACA, OL, OL95.

"Award Honorary Degrees to Lee Hastings Bristol, Jr." *Diapason* 52 (July 1961): 5.

> Bristol is awarded the honorary degree Doctor of Laws from Findlay College (Ohio), 25 May 1961, and from Missouri Valley College, Marshall, 3 June 1961.

"Dr. Lee Hastings Bristol, Jr." *Diapason* 59 (April 1968): 5.

> Resigns as president of Westminster Choir College, effective 30 June 1969.

Kyle, Marguerite K. "AmerAllegro." *Pan Pipes* 59/2 (1967): 66-67.

> Bristol received his L.H.D. degree from Temple University and the Episcopal Bishop of New Jersey's Medal of Honor.

63/2 (1974): 52.

> Westminster Choir College confers the Honorary Doctor of Fine Arts degree upon Bristol.

"Lee Hastings Bristol, III." *Diapason* 46 (July 1955): 32.

> Bristol is granted the honorary degree Doctor of Humanities, 6 June 1955, from Los Angeles Conservatory of Music and Art.

"Lee Hastings Bristol, Jr." *Diapason* 50 (July 1959): 5.

> Dickinson College, Carlisle, Penn., confers the honorary Doctor of Music degree upon Bristol, and Webber College, Babson Park, Fla., awards him the honorary Doctor of Letters degree.

"Lee Hastings Bristol, Jr." *Diapason* 60 (July 1969): 3.

> Bristol becomes the first executive secretary for the Joint Commission on Church Music of the Protestant Episcopal Church, effective 1 July 1969.

"Lee Hastings Bristol, Jr. (1923-79)." *Hymn* 30/4 (1979): 277.

A eulogy indexing the many accomplishments of Bristol, written by Alec Wyton, his colleague in the Episcopal Church.

"Lee Hastings Bristol New Head of Westminster." *Diapason* 53 (April 1962): 1.

Effective 1 March 1962, Bristol is named President of Westminster Choir College at age 38. Brief biography included.

"The New WCC President—Dr. Lee Hastings Bristol, Jr." *Choral Guide* 15 (September 1962): 10.

Announcement of Bristol's new position at Westminster Choir College, with a summary of his background as businessman, writer, composer, educator, and civic and religious leader.

"Notes from a Commuter's Train." *Music Journal* 12 (January 1954): 15.

Bristol talks about composing while in transit from Manhattan to Princeton.

[Obituary.] *American Organist* 13/10 (1979): 30.

Death notice includes a brief rendering of highlights in Bristol's life; tribute to follow in November issue.

[Obituary.] *Diapason* 70 (October 1979): 3.

Notice of Bristol's death in Syracuse, N.Y., at age 56; memorial service held 16 August 1979 in Princeton, N.J.

[Obituary.] *Journal of Church Music* 21 (November 1979): 9.

[Obituary.] *Hymn Society* 9/7 (1980): 135-36.

A thorough review of Bristol's life.

"Personals." *American Organist* 52 (July 1969): 27.

Bristol, retiring president of Westminster Choir College, Princeton, N.J., will be made a Fellow of the Royal School of Church Music. Accolades are given Bristol for his leadership at Westminster.

Robinson, Ray. "Lee Hastings Bristol, Jr. in Retrospect." *Journal of Church Music* 22 (September 1980): 16-17.

Indicates death date is 10 August 1979; a tribute to Bristol's life establishes him as one who invested his life in the lives of others.

————. **"Lee Hastings Bristol, Jr."** *American Organist* 13 (November 1979): 37.
A close look at Bristol's life.

"Variations on 'Old Hundredth.'" *Diapason* 42 (September 1951): 22.

> Announcement of the upcoming premiere of Bristol's lengthy organ work at St. Bartholomew's Church, New York, by organist Harold W. Friedell. Background and overall look at the work.

Radie Britain

B. Silverton, Tex., 17 March 1903; d. 23 May 1994, n.p. Studied piano at the American Conservatory in Chicago, B.M., 1924; studied music theory in Munich, Germany. On the faculty of the American Conservatory of Music, Chicago, 1938-ca. 1989. Received the international prize given by the Hollywood Bowl and the Juilliard Publication Award, 1930 and 1945, respectively, for *Heroic Poem*. Over 50 of her compositions have won international and national awards. Received the first national award given by the National League of American Pen Women for her *Rhapsodic Phantasy for Piano* and *Barcarola*. Honorary doctorate of music given by the Musical Arts Conservatory of Amarillo. The University of California, Los Angeles, music library houses her complete works. Her publications include *Major and Minor Moods*, *Lasso of Time*, *Adoration*, *Composer's Corner* (Hollywood: Highland Music, 1978).

AA73, ABD, AMH, AS66 [b. 1904], BB58, BB65, BB71, BB78, BB92, BDA, CACA, DN76, DN77, DN78, HHH, IWC, KTL, LMD, MHHH, NGA, PC71, PCM, REM, TCAC, WCH, WI62 [b. 1906], WI69 [b. 1906], X50, X56, X57, X60, X61, X62, X64, X65, X66, X67, X68, X69, X70, X71, X74, X75.

"American Composer Update." *Pan Pipes* 73/2 (1981): 24.

> Indication of sources in which Britain's name and biography appear.

Bailey, Walter B., and Nancy G. *Radie Britain: A Bio-Bibliography*. New York: Greenwood, 1990.

> Includes biography, bibliography, discography, works and performances, and a listing of works. Lists birthdate as 17 March 1899.

Drone, Jeanette, comp. **"American Composer Update."** *Pan Pipes* 75/2 (1983): 22-23.

> Britain receives a President's Achievement Award from Ronald Reagan.

Goss, Madeleine. *Radie Britain*. New York: Modern Music Makers, 1952. *

"Honors for Members." *ASCAP* 1/2 (1967): 18. *

> Includes information about *Cosmic Mist*.

Kyle, Marguerite K. "AmerAllegro." *Pan Pipes* 46 (January 1954): 32.

The Radie Britain Musical Foundation Fund is established to grant scholarships to worthy music students.

48 (January 1956): 38.

Britain wins First Prize in the National Pen Women's Contest.

50 (January 1958): 46.

Britain is given Award of Merit by the American Pen Women.

53/2 (1961): 45.

First Prize in the National American Pen Women's Competition is awarded to Britain.

55/2 (1963): 42.

Britain is recipient of the first national prize in a competition sponsored by the National Pen Women.

57/2 (1965): 49.

Britain wins the National First Prize from the National Pen Women.

59/2 (1967): 67.

Britain receives another first prize from the National League of American Pen Women.

63/2 (1971): 52-53.

Two national prizes for first place are accorded Britain by the National League of American Pen Women.

67/2 (1975): 48.

Britain receives ASCAP Award for 10th consecutive year; gives roster of sources in which Radie Britain is mentioned.

69/2 (1977): 35.

Originally for orchestra, Radie Britain made a version of *Pyramids of Giza* for organ, presented by Patricia Boos in Bowie, Md.

70/2 (1978): 34.

Britain named national music editor of *The Pen Woman*.

71/2 (1979): 28.

Britain's *Composer's Corner*, a collection of her articles, is published by Highland Music Company, Hollywood, Calif.

LePage, Jane Weiner. *Women Composers, Conductors, and Musicians of the Twentieth Century: Selected Biographies.* Metuchen: Scarecrow, 1980.

Includes Britain's biography and provides a list of works and discography.

"News in Brief." *Musical Courier* 156 (15 December 1957): 6. *

"Our Cover." *Music of the West* 12 (January 1956): 4. *

"Radie Britain." *Pan Pipes* 45 (January 1953): 42. *

47 (January 1955): 34.

Britain is the National Chairman of Music for the American Pen Women.

"Radie Britain." *Music of the West* 10 (June 1955): 15. *

"Radie Britain's Music." *Pan Pipes* 48 (January 1956): 25.

The 200th radio program on KPPC of the Pasadena Alumnae Chapter features Britain's *oeuvres*.

Rayner Brown

B. Des Moines, Iowa, 23 February 1912. B.M., 1938 and M.M., 1947, University of Southern California. Mentors include Ingolf Dahl, Hanns Eisler, Lucien Cailliet. Organ teacher, Los Angeles. Professor of music, Biola University, La Mirada, Calif., 1950-77; organist, Wilshire Presbyterian Church, Los Angeles, 1941-77.

ABD, BB78, BB92, CACA, DN73, DN76, DN78, KTL, OL95, TCH, X62, X70, X74.

"Composer's Works Premiered." *Diapason* 74 (October 1983): 7.

Robert Prichard premieres *Sonata for Organ and Brass Quintet* at Pasadena Presbyterian Church; William Beck and James Walker present the first hearing of *Sonata for Two Organs*, First Congregational Church, Los Angeles; Mary Preston performs *Sonata da piazza* for the first time; Janet Krellwitz premieres *Quattordici*, First Presbyterian Church, Garden Grove; *Passacaglia* is premiered by Mildred Kammeyer Barnes, Grace Lutheran Church, Culver City, Calif.; and *Quintelata* is premiered by Connie Grisham at Our Lady of Lourdes, Northridge.

"Here and There." *Diapason* 79 (October 1988): 3.

Sonata for Alto Saxophone, Percussion, and Organ Duet is premiered at Trinity Church, Wall Street in New York City, 2 April 1988. Cherry Rhodes and Ladd Thomas commissioned the work, which is dedicated to them.

"Here and There." *Diapason* 81 (January 1990): 3.

> Cherry Rhodes plays the premiere of Brown's *Sonata for Organ, No. 20*, at Grace Cathedral, San Francisco, 15 October 1989.

"Organ Recitals." *Diapason* 74 (July 1983): 15.

> Mary Preston premieres *Sonata da piazza* at Wilshire United Methodist Church, Los Angeles, February 7.

"Premieres." *American Organist* 26 (February 1992): 54.

> *Fioretti*, for two violins and organ, is premiered 6 October 1991, at First Baptist Church, Bakersfield, Calif. Jean and Donna Dodson played violins, accompanied by organist Phillip Dodson. The work is dedicated to the Dodsons.

"Premieres." *American Organist* 17 (November 1983): 45-46.

> *Sonata for Organ and Brass* is premiered by Robert Prichard at Pasadena Presbyterian Church. William Beck and James Walker perform the premiere of *Sonata for Two Organs* at First Congregational Church of Los Angeles.

"Premieres." *American Organist* 18 (September 1984): 33.

> *Koulu* is premiered by organist Mark F. Fackrell on April 9, First Methodist Church, Glendale, Calif.

"Premieres." *American Organist* 22 (October 1988): 50-51.

> The premiere of *Sonata for Alto Saxophone, Percussion, and Organ Duet* occurred on April 12 at Trinity Church, New York City. The commissioning duo—Cherry Rhodes and Ladd Thomas—requested the unusual combination of instruments. The work was dedicated to the duo.

"Premieres." *American Organist* 24 (Feburary 1990): 51.

> Cherry Rhodes performs the premiere of *Sonata for Organ, No. 20*, at Grace Cathedral, San Francisco, on September 15. The work, written for Ms. Rhodes, was the first prize winner in the Los Angeles AGO Chapter composition contest.

"Recital Programs." *Diapason* 74 (March 1983): 19.

> William Beck and James Walker premiere *Sonata for Two Organs* at First Congregational Church, Los Angeles, November 5.

"Steppin' Out: Premiered." *ASCAP in Action*, spring 1982, 50. *

> Brown's *Concerto No. 4*, for organ and wind orchestra is premiered.

Tusler, Robert L., comp. "**Rayner Brown: 80th Birthday Tribute.**" *Diapason* 83 (March 1992): 14-16.

A review of Brown's significant output of music: symphonies, concertos, choral works, large ensemble, chamber, piano, and organ works. A listing of his solo organ music and organ with instruments.

Paul J. Bunjes

B. Frankenmuth, Mich., 27 September 1914. M.M., University of Michigan; Ph.D., Eastman School of Music, 1966. On faculty, Concordia Teachers College, River Forest, Ill. Authored *The Service Propers Noted; The Introits . . .* (St. Louis: Concordia, 1960); *The Formulary Tones Annotated* (St. Louis: Concordia, 1965); *The Praetorius Organ* (St. Louis: Concordia, 1966). OL, OL95, X62, X70.

Hillert, Richard. "**Composers for the Church: Paul Bunjes.**" *Church Music* (St. Louis) 2 (1974): 15-26.

A scholarly overview of Bunjes's compositional style for various performing forces, includes a discussion on his background. A list of his works with dates and publishers and a list of organs he designed are included. Discussion about his liturgical music, hymn settings, chorale concertatos, chorale music, vocal music, organ music, and his critical editions of Brahms and Rhau are presented.

Wayne Burcham

B. Burlington, Iowa, 27 August 1943. Studied at Drake University; student of Gerhard Krapf at the University of Iowa, and Paul Fetler and Dominick Argento at the University of Minnesota; first prize winner in the AGO composition competition, 1973; director of music, Christ Church Lutheran, Minneapolis, 1969-71; since 1971, director of music at Holy Nativity Lutheran Church, Minneapolis. ABD, OL, OL95.

Belt, Byron. "**AGO/'80—Twin Cities Convention.**" *American Organist* 14 (August 1980): 25-26.

Burcham's *Suite for Organ after Baroque Masters* is one of two premieres presented at Evensong. A fun and splashy piece in its teasing treatment of Bach, Scarlatti, Couperin, and Vivaldi, it was "inappropriate" as a prelude, according to reviewer.

Stephen Douglas Burton

B. Whittier, Calif., 24 February 1943. Studied piano and theory at Oberlin; in Vienna, studied with Morris Browda at the Conservatory, 1957-60; classes in composition and conducting at the Mozarteum, Salzburg, 1962-65; directed Munich Kammerspiele, 1963-64; private study with Hans Werner Henze, 1962-66; Guggenheim Fellowship, 1969; additional study at Peabody Conservatory with Jean Eichelberger Ivey. Instructor, Catholic University of America; appointed associate professor of composition, George Mason University, Fairfax, Va., 1974.

ABD, OL, OL95, X68, X71, X74.

"A Capital Convention, Washington, D.C., June 28-July 2, 1982: Composers and Their Commissions." *American Organist* 16 (May 1982): 4.

An overview of Burton's *Homage to Johann Sebastian Bach*.

Foss, Lucas, et al. "Contemporary Music: Observations from Those Who Create It." *Music & Artists* 5/3 (1972): 18.

Burton expresses his views on composition in America today as being in a transitional stage and indicates that many music schools are bringing their educational programs up to date.

"Meet the Composer: Stephen Douglas Burton." *Instrumentalist* 26 (May 1972): 38-39.

A discussion of whether serious music will survive as a vital art, or exist only as a museum piece, and the responsibility of composer, performer, audience, and educator.

"1968 Winning Young Composers Named." *Music Clubs Magazine* 48/2 (1968): 37-38.

Burton receives first prize in Young Composers' Contest, 1968, in Classification I, III, IV, and also receives the Devora Nadworney Award. Detailed biography is provided.

Donald A. Busarow

B. Racine, Wisc., 10 April 1934. B.S., Concordia College, River Forest, Ill.; graduate studies at University of Michigan; received M.M. from Cleveland Institute of Music, 1964, and Ph.D. from Michigan State University, 1973. Organ study with Victor Hildner, Robert Noehren, Henry Fusner, and Corliss Arnold. Assistant professor of music, Concordia College, Milwaukee, 1972. In 1986, associate professor of music, chairman of the organ and church music departments, and director of graduate studies at Wittenberg University, Springfield, Ohio. Director of Wittenberg University choir and director of music at

St. Matthew Lutheran Church, Dayton, Ohio. Dissertation Abstract, 1974: "Melodies Associated with Chorale Texts by Martin Luther, as Found in *Das Babst Gesangbuch* (1545): A Study of Representative Musical Settings for Congregation, Choir and Organ, 1523-1959."

OL, OL95.

"Donald Busarow Assumes Duties at Concordia College, Milwaukee." *Diapason* 63 (September 1972): 10.

Busarow is named assistant professor of music, serving as organ and theory instructor; also serves as organ consultant for the Walcker Organ company of Germany.

"New Contribution Editors Named." *Journal of Church Music* 28 (September 1986): 45-46.

Biographical information provided on Busarow.

George Cacioppo

B. Monroe, Mich., 24 September 1927; d. Ann Arbor, 4 April 1984. University of Michigan, M.A., 1952: composition with Ross Lee Finney; with Leon Kirschner at Tanglewood; subsequently co-founded the ONCE Festival concerts in Ann Arbor, 1960.

ABD, BB71, BB78, BCL, CACA [b. 1926], JCN, KTL, OL, OL95, X64, X69.

Brown, Anthony. "An Interview with George Cacioppo." *Composer* (US) 8/17 (1976-77): 31-35.

An informative interview with Cacioppo; a discussion of the university's influence—at times adverse—on the creativity of the composer.

Finney, Ross Lee, et al. "Panel Discussion: Mixed Media Composition." *American Society of University Composers* 3 (1968): 123-45. *

James, Richard. "ONCE: Microcosm of the 1960s Musical and Multimedia Avant-Garde." *American Music* 5/4 (winter 1987): 359-90.

Participants in the Ann Arbor ONCE group (1957-69) made highly significant contributions to many of the most important trends in art music of the 1960s: electronic music, multimedia performance art, formal simultaneity, controlled improvisation, and film. Includes key figure George Cacioppo.

John Cage

B. Los Angeles, Calif., 5 September 1912; d. New York, 12 August 1992. Spent two years
at Pomona College. Composition student of Richard Buhling, 1930-31; student of Adolph
Weiss and Arnold Schoenberg, University of California, Los Angeles; studied with Henry
Cowell in New York, 1933. Studied Eastern philosophy with Gita Sarabhai and Zen
Buddhism with Daisetz T. Suzuki in the late 1940s. Guggenheim Foundation award,
1949; composer-in-residence for the University of Cincinnati, 1967, University of Illinois,
1967-69, and University of California, Davis, 1969. Music adviser to Merce Cunningham
Dance Co., 1942-87. Elected to the National Institute of Arts/Letters, 1968; received the
Commandeur de l'Ordre des Arts et des Lettres from the French government, 1982; Charles
Eliot Norton Professor of Poetry, Harvard University, 1988-89. Authored *Silence* (1961),
A Year from Monday (1967), *M* (1973), *Empty Words* (1979), and *X* (1983).

ABD, AMH, BB78, BB92, CACA, CACJ, DCM, DN77, HLM, JCN, KTL, MGGs, NG, OL95, TCH, VER, X50, X54,
X55, X56, X58, X59, X60, X61, X62, X69, X70, X71, X74.

Cogan, Robert. "In Memoriam John Cage." *Sonus* 13/2 (1993): 1-5.
> A tribute to John Cage.

"Convention Personalities." *American Organist* 18 (April 1984): 113.
> Cage's music is published by Henmar Press, a subsidiary of C. F. Peters; Cage serves as musical
> adviser for Merce Cunningham's dancers.

Gagne, Cole, and Tracy Caras. *Soundpieces: Interviews with American Composers.* Metuchen,
N.J.: Scarecrow, 1982.
> Furnishes a survey of current trends in American music; offers interviews with numerous
> composers, including Cage.

Gann, K. "Music: Dysfunctional Harmony." *Village Voice* 38 (14 September 1993): 96.
> Gann discusses myths that surround composers' creativity, including Cage's.

Gena, Peter, and Jonathan Brent, comps. and eds. *A John Cage Reader: In Celebration of His
70th Birthday.* New York: Peters, 1982.
> Chronological list of works through summer 1982 is included in this collection of essays.

Gustafson, Bruce. "AGO San Francisco: Some Perspectives." *Diapason* 75 (October 1984):
6, 8-9.
> *Souvenir for Organ* was premiered at the convention. The reviewer was "surprised to find
> Mr. Cage writing in straight-forward 'note' music."

Hughes, Edward D. "**New Beginnings.**" *Musical Times* 134 (January 1993): 14-15.

Hughes appraises the works and ideas of Cage, whose "work is relevant to new beginnings."

Kostelanetz, Richard. *John Cage.* New York: Praeger, 1970.

A biography related mostly in Cage's own words and writings. Includes a bibliography, discography, list of compositions, and books by Cage.

"**Obituaries.**" *Notes* 49/4 (1993): 1396.

Lists Cage's obituary notice.

Perloff, Marjorie, and Charles Junkerman, eds. *John Cage: Composed in America.* Chicago: University of Chicago Press, 1994.

A collection of papers presented at the Stanford Humanities Center, 1991-92. Discusses ethics, politics, and social views. Includes bibliography.

Pritchett, James. *The Music of John Cage.* Cambridge: Cambridge University Press, 1993.

Includes biographical information and bibliography.

Revill, David. *The Roaring Silence: John Cage—A Life.* New York: Arcade, 1992.

A biography, with bibliographical references and list of music.

Schaedler, Stefan, and Walter Zimmermann, eds. *John Cage: Anarchic Harmony.* Mainz: B. Schott, 1992. *

Schwartz, Elliott, and Barney Childs, eds. *Contemporary Composers on Contemporary Music.* New York: Holt, Rinehart & Winston, 1967.

Essays by composers from Debussy through the present include Cage.

Charles E. Callahan, Jr.

B. Cambridge, Mass., 27 September 1951. Studied at St. Paul Choir School, Boston; studied with Clarence Watters, George Faxon, Alexander McCurdy, Flor Peeters, Daniel Roth, William Watkins. Studied at Boston University and Curtis Institute; D.M.A., Catholic University of America, 1978; A.A.G.O., 1973 and Ch.M., AGO, 1975. Formerly professor/ composer-in-residence, Middlebury College, Vt.; faculty, resident composer, director of music, Knowles Memorial Chapel, Rollins College (Fla.); moved to Orwell, Vermont, where he composes full-time.

OL95.

"Here and There." *Diapason* 75 (December 1984): 4.

> Callahan premieres his own *Festal Fanfare*, op. 36, on November 7. The work was commissioned by Wesleyan College, W.V., where the first hearing occurred in Wesley Chapel.

"Here and There." *Diapason* 78 (August 1987): 3.

> Callahan's *Ragtime*, written for two organists at one organ, was featured in a recital of works commissioned since 1979 by Elizabeth and Raymond Chenault. The work was performed 29 May 1987 at Grace Episcopal Church in Charleston, S.C., for the Piccolo Spoleto Midnight Gala organ recital.

"Here and There." *Diapason* 81 (April 1990): 3.

> Raymond and Elizabeth Chenault premiered Callahan's *Evensong* based on "Ar hyd y nos" and Tallis's canon. The premiere was played at First Presbyterian Church, Greenville, S.C., on January 19.

"Premieres." *American Organist* 24 (April 1990): 69-70.

> Callahan's *Evensong* was premiered by the duo Raymond and Elizabeth Chenault, 19 January 1990, at First Presbyterian Church, Greenville, S.C.

"Premieres." *American Organist* 27 (April 1993): 52.

> *Organ Meditation on a Medieval Tune* was premiered by Randall Egan, 20 December 1992.

Ann Callaway

B. Washington, D.C., 28 October 1949. Studied with Alvin Etler at Smith College; George Crumb and George Rochberg at the University of Pennsylvania, M.A., 1974. Awarded the Fatman Fellowship, Smith College, 1971; grants from the New York State Council on the Arts and National Endowment for the Arts, 1975. Taught theory and composition, summers, Walden School, Vershire, Vt. Further studies with Grace Newman Cushman at Peabody Conservatory, and Jack Beeson at Columbia University.

CACA.

Benzinger, Mrs. W. P. "1970 Young Composers Contest, Calvacade for Creative Youth." *Music Clubs Magazine* 50/2 (1970-71): 28-29.

> Callaway receives first prize in Class I and second prize in Class II for the 1970 Young Composers Contest. Her education in theory/composition is provided.

"Here and There." *Diapason* 81 (September 1990): 3.

> Donald Joyce presented the European premiere of *Paraphrasis* (1981) in Bonn, at the Sinzig Festival for Contemporary Organ Music.

"Premieres." *American Organist* 27 (March 1993): 49.

> Donald Joyce premieres Callaway's *Water Garden—Reflections on Hildegard von Bingen* (1991) for organ and synthesizer in January 1992 at a concert sponsored by the Pasadena (Calif.) AGO Chapter.

Raver, Leonard. "New Music for Organ: A Report on the Fifty-eight Compositions Submitted for the Holtkamp/AGO Award 1983-84." *American Organist* 18 (April 1984): 166-70.

> Ann Callaway's *Paraphrasis* is highly regarded. Partial program notes about the piece and commission information are included.

Thomas Canning

B. 1911, n.p. Studied at Oberlin with Normand Lockwood, and at Eastman School of Music with Howard Hanson and Bernard Rogers; Fulbright grant recipient, 1961-62. Professor of music at Eastman; professor of music and composer-in-residence at the Creative Arts Center, University of West Virginia, Morgantown, 1963-78; now emeritus.

AA73, ABD, CACA, OL, OL95, X56, X61, X62, X66, X67, X68, X70, X71.

Bingham, Seth. "David Craighead." *American Organist* 43 (August 1960): 12.

> Craighead premieres Canning's *Sonata for Organ* (1960) at the AGO Convention, 27 June 1960, St. John's Episcopal Church, Detroit. An overview of the work is presented.

"The Composer." *Musical Courier* 16 (September 1961): 42-43.

> John Wesley's *Covenant Service* is set to music by Canning and is first performed 31 August 1961 at the University of Illinois.

"Concert Hall." *American Composers Alliance Bulletin* 10/3 (1962): 28.

> Canning's *Music for a Sermon* is premiered by organist Arthur Poister, 14 February 1960, at Hendricks Chapel, University of Syracuse, N.Y. Other Canning works are listed as being performed in 1960 by organists Allen I. McHose, Russell Wichman, and David Craighead.

Kyle, Marguerite K. "AmerAllegro." *Pan Pipes* 60/2 (1968): 64-65.

Premiere of *Four Percussion Improvisations with Organ Ostinati*, April 6-9 (1967), at Morgantown, W.V., by the composer and Michael Theis, percussionist.

62/2 (1970): 53-54.

Two Canning works premiered for the dedication of the Creative Arts Center of West Virginia University at Morgantown, 26 April 1969: *Canonic Piece for Two Organs* and *Variations and Fugue for Organ on a Hexachord by Alfred R. de Jaeger.*

67/2 (1975): 48-49.

Canning composes *Three Fanfares* for two trumpets, one trombone, and organ, for his daughter's wedding.

68/2 (1976): 44.

Announcement of the premiere of *Variations for Organ on "O for a Thousand Tongues to Sing,"* by Canning, 2 November 1975, by organist Larry Marietta at Wesley United Methodist Church, Morgantown, W.V.

70/2 (1978): 35.

Announcement of Canning's retirement from full-time teaching and the premiere of his *Galactic Journey* for organ and percussion, 29 March 1977.

"University-Community Leaders Honored." *Pan Pipes* 65/1 (1972): 6-8.

Mu Phi Alpha honors Canning's achievements at Epsilon Psi Chapter, Fairmont State College (Va.), 19 April 1972, with a presentation of his works; educational history provided.

Myron D. Casner

B. Williamsport, Penn., 1908; d. Mexico, N.Y., 9 September 1992. B.A., M.A., Wesleyan University, Middletown, Conn.; studied at the Royal College of Music and Royal College of Organists; chairman of the language department; organist at St. John's Episcopal Church, Sturgis, Mich.; and taught organ for 10 years at Goshen College, Goshen, Ind. Organ music and biography listed in Arnold's book.

OL, OL95.

[Obituary.] *Diapason* 84 (January 1993): 4.

Provides some biographical and career information.

Glenn Winston Cassler

B. Moundridge, Kans., 3 September 1906. Graduate of McPherson College (Kans.); B.M., Oberlin Conservatory; studied at the College of St. Nicholas, Kent, England; pupil of Ernest Bullock; studied at the Royal College of Music. Professor of music, St. Olaf College, Northfield, Minn., 1949-72; organist at St. John's Lutheran Church, Northfield, from 1950. Organ music listed in Arnold's book.

ABD, CACA, OL, OL95.

No bibliographical information located.

Augusta Cecconi-Bates

B. Syracuse, N.Y., 9 August 1933. Studied with Joseph McGrath, Syracuse, N.Y., and Robert Palmer, Cornell University. Director of Schola Italiana at Middlebury College (Vt.), 1956. Organist-choir director at St. Michael's, Central Square, N.Y., 1961-64; professorship at the Maria Regina College in Syracuse, 1964-65; music specialist for the Syracuse school district, since 1968; private music instructor, from 1976. Honorable mention in Stowe Institute Composition Contest, 1976; featured composer at the Norman Rockwell Festival in Dewitt, N.Y., 1976; in 1977, was featured composer and director for a concert of her own works sponsored by the Cherubini Society of Rochester, N.Y. Member of ASCAP and AMC.

CACA, IWC.

"American Composer Update." *Pan Pipes* 73/2 (1980): 25.
> Ceconni-Bates was composer-in-residence at Vermont Music and Arts Center, Lyndonville, Vt., in July 1980.

Drone, Jeanette, comp. "American Composer Update." *Pan Pipes* 75/2 (1983): 23.
> Cecconi-Bates's works are available from her directly; West Monroe, N.Y., address included.

John Anthony Celona

B. San Francisco, 30 October 1947. Student of Henry Onderdonk, San Francisco State College, and Iannis Xenakis, Indiana University; doctor of music degree, University of California at San Diego, with Kenneth Gaburo, 1977; dissertation was entitled "Structural

Aspects of Contemporary Music Notation and Command-String Notation—A New Music Notational System," *Dissertation Abstracts* 38 (May 1978): 6386A. Since 1978, on faculty at University of Victoria, British Columbia, Canada; music director, Open Space Art Gallery, Victoria. BMI Award, 1971; NEA grant, 1977.

ABD, CACA, OL, OL95.

"Convention Personalities." *American Organist* 17 (May 1983): 74.
    A brief biographical summary.

"A Measure of Success." *Music Educators Journal* 59 (November 1972): 102.
    Celona is a winner in the 1971 twentieth annual BMI Awards.

Raymond Hulet Chenault

B. 10 April 1950, n.p. B.M., Virginia Commonwealth University, 1972; M.M., University of Cincinnati Conservatory of Music, 1974; organ fellow, Washington National Cathedral, 1974-75; organist-choirmaster, All Saints Church, Atlanta, Ga., since 1975; teaching affiliate, Mercer University, since 1979; named an Outstanding Man of America, 1983.

OL95.

No bibliographical information located.

David Mark Cherwien

B. West Union, Iowa, 1 July 1957. B.M., Augsburg College, Minneapolis, 1979; graduate composition study with Dominick Argento; organ student of Heinrich Fleischer, Earl Barr, Paul Manz; studied at Berlin Church Music School, 1979-81, with Renate Zimmermann (improvisation), Karl Hochreiter (organ literature), Ernst Pepping (composition). Director of worship/music, First Lutheran Church, Richmond Beach, Seattle, 1981-87; instructor for service playing/improvisation, Elmhurst College (n.d.); director of music, Lutheran Church of the Good Shepherd, Minneapolis, since 1990.

OL95.

"Premieres." *American Organist* 22 (January 1988): 52.

> Cherwien's *Concertato on "Duke Street,"* for congregation, brass, percussion, organ, and choir, was premiered 11 October 1987 at Lutheran Church of the Good Shepherd, Moorhead, Minn. The work was commissioned by the Red River AGO Chapter.

"Premieres." *American Organist* 27 (February 1993): 42.

> *Blest, God All Glorious!*, a hymn concertato, was premiered 25 October 1992, Reformation Sunday, at St. James Lutheran Church, Gettysburg, Penn. The piece was commissioned in honor of Rev. Frederick Foltz and Rev. Edward Keyser, for their 25 years of service to St. James.

"Premieres." *Canadian Composer* 1/2 (1990): 24. *

"Premieres." *Canadian Composer* 2/2 (1991): 24. *

Clay Christiansen

B. 1949, n.p. B.A., Brigham Young University; studied with J. J. Keeler; master's degree, University of Utah; organ study with Alexander Schreiner. Organist, St. Mark's Episcopal Church, Salt Lake City, Utah; organist, Mormon Tabernacle, Salt Lake City, from 1982. OL, OL95.

"Appointments." *Diapason* 73 (October 1982): 9.

> Christiansen is appointed fourth Tabernacle organist at the Mormon Tabernacle, Salt Lake City, Utah.

"Here and There." *Diapason* 84 (November 1993): 3.

> Christiansen is featured on a new CD recording, *The Pipe Organ of the Mormon Tabernacle, Salt Lake City*, on the Klavier label. Works included are by Vierne, Elmore, Kabalevsky, Mendelssohn, Grieg, Bach, Christiansen, and others.

Rosemary Clarke-Naus

B. Daytona Beach, Fla., 23 June 1921. B.M., Stetson University, 1940, and M.M., Philadelphia Music Academy, 1941, and an organ diploma/M.M. from there in 1942; Ph.D., Eastman School of Music, 1950. Studied with Bernard Rogers, Robert Elwell, and

Harold Gleason. F.A.G.O., 1953. Associate professor of music at Stetson University, 1942-57; founded and directed Rosemary Clarke Conservatory, 1949-57; artist-in-residence, University of Dubuque, 1957-62; professor, 1962-75, and composer-in-residence, 1969-75, University of Wisconsin, Platteville; 1975, emeritus.

ABD, CACA, CACJ, CR, DN75, IWC, WCH.

No bibliographical information located.

Kenton Coe

B. Johnson City, Tenn., 12 November 1932. Studied with Quincy Porter and Paul Hindemith, Yale University: B.A., 1953. Studied with Boulanger at the Paris Conservatory, 1953-56. Won Fontainebleau prize for composition, 1953; French government grants, 1954-55; MacDowell fellowships, 1960, 1963.

ABD, CACA, OL, OL95, X71.

"Here and There." *Diapason* 71 (June 1980): 20.

> The world premiere of Coe's *Concerto for Organ, Strings, and Percussion* will occur 4 July 1980 at the Cathedral of Saint-Bertrand-de-Cominges, France, with Stephen Hamilton, organist; commission information given.

"Premieres." *American Organist* 24 (July 1990): 54.

> The Twin Cities premiere of Coe's *Fantasy for Organ* is played by Stephen Hamilton at Zion Lutheran Church in Minneapolis.

"Recital Programs." *Diapason* 70 (December 1979): 20-21.

> Kenton Coe's *Fantasy for Organ* is performed by organist-commissioning agent Stephen Hamilton for the premiere, September 25, Central Presbyterian Church, Bristol, Va.

Charles De Witt Coleman

B. Detroit, Mich., 29 January 1926; d. there, 22 April 1991. B.M., 1952, and M.M., 1954, Wayne State University; organ study with August Maekelberghe, Lode Van Dessel, Virgil Fox, and Marcel Dupré; composition with James Gibb, Ruth Wilie, and Dupré. For six years, minister of music at St. Cyprian's Episcopal Church, Detroit; for twenty years, minister of music, Tabernacle Baptist Church, Detroit. From 1958, head of his own publishing company.

CACA, OL, OL95.

[Obituary.] *American Organist* 25 (August 1991): 37.
> Indicates the funeral service for Coleman took place at Tabernacle Missionary Baptist Church, Detroit, on 27 April 1991.

Southern, Eileen. **"Conversation with Clarence E. Whiteman, Organ-Music Collector."** *Black Perspective in Music* 6/2 (fall 1978): 168-87.
> Whiteman's collection includes organ works by 14 black composers; Charles Coleman's music is part of the collection.

David Joseph Conte

B. Denver, Colo., 20 December 1955. B.M., Bowling Green (Ohio) University, 1977; composition student of Wallace DePue; M.F.A., 1981 and D.M.A., 1983, Cornell University; student of Karel Husa, Steven Stucky. Fulbright fellowship student of Nadia Boulanger, 1975-78. Taught composition, Interlochen Center for the Arts, summers 1979-81; faculty member, Cornell University; director of choral activities, Colgate University, 1984; faculty, American Conservatory, Fontainebleau, 1991; professor of composition, San Francisco Conservatory of Music, since 1985. Awarded R. Vaughan Williams Fellowship, 1989.

OL95.

No bibliographical information located.

John Cook

B. Maldon, England, 11 October 1918; d. Boston, Mass., 12 August 1984. B.M., 1939, Cambridge University, organ pupil of Boris Ord and David Willcocks; Doctor of Music, University of Durham, 1958; organist, Collegiate Church of the Holy Trinity, Stratford-on-Avon, 1949-54; organist, St. Paul's Cathedral, London, Ontario, 1954-56; organist, Church of the Advent, Boston, Mass., 1962-68. Served on the faculty at MIT, Cambridge, Mass., 1965-82.

ABD, BBCpo, OL95, X53, X54, X60.

Angel, Clark. "Concerto for Organ and Brasses." *American Organist* 43 (August 1960): 22-23.

Fanfare for Organ and Brass receives its premiere by Marilyn Mason and the Brass Ensemble of the University of Michigan at the AGO Convention, 1960.

Banta, Lorene. "Recitals and Concerts." *American Organist* 49 (October 1966): 9.

A Fantasy receives its premiere performance played by George Faxon at Memorial Music Hall, Methuen, Mass., 10 August 1966; the work was commissioned by Faxon.

Bingham, Seth. "Marilyn Mason Plays New Work by John Cook." *Diapason* 50 (October 1959): 16.

Flourish & Fugue, for Organ receives its premiere by Marilyn Mason, who commissioned it and to whom the work is dedicated. The reviewer calls it "a stunning new composition."

Cabena, Barrie. "A Tribute to John Cook." *American Organist* 19 (January 1985): 55.

Cook, who died 12 August 1984 from diabetes, is eulogized.

[Obituary.] *American Organist* 18 (November 1984): 47-48.

Cook's death notice released with past positions listed.

[Obituary.] *Diapason* 75 (November 1984): 5.

Death notice for John Cook indicates his interest in both church and theater music.

[Obituary.] *Variety* 316 (29 August 1984): 111.

Obituary notice for Cook indicates he was 66 and on the faculty at MIT; he composed for both the theater and church.

[Obituary.] *Musical Times* 125 (December 1984): 719.

Provides information about Cook's death in Boston; cites his position from 1961-68 as music director at the Church of the Advent, Boston.

"Recitals and Concerts." *American Organist* 43 (January 1960): 27-28.

St. Paul's Chapel, Columbia University, New York, is the stage for the premiere of Cook's *Flourish & Fugue* by organist Marilyn Mason, who commissioned the work. The performance occurred on 15 July 1959, and the review indicated it was "a thrilling piece."

"TAO Report on AGO Biennial Convention, Philadelphia, June 22-26." *American Organist* 47 (August 1964): 19.

Marilyn Mason, organist, performs the world premiere of Cook's *Capriccio for Organ and Strings* (1964), 22 June 1964. A brief description of the work follows.

Paul Cooper

B. Victoria, Ill., 19 May 1926; d. Houston, Tex., 4 April 1996. B.A., 1950, M.A., 1953, and D.M.A., 1956, University of Southern California with Ernest Kanitz; private student of Nadia Boulanger in Paris, 1953-54; also studied with Halsey Stevens and Roger Sessions. Professor of music, University of Michigan, 1955-67, composer-in-residence at University of Cincinnati, 1968-74, and at Rice University in Houston from 1974. Held two Guggenheim fellowships, 1965 and 1972, and served as visiting professor at the Royal Academy of Music in Stockholm, 1985, and at the Royal Conservatory of Music, Copenhagen, 1988; received two Rackham Research Fellowships, University of Michigan, and was also the United States cultural representative for the State Department in Yugoslavia. Published *Perspectives in Music Theory* (New York: Dodd, Mead, 1973; 2nd ed., New York and London: Harper & Row, 1981).

AA73, ABD, ASUC, BB78, BB92, CACA, CACJ, DN78, IWW92, NG, NGA, OL, OL95, WHP84, X62, X67, X68, X69, X70, X71, X74.

"Appointments." *American Organist* 51 (June 1968): 21.

Cooper is appointed professor of composition and theory and composer-in-residence at the University of Cincinnati College-Conservatory of Music; biography.

"Here and There." *Diapason* 76 (June 1985): 3.

Cooper's *In nomine* is premiered by Charles Benbow, the organist who also commissioned the work; overview of the one-movement sectional piece is provided.

Kyle, Marguerite K. "AmerAllegro." *Pan Pipes* 61/2 (1969): 48.

Cooper receives ASCAP award and is appointed composer-in-residence at the University of Cincinnati.

64/2 (1972): 49.

Fourth consecutive ASCAP award presented to Cooper.

66/2 (1974): 46.

Announcement that Cooper's *Variants*, for organ, is published by J & W Chester, London; ASCAP recipient; receives second Guggenheim fellowship.

67/2 (1975): 49-50.

Cooper receives the ASCAP Standard Award; appointed professor of music and composer-in-residence at Shepherd School of Music, Rice University. In preparation are two workbooks to accompany *Perspectives in Music Theory*.

71/2 (1979): 29.

Requiem for Organ and Percussion is premiered by Leonard Raver, organist, and Richard Brown, percussionist; the work is published by J & W Chester, London.

75/2 (1983): 24-25.

Cooper's *Concerto for Organ and Orchestra* is premiered June 1982 by organist Clyde Holloway at Christ Church Cathedral, Houston.

87/2 (1995): 18.

The American Guild of Organists national convention in Dallas included the first performance of *Three Alleluias for Solo Organ*, commissioned by the AGO, with Marilyn Keiser performing at the organ. After the premiere, Keiser performed the work, published by G. Schirmer, five additional times in the United States and Canada.

"Music Journal's 1972 Gallery of Living Composers." *Music Journal* 30 (Annual 1972): 38.

An introduction to the composer.

"Premieres." *American Organist* 19 (June 1985): 42.

In nomine receives its premiere on 16 March 1985 by organist Charles Benbow at Alice Tully Hall, New York.

"Prizes and Premieres." *Musical America* 84 (July 1964): 60.

Concerto for Harpsichord and Organ was given its New York premiere by Harold Chaney and Robert Huddleston, St. Michael's Church, 26 May 1964.

"Recitals." *American Organist* 19 (August 1985): 60.

Notice of Charles Benbow performing the premiere of Cooper's organ work *In nomine*.

William Benjamin Cooper

B. Philadelphia, Penn., 14 February 1920; d. New York, 25 May 1993. Studied at Lincoln University (Penn.), 1942-43; in the U.S. armed forces as chaplain's assistant, 1943-45; studied at Trinity College of Music, London, 1945-46; organist at St. Barnabas' Episcopal Church, Philadelphia, 1946-48; organist at St. Augustine's Episcopal Church, Philadelphia, 1948-51; B.M., 1951, and M.M., 1952, Philadelphia Musical Academy; further study at the School of Sacred Music, Union Theological Seminary, Columbia University, Fordham

University, and Manhattan School of Music. Organ student of Rollo Maitland, Dr. Ellingford (London), Claire Coci, Donald Coats, Arden Whitacre; composition with Stephan Wolpe, Julius Higman, and Harold Friedell. Since 1958, he has taught at Wadleigh Intermediate School, Bennett College (N.C.), Hampton Institute (Va.), and Mercy College (White Plains, N.Y.); organist, St. Philip's Episcopal Church, New York, 1953-74; since 1975, organist, St. Martin's Episcopal Church, New York. Organ music listed in Arnold's book.

ABD, AFR, CACA, OL, OL95.

Southern, Eileen. "Conversation with Clarence E. Whiteman: Organ-Music Collector." *Black Perspective in Music* 6/2 (fall 1978): 168-87.

> Whiteman's collection includes organ works by 14 black composers; Cooper's music is part of the collection.

Aaron Copland

B. Brooklyn, N.Y., 14 November 1900; d. North Tarrytown, N.Y., 2 December 1990. Pupil of Nadia Boulanger, 1921-24. Also studied with Rubin Goldmark, New York. First Guggenheim awarded a composer, 1925; won RCA Victor Award; Pulitzer Prize, 1945; New York Music Critics' Circle Award, 1945, 1947; numerous honorary doctorates, from Princeton, Brandeis, Wesleyan, Temple, Harvard, Rutgers, Ohio State, New York, Columbia, and York Universities. Organized the Yaddo Festivals; founder of the American Composers Alliance, 1937; Charles Eliot Norton lecturer at Yale; head of composition, 1940-65, and faculty chair, 1957-65, Berkshire Music Center. Authored *What to Listen for in Music* (New York: MacGraw-Hill, 1939; 2nd ed., 1957); *Music and Imagination* (Cambridge: Harvard University Press, 1952); *The New Music, 1900-1960* (rev. and enl. ed., New York: Norton, 1968); with Vivian Perlis, *Copland Since 1943* (New York: St. Martin's, 1989).

AA73, ABD, AMH, AS66, ASC, BB58, BB65, BB71, BB78, BB92, BBCch, BBCpo, BDA, CA1, CACA, CC92, CDC, DCM, DDM, DN70, DN74, EDM, EMS, EVM, GD54, HHH, HLM, IMD, IMD2, JCN, KTL, LMD, LMU, MEH, MGG, MHHH, NCE, NG, NGA, OL, OL95, PC71, PCM, REM, SML, TCAC, TSC, VER, WI69, WTM, X50, X51, X52, X53, X55, X56, X57, X58, X59, X60, X61, X62, X64, X65, X66, X67, X68, X69, X70, X71, X74.

"Aaron Copland." *Pan Pipes* 44 (January 1952): 27. *

"Aaron Copland." *Pan Pipes* 45 (January 1953): 45. *

"Aaron Copland." *Canon* 13 (May-June 1960): 239-40.

> A summary of Copland's career to date; honors indicated.

"Aaron Copland." *Composers of the Americas* 1 (1955): 26-35.

Brief biography in Spanish and English is followed by a chronological catalog of his works; included are duration and publishers of the works and a bibliography of articles and books by Copland.

"Aaron Copland on the Composer's Craft." *International Musician* 47 (May 1949): 34. *

"Aaron Copland; Chronological Catalog of the Works of the American Composer." *Musica y artes* 57-58 (November-December 1954): 33-38. *

Berger, Arthur. *Aaron Copland.* London: Oxford University Press, 1953; reprint, New York: Da Capo, 1987 and 1990.

List of works and recordings; a select bibliography of articles on and references to Copland are included in this biography.

————. **"Aaron Copland, 1900-1990."** *Perspectives of New Music* 30/1 (1992): 296-98.

A brief overview of Copland's life and music.

Bernstein, Leonard. **"Aaron Copland: An Intimate Sketch."** *High Fidelity/Musical America* 20 (November 1970): 53-55.

Bernstein relates how he and Copland met, performed their works for one another, and Copland's forays into dodecaphonic music.

Blanks, F. R. **"Aaron Copland, a Vital Force in American Music."** *Canon* 12 (August 1958): 413-15.

Discusses how Copland's importance as a composer increased after he returned to the United States in 1921. Two basic ingredients exist in his music: 1) a desire to infuse a distinctive American quality into the music and 2) the concept of *Gebrauchsmusik*, the idea of practical music.

Butterworth, Neil. *The Music of Aaron Copland.* New York: Universe Books, 1986.

Includes list of compositions and bibliography.

Dickinson, Peter. **"Copland: Early, Late and More Biography."** *Musical Times* 131 (November 1990): 582-85.

Vivian Perlis and Copland combine forces for his latest biography, *Copland Since 1943* (New York: St. Martin's Press, 1989). The book "intercalates reminisces by Copland with interviews from colleagues and friends."

Evans, Peter. **"The Thematic Technique of Copland's Recent Works."** *Tempo* 51 (spring-summer 1959): 2-13.

A scholarly article on how Copland recycles segments from his early works to play significant roles in later *oeuvres*, and Copland's ideas about dodecaphonic approaches to composition.

Gagne, Cole, and Tracy Caras. *Soundpieces: Interviews with American Composers.* Metuchen, N.J.: Scarecrow, 1982.

Provides a survey of current trends in American music by offering interviews with numerous composers, including Copland.

Goldman, Richard Franko. "Aaron Copland." *Musical Quarterly* 47/1 (1961): 1-3.

A salute to Copland on his sixtieth birthday; an overview of his compositional styles is presented.

Harrison, Jay S. "The New York Music Scene." *Musical America* 84 (31 May 1964): 30.

The Boston Symphony Orchestra performs Copland's *Symphony for Organ and Orchestra* with organist Berj Zamkochian, 3 April 1964. The work, which essentially integrates the organ and orchestra, is dedicated to Nadia Boulanger.

Hitchcock, H. Wiley. "Aaron Copland and American Music." *Perspectives of New Music* 19 (1980-81): 31-33.

An overview of Copland's long and successful career as composer, teacher, writer, publisher, promoter, and organizer of American music.

Horowitz, Is. "Noted Composer Aaron Copland Dead at Age 90." *Billboard* 102 (15 December 1990): 8, 81.

Obituary notice; highpoints of Copland's life.

Kay, Norman. "Copland, All-American Composer." *Music & Musicians* 14 (September 1965): 21-24.

A detailed account of Copland's stylistic development.

Kirkpatrick, John. *The New Grove Twentieth-Century American Masters.* New York: Norton, 1988.

Includes Copland's life and works.

Kyle, Marguerite K. "AmerAllegro." *Pan Pipes* 52/2 (1960): 42.

Copland receives honorary doctorate of music degrees from Temple University and the University of Hartford.

54/2 (1962): 42.

MacDowell Medal awarded to Copland at Peterborough, N.H.

56/2 (1964): 49.

Symphony for Organ and Orchestra is published by Boosey & Hawkes.

57/2 (1965): 51.

Copland is awarded the Presidential Medal of Freedom by Lyndon Baines Johnson at the White House, 4 September 1964; three honorary degrees accorded him in 1964 from Syracuse University, the University of Rhode Island, and the University of Michigan.

60/2 (1968): 66.

Received an honorary D.F.A. from Jacksonville University and the Doctor of Music degree from Rutgers.

61/2 (1969): 48.

The *Organ Symphony* is recorded by E. Power Biggs and the New York Philharmonic, Leonard Bernstein conducting, on Columbia Records.

64/2 (1972): 49.

Copland receives honorary degrees from Columbia University, New York University, and York University, England.

[Obituary.] *Variety* 341 (10 December 1990): 101.

Copland's obituary cites numerous awards and honors accorded him.

[Obituary.] *American Organist* 25 (March 1991): 50.

Indicates Copland wrote his first symphony with a substantial organ part for his teacher, Nadia Boulanger, to play. He later revised the work without an organ part as Symphony No. 1.

[Obituary.] *Notes* 48/4 (1992): 1208.

Peare, Catherine Owens, and Mircea Vasiliu. *Aaron Copland: His Life.* New York: Holt, Rinehart & Winston, 1969.

A biography of Copland, whose music encompasses many forms including opera, ballet, symphony, and concerto.

Rosenberg, Deena, and Bernard Rosenberg. *The Music Makers.* New York: Columbia University, 1979.

This first publication for the Project for the Oral History of Music in America incorporates 32 accounts by individuals representing various aspects of serious musical life in contemporary America, and includes Copland.

Schwartz, Elliott, and Barney Childs, eds. *Contemporary Composers on Contemporary Music.* New York: Holt, Rinehart & Winston, 1967.

Essays by composers from Debussy to the present; contains an article by Copland.

Scott-Maddocks, D. "Aaron Copland." *Music & Musicians* 8 (June 1960): 25. *

Skowronski, JoAnn. *Aaron Copland: A Bio-Bibliography.* Westport, Conn.: Greenwood, 1985.

Includes biography, bibliography, discography, works and performances, and listing of works.

Smith, Julia Frances. "**Aaron Copland: His Work and Contribution to American Music: A Study of the Development of His Musical Style and an Analysis of the Various Techniques of Writing He Has Employed in His Works.**" Ph.D., New York University, 1952. *Dissertation Abstracts* 13 (January 1953): 103-41.

Later published, New York: Dutton, 1955.

Smith, Rollin. "**American Organ Composers.**" *Music* (AGO) 10 (August 1976): 18.

A list of compositions by significant organ composers in the United States includes Copland's *Symphony for Organ and Orchestra*, dedicated to Boulanger, and his only organ solo entitled *Episode* (Gray, 1941); brief descriptions of both.

Sneerson, Grigorij. *Portrety amerikanskyh kompozitorov* (Portraits of American Composers). Moskva: Muzyka, 1977.

Biographical portraits of nine American composers and discussions of their music and its place in contemporary music history includes information about Copland.

R. Evan Copley

B. Liberal, Kans., 22 March 1930. Composition student of Owen Reed at Michigan State University. On faculty at Iowa Wesleyan College, 1958-64; Oklahoma State University, 1965-68; since 1968, at the University of Northern Colorado.

ABD, CACA, CACJ, OL, OL95.

Studebaker, Donald. "**R. Evan Copley: Portrait of a 20th-Century Composer-Church Musician.**" *American Organist* 24 (January 1990): 74-75.

An overview of Copley's compositions; selected list of works and examples of his writing are included.

Robert Crandell

B. Hornell, N.Y., 10 January 1910; d. Battle Creek, Mich., 19 September 1976. Numerous years as organist-director of music at Brooklyn's First Presbyterian Church and Packer Collegiate Institute, Brooklyn, N.Y. B.M., University of Michigan, 1932; S.M.M., Union

Theological Seminary, 1936; later joined the faculties of both as teacher of composition and theory. Further study in Paris with Nadia Boulanger. Composition pupil of Hunter Johnson, Edwin Stringham, and Roy Harris; organ student of Paul Alwardt, Clarence Dickinson, and Hugh Porter. Taught theory, University of Michigan, 1932-34; appointed to the faculty, 1951, and director of the music department, 1963, Packer Collegiate Institute; lecturer, Union Theological Seminary, 1962-71.

ABD, CACA, OL, OL95.

Baker, Robert. [Obituary.] *Music* (AGO) 19 (December 1976): 56.
Crandell's death notice includes an appendix of published works.

Bingham, Seth. "Organ Personalities." *American Organist* 46 (November 1963): 11.
Brief mention of Crandell's *Carnival Suite*, his position at Brooklyn's First Presbyterian Church, and as director of the Packer Collegiate Institute.

"Carnival, a Suite for Organ." *American Organist* 33 (October 1950): 324.
Published by H. W. Gray, Crandell's work is reviewed as "recital music that seems to need the concert hall."

"Carnival, a Suite for Organ." *Diapason* 41 (November 1950): 23.
Announcement that this work was published by H. W. Gray; an overview of the work is presented.

Robert Crane

B. Winchester, Mass., 24 December 1919. Studied with Normand Lockwood, Oberlin Conservatory of Music, B.M.; with Nadia Boulanger at the Longy School of Music; with Bernard Rogers and Howard Hanson at the Eastman School of Music, Ph.D., 1960. Associate professor of music at University of Wisconsin School of Music, from 1950. Dissertation is a cantata, *Peter Quince at the Clavier*, for solo soprano, solo tenor, and orchestra.

ABD, CACA, CACJ, OL, OL95, PCM, X54, X62, X64, X68.

Kyle, Marguerite K. "AmerAllegro." *Pan Pipes* 51 (January 1959): 57.
Crane's *Chorale Prelude for Organ and Brass Quartet on "Wachet auf"* is premiered at Calvary Lutheran Church, Madison, Wisc.; his *Chorale Prelude on "Lanier"* is published by Carl Fischer.

56/2 (1964): 49-50.

Crane's *Fantasy for Organ on "Lauda Sion Salvatorem"* is premiered by organist James Kriewald in Madison, Wisc., 11 December 1963.

"Personals." *American Organist* 51 (June 1968): 23.

Crane, professor of music at the University of Wisconsin, is honored with a festival of his musical compositions, 9-12 May 1968, presented by students at Defiance (Ohio) College.

"Talk About Music." *Music Journal* 12 (September 1954): 3.

Crane wins Phi Mu Alpha Sinfonia composition contest with his *Sonatina 1952*.

Thomas C. Crawford

B. Harrisburg, Penn., 12 March 1956. Graduated from the Eastman School of Music, B.M., 1978; full fellowship to Columbia University, master's degree, 1980. Organ studies with Russell Saunders, John Ditto, and Terry Yount; composition with Fred Lehrdahl, George Edwards, Joseph Schwantner, and Samuel Adler. Received the Sernaffasky Prize, 1977; Howard Hanson Prize, 1978; was the winner of the Holtkamp Organ Composition Competition in 1979 and 1980; and numerous commissions. Organist-choirmaster at Holy Trinity Church, Webster, N.Y., 1979; director of music at St. Paul's Episcopal Church, Fairfield, Conn., since 1979.

BBCpo, OL, OL95, X51.

"Appointments." *Diapason* 70 (September 1979): 6.

Crawford is appointed director of music at St. Paul's Episcopal Church, Fairfield, Conn.; two commissions by organist John Holtz are listed: *Ashes of Rose* and *Mélange*.

"Names." *Music Journal* 37 (January 1979): 32.

Hinshaw will publish Crawford's winning piece, *Mélange*, from the First Annual Holtkamp Organ Composition Contest, 1978; commission information included.

Paul Creston

B. New York, 10 October 1906; d. San Diego, 24 August 1985. *Né* Giuseppe Guttoveggio. Entirely self-taught in harmony, orchestration, and composition. Studied piano with Randegger and Déthier, and organ with Pietro Yon. He began composing as a child;

served as theater organist in silent movies and also held teaching positions at various colleges in New York. Guggenheim Fellowship, 1939. Lectured in Israel and Turkey under the auspices of the State Department. Professor of composition and orchestration at New College of Music, 1964-68, and Central Washington University, 1968-76. In 1976, he moved to San Diego. Authored *Principles of Rhythm* (New York: Belwin-Mills, 1964; paperback, 1976), *Creative Harmony* (New York: Belwin-Mills, 1970), and numerous articles. BB92, CACA, IWW92, NGA, OL, OL95.

"The AGO National Convention, Washington, D.C., 1982." *Diapason* 73 (September 1982): 15.

James Moeser premieres Creston's *Symphony No. 6*, a work commissioned for the convention and performed at the John F. Kennedy Center for the Performing Arts, Washington.

"A Capital Convention, Washington, D.C., June 28-July 2: Composers and Their Commissions." *American Organist* 16 (May 1982): 4.

Creston writes *Symphony No. 6*, op. 118, for organ and orchestra, to glorify the organ, not the performer—a one-movement composition; fairly complete description of the work.

"Convention Event." *American Organist* 16 (April 1982): 80.

An introduction to the composer.

Kyle, Marguerite K. "AmerAllegro." *Pan Pipes* 53/2 (January 1961): 48.

Creston's *Suite for Organ* and *Fantasia for Organ* are published by Ricordi.

55/2 (1963): 44.

Creston is elected Life Fellow of the International Institute of Arts and Letters.

59/2 (1967): 68-69.

Rapsodia Breve, for pedals alone, is published by Franco Colombo.

69/2 (1977): 39.

Creston's *Rhapsodie*, for organ and saxophone, was premiered in London by Jean-Marie Londeix and Martin Jones, 31 July 1976.

Mitchell, Howard. "The Hallmark of Greatness." *Musical Courier* 154 (15 November 1956): 9-10.

Information about Creston's writing and honors received.

[Obituary.] *American Organist* 19 (November 1985): 86.

Creston dies in San Diego, 24 August 1985.

[Obituary.] *Clavier* 24/10 (1985): 32-33.

> A personal glimpse of the composer by friend Claudette Sorel.

"Paul Creston." *Composers of the Americas* 4 (1958): 58-69.

> Brief biography in Spanish and English is followed by a list of works to date; indicates publishers, performing times, and notes about the work—e.g., premiere date and commission information.

"Paul Creston." *Pan Pipes* 43 (December 1950): 115. *

> 44 (January 1952): 27. *

> 45 (January 1953): 45-46. *

"Recitals and Concerts." *American Organist* 42 (October 1959): 349-50.

> Marilyn Mason plays the first performance of Creston's *Suite for Organ* on the West Coast at the Alfred Hertz Memorial Hall of Music, University of California, Berkeley, 12 April 1959. Mason commissioned the work and it is dedicated to her.

Simmons, Walter. "Paul Creston: Maintaining a Middle Course." *Music Journal* 34 (December 1976): 12-13.

> Denotes the year 1927 as the beginning of using the name Paul Creston. He relates his credo: "All parameters of music should be given due consideration to attain perfect balance when composing."

Slomski, Monica Jane. *Paul Creston: A Bio-Bibliography.* Westport, Conn.: Greenwood, 1994. *

————. **"Paul Creston: The Man and His Music with an Annotated Bibliography of His Works."** D.M.A., University of Missouri-Kansas City, 1987. *Dissertation Abstracts* 49 (November 1988): 994A-95A.

> Describes Creston's life and work as a composer and theorist; an overview of rhythmic, formal, melodic, harmonic, and scoring techniques; annotated bibliography of his works.

George Crumb

B. Charleston, W.Va., 24 October 1929. B.M., Mason College (W.Va.), 1950; M.M., University of Illinois, 1953; D.M.A., University of Michigan, 1959, where he was a student of Ross Lee Finney. Studied with Boris Blacher at Berlin Hochschule für Musik. Taught at the University of Colorado, 1959-64; University of Pennsylvania, since 1965; in 1983,

Crumb was named Annenberg Professor of the Humanities there. Received grants from the Koussevitzky Foundation, 1965; Guggenheim Foundation, 1967 and 1973; elected to the American Academy of Arts & Letters, 1967; won the Pulitzer Prize, 1968.

ABD, AMH, BB78, BB92, BBCch, CACA, CACJ, DCM, JCN, KTL, MGGs, NG, NGA, OL95, TCH, X69, X70, X71, X74.

Belt, Byron. **"AGO National Convention, San Francisco 1984."** *American Organist* 18 (August 1984): 28-33.

Crumb's *Pastoral Drone* is premiered at the convention by David Craighead.

Borroff, Edith. *Three American Composers.* Lanham, Md.: University Press of America, 1986.

Crumb, Finney, and Irwin Fischer are discussed in this book. Crumb's biographical data is presented, and his music, in general, is discussed. At the onset, an overview of fifty years as a time of change is given in this scholarly tome.

"Convention Personalities." *American Organist* 18 (April 1984): 115.

Crumb was a student of Boris Blacher at the Hochschule für Musik, Berlin; received his D.M.A. in composition, under Ross Lee Finney, at the University of Michigan. Crumb has taught at the University of Pennsylvania, University of Colorado, Harvard, and Berkshire Music Center, Tanglewood. He received a Pulitzer Prize in 1968 for *Echoes of Time and the River*, and awards from UNESCO, the Guggenheim and Rockefeller Foundations.

Crumb, George. *George Crumb: Profile of a Composer.* New York: C. F. Peters, 1986. Introduction by Gilbert Chase; compiled and edited by Don Gillespie.

In essence, an autobiography.

Gagne, Cole, and Tracy Caras. *Soundpieces: Interviews with American Composers.* Metuchen, N.J.: Scarecrow, 1982.

Furnishes a survey of current trends in American music; offers interviews with numerous composers, including Crumb.

Gustafson, Bruce. **"AGO San Francisco: Some Perspectives."** *Diapason* 75 (October 1984): 6, 8-9.

Crumb's *Pastoral Drone* is "austerely strong."

Robert Cuckson

B. Australia, 1942. Concert pianist who has composed for organ; lives and teaches in New York. Organ music and biography listed in Arnold's book

OL, OL95.

No bibliographical information located.

Robert Milton Cundick

B. Salt Lake City, 26 November 1926. Attended the University of Utah: B.F.A., 1949; M.F.A., 1950; Ph.D., 1955. Joined faculty there, 1948-56, then joined Brigham Young staff, 1956-79. Organ studies with Alexander Schreiner and Robert Munns, and composition with Leroy J. Robertson. In 1965-91, he served as one of the organists at the Mormon Tabernacle. Won the S. Lewis Elmer Awards, 1971. With N. Dayley, he authored *Music Manuscript: A Practical Guide* (Orem, Utah: Sonos Music Resources, n.d.).

ABD, OL, OL95.

Basch, Peter J. "Robert Cundick." *Music* (AGO) 4 (September 1970): 26-27.

An interview with Cundick elicits information about his organ compositions and approach to composition, in general; education information listed.

"Changes at Salt Lake." *Diapason* 56 (September 1965): 4.

Cundick, with Roy M. Darley, is named one of the Mormon Tabernacle organists upon the retirement of Frank W. Asper.

"Here and There." *Diapason* 83 (January 1992): 3.

Cundick retired, effective December 1991, after more than 26 years of service for the Mormon Tabernacle Choir. Upon retirement, Cundick and his wife accepted an invitation from Brigham Young University to act as directors of hosting at the university's Jerusalem Center for Near Eastern Studies, in Israel. Includes career highlights.

W. Lawrence Curry

B. Parnassus, Penn., 19 March 1906; d. 26 February 1966. Phi Beta Kappa graduate, B.A., University of Pennsylvania, 1938. M.S.M. and S.M.D., Union Theological Seminary, 1945. Dissertation is a cantata, *Thy Kingdom Come*. Taught piano and conducting at Beaver College (Glenside, Penn.), 1929-39, and later was chairman of the department for thirty years; conductor, Matinee Musical Chorus, 1947-55; conductor, Fortnightly Male Chorus, 1951-59; music editor of Westminster Press; director of music at First Methodist Church, Germantown, Penn.

ABDad, CACA, OL, OL95.

Curry, W. Lawrence. *Worship and Hymns for All Occasions.* Philadelphia: Westminster, 1968. *

"Dr. and Mrs. Curry Announce Busy Schedule for Summer." *Diapason* 46 (May 1955): 25.
Itinerary for recitals and workshops given by the Currys is announced.

[Obituary.] *Diapason* 57 (April 1966): 40.
Curry's death notice provides biographical information.

[Obituary.] *Journal of Church Music* 8 (May 1966): 20-21.
Curry's death date is listed as 25 February 1966; "he taught his congregation how to sing."

Williams, L. R. "More of Who's Who!" *Church Musician* 15 (February 1964): 6-7. *

"W. Lawrence Curry." *Diapason* 42 (October 1951): 37.
Curry is appointed conductor of the Fortnightly Club of Philadelphia; lists his other positions.

"W. Lawrence Curry to Lead 2 Summer Choir Schools." *Diapason* 41 (February 1950): 10.
Curry is appointed music educator for the Presbyterian Board of Christian Education, and will
lead two schools for organists and choir directors, introducing new material for service needs.

Curtis Otto Bismarck Curtis-Smith

B. Walla Walla, Wash., 9 September 1941. Piano study with David Burge at Whitman
(Wash.) College, 1960-62; with Gui Mombaerts at Northwestern University, B.M., 1964,
and M.M., 1965; with Kenneth Gaburo, 1966, University of Illinois, Champaign-Urbana;
and with Bruno Maderna, 1972, Berkshire Music Center, Tanglewood. Taught at Western
Michigan University, 1968-76 as associate professor, and 1977-90 as full professor. Honors:
Koussevitzky Prize, 1972; Gold Medal of Concorso Internazionale di Musica e Danza G.
B. Viotti, 1975; NEA grants; Prix du Francis Salabert, 1976; ASCAP awards; Guggenheim
fellowship, 1978-79; American Academy and Institute of Arts and Letters award, 1978;
Michigan Council for the Arts grants, 1981 and 1984.

BB92, CACA, CC92, DN78, IWW92, NGA, OL, OL95.

Hertzog, Christian. "Curtis-Smith, Curtis." *Contemporary Composers* (CC92).
A review of Curtis-Smith's style, brief presentation on *Masquerades* (1978) for organ, and
comments from the composer. Other works for organ include *Gargoyles* (1978) and *Variations
on Amazing Grace* (1983).

Noel George DaCosta

B. Lagos, Nigeria, 27 December 1929, of Jamaican parentage. At 11, came to New York; studied at Queens College, B.A., 1952, and Columbia University, M.M., 1956. DaCosta is named a Fulbright scholar in music composition with Luigi Dallapiccola, 1958. Taught at Hampton Institute, 1963-66, Queens College, and Hunter College. Appointed to the faculty at Rutgers College (N.J.) as associate professor of music, 1970; since 1984, he has served on the faculty as violinist, composer, and instructor. NEA grants received in 1974, 1977, 1980.

ABD, AFR, BCS, BDA, CACA, CACJ, IWW92, NGA, OL, OL95.

Laidman, Janet Loretta. **"The Use of Black Spirituals in the Organ Music of Contemporary Black Composers as Illustrated in the Works of Three Composers."** Ed.D., Columbia University Teachers College, 1989. *Dissertation Abstracts* 52 (August 1991): 460A.

DaCosta's *Spiritual Set* includes written symbols for improvisation. His work is analyzed for melodic, harmonic, rhythmic, formal, and stylistic elements. Includes biographical information and a comparison and summary of pieces is provided; appendix lists other black composers who incorporate spirituals into their works.

McDaniel, Lorna. **"Out of the Black Church."** *American Organist* 13 (May 1979): 34-38.

An in-depth look at DaCosta's *Spiritual Set*, for organ.

_____. *"Ukom Memory Songs."* *American Organist* 18 (February 1984): 35.

A scholarly article on the "ukom," and DaCosta's transposition of beats into modes in his work entitled *Ukom Memory Songs*.

Southern, Eileen. **"Conversation with Clarence E. Whiteman: Organ-Music Collector."** *Black Perspective in Music* 6/2 (fall 1978): 168-87.

The organ music of DaCosta is part of Whiteman's extensive collection, which includes the organ works of 14 black composers.

Leon Dallin

B. Silver City, Utah, 26 March 1918. B.M., M.M., with Howard Hanson and Bernard Rogers at Eastman; Ph.D., with Miklós Rosza and Ernest Kanitz, University of Southern California, 1946. On faculty at Colorado State University, 1946; University of Southern

California, 1946-48; Brigham Young University, 1948-55; California State University, Long Beach, since 1955. Books authored include *Techniques of 20th-Century Composition* (Dubuque, Iowa: Wm. C. Brown, 1957); *Foundations in Music Theory* (Belmont, Calif.: Wadsworth, 1962); and *Introduction to Music Reading—A Program for Personal Instruction* (Glenview, Ill.: Scott, Foresman, 1966).

ABD, CACA, CACJ, IWW92, OL, OL95, X62, X66, X67, X68, X69, X70, X71.

Kyle, Marguerite K. "AmerAllegro." *Pan Pipes* 56/2 (1964): 50.

    Dallin is appointed academic editor of music for the publisher Scott, Foresman, and Co.

Pamela Decker

B. 1955. Fulbright grant received for study at Musikhochschule, Lübeck, 1980. Graduated from Stanford with B.A., M.A., and, in 1982, D.M.A. Studied organ with Herbert Nanney, John Walker, Hans Gibhard, and Uwe Roeke, and composition with Leland Smith, Jens Rohwer, Roland Ploeger, and Julio Estrada. Taught at University of the Pacific, Stockton, Calif., and was organist at University of the Pacific in Stockton and St. Bede's Episcopal Church in Menlo Park. Currently, director of music at St. James' Episcopal Church in Dexter, Mich. Won 2nd prize in the AGO Organ Composition Contest—New Music Project of the Los Angeles chapter of the AGO—for her *Toccata*, 1989. Her dissertation is entitled "A Transcription for Organ of the *Concerto Grosso No. 1* for String Orchestra with Piano Obbligato (1924/25) by Ernest Krenek," *Dissertation Abstracts* 43 (October 1982): 967A.

A composite biography was produced from *American Organist* articles: 18 (April 1984): 15, and 24 (December 1990): 59.

"Convention Personalities." *American Organist* 18 (April 1984): 115.

    An introduction to organist-composer Pamela Decker; lists her educational experience.

"Here and There." *Diapason* 81 (February 1990): 3.

    Decker released a new CD recording entitled *Toccata*, produced by Arkay Records. Repertory includes toccatas by Buxtehude, Bach, Muffat, Decker, Heiller, and others.

"Here and There." *Diapason* 81 (December 1990): 3.

    Toccata for Organ will be published by C. F. Peters.

"Here and There." *Diapason* 85 (June 1994): 3.

    Decker is invited to perform at the Eighth International Organ Festival in Tallinn, Estonia, in August. She also received a grant from Arts International to assist in funding.

"Honors." *Diapason* 71 (September 1980): 7.

> Decker receives Fulbright grant to study in Germany, 1980-81.

"Mixtures." *American Organist* 24 (December 1990): 59.

> Decker has signed a contract with C. F. Peters for the publication of her *Toccata for Organ*. Brief biographical notes.

"Premieres." *American Organist* 22 (February 1988): 43.

> *Toccata* is premiered 28 February 1988 by organist Gwen Adams for the San Jose (Calif.) AGO chapter; *Passacaglia* is published by Hindon Publications.

Norman Dello Joio

B. New York, 24 January 1913. Attended City College, CUNY; spent three years at Juilliard, then to Yale University to study with Bernard Wagenaar and Paul Hindemith. Wins Elizabeth Sprague Coolidge Award, 1937. Two Guggenheim Awards, 1944 and 1966. Taught at Sarah Lawrence College, 1944-50; professor of composition, Mannes College, New York, 1956-72; founder-chairman of the policy committee for the Contemporary Music Project for Creativity in Music Education, 1959-72; dean of the School of the Arts, Boston University, 1972-78; after a sabbatical year, he returned to the Boston University faculty. Won the Pulitzer Prize, 1957, for his *Meditation on Ecclesiastés*. Organ study was with Pietro Yon, his godfather.

AA73, ABD, AMH, ASC, ASUC, BB58, BB65, BB71, BB78, BB92, BBCh, BBCpo, BDA, BMI, CA9, CACA, CACJ, CC92, DCM, DDM, DN73, EDM, EVM, GD54, HHH, HLM, IMD, IWW92, KTL, LMD, MEH, MGG, NCE, NG, NGA, OL, OL95, PC71, PCM, REM, TCAC, VER, WI62, WI69, WTM, X50, X51, X52, X53, X54, X55, X56, X57, X58, X59, X60, X61, X62, X64, X65, X66, X67, X68, X69, X70, X71, X74.

"American Composer Update." *Pan Pipes* 73/2 (1980): 26.

> Dello Joio receives an honorary doctor of music degree from the University of Susquehanna (Penn.).

Bumgardner, Thomas A. *Norman Dello Joio.* Boston: Twayne, 1986.

> Provides biographical information, a chronology, selected bibliography, catalog of musical works, and a discography. The works are divided into categories for discussion.

"Composers in Focus." *BMI: The Many Worlds of Music*, winter 1976, 19-20.

> Lists Dello Joio's three-generation Italian-organist ancestry; discusses his background and influences on his music, commissions, and his styles of writing.

"Dello Joio Wins Pulitzer Prize." *Musical America* 77 (June 1957): 35.

Dello Joio is awarded the Pulitzer Prize for 1957 for his score *Meditations on Ecclesiastés*. Includes biography.

"Dello Joio Writes New Work for SMU Organ." *American Organist* 48 (December 1965): 26.

Nita and Jake Akin and the Aeolian-Skinner Company commission Dello Joio to write *Laudation*, which is performed on the inaugural recital of the Aeolian-Skinner organ at Southern Methodist University, 15 October 1965.

Downes, Edward. "The Music of Norman Dello Joio." *Musical Quarterly* 48/2 (1962): 149-72.

A scholarly, in-depth approach to Dello Joio's compositional development.

Kyle, Marguerite K. "AmerAllegro." *Pan Pipes* 49 (January 1957): 42-43.

Dello Joio is professor of music at Mannes College of Music, New York.

50 (January 1958): 48.

Dello Joio wins Pulitzer Prize for *Meditations on Ecclesiastés*.

56/2 (1964): 51.

Dello Joio is named chairman of the joint committee for the MENC and the Ford Foundation project for contemporary music in education.

61/2 (1969): 49.

Honorary doctor of music degree is conferred by the University of Cincinnati.

62/2 (1970): 57.

Antiphonal Fantasy, for organ, brass, and strings, is published by E. B. Marks.

McCandless, William Edgar. "Cantus Firmus Techniques in Selected Instrumental Compositions." Ph.D., Music Theory, Indiana University, 1974.

Discusses traditional cantus firmus sources and techniques. Analyzes the textural, rhythmic, and tonal treatments of pre-existent melodies in ten twentieth-century compositions including Dello Joio's *Variations, Chaconne, and Finale*.

Meier, Ann. "An Interview with Norman Dello Joio." *Music Educators Journal* 74 (October 1987): 53-56.

The importance of placing composers in the schools, and the importance of communicating one's expertise but not one's aesthetics are discussed; awards are listed.

"Norman Dello Joio." *Pan Pipes* 43 (December 1950): 116. *

"**Norman Dello Joio.**" *Pan Pipes* 44 (January 1952): 28. *

"**Norman Dello Joio.**" *Pan Pipes* 45 (January 1953): 46-47. *

"**Norman Dello Joio.**" *Pan Pipes* 47 (January 1966): 39, 43.

> Dello Joio receives two commissions: one from the Elizabeth Sprague Coolidge Foundation and one from the Koussevitzky Foundation; brief biography included.

"**Norman Dello Joio.**" *Composers of the Americas* 9 (1963): 41-50.

> A brief biography in Spanish and English is followed by a list of his works, with notes about duration, publishers, and commission information.

"**Premieres.**" *Music Journal* 24 (March 1966): 16.

> Dello Joio's *Antiphonal Fantasy* receives its world premiere by organist Richard Ellsasser with the Philadelphia Orchestra led by Eugene Ormandy, 29 September 1965.

"**Premieres.**" *BMI: The Many Worlds of Music*, December 1965, 12.

> *Laudation* receives its world premiere.

Sabin, Robert. "**Norman Dello Joio.**" *Musical America* 70 (1 December 1950): 9 + .

> A detailed look at the influences upon Dello Joio as a composer, and his means of composition.

Stefania Bjørnson Denbow

B. Minneapolis, Minn., 28 December 1916. Studied at the University of Minnesota, B.M., 1937, and M.A., 1939. Organ study with Arthur Poister; studied composition with James Stewart and Karl Ahrend, Ohio State University. Mu Phi Epsilon Awards 1972, 1973, 1977; National Federation of Music Clubs special award of merit, 1976. Finalist in the Festival of Contemporary Music, Marshall University. Former organist-choir director in Annapolis, Md., and Athens, Ohio. Private piano and organ teacher. Organ music listed in Cohen's book.

ABD, CACA, DN76, DN77, IWC, WCH.

No bibliographical information located.

David Diamond

B. Rochester, N.Y., 9 July 1915. Studied at Cleveland Institute. Studied composition with Bernard Rogers at Eastman, 1930-34; private work with Roger Sessions in New York; studied with Nadia Boulanger, Paris, 1937. Received the Juilliard Publication award, three Guggenheim fellowships (1938, 1942, 1958); American Academy in Rome award; the Paderewski Prize; a grant from National Academy of Arts & Letters; and ASCAP-Stravinsky Award, 1967. Fulbright professor, University of Rome, 1951; moved to Florence, 1953-65, with brief appointments at the University of Buffalo in 1961 and 1963. Returned to the United States in 1965. On faculty at Manhattan School of Music, 1965-68; visiting professor, University of Colorado, Boulder, 1970; on faculty at Juilliard since 1973.

ABD, AMH, BB78, BB92, BBCh, BBCpo, BDA, CACA, DCM, HLM, KTL, NG, OL95, TCH, X50, X51, X52, X53, X54, X55, X56, X57, X58, X60, X61, X62, X69, X70, X71, X74.

Kimberling, Victoria J. *David Diamond: A Bio-Bibliography.* Metuchen, N.J.: Scarecrow, 1987.
  Includes biography, bibliography, discography, works and performances, and listing of works.

"Recitals." *American Organist* 22 (August 1988): 61.
  Leonard Raver performs the premiere of Diamond's *Symphony for Organ* on 15 March 1988, at Alice Tully Hall, Lincoln Center, New York City.

Schwarz, K. Robert. "Ringing True." *Musical America* 110 (November 1990): 20-24.
  Diamond, along with Howard Hanson, Walter Piston, and Virgil Thomson, is discussed as a composer synonomous with "American Classical music." The article considers this "lost" generation of composers who write tonal music.

Edward Diemente

B. Cranston, R.I., 27 February 1923. Educated at Boston University, yet graduated from Hartt College of Music, B.M.; M.M. from Eastman School of Music. Studied with Edward Hall Broadhead, Luman Bunnell, and Catharine Crozier. Joined Hartt College faculty, 1948; appointed director for the Electronic Music Studio, 1970; and named professor and chairman of the composition and theory departments at Hartt College of Music, since 1982; music director and organist, Cathedral of St. Joseph, Hartford, since 1961. Recipient of several ASCAP awards.

AA73, ABD, CACA, CACJ, CPM, DN76, DN77, OL, OL95, PC71, PCM, X62, X64, X65, X67, X68, X69, X70, X71, X74.

"AGO National Convention, Washington, D.C., 1982." *Diapason* 73 (September 1982): 6.

The premiere of *Cantos* is performed by Robert Noehren at St. John's Church, Lafayette Square; the work was commissioned for the convention.

Black, George. "Another View of the Contemporary Workshop." *Music* (AGO) 7 (September 1973): 38-39.

Elizabeth Sollenberger played Diemente's *Diary, Part I* (1972), written for this workshop, in a pointillistic fashion, reminiscent of fragmented diary writing; an unscheduled performance of Diemente's work *The Eagles Gather*, for organ, percussion, and tape, was played by organist Stuart Smith.

"A Capital Convention, Washington, D.C., June 28-July 2, 1982: Composers and Their Commissions." *American Organist* 16 (May 1982): 5.

An overview of *Cantos*, four pieces for the organ, is presented; "the surface sound of *Cantos* is the vocabulary of non-serial 12-tone music."

"Contemporary Composers and Their Works." *Music & Artists* 4/2 (1971): 5.

Brief biography; Diemente is recipient of Pittsburgh Feehan Federation award and is organist at the Hartford Cathedral of St. Joseph; the premiere of his *Magnificat* for two choruses and organ occurred March 17.

"Convention Event." *American Organist* 16 (April 1982): 101.

An introduction to Diemente's background and how it influences his writing.

"Edward P. Diemente." *Diapason* 52 (October 1961): 11.

Diemente is appointed director of music and organist at St. Joseph's Cathedral, Hartford, effective 1 September 1961.

Foss, Lukas, et al. "Contemporary Music: Observations from Those Who Create It." *Music & Artists* 5/3 (1972): 19-20.

Diemente indicates that "we are in a liberation movement . . . ideologies are replaced by freedom . . . composers . . . are redefining music. . . . Sound rather than syntax . . . an exciting, poetic time to be alive."

Kyle, Marguerite K. "AmerAllegro." *Pan Pipes* 49 (January 1957): 43.

Diemente receives first and second prizes in Wassili Leps Foundation Award from Brown University.

50 (January 1958): 49.

Diemente is named co-chairman, department of theory at Hartt College.

53/2 (1961): 50.

Diemente serves as assistant chairman of the Institute of Contemporary American Music.

54/2 (1962): 45.

Diemente is appointed chairman for the Institute of American Music and chairman of the theory and composition department at Hartt College; also named music director-organist at St. Joseph's Cathedral, Hartford.

56/2 (1964): 52.

Fanfare "Gaudeamus" is introduced by John Doney, 26 June 1963, at the AGO Regional Convention in Hartford, Conn.

59/2 (1967): 70.

Published are Diemente's *Two Trumpet Tunes for Organ*, *Organ Fantasy*, *Four Pieces for Organ*, and *Psalm 4 and Psalm 90 for Organ*, all by GIA.

60/2 (1968): 67.

Diemente wins first prize for choral and organ work from the Feehan Foundation, Pittsburgh; GIA publishes *Three Versets for Organ*.

63/2 (1971): 54-55.

Publication of *Two Preludes for Organ* by World Library Publishers, Cincinnati, is announced.

64/2 (1972): 51.

Premiere of *The Eagles Gather*, for organ, percussion, and tape, occurs 17 June 1971, with organist John Holtz and percussionist Richard Lepore performing.

65/2 (1973): 48.

Leonard Raver premieres Diemente's *Hosanna I for Organ and Tape* at Hartt College, 9 June 1972.

66/2 (1974): 48.

Premiere of Diemente's *Diary, Part I*, is performed by Elizabeth Sollenberger, Trinity Church, New York, and is published along with *Seven Things from the Box of Magic*, for organ, percussion, and tape, by Seesaw Music.

67/2 (1975): 51.

Diemente is named director of the University of Hartford's Electronic Studio; receives Distinguished Alumnus Award, 1974, University of Hartford.

68/2 (1976): 46-47.

Diemente receives a commission from organist John Holtz, who performed the premiere, for *Orenda*, at Trinity College Chapel, Hartford.

69/2 (1977): 41.

ASCAP Standard award, Vincent Coffin Grant, and Connecticut Arts Foundation Grant are presented to Diemente.

70/2 (1978): 38.

ASCAP award is presented to Diemente.

"Various Festival Programs." *Diapason* 64 (August 1973): 17.

> *Diary, Part I* is performed by Elizabeth Sollenberger; *Seven Things from the Box of Magic* receives its 1973 premiere by organist Edward Clark and percussionist Douglas Jackson.

Emma Lou Diemer

B. Kansas City, Mo., 24 November 1927. B.M., 1949, and M.M., 1950, in composition, Yale University; Ph.D., in composition, Eastman School of Music, 1960. Pupil of Donovan and Hindemith, Yale University; Toch and Sessions, Berkshire Music Center, Tanglewood; and Rogers, Hanson, and Craighead at Eastman. Composer-in-residence for the Ford Foundation Young Composers Project, Arlington, Va., 1959-61; taught on the faculties of the University of Maryland, 1965-70, and the University of California at Santa Barbara, 1971-91. Currently organist at First Presbyterian Church, Santa Barbara, and composer-in-residence, Santa Barbara Symphony.

ABD, AS66, BB92, CACA, CACJ, CAP, CC92, CR, DN74, DN77, DN78, IWC, IWW92, NGA, OL, OL95, PC71, PCM, TCH, WCH, X57, X62, X65, X68, X71, X74.

"American Composer Update." *Pan Pipes* 87/2 (1995): 21.

> Diemer's *God with Us* is published by Sacred Music Press and her *Fantasie*, also for organ, is recorded by Christa Rakich on AFKA Records, *Organ Music by Women*.

Bender, James F. "Three American Composers from the Young Composer Project: Style Analysis of Selected Works by Emma Lou Diemer, Donal Martin Jenni and Richard Lane." Ph.D., New York University, 1988. *Dissertation Abstracts* 50 (July 1989): 14A.

> Bender concentrates on Diemer's vocal works, but delineates the evolution of her style through her melodic lines; her basic development came through the shortening of motivic modules.

Brown, Cynthia Clark. "Emma Lou Diemer: Composer, Performer, Educator, Church Musician." D.M.A., Southern Baptist Theological Seminary, 1985. *Dissertation Abstracts* 46 (March 1986): 2478A.

Included are a catalog of her works and a discography; the work details her contributions to 20th-century composition, performances, education, and church music; biography.

Diemer, Emma Lou. "Fantasies and Improvisations." *Journal of Church Music* 23 (September 1981): 14-18.

Diemer discusses her improvisations from the 1950s to the present, and describes various works suitable for church.

_____. "Loneliness of the Long Distance Organ Composer." *American Organist* 16 (September 1982): 45-47.

Diemer gives her general approach to composition and discusses her personal style. Lists her published organ music; details about *Declarations* (1973), for organ, are provided.

_____. "My Life as a Composer." *Piano Quarterly* 33/129 (1985): 58-59.

Diemer comments on women's role in music, in university life, and as a composer, with tips on publication.

Drone, Jeanette, comp. "American Composer Update." *Pan Pipes* 75/2 (1983): 25-26.

Declarations and *Toccata and Fugue for Organ* are recorded on Capriccio Records, distributed by CRI.

"Emma Lou Diemer Is Winner in St. Mark's Competition." *Diapason* 48 (June 1957): 6.

Diemer, organist of Central Presbyterian Church, Kansas City, Mo., wins the 1956 St. Mark's Composers Competition, Philadelphia, for *A Festival Voluntary* based on a given theme.

"Here and There." *Diapason* 67 (July 1976): 11.

Diemer performs a recital of works by women; premieres her own *Pianoharpsichordorgan*, a taped composition, 25 April 1976, at the University of California, Santa Barbara.

Hinshaw, Donald G. "Contemporary Composers: Emma Lou Diemer." *Journal of Church Music* 18 (September 1976): 13-15.

An introduction to Diemer, an imaginative composer, whose style is discussed and list of works is provided.

Hubler, Lyn Helen. "Women Organ Composers from the Middle Ages to the Present: With Performance Suggestions for Selected Works." D.M.A., Stanford University, 1983.

A survey; Diemer and her works are included. Appendix lists the names, dates, and nationalities of 220 women organ composers.

LePage, Jane Weiner. *Women Composers, Conductors, and Musicians of the Twentieth Century: Selected Biographies.* Metuchen, N.J.: Scarecrow, 1980.

Includes the biography of Diemer, lists her works and provides a discography.

"Music Journal's Gallery of Living Composers." *Music Journal* 31 (annual, 1973): 91-95.

Biography; major prizes and awards listed, major works listed, and current address provided.

Naus, Thomas. "The Organ Works of Emma Lou Diemer." Ph.D., Michigan State University, 1991. *Dissertation Abstracts* 52 (October 1991): 3472A.

A stylistic and theoretical study of her organ works; includes biography, chronological catalog of her work, discography, a matrix for *Declarations*, her only serial work, and a general plan for *Church Rock*, an improvisational work for organ and tape.

"Pipings." *American Organist* 27 (December 1993): 50.

Diemer is guest composer at the Third Festival of Women Composers, 23-27 March 1993, at Indiana University of Pennsylvania. One recital was devoted to her organ works.

"Premieres." *Music Journal* 32 (December 1974): 26.

Premiere of Diemer's *Declaration* for organ at the University of California, Santa Barbara, by the composer.

"Premieres." *Music Educators Journal* 63 (September 1976): 23.

On 25 April 1976, Diemer's *Pianoharpsichordorgan* is premiered at Lotte Lehman Concert Hall, University of California, Santa Barbara.

"Premieres." *American Organist* 19 (March 1985): 144-45.

Diemer's *Concert Piece for Organ and Orchestra* is premiered 25 February 1985, with the University of Oregon Symphony led by Karen Kaltner and with the composer at the keyboard, at the West Coast Women Conductor-Composer Symposium.

"Premieres." *American Organist* 20 (December 1986): 40.

Diemer performs the premiere of her *Church Rock*, for organ and tape, with two other premieres, at the National City Christian Church, Washington, D.C., for the tenth anniversary of American Women Composers.

John H. Diercks

B. Montclair, N.J., 19 April 1927. Studied with Herbert Elwell, Oberlin, B.M.; Bernard Rogers, Alan Hovhaness, and Howard Hanson, Eastman School of Music, M.M. and

Ph.D., 1960. Dissertation: "Suite No. 2." Awards include Southern Foundation fellowship, 1958; Danforth Foundation grants; MacDowell fellowship; ASCAP awards; and NEA grant. On faculty at the College of Wooster (Ohio), 1950-54; since 1954, Hollins College (Va.). Music critic of the *Roanoke Times* since 1962. Author of two chapters in *Teaching Piano*, edited by D. Agay (Yorktown Press, n.d.).

ABD, CACA, IWW92, OL, OL95, PC71, PCM, SCL, X62, X66, X67, X68, X69, X70.

"Five Questions: 55 Answers." *Composer* (US) 7/16 (1976-77): 16-25. *

Kyle, Marguerite K. "AmerAllegro." *Pan Pipes* 49 (January 1957): 43.

Diercks is appointed to Hollins College (Va.) faculty.

53/2 (1961): 50.

Diercks received a Ph.D. in composition from the Eastman School of Music, and also a Danforth grant to study Oriental music.

54/2 (1962): 45.

Diercks is employed as music critic for the *Roanoke Times*.

55/2 (1963): 45.

Six Sacred Organ Compositions by Diercks is published by Abingdon Press.

56/2 (1964): 52.

Organist Edmund Wright premieres Diercks's *Six Sacred Organ Compositions* in February.

58/2 (1966): 58.

Concordia publishes Diercks's *Prelude for Organ*.

60/2 (1968): 67.

Publication of Diercks's *Prelude on "O Day of Rest"* is announced by Concordia.

70/2 (1978): 38.

Diercks is awarded a National Endowment for the Humanities grant for study in ethnomusicology at the University of Washington.

Richard W. Dirksen

B. Freeport, Ill., 1921. Graduated *magna cum laude* from Peabody Conservatory of Music, 1942; honorary Doctor of Fine Arts degree from George Washington University, 1980. Served for over 40 years in various capacities at Washington, D.C.'s National Cathedral—as assistant, 1942; associate organist and choirmaster, 1947; and director of the program and organist-choirmaster, 1977-88. Conductor of the Cathedral Choral Society and the Choral Arts Society. Now retired.

ABD, CACA, OL, OL95, PCM, X58, X60, X62, X69, X74.

"Appointments." *American Organist* 52 (February 1969): 23.

> Dirksen is appointed chancellor of the College of Church Musicians, Washington Cathedral, 1 February 1969. Includes Dirksen's educational background.

"Convention Event." *American Organist* 16 (April 1982): 139.

> Includes a biography of Dirksen.

"Dirksen Named to Newly Created Cathedral Post." *Diapason* 56 (December 1964): 25.

> Dirksen named director of the Advance Program; will coordinate religious and secular activities and study ways to enlarge the program.

Ellinwood, Leonard. "The Music of Washington Cathedral." *Organ Institute Quarterly* 7 (spring 1957): 11-17.

> An article describing the musical happenings at the Cathedral; pp. 15-16 describe Dirksen's duties.

Anthony Donato

B. Prague, Neb., 8 March 1909. Studied at the Eastman School of Music with Howard Hanson, Bernard Rogers, and Edward Royce, B.M., 1931; M.M., 1937; Ph.D, 1947. Taught violin at Drake University, 1931-37; Iowa State Teachers College, 1937-39; University of Texas, 1939-46; Northwestern University, 1947-77. Fulbright grant to study in England, 1951-52. Published *Preparing Music Manuscript* (Englewood Cliffs, N.J.: Prentice-Hall, 1963).

ABD, AMH, AS66, ASC, ASUC, BB58, BB71, BB78, BB92, BBCh, CA15, CACA, CACJ, KTL, LCI, LMD, MHHH, NGA, OL, OL95, PC71, PCM, TCAC, X50, X51, X53, X54, X55, X56, X57, X59, X62, X64, X65, X66, X67, X68, X69, X70, X74.

"Anthony Donato." *Pan Pipes* 43 (December 1950): 118. *

"Anthony Donato." *Pan Pipes* 45 (January 1953): 47. *

"Anthony Donato." *Composers of the Americas* 15 (1969): 78-89.

> A brief biography in Spanish and English; an annotated list of works follows.

Kyle, Marguerite K. "AmerAllegro." *Pan Pipes* 48 (January 1956): 42.

Two *Pastels* for organ are published by Mercury Music.

54/2 (1962): 45.

Donato is a fellow of the Huntington Hartford Foundation, Pacific Palisades, Calif.

66/2 (1974): 48-49.

Donato's *Two Windsongs* for soprano and organ are premiered in Evanston, Ill., 7 November 1973, by Norico and Karel Paukert.

"Two Pastels for Organ." *Notes* 14 (September 1957): 610.

A review of Donato's new work, *Two Pastels* for organ. Although the works are brief, they are considered to be quality works; brief overview of the pieces.

George W. Drumwright, Jr.

B. Washington, D.C., 3 June 1952. Student at Peabody Conservatory, 1972-74; organ student of Edith Ho and William Watkins; composition with Lawrence Moss; B.M. in composition, 1977, and M.M. in composition, 1979, from the University of Maryland. Since 1983, organist-director of music, Calvary Baptist Church, Washington, D.C. Organ music listed in Arnold's book.
OL, OL95.

No bibliographical information located.

Marion Dunn

B. 19—, n.p. *Bells in the Starry Night*, for organ, won the composition prize awarded by Schulmerich.
CR.

No bibliographical information located.

Paul Earls

B. Springfield, Mo., 9 June 1934. B.M., M.M., and Ph.D., from Eastman School of Music. Student of Bernard Rogers and Howard Hanson. Associate professor of music, Duke University, 1965-72; fellow at the Center for Advanced Visual Studies, 1970; visiting associate professor and lecturer in humanities, MIT, 1972-74; since 1972, lecturer in media and the performing arts, Massachusetts College of Art. Also briefly on other faculties: Southwestern Missouri State College, Chabot College, University of Oregon, and the University of Lowell, Mass. Recipient of the Benjamin Prize, 1958; Guggenheim grant, Fulbright grant, MacDowell and Yaddo Colony fellow; Huntington Hartford Foundation and Mary Duke Biddle Foundation grants.

AA73, ABD, ASUC, CACA, CACJ, IWW92, OL, OL95, X68, X70, X71, X74.

"American Composer Update." *Pan Pipes* 75/2 (1983): 26.

Earls is a fellow at MIT Center for Advanced Visual Studies.

Kyle, Marguerite K. "AmerAllegro." *Pan Pipes* 63/2 (1971): 55-56.

On leave from Duke University, 1970-72, Earls is a fellow at MIT Center for Advanced Visual Studies; awarded a Guggenheim grant, 1970-71.

65/2 (1973): 49-50.

Ione Press (E. C. Schirmer) publishes Earls's *Huguenot Variations for Organ* and *Nun danket Fantasy*, for organ.

67/2 (1975): 52.

Earls is a National Endowment for the Arts Fellowship Grant recipient.

70/2 (1978): 39.

Earls is the 1976-77 composer-in-residence at the University of Lowell, Mass.; recipient of an NEA grant.

Cecil Effinger

B. Colorado Springs, Colo., 22 July 1914; d. Boulder, Colo., 22 December 1990. Studied mathematics at Colorado College, B.A., 1935; harmony and counterpoint with Frederick Boothroyd, Colorado Springs, 1934-36; composition with Bernard Wagenaar, New York, 1938, and Nadia Boulanger, 1939, in Fontainebleau, where he was awarded the Stoval

Composition prize. Also, winner of the Naumburg Recording Award. Oboist in Colorado Springs Symphony Orchestra, 1933-41, Denver Symphony Orchestra, 1937-41, and Colorado School for the Blind, 1935-41. During World War II, conducted 506th Army Band, then taught at American University in France; Colorado College, 1946-48; music editor, *Denver Post*, 1947-48; head of composition department and composer-in-residence at the University of Colorado, Boulder, 1948-84. In 1954, he patented a practical music typewriter as the "Musicwriter" and has designed the "Tempo-Watch."

AA73, ABD, AS66, BB58, BB78, BB92, CACA, CACJ, EVM, GD54, HHH, KTL, LMD, MHHH, NG, NGA, OL, OL95, PC71, PCM, REM, TCAC, TCH, VER, X55, X56, X58, X60, X62, X64, X65, X66, X67, X68, X70, X71, X74.

Bingham, Seth. "Organ Personalities." *American Organist* 46 (November 1963): 12.

> A personal note from Bingham about his relationship with Effinger, whose *Organ and Orchestra Concerto* is mentioned.

"Cecil Effinger." *Pan Pipes* 45 (January 1953): 50. *

Kyle, Marguerite K. "AmerAllegro." *Pan Pipes* 55/2 (1963): 47.

> Effinger's *Fanfare for Organ* is in preparation for publication.

63/2 (1971): 56.

> Effinger received a faculty fellowship, 1969-70, to take leave from the University of Colorado to compose.

McCray, James. "American Choral Music with Organ: The Music of Cecil Effinger." *American Organist* 24 (July 1990): 76-81.

> A background of Effinger's life and a detailed look at his works with organ; anthems, cantatas, and oratorios; list of works follows.

[Obituary.] *American Organist* 25 (March 1991): 50.

> Effinger's inventions are noted. Lists several teaching positions he held, and indicates he was oboist with the Colorado Springs Symphony Orchestra, 1932-41, and served as music editor for the *Denver Post* in 1946-48.

[Obituary.] *Diapason* 82 (March 1991): 5.

> Includes the same information as above; however, dates at the *Denver Post* read 1947-48. Appointed professor and head of the composition department at the University of Colorado, 1948; named professor emeritus and appointed composer-in-residence in 1981, serving until 1984.

[Obituary.] *Notes* 47/4 (1991): 1086.

[Obituary.] *Notes* 48/4 (1992): 1209.

"Oremus, Prelude on 'Our Father, Who Art in Heaven,' for Organ." *Notes* 10 (September 1953): 685.

> Effinger's organ work *Oremus* is published by Gray; description of the work is included.

Guy H. Eldridge, Jr.

B. 1904; d. 1976.
OL.

No bibliographical information located.

Merrill Ellis

B. Cleburne, Texas, 9 December 1916; d. 21 July 1981. Studied with Roy Harris at the University of Oklahoma, Spencer Norton, and Charles Garland. M.M. from the University of Missouri. Taught music theory and music history at Joplin Junior College, Joplin, Mo., and North Texas State University (NTSU), Denton, Texas. Became director of the electronic laboratory, NTSU. Recipient of ASCAP awards and numerous commissions.

AA73, ABD, AMH, CACA, DN78, JCN, OL, OL95, X62, X65, X66, X67, X68, X69, X70, X71, X74.

"American Composer Update." *Pan Pipes* 73/2 (1981): 28.

> Ellis receives an ASCAP award and a research grant from North Texas State University.

Kyle, Marguerite K. "AmerAllegro." *Pan Pipes* 51 (January 1959): 60.

> Premiere of Ellis's *Organ Toccata* is performed 1 May 1958 by organist Martha Pate, Kansas State Teachers College, Pittsburg.

55/2 (1963): 47.

> Ellis joins the North Texas State University faculty.

56/2 (1964): 54.

> Ellis is awarded the Harvey Gaul Composition Prize in June for his *Organ Fantasy*.

58/2 (1966): 59-60.

Ellis is named director of a grant to build and establish an electronic composition research laboratory at NTSU.

59/2 (1967): 71-72.

Ellis receives ASCAP award, 1966.

60/2 (1968): 69.

ASCAP award, 1967.

63/2 (1971): 56.

Ellis is awarded an NTSU research grant "to improve and operate the NTSU Electronic Music Center"; ASCAP award.

64/2 (1972): 53.

ASCAP award; research grant from NTSU.

66/2 (1974): 50.

Ellis is named director of Electronic Music Center; ASCAP award; faculty research grant from NTSU.

70/2 (1978): 39-40.

Hinshaw publishes *Organ Toccata*.

71/2 (1979): 31.

ASCAP award; NTSU faculty research grant continues for Ellis.

Robert Hall Elmore

B. Ramaputnam, India, to American missionary parents, 2 January 1913; d. Ardmore, Penn., 22 September 1985. B.M., University of Pennsylvania, 1937. Received the degrees of Licentiate of the Royal College of Music of London in organ, piano, and accompanying, and as an Associate of the Royal College of Organists. Organ study with Pietro Yon, E. F. Easterday, and Ralph Kinder; composition with Harl McDonald. Received the Nitsche Prize from the University of Pennsylvania, and was first recipient of the Thornton Oakley Medal for achievement in the creative arts, 1936. Taught organ at Clarke Conservatory of Music, 1936-53; the Musical Academy in Philadelphia, from 1939; and on the faculty at the University of Pennsylvania, 1940 until his death.

AA73, ABD, AMH, AS66, ASC, BB58, BB78, BB92, BBCpo, CACA, KTL, OL, OL95, PC71, PCM, X52, X53, X54, X58, X60, X62, X64, X66, X67, X68, X69, X70, X74.

"American Composer Update." *Pan Pipes* 73/2 (1981): 28-29.

Elmore's *Sonata for Organ* is published by Flammer.

75/2 (1983): 26-27.

Elmore plays several recitals and performs organ dedications in two churches.

"AOPC honors Elmore." *American Organist* 48 (October 1965): 25.

Honorary life membership is presented to Elmore from the American Organ Players' Club of Philadelphia. A recital of his organ works was performed by Lewis Bruun.

Bingham, Seth. "Elmore Plays in New York City." *Diapason* 46 (May 1955): 13.

Elmore is proclaimed "brilliant" in his New York recital at St. Thomas Church, 28 March 1955, performing works from Bach to his own *Rhythmic Suite*.

_____. **"Estelle Borhek Jonston Memorial Music Festival."** *American Organist* 47 (December 1964): 8-9.

A laudatory review of the festival, and especially so of Elmore's composition *Psalm of Thanksgiving* (1959) for two choirs, two brass and percussion ensembles, and two organs, plus his new *Concerto for Organ, Brass, and Percussion* (1964).

_____. **"Organ Personalities."** *American Organist* 46 (November 1963): 13.

Elmore's biography is briefly delineated, and also mentions the composer is active as a performer.

"Central Moravian Church Appoints Robert Elmore." *Diapason* 46 (October 1955): 22.

Elmore is appointed organist-choirmaster in Bethlehem, Penn., at Central Moravian Church.

Elmore, Robert. "Art for the Lord's Sake." *American Organist* 43 (June 1960): 22, 28, 30.

Elmore discusses "art for the Lord's sake" in church music, not "art for art's sake." He underscores the idea of using one's talents from God for God, through composition or performance.

"Elmore Made Life Member of Philadelphia Group." *Diapason* 56 (August 1965): 3.

Elmore is named a life member in the American Organ Players' Club of Philadelphia, 2 May 1965, when a recital was held in his honor.

Kyle, Marguerite K. "AmerAllegro." *Pan Pipes* 50 (January 1958): 52.

Flammer publishes *Fantasy on Nursery Tunes*.

51 (January 1959): 60.

Two organ works are published: *Three Meditations on Moravian Hymn-Tunes* (Flammer) and *Meditation on an Old Covenanters' Tune* (Gray); honorary degrees conferred on him are Doctor of Laws, Alderson-Broaddus College, and Doctor of Humane Letters, Moravian College.

55/2 (1963): 47-48.

Elmore's *Invocation for Organ and String Orchestra* premiered at the Festival of Music, Central Moravian Church, Bethlehem, Penn., 4 November 1962.

56/2 (1964): 54.

Two works published: *Alla Marcia* (Flammer) and *Meditation on "Veni Emmanuel"* for organ and brass quartet (J. Fischer).

58/2 (1966): 60.

More Elmore works published for organ: *Concerto for Organ, Brass, and Percussion* (Gray) and *Twelve Interludes* (Elkan-Vogel); American Organ Players' Club presented him a life membership, 22 May 1969.

59/2 (1967): 72.

Elmore's *Chorale Preludes* are premiered by him on 2 October 1966.

64/2 (1972): 53.

Premiere of Elmore's arrangement of Mussorgsky's *Pictures at an Exhibition* for organ and percussion occurred 6 December 1970 as part of the dedicatory recital at Tenth Presbyterian Church, Philadelphia; premiere of *Chorale-Fantasie* for two choirs and two organs took place on 25 April 1971 at First Presbyterian Church, Moorestown, N.J.

65/2 (1973): 50-51.

Pavane is recorded at Calvary Baptist Church, New York.

69/2 (1977): 44.

Sonata for Organ in C Major is premiered 12 December 1976 at Tenth Presbyterian Church, Philadelphia, by organist Norman MacKenzie.

70/2 (1978): 40.

Premiere of *Concertino for Trumpet and Organ* was performed 20 April 1977 at Curtis Institute of Music, Philadelphia.

71/2 (1979): 31.

Sonata for Organ is published by Flammer; Elmore celebrates ten years as director of music at Tenth Presbyterian Church, Philadelphia.

Lange, Stephen R. **"An Analysis of Concerto for Brass, Organ and Percussion by Robert Elmore, Concerto for Brass and Organ by Seth Bingham, and Concerto for Organ and Brasses by Normand Lockwood."** Ph.D., Michigan State University, 1978. *Dissertation Abstracts* 39 (September 1978): 1182A. *

Ness, J. Earl. **"Recitals and Concerts."** *American Organist* 43 (October 1960): 24.

Favorable review of Elmore's recital at First Presbyterian Church, Philadelphia, 27 April 1960.

[Obituary.] *American Organist* 20 (January 1986): 55.

Elmore dies on the way home after the morning service, 22 September 1985, Ardmore, Penn.

[Obituary.] *Diapason* 77 (January 1986): 3.

Death notice; brief highlights in Elmore's life.

"The Organs in Central Moravian Church." *American Organist* 41 (November 1958): 418 + . *

Includes information on Elmore's *Chorale Prelude on Seelenbräutigam.*

Owen, Barbara. "Recitals and Concerts." *American Organist* 43 (April 1960): 24.

A review of Elmore's recital at St. Stephen's Episcopal Church, Providence, R.I.; his composition *Jesus Makes My Heart Rejoice* is panned.

"Recitals and Concerts." *American Organist* 45 (January 1962): 20.

Three Psalms is introduced by the composer in the Memorial Music Festival, held on 5 November 1961 at Central Moravian Church, Bethlehem, Penn. Elmore, with this work, reached "a new high level of musical eloquence."

"Robert Elmore." *American Organist* 32 (September 1949): 311-12.

Biography; a listing of published organ works to date, and a mention of other areas in which he writes.

"Robert Elmore." *Pan Pipes* 44 (January 1952): 29. *

"Robert Elmore." *Pan Pipes* 45 (January 1953): 50. *

"Robert Elmore." *Pan Pipes* 47 (January 1955): 45.

Rhapsody for organ and brass is premiered 17 January 1954, Syracuse University, by organist Arthur Poister. Elmore premieres *Two Portraits* for organ and string quartet, 4 August 1954, Washington Memorial Chapel, Valley Forge, Penn.; *Suite in Rhythm* and *Rhumba* are published by St. Mary's Press. Elmore records some of his organ works on Canterbury Records.

"Robert Elmore." *Diapason* 61 (December 1969): 3.

Elmore is named music director and organist for Tenth Presbyterian Church, Philadelphia.

"Robert Elmore Composes Score for Religious Film." *Diapason* 44 (August 1953): 25.

A two-hour score for organ and chamber orchestra is composed by Elmore for a film entitled *The Living Church*, distributed by Westminster Press.

"Robert Elmore Honored." *American Organist* 49 (February 1966): 23.

Elmore is honored for ten years of service as organist-choir director at Central Moravian Church, Bethlehem, Penn., 20 December 1965. Condensed biography included.

"Robert Elmore, Organist and Composer." *Diapason* 45 (December 1953): 4.

Elmore presents a dedicatory recital at St. Stephen's Church, Philadelphia; Galaxy publishes his *Night of the Star* for organ.

"Robert Elmore, Whom Two Colleges Honor." *Diapason* 49 (August 1958): 4.

Two honorary degrees accorded Elmore: Alderson-Broaddus College (Phillipi, W.V.) confers on him the L.L.D., 2 June 1958, and Moravian College confers the L.H.D. on 8 June 1958.

"Robert H. Elmore, 1913-1985." *Journal of Church Music* 28 (February 1986): 27.

An obituary for Elmore, with a summary of his career.

"Rhumba and Rhythmic Suite." *Diapason* 45 (August 1954): 23.

St. Mary's Press debuts with two Elmore works—*Rhumba* and *Rhythmic Suite*—and his anthology entitled *Graveyard Gems*, all for organ.

Spicer, David. "Robert H. Elmore, An Appreciation." *Diapason* 77 (March 1986): 17.

A complete review of Elmore's life.

"Two New Works by Elmore Are Heard in Valley Forge." *Diapason* 45 (October 1954): 19.

Two Portraits, for organ and string quartet, is premiered 4 August 1954, Washington Memorial Chapel, Valley Forge, Penn. The second work is *Plaint*, for contralto and string quartet.

Wetzler, Robert P. "Contemporary Composers." *Journal of Church Music* 12 (April 1970): 22.

A look at Elmore as composer, performer, and teacher.

James Engel

B. Milwaukee, Wisc., 21 March 1925; d. Minneapolis, Minn., 17 April 1989. Educated at Concordia College, River Forest, Ill., B.M., 1945; M.M., Northwestern University, 1951; and further graduate studies at the University of Wisconsin, Madison. Organ student of Frederick Marriott and Thomas Matthews. Chair, music department, Concordia College,

Milwaukee, 1957-70; director of choral activities, Fox Valley Academy, Appleton, Wisc., 1970-72; professor of organ and music theory, Dr. Martin Luther College, New Ulm, Minn., 1975-89. Editor of the new hymnal project of the Wisconsin Evangelical Lutheran Synod. Author of *An Introduction to Organ Registration* (St. Louis: Concordia, 1986).

OL, OL95, WWAM-Cl.

[Obituary.] *American Organist* 23 (October 1989): 65.

> Biographical information provided; works were published by Concordia, Augsburg/Fortress, Northwestern, Morning Star, and Chantry Press.

[Obituary.] *Diapason* 80 (September 1989): 4.

> Biographical information provided; lists publishers of Engel's works.

[Obituary.] *Notes* 46/4 (1990): 930.

> Date of death; cites source for his biography: *Who's Who in American Music: Classical.*

Donald Erb

B. Youngstown, Ohio, 17 January 1927. After serving in the U.S. Navy, enrolled at Kent State University to study trumpet, and had courses in composition with Harold Miles and Kenneth Gaburo, B.S., 1950; entered Cleveland Institute of Music, 1950, in Marcel Dick's class and received his M.M., 1953; studied with Nadia Boulanger in Paris, 1952. Employed as faculty member of Cleveland Institute of Music, 1953. Studied composition with Bernhard Heiden at Indiana University, doctorate received in 1964; assistant professor of composition, Bowling Green State University, 1964-65; Guggenheim fellowship grant, 1965. Visiting assistant professor for research in electronic music, Case Institute of Technology, Cleveland, 1965-67; composer-in-residence, Cleveland Institute of Music, 1966-81; visiting professor of composition at Indiana University, 1975-76. In 1969-74, staff composer at Bennington Composers Conference in Vermont. Held the Meadows Professor of Composition chair, Southern Methodist University, Dallas, 1981-84; professor of music, Indiana University, 1984-87; professor of composition, Cleveland Institute of Music, from 1987. President of American Music Center, 1982-86. Composer-in-residence for the St. Louis Symphony Orchestra, 1988-90.

ABD, AMH, ASUC, BB71, BB78, BB92, CACA, CACJ, CC92, DCM, DN75, DN77, DN78, IWW92, KTL, NG, NGA, OL, OL95, PC71, TCH, X60, X61, X62, X66, X67, X68, X69, X70, X71, X74.

"Composers in Focus." *BMI: The Many Worlds of Music*, winter 1976, 20-21.

A discussion of Erb's style and the use of tape in his compositions. Mention is made of his Ford Foundation fellowship and Rockefeller and Guggenheim grants.

"Contemporary Composers and Their Works." *Music & Artists* 4/2 (1971): 5.

A brief biography that includes awards and honors, current position, and with whom he records.

"Donald Erb." *International Trombone Association* 13/2 (1985): 11-12.

Biographical information; Erb mixes his technical knowledge with jazz and electronic sounds.

Felder, D. "An Interview with Donald Erb." *Composer* (US) 10-11 (1980): 43-52. *

"Honors and Appointments." *Instrumentalist* 45 (November 1990): 10.

Erb receives a $25,000 grant from the NEA for composing.

"In the Press." *BMI: The Many Worlds of Music*, March 1969, 18-19.

Erb is interviewed; he states that the artist of the future is going to feel at home with electronics [synthesizers, use of tape, and the like].

Jacobson, Robert. "Donald Erb." *BMI: The Many Worlds of Music*, June 1971, 9.

A look into the educational and compositional background, with philosophical statements about his compositions.

Kratzenstein, Marilou, and Bruce Gustafson. "The Minneapolis-St. Paul AGO Convention." *Diapason* 71 (August 1980): 3.

Karel Paukert performs *Nebbiolina* at University Lutheran Church of Hope. Erb's work is scored for an organist (who also plays percussion) and eight bell ringers.

Kyle, Marguerite K. "AmerAllegro." *Pan Pipes* 61/2 (1969): 51.

Erb receives a five-year contract from Presser for the publication of all of his music; a Rockefeller grant recipient, he will be composer-in-residence for the Dallas Symphony, 1968-69.

Lipp, Charles. "Meet the Composer: An Interview with Donald Erb." *Instrumentalist* 33 (February 1979): 92-94.

A discussion of Erb's start in composition; when to start students' compositional skills; stresses listening and knowledge of music in grade school; it is important to be performing, also.

Pozzi Escot

B. Lima, Peru, 1 October 1933. Studied composition with Andrés Sás at the Sás-Rosay Music Academy in Lima, 1949-53; with William Bergsma at the Juilliard School; and Philipp Jarnach in Hamburg, Germany. Emigrated to the U.S. in 1953, and became a naturalized citizen, 1963. Received four MacDowell fellowships; grants from the German government and from the Ford Foundation; fellow at Radcliffe Institute, 1968-69; in 1956, named laureate composer of Peru; advisor-lecturer, by invitation of the U.S. State Department and the Ministry of Culture of Peru, 1972. Lectured at the Universities of Peking and Shanghai, 1984. Taught theory and composition at New England Conservatory, and in 1972 was assistant professor and director of the electronic studio at Wheaton College, Norton, Mass. Authored *Music in America* (Bloomington: Indiana University Press, n.d.); *Perspectives of New Music* (Princeton, N.J.: Princeton University Press, n.d.); *Sonic Design: The Nature of Sound and Music*, with Robert Cogan (Englewood Cliffs, N.J.: Prentice-Hall, 1976); *Sonic Design: Practice and Problems*, with Robert Cogan (Englewood Cliffs, N.J.: Prentice-Hall, 1981); and *Twentieth Century Sound: Techniques and Vision* (Berkeley: University of California Press, Berkeley, n.d.).

IWC, IWW92, NGA.

Cogan, Robert. *New Images of Musical Sound.* Cambridge, Mass.: Harvard University, 1984.

> The author and Pozzi Escot shared the work of developing an analytic theory of tone color in music, which is related to sonic oppositional analysis used in linguistics.

Delio, Thomas. "Sound, Gesture and Symbol: The Relation between Notation and Structure in American Experimental Music." *Interface* 10/3-4 (1981): 199-219.

> Article defines two categories of structure and notation (behaviorism and pluralism) and explores late 20th-century works in connection with these categories. Escot's *Neyrac lux* falls in the pluralist category.

_____, **ed.** *Contiguous Lines: Issues and Ideas in the Music of the 60s and 70s.* Lanham, Md.: University Press of America, 1984.

> The eight essays on contemporary music by various authors includes an essay by Escot on non-linearity.

"Martha Folts Recital." *Diapason* 67 (August 1976): 4.

> Folts presents Escot's *Fergus Are*; the work is described as a number of geometric designs drawn by the composer on a mathematical basis.

Alvin Derald Etler

B. Battle Creek, Iowa, 19 February 1913; d. Northampton, Mass., 14 June 1973 (some sources give June 13 as date of death). B.M., Yale School of Music, 1944; composition study with Paul Hindemith. Further study for oboe at the University of Illinois and Western Reserve. Oboist, Indianapolis Symphony Orchestra, 1938-40; taught at Yale University, 1942-46; Cornell University, 1946-67; University of Illinois, 1947-49. On faculty at Smith College, Northampton, Mass., from 1949 until his death. Author of *Making Music—An Introduction to Theory* (New York: Harcourt Brace Jovanovich, 1974).

ABD, AMH, BB58, BB65, BB71, BB78, BB92, BMI, CACA, DCM, EDM, IMD, KTL, LMD, NG, NGA, OL, OL95, PC71, PCM, REM, TCAC, TCH, X51, X55, X56, X57, X58, X59, X62, X65, X66, X67, X68, X70, X71, X74.

[Obituary.] *High Fidelity/Musical America* 23 (September 1973): MA17.
Etler dies on 14 June 1973.

[Obituary.] *Musical Times* 114 (December 1973): 1269.
The death date here is given as 13 June 1973; also includes a notice that his book will be published soon.

[Obituary.] *Variety* 271 (20 June 1973): 63.

Shelden, Paul M. "Alvin Etler (1913-1973)—A Look at the Career of a Significant Twentieth-Century Composer of Music for Wind Instruments." *Wood World Brass* 18/6 (1979): 9-10.
Etler says that he writes for the performer to communicate and present drama; briefly describes his early, middle, and late periods regarding works for winds.

_____. "Alvin Etler (1913-1973): His Career and the Two Sonatas for Clarinet." D.M.A., University of Maryland, 1978.
A biographical account that includes information on his career and his two clarinet sonatas.

Stroh, Virginia L. "The Oboe-Playing Composer." *Woodwind World* 2 (May 1958): 7.
Etler is applauded by conductor George Szell for his fine new work, *Concerto in One Movement*. A biographical article, it includes prizes he has won, works he has composed, and his future plans.

Nancy Plummer Faxon

B. Jackson, Miss., 19 November 1914. Piano student of Mrs. J. L. Roberts; B.S., Millsaps College; M.M. in piano, 1938, and M.M., 1941, in voice, Chicago Musical College. Student of Rudolf Ganz, piano; Mme. Nelli Gardini, voice; and Max Wald, composition. Soloist, Sorrenton Opera Company, 1938; voice instructor, Ward-Belmont College, Nashville, Tenn., 1941-42; organist-choirmaster, Wheaton Methodist Church, Evanston, Ill., 1943-44; piano and music theory teacher at Millsaps College, 1945-46; organist-choirmaster, Church of the Redeemer, Chestnut Hill, Mass., 1950-51; and theory instructor, Chaloff School of Music, Boston, 1950-51. Won first prize, National Composers Congress, 1941.

OL, OL95, WWAM-Cl.

"NPF Receives Orah Ashley Lamke Award." *Triangle* 81/1 (1986): 3 + . *

"Pipings." *American Organist* 24 (February 1990): 48.

> Faxon was honored by a special program of her music, performed under the artistic direction of her husband, George, at Old South Church, Boston, on 16 November 1989. The concert included her *Toccata* for organ.

"Tribute Honors Composers, Raises Scholarship Fund." *Triangle* 77/4 (1983): 5. *

Richard Felciano

B. Santa Rosa, Calif., 7 December 1930. Studied with Darius Milhaud, Mills College; courses at Paris Conservatory; lessons with Luigi Dallapiccola in Florence, Italy, 1958-59; Ph.D., University of Iowa, 1959. Guggenheim fellowship, 1969; two fellowships from the Ford Foundation, 1964 and 1971-73; American Academy of Arts and Letters Award, 1974; Fulbright, NEA, and Rockefeller grants. Faculty member, Lone Mountain College, San Francisco, 1959-67; resident composer at the National Center for Experiments in Television in San Francisco, 1967-71; resident composer for the city of Boston, 1971-73; now on the music faculty, University of California, Berkeley.

ABD, BB78, BB92, CACA, CC92, IWW92, KTL, NGA, OL, OL95, PC71, PCM, X65, X69, X70, X71, X74.

Fried, Alexander. "A Surprising Organ Recital." *American Music Digest* 1 (October 1969): 5.

> On 9 May 1969, organist Lawrence Moe performs the premiere of *Glossolalia* at Hertz Hall, University of California, Berkeley. The work is scored for percussion, voice, tape, and organ.

Haller, William. "Organ Works of the Avante-Garde [sic]." *Clavier* 13/4 (1974): 33-36.

> A discussion of influential American composers on avant-garde works; includes mention of Felciano's *God of the Expanding Universe*.

Little, Jeanie R. "Serial, Aleatoric, and Electrical Techniques in American Organ Music Published between 1960 and 1972." Ph.D., University of Iowa, 1975. *Dissertation Abstracts* 36 (June 1978): 7722A.

This scholarly, in-depth work analyzes in detail Felciano's works for organ and electronic tape, among other composers' works.

"Mixtures." *American Organist* 25 (March 1991): 49.

Felciano's 60th birthday was celebrated on 2 December 1990 in San Francisco, with a retrospective concert of his music that featured two unpublished works by the composer, performed by Fred Tulan.

"Premieres." *American Organist* 21 (April 1987): 57.

Concerto for Organ and Orchestra is premiered by organist Lawrence Moe with the University Symphony of the University of California, Berkeley, 21 November 1985; program notes are given for the one-movement work.

Rimmer, Frederick. "Adventurous Attitudes: Some Recent Organ Music." *Organists' Review* 60/241 (1976): 15-17.

Felciano's *Ekāgrata* is discussed as one of the new adventurous organ works by an American. Matthias Bamert's *Organism* and Anthony Newman's *Bhajebochstiannanas* are the other American works discussed and outlined. Some Scandinavian, Polish, and British composers are also included.

Wells, Frederick. "Far West AGO Convention." *American Organist* 50 (September 1967): 10-11.

Felciano gives a lecture on his new work *Glossolalia*, for electronic tape, organ, percussion, and a male voice.

Wyton, Alec. "An Interview with Richard Felciano." *Church Music* (London) 3/16 (1972): 13-15.

Information about *Glossolalia* is related; the use of electronic sound and other kinds of medium are discussed for use in worship. "Music tends to effect human beings on the most fundamental level."

_____. **"An Interview with Richard Felciano."** *Music* (AGO) 4 (November 1970): 44-47.

Felciano talks about his compositional style, the use of electronic sound, and music in worship; he comments on how "music tends to effect human beings on the most fundamental level." *Glossolalia*, for baritone, tape, percussion, and organ, is highlighted.

William Ferris

B. Chicago, Ill., 26 February 1937. Studied composition with Alexander Tcherepnin, De Paul University School of Music, 1955-60; private lessons with Leo Sowerby at the American Conservatory in Chicago, 1957-62; organ study with Arthur Becker; and choral conducting with Paul Stassevitch. Founded William Ferris Chorale, 1960, specializing in Renaissance and 20th-century music. Organist of Holy Name Cathedral, Chicago, 1954-58 and 1962-64, and director of music, Sacred Heart Cathedral, Rochester, N.Y., 1966-71; joined the faculty of American Conservatory of Music in Chicago, 1973.

ABD, BB78, BB92, CACA, IWW92, OL, OL95, X70, X71.

Kohlenberg, Lee. "New Organ Work in Chicago." *American Organist* 17 (March 1983): 62-63.

Commissioned by the Chicago Symphony Orchestra, a one-movement work, *Acclamations*, for organ and orchestra, is introduced at Orchestra Hall, 27-29 January 1983. The work is analyzed in depth. Ferris is organ soloist.

Kyle, Marguerite K. "AmerAllegro." *Pan Pipes* 70/2 (1978): 40.

Ferris receives commission to orchestrate Sowerby's *Organ Concerto* (op. post.).

71/2 (1979): 31-32.

Ferris is cited in the new edition of *Baker's Biographical Dictionary of Music and Musicians.*

McKenna, Edward J. "Major Catholic Composers: A Critical Evaluation." *American Organist* 18 (June 1984): 43.

Ferris is Sowerby's principal successor in Catholic and Episcopalian music.

Mamula, Stephen. "Selected American Composers: A Profile and Analysis." *American Record Guide* 45 (May 1982): 4-5.

Concerto Piece for Organ and String Orchestra (1963) is finally premiered by the Boston Symphony Orchestra; Ferris also writes compositions in large and dramatic forms; composes with eclectic harmonies; lists publishers of his works.

"William Ferris." *American Organist* 49 (October 1966): 29.

Ferris is appointed organist and choral director of the Cathedral of the Sacred Heart, Rochester, N.Y.; provides brief biograhy and notice that his work *Concert Piece for Organ and String Orchestra* will be premiered by organist Berj Zamkochian in the upcoming season, with the Boston Symphony Orchestra.

"William Ferris." *Diapason* 57 (October 1966): 15.

> Ferris is appointed organist and choir director, Cathedral of the Sacred Heart, Rochester, N.Y., effective September 1. Provides a summary of his personal and professional backgrounds.

"William Ferris." *Diapason* 61 (October 1970): 11.

> Ferris wins the Leo Sowerby Memorial Composition Contest sponsored by the Chicago AGO for his cantata *Out of Egypt*.

Paul Fetler

B. Philadelphia, Penn., 17 February 1920. Family moved to Europe soon after his birth and he had early music studies in Latvia, the Netherlands, Sweden, and Switzerland. Returned to U.S., 1939, and studied briefly at Chicago Conservatory of Music; also, composition study with David Van Vactor, Northwestern University, B.M., 1943. Served in World War II as liaison officer and Russian interpreter; became a student of Sergiu Celibidache. Back to the U.S., 1946; studied with Quincy Porter and Paul Hindemith at Yale University, M.M., 1948. In 1948, joined the music faculty at University of Minnesota, where he earned his Ph.D. in 1956, and became a permanent faculty member. Guggenheim grant awarded, 1953; returned to Berlin for study with Boris Blacher, 1960; three NEA grants: 1975, 1977, 1980. Recipient of a Ford Foundation grant and Alice M. Ditson Award.

ABD, AMH, BB92, CACA, CACJ, OL, OL95, PC71, PCM, TCH, X51, X58, X60, X62, X64, X65, X68, X70, X71.

Kyle, Marguerite K. "AmerAllegro." *Pan Pipes* 46 (January 1954): 38.

> Fetler receives a Guggenheim fellowship for 1953-54.

49 (January 1957): 46.

> Fetler receives his Ph.D. from the University of Minnesota, and remains there to teach theory and composition as assistant professor.

50 (January 1958): 52.

> Fetler is appointed assistant professor of theory and composition at the University of Minnesota, Minneapolis.

53/2 (1964): 52.

> Fetler receives his second Guggenheim award.

60/2 (1968): 69.

> Concordia publishes *Two Choral Preludes* by Fetler in *The Parish Organist*.

63/2 (1971): 56-57.

Announcement of publication of Fetler works: *How Wonderful Thou Art* and *Noel*, both for organ and both published by Augsburg.

67/2 (1975): 54.

Augsburg publishes *Toccata*, for organ.

69/2 (1977): 44.

Fetler receives an NEA grant and a Certificate of Merit from Yale's Alumni Association.

"University of Minnesota Professor Receives Certificate of Merit from Yale University." *School Musician* 47 (January 1976): 15.

For his contribution and service in the field of music, Fetler receives a certificate of merit from Yale University, where he received his B.A., 1947, and M.A., 1948.

Wetzler, Robert P. "Contemporary Composers." *Journal of Church Music* 12 (June 1970): 11.

Son of a Russian Protestant missionary, Fetler's personal and educational backgrounds are summarized.

Ross Lee Finney

B. Wells, Minn., 23 December 1906; d. Carmel, Calif., 5 February 1997. Studied at the University of Minnesota with Donald Ferguson; B.A., 1927, Carleton College; to Paris for study with Nadia Boulanger, 1928; returned to U.S., enrolled at Harvard and studied with Edward Burlingame Hill; instructive sessions with Roger Sessions. In 1929-49, on faculty of Smith College; concurrently taught at Mount Holyoke College, 1938-40. In 1931-32, to Vienna for lessons with Alban Berg; in 1937, studied with Gian Francesco Malipiero in Asolo. Taught composition at Hartt School of Music, Hartford, Conn., 1941-42; Amherst College, 1946-47. Won two Guggenheim fellowships, 1937 and 1947, and the Pulitzer traveling fellowship, 1937. Visiting lecturer at University of Michigan, Ann Arbor, 1948-49; composer-in-residence and professor and served as chair of composition department from 1949; emeritus in 1973; he established an electronic music laboratory there.

AA73, ABD, AMH, AS66, ASUC, BB58, BB65, BB71, BB78, BB92, BBCch, BBCpo, BDA, CA11, CACA, CACJ, CC92, CPM, DAS, DCM, DN72, EDM, HHH, IMD, IWW92, JCN, KTL, LMD, MGGs, MHHH, NG, NGA, OL, OL95, PC71, PCM, PET, REM, TCAC, WI62, WI69, X50, X51, X52, X53, X54, X55, X56, X57, X58, X59, X60, X61, X62, X64, X65, X66, X67, X68, X69, X70, X71, X74.

Borroff, Edith. *Three American Composers.* Lanham, Md.: University Press of America, 1986.

Finney, Irwin Fischer, and George Crumb are focused on in this book. Finney's biographical data is presented, his music in general, his songs, chamber music, piano, choral, and large instrumental works are discussed as is total serialism. At the onset, an overview of fifty years as a time of change is given in this scholarly tome.

Cooper, Paul. **"The Music of Ross Lee Finney."** *Musical Quarterly* 53/1 (1967): 1-21.

A detailed analysis of Finney's work, including his philosophy on the "Principle of Complimentarity"—that is, no work of art is understood or analyzed from a single perspective.

Gagne, Cole, and Tracy Caras. *Soundpieces: Interviews with American Composers.* Metuchen, N.J.: Scarecrow, 1982.

Finney is interviewed in this survey of current trends in American music. Biographical sketch, photograph, and list of works through 1980 are included.

Goossen, Frederic, ed. *Thinking About Music: The Collected Writings of Ross Lee Finney.* Tuscaloosa: University of Alabama Press, 1991.

Includes bibliography and reference sources.

Hitchcock, H. Wiley. **"Ann Arbor, Michigan."** *Musical Quarterly* 48/2 (1962): 244-48.

Finney's impact on his students, especially those who organized ONCE to promote new music, is imparted.

Hitchens, Susan Hayes. *Ross Lee Finney: A Bio-Bibliography.* Westport, Conn.: 1996.

The definitive source-book.

Kyle, Marguerite K. **"AmerAllegro."** *Pan Pipes* 48 (January 1956): 49.

Finney is awarded a Rockefeller Foundation grant for January through September 1956.

49 (January 1957): 47.

Finney is composer-in-residence at the University of Michigan; recipient of a Rockefeller Foundation grant and other awards.

51 (January 1959): 61.

Finney continues as composer-in-residence at the University of Michigan.

52/2 (1960): 48-49.

Finney serves as composer-in-residence at the American Academy in Rome, 1960.

55/2 (1963): 49.

Finney is inducted into the National Institute of Arts and Letters.

56/2 (1965): 55.

A Fulbright takes Finney to Paris, June-July; *Hymn, Fuguing and Holiday* is published by C. Fischer.

58/2 (1966): 60-61.

Finney is guest composer at University of Kansas Symposium of Contemporary American Music.

61/2 (1969): 51.

So Long as the Mind Keeps Silent is premiered by Robert Noehren at First Unitarian Church, San Francisco, and is recorded by Noehren on Lyrichord.

62/2 (1970): 59-60.

Five Fantasies for Organ published by C. F. Peters.

63/2 (1971): 57.

Same information as in the previous item.

64/2 (1972): 54.

Same information as in the previous item.

67/2 (1975): 54.

Finney receives a Rockefeller Foundation grant for residence at Villa Serbelloni in Bellagio, Italy.

Little, Jeanie R. **"Serial, Aleatoric, and Electrical Techniques in American Organ Music Published between 1960 and 1972."** Ph.D., University of Iowa, 1975. *Dissertation Abstracts* 36 (June 1978): 7722A.

This scholarly, in-depth work analyzes in detail Finney's *Five Fantasies*, among other composers' works.

Parks, Anne. **"The Five Fantasies for Organ of Ross Lee Finney."** *Diapason* 68 (December 1976): 4-5.

The first of a two-part article presents a background and a scholarly approach to reviewing Finney's *Five Fantasies* (1966-69).

————. **"The Five Fantasies for Organ of Ross Lee Finney."** *Diapason* 68 (April 1977): 1, 16-17.

The conclusion of a detailed analysis.

"Ross Lee Finney." *Pan Pipes* 43 (December 1950): 119. *

44 (January 1952): 29-30. *

45 (January 1953): 51. *

47 (January 1955): 43, 45.

Brief biographical information; composer-in-residence at the University of Michigan.

"Ross Lee Finney." *Composers of the Americas* 11 (1965): 22-32.

A brief biography in Spanish and English is followed by a listing of Finney's works to date, with notes regarding commissions, duration of the work, and premieres.

"Ross Lee Finney." *American Music Teacher* 25/2 (1975): 32.

A brief introduction to the composer and mention of his honors, awards, and prizes.

Irwin Fischer

B. Iowa City, Iowa, 5 July 1903; d. Wilmette, Ill., 7 May 1977. Graduated 1924, University of Chicago; studied organ with Middelschulte, piano with Louise Robyn, composition with Adolf Weidig at American Conservatory, Chicago, M.M., 1930; studied composition briefly with Boulanger in Paris, 1931, and Kodály in Budapest, 1936; conducting lessons with Paumgartner and Malko at Salzburg Mozarteum, 1937. In 1928, joined the faculty of American Conservatory, Chicago. Organist with the Chicago Symphony Orchestra, 1944-67. Authored *A Handbook of Modal Counterpoint*, with Stella Roberts (New York: Free Press, 1965; Macmillan, 1967).

AA73, ABD, AMH, BB92, CACA, CACJ, NG, NGA, OL, OL95, X55, X61, X62, X64, X65, X66, X67, X68, X69, X70, X71, X74.

Borroff, Edith. *Three American Composers.* Lanham, Md.: University Press of America, 1986.

A microscopic view of music in the last fifty years, centering on Fischer, Finney, and Crumb. Details about Fischer's music, songs, biblical songs, piano, organ, chamber orchestral, band and other works are given. Fischer's *Concerto: Chorale Fantasy*, for organ, is highlighted.

"Choral Fantaisie [sic] for Organ and Orchestra." *Musical Courier* 151 (15 January 1955): 30-31.

Irwin Fischer's *Choral Fantasy for Organ and Orchestra* received its world premiere Christmas week, 1954, by Mario Salvador, organist of St. Louis Cathedral, with the St. Louis Symphony. General description of the work is supplied.

Devries, René, and Dosha Dowdy. **"Chicago."** *Musical Courier* 159 (March 1959): 29.

Fischer, as organist of the Chicago Symphony Orchestra, performed in Honegger's *Christmas Cantata* and Respighi's *Roman Festivals*.

Kyle, Marguerite K. "AmerAllegro." *Pan Pipes* 51 (January 1959): 61.

Fischer is organist for the Chicago Symphony Orchestra and on the faculty at the American Conservatory of Music and Cosmopolitan School of Music.

52/2 (1960): 49.

Highgate Press publishes *Chorale Prelude on "Jesu, meine Freude."*

53/2 (1961): 53.

Fischer is composer-in-residence, American Academy in Rome, 1966.

67/2 (1975): 54.

Fischer is named Dean of the Faculty, American Conservatory of Music, Chicago.

[Obituary.] *Pan Pipes* 70/1 (1977): 27.

A notice of Fischer's death reveals that he studied with Kodály in Budapest; positions held are listed.

Beatrice Hatton Fisk

B. Henley-on-Thames, England, 20 September 1903; d. New London, Conn., 8 July 1977. Emigrated to the U.S., 1914. Student of Aurelio Giorni, Melchiorre Mauro-Cottone, T. Tertius Noble, Bruce Simonds, and Robert Baker. Author of *Keyboard Fundamentals*, a three-volume manual of piano instruction. Organist at First Church of Christ Congregational Church, New London, for fifteen years; organist-choir director, St. James Episcopal Church, New London, 1950-66; organist, First Church of Christ, Scientist, New London, 1968-71.

OL, OL95.

[Obituary.] *Music* (AGO) 11 (October 1977): 29.

The obituary provides biographical information and career summary.

Heinrich Fleischer

B. Eisenach, Germany, 1 April 1912. A direct descendant of Martin Luther, he studied at Weimar, and was Straube's colleague and student at the University of Leipzig, 1937-48, Ph.D. He taught at Valparaiso University and the University of Chicago, among other positions. While in Germany, he was organ professor at Leipzig State Academy of Music and organist at Leipzig University (St. Paul's University Church). Fled East Germany to escape arrest in 1949 and came to the United States.

OL, OL95.

Angel, Clark. "Recitals and Concerts." *American Organist* 44 (April 1961): 27-28.

A critical review of Fleischer's dedicatory recital of the new Schlicker organ at Grace Lutheran Church, Eau Claire, Wisc., 20 November 1960.

"Dr. Heinrich Fleischer." *Music News* 42 (October 1950): 15.

Fleischer, on the music faculty at Valparaiso University as professor of organ, is appointed to the faculty of Chicago Musical College. He will head the organ department and offer courses in advanced musicology.

"Fleischer Observes Tenth Anniversary in America." *Diapason* 50 (August 1959): 30.

August 10 is the tenth anniversary of Fleischer's emigration to the U.S., at the invitation of Valparaiso University (Ind.); served as professor of organ and church music at Valparaiso until 1957; currently university organist and lecturer in music at the University of Chicago.

"Heinrich Fleischer." *Music News* 42 (May 1950): 20.

A review of Fleischer's Palm Sunday recital at the Rockefeller Memorial Chapel of the University of Chicago. Program is listed. "Few organists have both Fleischer's technical equipment and great interpretative gifts."

"Heinrich Fleischer." *Diapason* 55 (April 1964): 20.

Summary of Fleischer's career; he will be guest artist at the National Convention of the Royal Canadian College of Organists, Winnipeg, August 24-27.

"Here and There." *Diapason* 83 (June 1992): 3.

Fleischer presented two lectures on the topic "The Training and Office of the Lutheran Church Musician, Past and Present" at Dr. Martin Luther College, New Ulm, Minn., on March 26.

"Marriott Resigns at University of Chicago; Fleischer, Lawson Named." *Diapason* 44 (August 1953): 4.

Fleischer to serve as chapel organist and James R. Lawson as carillonneur at the University of Chicago, succeeding Frederick Marriott.

"Recital by Dr. Fleischer in Chicago Church, January 7." *Diapason* 42 (January 1951): 8.

Announcement of Fleischer's recital program to be played at Salem Lutheran Church; summary of his background given.

"Recitals and Concerts." *American Organist* 40 (June 1957): 194.

> Fleischer performs at Harvard's Memorial Chapel, Cambridge, Mass., 12 March 1957. Reviewer Melville Smith was not impressed with his program. It "was not one of absorbing interest . . . none of the music was particularly rewarding. . . ." Bach, Buxtehude, Langlais, Messiaen, and Reger were the composers represented on the recital.

Schenk, Kathryn E. "Heinrich Fleischer: The Organist's Calling and the Straube Tradition." Ph.D., University of Minnesota, 1989. *Dissertation Abstracts* 51 (December 1990): 1824A.

> An examination of Fleischer's life and career in the context of social, political, religious, and artistic movements in Germany (1912-49) and in the United States (after 1949); she explores his philosophy of teaching and performing, especially as it relates to the philosophy of his mentor, Karl Straube.

Wells, Frederick. "Far-Western Regional AGO Convention." *American Organist* 46 (September 1963): 9.

> Fleischer is opening-night recitalist for the convention; highly favorable review is rendered.

Lukas Foss

(*Né* Fuchs.) B. Berlin, Germany, 15 August 1922. Piano and theory study with Julius Goldstein-Herford. Family moved to Paris when Nazis took power in Germany; studied piano there with Lazare Lévy, composition with Noël Gallon, orchestration with Felix Wolfes, and flute lessons with Louis Moÿse. Emigrated in 1937 to the U.S.; enrolled at Curtis Institute of Music, Philadelphia, for piano study with Isabelle Vengerova, composition with Rosario Scalero, and conducting with Fritz Reiner. Summers spent at Tanglewood, where he studied conducting with Koussevitzky at the Berkshire Music Center; advanced composition course with Hindemith at Yale, 1939-40. Naturalized U.S. citizen, 1942. Guggenheim fellowship, 1945 and 1960; Fulbright fellowship, 1950-52; taught composition at the University of California, Los Angeles, 1953-62, and there established the Improvisation Chamber Ensemble to perform music of "controlled improvisation." Appointed music director for Buffalo Philharmonic, 1963-70; music director of the American-French Festival at Lincoln Center, New York, 1964-65; principal conductor of the Brooklyn Philharmonia, 1971; director of Milwaukee Symphony Orchestra, 1981, and in 1986 resigned and was made conductor laureate; held Brooklyn post until 1990. Elected a member of the American Academy and Institute of Arts and Letters in 1983.

ABD, AMH, AS66, ASC, BB58, BB65, BB71, BB78, BB92, BBCch, BBCpo, BDA, CA7, CACA, CC92, CME, DCM, DDM, EDM, EVM, GD54, HHH, HLM, IMD, IMD2, IWW92, JCN, KTL, LMD, LMU, MEH, MGG, MHHH, NCE, NG, NGA, OL, OL95, PC71, PCM, REM, SML, TCAC, TCH, VER, WI62, WTM, X50, X51, X52, X53, X54, X55, X56, X57, X58, X60, X61, X62, X64, X65, X66, X67, X68, X69, X70, X71, X74.

Bassin, Joseph P. "An Overview of the Third Period Compositional Output of Lukas Foss, 1976-83." Ed.D., Columbia University Teachers College, 1987. *Dissertation Abstracts* 48 (January 1988): 1573A-74A.

Based upon interviews with the composer, Bassin discusses the compositional devices Foss used at this time in detail.

Christensen, Louis. "An Interview with Lukas Foss." *Numus-West* 2/2 (1975): 51-52.

A discussion about improvisation, theatrical elements in his music, and symbolism; a list of 55 works by Foss is included.

"Classified Chronological Catalog of Works by the U.S. Composer Lukas Foss." *Boletin interamerican de musica* 25 (September 1961): 40-44.

A catalog of Foss's works, chronologically listed.

Drone, Jeanette, comp. "American Composer Update." *Pan Pipes* 75/2 (1983): 27-28.

Foss is recently appointed music director of the Milwaukee Symphony Orchestra.

"Etudes for Organ." *Source* 2/2 (1968): 29-33.

Foss's biography, a recording and score of the *Etudes*, and a performing guide from the composer are included.

Foss, Lukas. "Contemporary Music: Observations from Those Who Create It." *Music & Artists* 5/3 (1972): 11-23.

Lukas Foss discusses various aspects of contemporary music regarding the orchestra, conductor, student, composer, notation, and even the audience.

Gagne, Cole, and Tracy Caras. *Soundpieces: Interviews with American Composers.* Metuchen, N.J.: Scarecrow, 1982.

Interview with Foss discusses the current trends in American music.

Gräter, M. "Lukas Foss—ein amerikanischer Musik." *Melos* 21 (December 1954): 340-41. *

Haller, William. "Organ Works of the Avante-Garde [sic]." *Clavier* 13/4 (1974): 33-36.

A discussion of influential American composers on avant-garde works; includes Foss as instrumental in new philosophies, one being the expanded traditional notation that allows the performer freedom to make choices; and cites his *Etudes for Organ*.

Hatten, Robert S. "An Evening with Lukas Foss." *Indiana Theory Review* 1/1 (1977): 44-47.

A discussion with Foss on the idea of improvisation as composing—is it good or bad; often the performer does not desire the freedom to improvise.

Houkom, Alf S. "Lukas Foss and Chance Music." *Music* (AGO) 2 (February 1968): 10.

Foss's *Etudes for Organ* is a work "utilizing only particular aspects of aleatoricism for each etude," which alleviates monotony in the work.

Kupferberg, H. "Lukas Foss." *Ovation*, April 1984. *

Kyle, Marguerite K. "AmerAllegro." *Pan Pipes* 46 (January 1954): 39.

Foss is associate professor at the University of California, Los Angeles.

50 (January 1958): 53.

Foss receives an honorary doctorate of music from Los Angeles Conservatory.

55/2 (1963): 50.

Elected to the Institute of Arts and Letters.

56/2 (1964): 56.

Becomes music director and conductor of the Buffalo Philharmonic.

66/2 (1974): 52.

Foss, previously professor of composition at Manhattan School of Music, is currently teaching at SUNY-Buffalo and is also director of the Center for Creative and Performing Arts.

"A List of the Music by Lukas Foss." *Boston Symphony Concert Bulletin* 18 (10 March 1950): 988 + . *

Little, Jeanie R. "Serial, Aleatoric, and Electrical Techniques in American Organ Music Published between 1960 and 1972." Ph.D., University of Iowa, 1975. *Dissertation Abstracts* 36 (June 1978): 7722A.

This scholarly, in-depth work analyzes in detail Foss's chance work for organ, among other composers' works.

"Lukas Foss." *Pan Pipes* 43 (December 1950): 119. *

44 (January 1952): 30. *

"Lukas Foss." *Variety* 21 (22 April 1959): 82. *

"Lukas Foss." *Composers of the Americas* 7 (1961): 17-23.

A brief biography in Spanish and English is followed by a catalog of his works to date, with annotations.

"Music Journal's 1972 Gallery of Living Composers." *Music Journal* 30 (Annual 1972): 42.

Brief biography; education, honors and awards, and major works listed.

Pace, R. **"Lukas Foss: Wild Thing."** *Ear* 13 (December/January 1988-89): 25. *

Perone, Karen L. *Lukas Foss: A Bio-Bibliography.* New York: Greenwood, 1991.

Biography, bibliography, works and performances, and discography are included.

"Personals." *American Organist* 52 (March 1969): 28.

Harold Chaney, organist, joined the Pro Arte Symphony Orchestra for the world premiere of *Waves* in Carnegie Hall, 20 January 1969.

"Premieres." *Music Journal* 26 (January 1968): 14.

Four Etudes for Organ with Two Assistants by Foss is premiered by Robert F. Triplett for an inaugural recital on the new organ in King Chapel at Cornell.

"11th in Our Series of American Composers." *Music Clubs Magazine* 38 (April 1959): 63.

A salute to Lukas Foss, with an announcement that the Music Clubs Federation has commissioned him to write an orchestral work, *Variations*. Included are biographical information and statements about some of his philosophies.

Isadore Freed

B. Brest-Litovsk, Russia, 26 March 1900; d. Rockville Centre, N.Y., 10 November 1960. Came to U.S. at an early age; graduated from University of Pennsylvania, B.M., 1918. On Curtis Institute of Music faculty, 1924-25. Studied with Josef Hofmann and Ernest Bloch; Louis Vierne and Vincent d'Indy in Paris; returned to U.S., 1934. Founder and conductor of the Philadelphia Chamber Orchestra, 1934-37; founder of the first American Composers' Laboratory, Philadelphia, 1934, enabling creative artists to hear their own works; taught at Temple University, 1937-46. Honorary doctor of music degree from New York College of Music, 1943; in 1944, appointed head of music department, Hartt College of Music, Hartford, Conn. Authored *Harmonizing the Jewish Modes* (New York: Sacred Music Press, 1958).

ABD, ASC, BB58, BB65, BB71, BB78, BB92, BBCh, BDA, CACA, CPM, DCM, EDM, EJM, EVM, HHH, KTL, MGGs, MHHH, MJM, NG, NGA, OL, OL95, REM, TCAC, WI62, WI69, X50, X51, X52, X54, X55, X56.

"AmerAllegro." *Pan Pipes* 43 (January 1950): 39. *

"Claire Coci Plays Freed's New Fantasy with Strings." *Diapason* 46 (April 1955): 1.

Antiphonal Fantasy is dedicated to performer Coci, who premiered the work with the Phoenix String Quartet at Town Hall, New York, 19 March 1955.

"Isadore Freed." *Pan Pipes* 43 (December 1950): 119-20. *

44 (January 1952): 30. *

45 (January 1953): 51. *

47 (January 1955): 46.

Antiphonal Fantasy for organ and strings will be heard this spring on Claire Coci's tour in America.

Kyle, Marguerite K. "AmerAllegro." *Pan Pipes* 48 (January 1956): 50.

Claire Coci and the Phoenix Quartet premiere *Antiphonal Fantasy*, 19 March 1955, Town Hall, New York.

49 (January 1957): 48.

Freed is chairman of the department of composition and theory at Hartt College; continues as chairman for the Institute of Contemporary American Music.

50 (January 1958): 54.

Gives information on previous positions held by Freed, premieres, publications, and recordings of his work.

51 (January 1959): 63.

Freed continues as chairman of composition and theory departments at Hartt College; professor of sacred music at Hebrew Union College, New York.

52/2 (1960): 50.

Psalm 150, commissioned by the Pittsburgh AGO, is premiered in February 1959.

[Obituary.] *Musical America* 80 (December 1960): 96.

Death notice; highlights of his life given.

[Obituary.] *Variety* 220 (23 November 1960): 71.

[Obituary.] *International Musician* 59 (January 1961): 39.

Death date given as November 11; summary of background.

[Obituary.] *Musical Courier* 163 (January 1961): 9.

> Death notice; highlights of his life provided.

"Six Liturgical Pieces." *Diapason* 44 (December 1952): 23.

> Published by Transcontinental Music, Freed's treatment of Jewish themes are considered "clever writing" but not difficult.

Soltes, Avraham. *Off the Willows: The Rebirth of Modern Jewish Music.* New York: Bloch, 1970.

> Documents the rebirth of Jewish music in the past two generations. Key figures included Freed, who helped to bring about this phenomenon.

Steinhauer, Erwin. *A Jewish Composer by Choice: Isadore Freed, His Life and Work.* New York: n.p., 1961. *

Harold Friedell

B. Jamaica, Long Island, N.Y., 11 May 1905; d. Hastings-on-Hudson, N.Y., 17 February 1958. Attended Juilliard and Union Theological Seminary. His teachers were David McK. Williams, Clement Gale, and Bernard Wagenaar. Organist-choirmaster of Calvary Episcopal Church, 1934-46; St. Bartholomew's Church, New York, 1946-58; on the faculties of Union Theological Seminary, Juilliard, and the Guilmant Organ School. Honorary doctor of music degree from Missouri Valley College, Marshall.

ABD, BB92, OL, OL95.

Berry, Ray. **"Harold W. Friedell, 1906-58."** *American Organist* 41 (March 1958): 103.

> Friedell's death, 17 February 1958, is announced. Lists his career positions.

"Heart Attack Fells Dr. Harold Friedell." *Diapason* 49 (March 1958): 1.

> Death comes to Friedell, 17 February 1956; summary of his life and career.

"Missouri College Gives Doctorate to Friedell." *Diapason* 48 (September 1957): 1.

> Honorary doctor of music degree is presented to Friedell from Missouri Valley College, 1 June 1957.

Herbert Fromm

B. Kitzingen, Germany, 23 February 1905. Private study with A. Reuss, Munich; conducted at the Civic Theater in Bielefeld, 1930, and at Würzburg, 1931-33. Came to the U.S. in 1937. Organist at Temple Beth Zion, Buffalo, 1937-41; music director, Temple Israel, Boston, 1941-73. Authored *Seven Pockets* (Ardmore, Penn.: Dorrance, 1977) and *On Jewish Music: A Composer's Views* (New York: Bloch, 1978).

AA73, ABD, AS66, BB78, BB92, BDA, CACA, EJM, IMD, KTL, OL, OL95, TCH, X57, X62, X64, X65, X66, X67, X68, X69, X70, X71, X74.

"American Composer Update." *Pan Pipes* 75/2 (1983): 28.

> *Ten Studies for Organ* is published by Transcontinental Music; *Organ Partita* to be recorded on Musique Internationale.

Kyle, Marguerite K. "AmerAllegro." *Pan Pipes* 49 (January 1957): 48-49.

> George Faxon performs the premiere of *Fantasy for Organ* at Riverside Church, New York.

51 (January 1959): 63.

Transcontinental publishes Fromm's *Suite of Six Pieces for Organ*.

52/2 (1960): 50.

Suite for Organ is premiered by Ludwig Altman.

55/2 (1963): 50-51.

George Faxon premieres *Mornings Will I Seek Thee*, organ solo, and *Music* and *Processional*, for two trumpets and organ, 4 February 1962 at Trinity Church, Boston; *Partita for Organ* is published by E. C. Schirmer.

56/2 (1964): 57.

Transcontinental publishes Fromm's *Silent Devotion* and *In Memoriam*, both for organ.

57/2 (1965): 58.

Fromm is recipient of an ASCAP award.

58/2 (1966): 62-63.

Fromm's *Prelude on High Holiday Motifs* is commissioned by Temple Emanu-El, New York, and premiered there by John Houston, 21 February 1965; ASCAP award.

59/2 (1967): 74.

Fromm's *Organ Sonata: Days of Awe* receives its premiere by Lois Jungas, St. Paul's Cathedral, Boston, 4 December 1966.

60/2 (1968): 72.

Partita for Organ is premiered 27 February 1967, at Trinity Church, Boston; and also *Organ Fantasy on "Kol Nidre"* by organist Ludwig Altman at Temple Emanu-El, San Francisco, 16 April 1967. Fromm receives an ASCAP award for 1967-68.

61/2 (1969): 54.

Transcontinental publishes Fromm's *Organ Sonata: Days of Awe*; Robert Noehren records *Partita for Organ on "Let All Mortal Flesh"* on Lyrichord; ASCAP award; Fromm named editor of a new hymnal for the Union of the American Hebrew Congregations.

62/2 (1970): 61.

ASCAP award, 1969-70; completes the manuscript of a new hymnal for the American Reform Synagogue.

70/2 (1978): 42.

Fromm's *Seven Pockets* is published by Dorrance in Philadelphia; New York City's Bloch published *On Jewish Music*; ASCAP award.

David Maulsby Gehrenbeck

B. St. Paul, Minn., 30 June 1931. Organist, First Presbyterian Church, White Bear Lake, Minn., 1947-51; organist, Merriam Park Presbyterian Church, St. Paul, 1951-53. B.A., Macalester College, St. Paul, Minn., 1953. Organist-choirmaster, Westminster Presbyterian Church, Albuquerque, N.M., 1954-55. M.S.M., 1957, and S.M.D., 1971, Union Theological School; studied with Searle Wright and Seth Bingham. Minister of music, First Presbyterian Church, Caldwell, N.J., 1957-61; assistant organist-choirmaster, Fifth Avenue Presbyterian Church, New York, 1961-62; instructor of sacred music, 1965-70, and assistant professor of organ and sacred music, 1970-71, Union Theological Seminary, New York; director of music, Broadway Presbyterian Church, New York, 1966-71; assistant professor, 1971-74, and associate professor of organ and sacred music, from 1974, Illinois Wesleyan University; since 1973, organist-choirmaster, First United Methodist Church, Normal, Ill. His dissertation is entitled "*Motetti de la Corona*: A Study of Ottaviano Petrucci's Four Last-Known Motet Prints (Forrombrone, 1514, 1519), with 44 Transcriptions" (Union Theological Seminary, January 1972).

ABD, CACA, OL, OL95.

Bingham, Seth. "Recitals and Concerts." *American Organist* 47 (January 1964): 11.

Gehrenbeck is highly praised for his two recitals of Bach works at James Memorial Chapel, Union Theological Seminary, New York.

Philip Gehring

B. Carlisle, Penn., 27 November 1925. A.B. and B.M. from Oberlin; M.M. and Ph.D., 1964, from Syracuse University. Organ student of Fenner Douglass, Arthur Poister, and André Marchal; composition student of Herbert Elwell and Ernst Bacon. Organist-choirmaster, Kimball Memorial Lutheran Church, Kannapolis, N.C., 1950-53; taught at Davidson College (N.C.), 1952-58; since 1958 on faculty at Valparaiso University. His dissertation is "Improvisation in Contemporary Organ Playing" (*Dissertation Abstracts* 25 [September 1964]: 1956-57). Second prize, AGO improvisation contest, 1966; winner in the AGO national improvisation contest, 1977. With Donald Ingram, he authored *The Church Organ: A Guide to Its Selection* (Valparaiso: Lutheran Society for Worship, Music & the Arts, 1973).

ABD, CACA, OL, OL95.

"Here and There." *Diapason* 83 (July 1992): 4.

> The Association of Lutheran Church Musicians released a new Parish Study Series that includes Gehring's series on *The Organ*.

"Philip Gehring." *Diapason* 62 (May 1971): 3.

> Gehring is invited to participate in the Haarlem International Organ Concourse, July 7-9, at St. Bavo Church, Haarlem, Holland; includes his recital itinerary in Europe.

"Recitals and Concerts." *American Organist* 41 (December 1958): 466-67.

> On 15 July 1958, Gehring performs a recital at the Summer Organ Festival, Crouse College Auditorium, Syracuse University. Traditional fare was played with the exception of Gardner Read's *Toccata* (from *Suite for Organ*). "An outstanding recital."

Hugo Gehrke

B. Mayville, Wisc., 1912; d. San Mateo, Calif., 15 February 1992. Graduated from Concordia College, River Forest, Ill., received M.Mus. from Northwestern University; honorary doctorate awarded from Concordia College, Seward, Neb., 1975. Professor of music, Concordia College, Oakland, Calif.; emeritus professor, Concordia College, Milwaukee, Wisc. Organ music and biography listed in Arnold's book.

OL, OL95.

[Obituary.] *Diapason* 83 (April 1992): 6.

> Obituary provides biographical information, including positions held and his schooling. Also lists organs he designed.

[Obituary.] *American Organist* 26 (June 1992): 46-47.

> Includes the same information listed above.

Wells, Frederick. "Far West AGO Convention." *American Organist* 50 (September 1967): 10-11.

> Gehrke's two performances of German chorales by German and American composers are given high marks.

Vittorio Giannini

B. Philadelphia, Penn., 19 October 1903; d. New York, 28 November 1966. Sent to Italy at age 10 to study at the Conservatory of Milan, 1913-17; returning to U.S., studied with Martini and Trucco in New York; Juilliard graduate school studies with Rubin Goldmark in composition and Hans Letz in violin, 1925; won American Prix de Rome, 1932. Appointed to faculty of Juilliard School of Music, 1939, to teach composition and orchestration; in 1941, he instructed music theory also; appointed professor of composition at Curtis Institute of Music, Philadelphia, 1956; also taught at Juilliard, 1939-66, and the Manhattan School of Music, 1941-66. President of North Carolina School of the Arts, Winston-Salem, from 1965 until the time of his death. Recipient of numerous honorary doctorate degrees.

ABD, AS66, ASC, BB65, BB71, BB78, BBCch, BDA, CACA, CPM, DCM, EDM, EVM, GD54, HHH, IMD, KTL, LMD, MGG, MGGs, MLA23/4, NG, NGA, OL, OL95, REM, TCAC, X51, X52, X53, X54, X55, X56, X57, X58, X60, X61, X62, X64, X65, X66, X67, X68, X69, X70, X71.

Bechtel, Donald. "A Bibliography of the Works of Vittorio Giannini." M.A., Music, Kent State University, 1972.

> Arranges works by genre, indicates publishers, source of citation, duration of performance, and date of publication. Brief biography.

Mark, Michael L. "The Life and Works of Vittorio Giannini (1903-66)." Ph.D., Catholic University of America, 1970. *Dissertation Abstracts* 31 (1970): 1311A. *

[Obituary]. *Variety* 245 (30 November 1966): 64, 245.

Obituary cites Giannini's passing; he was president of North Carolina School of the Arts.

[Obituary.] *Clavier* 6/1 (1967): 52.

Death notice for Vittorio Giannini, composer of piano and organ concertos; lists highlights of his life.

[Obituary.] *Music Educators Journal* 53 (February 1967): 16.

Notice of Giannini's death; indicates he served on the Committee for the Contemporary Music Project for Creativity in Music Education of the MENC.

[Obituary.] *Musical Times* 108 (January 1967): 64.

Parris, Robert. "Vittorio Giannini and the Romantic Tradition." *Juilliard Review* 4 (September 1957): 32-46.

A detailed, scholarly review of Giannini's compositional method and style: cadences, embellishments, and harmonic, melodic, and rhythmic construction; lists prizes, awards, and his works.

Schauensee, Max de. "The Gianninis, Portrait of a Prodigious Philadelphia Family." *Opera News* 28 (11 April 1964): 14-16.

A history of Vittorio Giannini's family that led him to music composition.

Thomas Gieschen

B. Wauwatosa, Wisc., 11 July 1931. B.S.E., with Paul Bunjes, Concordia College, River Forest, Ill., 1952. Graduate study at the University of Michigan, with Robert Noehren, 1953-54. M.M., 1958, and D.M.A., 1968, with Barrett Spach, Northwestern University. Teacher and minister of music, Gethsamane Lutheran Church, Detroit, 1952-55. Teacher, minister of music, Emmaus Lutheran Church, Milwaukee, 1955-57. Since 1957, professor of music, Concordia College, River Forest, Ill. Organ music and biography listed in Arnold's book.

OL, OL95.

No bibliographical information located.

Milton Gill

B. 1932; d. 25 October 1968, in a plane crash at the Lebanon, N.H. airport. Graduate of Princeton University, 1959, student of Roger Sessions and Carl Weinrich. Assistant professor of music and college organist at Dartmouth from 1959; named chairman of the music department, 1965; studied in Hamburg, Germany, with Heinz Wunderlich, on a Dartmouth faculty fellowship, 1964-65.

ABD, ASUC, OL, OL95, PCM, X64, X65, X68.

"Milton Gill." *Diapason* 55 (October 1964): 33.

Gill is awarded a Dartmouth faculty fellowship for 1964-65, to compose, study organ, and travel in Europe. Biographical data included.

"Milton Gill." *Diapason* 57 (December 1965): 41.

Gill named chairman of the music department at Dartmouth College, September 1965.

[Obituary.] *Diapason* 60 (December 1968): 16.

Notice of Gill's death in an airplane crash, 25 October 1968, at the Lebanon, N.H., airport.

Noel Goemanne

B. Poperinge, Belgium, 10 December 1926. Graduate of the Lemmens Institute, 1948; graduate work at Conservatoire Royal in Liège. Organ study with Flor Peeters, Staf Nees, Jules Van Nuffel, and Marius De Jong; other studies with Pierre Frodese and Charles Hens. Became a U.S. citizen, 1959. Joined faculty of Tarrant County Junior College, Ft. Worth, 1976; organist-choir director, Christ the King Catholic Church, Dallas, since 1977. Honorary doctorate of music degree from St. Joseph's College (Ind.). Authored *The Piano: A Necessary Foundation for the Study of the Organ* (n.p.: author, 1968); *Liturgical Music in the Philippines* (n.p.: author, 1971); and *The Bernstein Mass—Another Point of View* (New York: Sacred Music Press, 1973). Recipient of the papal medal and *Pro ecclesia* award.

ABD, CACA, OL, OL95, X74.

"Honored." *Music* (AGO) 11 (June 1977): 37.

Goemanne receives the *Pro ecclesia et pontifice* medal from Pope Paul for his exemplary service to the church.

"Introducing a Person of Note." *Pastoral Music* 8/1 (1983): 37. *

"Members in Profile." *Sacred Music* 103/1 (1976): 43.

A summary of Goemanne's background.

"News." *Sacred Music* 105/3 (1978): 27.

Goemanne's *Partita on an American Shaker Melody, "Lord of the Dance"* is premiered by Clay Christiansen at St. Mark's Cathedral, Salt Lake City, Utah, 15 October 1978.

"News." *Sacred Music* 110/1 (1983): 27. *

Includes information about Goemanne's *Ave maris stella.*

"News." *Sacred Music* 106/1 (1979): 33.

Clay Christiansen performs the premiere of Goemanne's *Partita on an American Shaker Melody*, 15 October 1978, Salt Lake City, at St. Mark's Cathedral.

"News and Honors." *ASCAP* 6/2 (1974): 36.

Goemanne's *This Is the Day*, commissioned by the AGO, was premiered at Fort Worth's First Presbyterian Church, 14 May 1974.

"Noel Goemanne." *Diapason* 46 (August 1955): 29.

Goemanne is appointed organist-choirmaster of St. Rita's Catholic Church, Detroit.

"Noel Goemanne." *Diapason* 59 (October 1968): 22.

Goemanne is appointed director of music, St. Monica's Catholic Church, and Holy Trinity Seminary, Dallas.

"Noel Goemanne, Belgian Organist, at Texas Church." *Diapason* 44 (March 1953): 16.

Goemanne appointed organist-choirmaster at St. Mary's and Our Lady of Lourdes Church, Victoria, Texas.

"Noel Goemanne Premiere." *Diapason* 64 (May 1973): 19.

Goemanne premieres his *Fanfare for Festivals*, 10 June 1973.

"Noel Goemanne's Works Premiered by Clay Christiansen." *Ceol* 18/1 (1979): 52. *

Includes information about the premiere of *Partita on a Shaker Melody.*

"Organ Piece Premiered." *Clavier* 20/4 (1981): 47.

> Goemanne's *Trilogy* is premiered by the man who commissioned it, Gerald Johnson, at First Presbyterian Church, Monticello, Ark., in December; the work will be published by Shawnee Press.

"Pipings." *American Organist* 27 (April 1993): 51.

> Goemanne's *Trilogy for Dallas*, commissioned by the Dallas Symphony Association for the new Fisk organ of the Symphony Center in Dallas, will be published by CPP/Belwin and released in 1993.

"Premieres." *American Organist* 28 (April 1994): 49.

> *Trilogy for Dallas* will be premiered by organist Paul Riedo, organist for the Dallas Symphony Orchestra, in recitals 14-17 April 1994. The 15-minute composition was written for the new Fisk organ, known as the Lay Family Organ, at the Meyerson Symphony Center.

"Premieres." *American Organist* 29 (February 1995): 52.

> Two works are premiered on 24 December 1994, at the Church of Christ the King, Dallas. *Three Fantasies for Christmas* for organ solo and *Variations on the "Lord of the Dance"* for trumpet and organ were performed by organist-composer Noel Goemanne and trumpeter Richard Ginagiulio.

"Stepping Out." *ASCAP*, spring 1981, 40.

> *Trilogy*, by Goemanne, receives its premiere on 14 December 1980, at the University of Arkansas, Monticello.

Van Remoorte, Julien. *Noel Goemanne: Componist-Orgelist.* Flanders: n.p., 1968. *

Jack C. Goode

B. Marlin, Texas, 20 January 1921. B.M., Baylor University, 1942; further study at Tulsa University, 1946; M.M., American Conservatory of Music, 1947; additional study in the summer of 1957 at Berlin Hochschule. Taught as professor of music, Northwestern University, 1949-50; Wheaton College, 1950-68; American Conservatory of Music, since 1968. Authored *Pipe Organ Registration* (New York: Abingdon, 1964).

ABD, CACA, LCI, OL, OL95, PC71, X65, X66, X67, X69, X74.

Kyle, Marguerite K. "AmerAllegro." *Pan Pipes* 52/2 (1960): 51.

> *Fancy for the Trumpet Stop* is premiered by Frederick Swann, July 28, at Riverside Church, New York; it is accepted for publication by H. W. Gray.

55/2 (1963): 51.

Improvisations on Hymn Tunes for Organ is published by Hope; *Processional* and *Magnificat* are published by Abingdon.

57/2 (1965): 59.

Goode's book on pipe organ registration is published, 1964.

58/2 (1966): 64.

Pipe Organ Registration and *Homage à Couperin* are published by Abingdon, and *Preludes on Hymn Tunes* is published by Hope; Goode goes to Paris for coaching with Marie-Claire Alain, and to Hamburg for study with Heinz Wunderlich.

59/2 (1967): 76.

The premiere of Goode's *Homage à Couperin* is given by the composer at Wheaton College, 23 March 1966.

Joseph Goodman

B. New York, 28 November 1918. B.A., Johns Hopkins University, 1938; studied with Paul Hindemith at Yale, 1945; M.A., Harvard University, 1948, with Walter Piston; Fulbright award to study in Venice with Gian Francesco Malipiero, 1950-51. Professor of music, Queens College, CUNY, 1952-53, and 1955; instructor in music, Brooklyn College, CUNY, 1953-55; head of the composition department, Union Theological Seminary School of Sacred Music, 1959-73.

ABD, CACA, CACJ, DN77, IWW92, OL, OL95, PC71, PCM, X50, X51, X56, X65, X68, X74.

"Here and There." *Diapason* 73 (February 1982): 11.

Premiere of Goodman's *Trio for Organ, Flute, and Cello* is performed in Stillwater by Oklahoma State University faculty members Gerald Frank, Gwen Powell, and Evan Tonsing.

"Honors for Members." *ASCAP* 2/3 (1968): 36.

Fantasy for organ was premiered by James Tallis at the National AGO Convention in Boulder, Colo., 4 July 1968.

Jones, Bruce. "Florida Conclave." *Music* (AGO) 8 (February 1974): 32-35, 53.

Goodman's *Concerto for Organ and Orchestra* is premiered by Gerre Hancock, organist; a brief description of the three-movement work is provided. Written in 1964, it finally receives its premiere a decade later.

"Steppin' Out: Premiered." *ASCAP*, spring 1982, 50.

> Announcement that the premiere of Goodman's *Trio for Organ, Flute, and Cello* occurred in Stillwater, Okla.

Dianne Goolkasian-Rahbee

B. Somerville, Mass., 9 February 1938. Studied with her mother, Antoine Louise Moeldner, a pupil of Paderewski; also at Juilliard with Joseph Bloch, Alton Jones, Hugo Weisgall, Vittorio Giannini, Robert Starer, and Arnold Fish; privately with David Saperton, piano with Lily Dumont, Russell Sherman, Veronica Jochum Von Moltke, and composition with John Heiss; and at the Mozarteum in Salzburg with Enrico Mainardi.
WWAM-Cl.

No bibliographical information located.

Jacob Frederic Goossen

B. St. Cloud, Minn., 30 July 1927. B.A., 1949, M.A., 1950, and Ph.D., 1954, University of Minnesota, Minneapolis; further study at the Longy School of Music, Cambridge, Mass. Teachers include Donald Ferguson, James Aliferis, William Lindsay, Arthur Shepherd, and Melville Smith. Goossen was on the music faculties of the University of Minnesota, 1953-54; Berea College, 1955-58; and the University of Alabama, since 1958, teaching composition, and is now director of graduate studies.
ABD, CACA, OL, OL95, WWAM-Cl, X68.

"Composer Profile: Frederic Goossen." *National Association of College Wind and Percussion Instructors* 37/4 (1989): 42-43.

> A profile of Goossen's educational history; indicates that his compositional style centers around motivic construction; lists publishers, record labels, and selected works.

Kyle, Marguerite K. "AmerAllegro." *Pan Pipes* 55/2 (1963): 51.

> Goossen completed *Toccata for Organ* with a grant from the University of Alabama.

56/2 (1964): 58.

Toccata for Organ will be premiered 20 March 1964, by Warren Hutton, University of Alabama, Tuscaloosa.

61/2 (1969): 55.

Announcement that American Composer Alliance publishes Goossen's works.

Richard T. Gore

B. Takoma Park, Md., 25 June 1908; d. Wooster, Ohio, 15 December 1994. Received B.A., 1933, and M.A., 1938, from Columbia University; additional study in Berlin at the University and at the Hochschule für Musik; Ph.D. in theory from Eastman School of Music, 1956. Studied composition with Seth Bingham. Served as organist for Cornell University. Taught at Mt. Holyoke College, 1938-39; Cornell University, 1939-45; and College of Wooster (Ohio), 1945-74.

ABD, CACA, OL, OL95.

Boeringer, James. *The Works of Richard T. Gore.* Springfield, Ohio: Chantry Music, 1974. *

"Dr. Richard T. Gore." *Diapason* 55 (April 1964): 3.

Gore observes his fortieth year as organist with a recital, 11 February 1964, at Wooster's Memorial Chapel.

[Obituary.] *Diapason* 86 (March 1995): 4.

Highlights of Gore's education and career are provided in the obituary.

[Obituary.] *American Organist* 29 (March 1995): 54.

Detailed obituary presents information about Gore's career, education, and compositions.

"Richard T. Gore." *Diapason* 40 (January 1949): 3.

Gore presents a recital, 28 November 1948, at First Presbyterian Church, East Liverpool, Ohio, performing his work on *Lasst uns erfreuen.*

"Richard T. Gore." *Diapason* 46 (September 1955): 32.

Gore completes ten years as head of the music department at the College of Wooster; he has completed his Ph.D. requirements at Eastman.

Jack S. Gottlieb

B. New Rochelle, N.Y., 12 October 1930. Studied with Karol Rathaus, Queens College (CUNY), B.A., 1953, and with Irving Fine, Brandeis University, M.F.A., 1955; Berkshire Music Center, Tanglewood with Blacher and Copland; University of Illinois with Burrill Phillips and Robert Palmer, D.M.A., 1964. From 1958-66, assistant to Leonard Bernstein at the New York Philharmonic; music director, Congregation Temple Israel, St. Louis, 1970-73; appointed composer-in-residence, School of Sacred Music, Hebrew Union College, New York, 1973-77. Recipient of a National Endowment for the Arts grant, 1976. In 1977-79 editorial associate with a music publisher; in 1979 he began his own publishing company. Compiled *Leonard Bernstein: A Complete Catalog of His Works* (New York: Amberson Enterprises, 1978). His dissertation is entitled "The Music of Leonard Bernstein: A Study of Melodic Manipulation" (*Dissertation Abstracts* 36 [1964]: 12-7355).

AA73, ABD, AS66, BB65, BB71, BB78, BB92, CA9, CACA, DCM, DN72, IWW92, LMD, NGA, OL, OL95, PC71, PCM, X57, X61, X62, X64, X65, X66, X67, X68, X70, X71, X74.

"American Composer Update." *Pan Pipes* 73/2 (1981): 30.
> Gottlieb is listed in the 1980 edition of *Who's Who in American Jewry*.

Drone, Jeanette, comp. "American Composer Update." *Pan Pipes* 75/2 (1983): 29.
> Lists references that cite his biography.

"Jack Gottlieb." *Composers of the Americas* 9 (1963): 74-78.
> A brief biography in Spanish and English is followed by an annotated catalog of his works.

Kyle, Marguerite K. "AmerAllegro." *Pan Pipes* 51 (January 1959): 64.
> Ford Foundation Grant recipient; completes D.M.A. from the University of Illinois; and is assistant to Leonard Bernstein.

63/2 (1971): 60.
> Gottlieb is appointed music director at Temple Israel, St. Louis; also director of the Religious School music program; and is a founding member of the St. Louis Circle of Jewish Music.

66/3 (1974): 53.
> Gottlieb resigns from Temple Israel; he is named director of special events and composer-in-residence, School of Sacred Music, Hebrew Union College, New York.

68/2 (1976): 52-53.
> Premiere of Gottlieb's *Organ Postlude on "Shofeit Kol Ha-Aretz"* is given by Sylvia Plyler; MacDowell Colony resident.

70/2 (1978): 43.

Gottlieb leaves Hebrew Union College and joins the firm of Amberson Enterprises to handle Leonard Bernstein's business activities; ASCAP award.

71/2 (1979): 33.

Gottlieb establishes his own publishing company, Theophilus Music.

Lemmon, Alfred E. "Jack Gottlieb at 50." *American Organist* 15 (June 1981): 37.

A tribute to Gottlieb's career as composer; a performance of his works honors him.

"Young Composers Contest Award." *Music Clubs Magazine* 37 (September 1957): 40.

Wins a first prize in the 1957 Young Composers Contest and also the Devora Nadworney Scholarship. Music education is provided along with previous awards and *oeuvres*.

Elizabeth Davies Gould (Hochman)

B. Toledo, Ohio, 8 March 1904. Her second marriage is to Hochman, but she continues to use surname Gould. Studied at the University of Toledo, Oberlin, 1922-24, and the University of Michigan, B.A., and M.A. in 1926, with Artur Schnabel and Guy Maier. In 1965, she won first prize from Delta Omicron. Named one of ten leading women composers by the National Council of Women of the United States, 1963; received Arthur Shepherd award, 1969; winner of six first prizes and two special citations in Mu Phi Epsilon contests. Teaches privately.

ABD, AS66, CACA, CR, ICW, PC71, PCM, WCH, X53, X54.

"Elizabeth Gould Honored at Oberlin." *Triangle* 74/2 (1980): 13.

A recital of Gould's music with the presentation of a Steinway concert grand piano to the Oberlin Conservatory of Music in her name honors Gould; biographical information provided.

"Elizabeth Gould Hochman Honored with 80th Birthday Concert." *Triangle* 78/3 (1984): 18. *

Karen Jean Griebling-Long

B. Akron, Ohio, 31 December 1957. B.M., Eastman School of Music, with Francis Tursi, Samuel Adler, Warren Benson, and Joseph Schwantner, 1980; M.M., University of

Houston, with Lawrence Wheeler, Milton Katims, Michael Horvit, Donald Granth, and Donald Wright, 1982; D.M.A., University of Texas at Austin, 1986. Violist, Houston Ballet Orchestra, 1980-82; Texas Chamber Orchestra, 1980-82. Won the Seven Year Composition Contest award from the National Federation of Music Clubs, 1976; ASCAP, 1982.

BB92, WWAM-Cl.

No bibliographical information located.

Lester H. Groom

B. Chicago, Ill., 19 January 1929. Studied at Wheaton College with his father, Lester W. Groom, and Malcolm Bensen, B.M., 1951; Northwestern University, studied with Barrett Spach, M.M., 1952; American Conservatory of Music, composition with Stella Roberts, 1953-54. Taught briefly at Moody Bible Institute; on faculty at Blue Mountain College (Miss.), 1957-62; Baker University (Baldwin City, Kans.), 1962-67; and since 1968, Seattle Pacific University and organist-choirmaster, Church of the Epiphany, Seattle, Wash. Professor emeritus from 1991, Seattle Pacific University.

IWW92, OL, OL95.

"The Late Lester W. Groom, Whose Son Succeeds Him." *Diapason* 41 (September 1950): 8.

Diapason made a prediction twenty-one years ago that Lester H. Groom would be a leader of another generation, coming from such a musical family; now Groom, upon his father's death, succeeds him at First Congregational Church, Chicago.

"Lester Groom." *American Organist* 55 (August 1969): 20.

Groom's appointment as assistant professor of music at Seattle Pacific College, Seattle, Wash., is announced; gives recent positions held.

"Lester H. Groom." *Diapason* 54 (February 1963): 40.

Groom is appointed to Baker University (Baldwin City, Kans.) faculty and becomes organist at First United Methodist Church there.

"Lester H. Groom." *Diapason* 59 (January 1968): 17.

Groom is appointed organist-choirmaster of the Church of the Epiphany, Seattle, Wash.

Raymond H. Haan

B. Falmouth, Mich., 26 April 1938. Studied at Calvin College, A.B., 1959; University of Michigan, M.A., 1972. Director of music, Cutlerville East Christian Reformed Church, Grand Rapids, Mich., since 1960. ASCAP award.

OL, OL95, WWAM-Cl.

"Premieres." *American Organist* 26 (October 1992): 52.

> Haan's *Variations on St. Thomas* for organ, commissioned to honor the 150th anniversary of First Congregational Church, Wauwatosa, Wisc., is premiered.

Edmund Thomas Haines

B. Ottumwa, Iowa, 15 December 1914; d. Bronx, N.Y., 3 July 1974. Studied at the University of Missouri, Kansas City; Eastman School of Music, with Howard Hanson and Bernard Rogers, Ph.D., 1941; studied also with Aaron Copland and Roy Harris. Pulitzer award, 1941; Ford Foundation grant, 1958; recipient of two Guggenheim grants and two Fulbright grants. Taught at the University of Michigan, 1941-47; Sarah Lawrence College, 1948-74.

ABD, AMH, AS66, CACA, MHHH, OL, OL95, PCM, TCAC, WI62, X59, X66, X67, X68, X69, X70.

[Obituary.] *Variety* 275 (17 July 1974): 110.

> Obituary notice; Pulitzer award winner; taught on the Sarah Lawrence College faculty; previous positions were at the University of Missouri-Kansas City, Eastman, and the University of Michigan.

"Promenade Air and Toccata." *American Organist* 32 (February 1949): 42.

> Haines's *Promenade Air and Toccata* is winner of the AGO publisher's prize and will be published by J. Fischer; the work is described as "distinctly cubistic music."

"Promenade Air and Toccata." *American Organist* 32 (March 1949): 78.

> Reviewer highly dislikes this work by Haines, and thought the judges could do a better job of selecting a winning composition from the numerous efforts submitted.

Paul Robert Hamill

B. 1930. B.M. in organ, Boston University; M.A. from Wesleyan University, Middletown, Conn., 1956; organ study with Frederick Johnson, George Faxon, and Samuel Walter; composition with Richard Winslow and Gerald Jaffe. In 1957, appointed to the music faculty of Woodmere Academy, Woodmere, Long Island, N.Y. Compiled *Church Music Handbook, 1982-83* (New York: Pilgrim, 1982).

ABD, OL, OL95.

"Paul Hamill Receives New Long Island Faculty Post." *Diapason* 48 (July 1957): 7.

> Hamill is appointed to the music faculty of Woodmere Academy, Woodmere, Long Island, N.Y.

George Calvin Hampton

B. Kittanning, Penn., 31 December 1938; d. Port Charlotte, Fla., 5 August 1984. Organ studies with Joseph Wood and Richard Hoffman at Oberlin College Conservatory of Music, B.M., 1960; studied at Syracuse University with Arthur Poister, M.M., 1962. Taught at Salem College, Winston-Salem, N.C., 1960-61; Choate School, 1969-70. Organist, St. Peter's Church, Cazenovia, N.Y., 1961-62; organist-choirmaster at New York's Calvary Episcopal Church (it later merged with Holy Communion and St. George's), from 1963 until his death in 1984.

ABD, BB92, CACA, MLA41/4, OL, OL95, X62, X67, X68, X70, X71.

"Alla Breve." *American Organist* 26 (November 1992): 43.

> *Five Dances for Organ* and *Three Pieces for Organ* are published by E. C. Schirmer and include explanatory notes by Wayne Leupold.

Belt, Byron. "AGO/80—Twin Cities Convention: Stimulating, Inspiring, Exhausting." *American Organist* 14 (August 1980): 26.

> Hampton's *Concerto in E Major for Organ and Strings* is a brief concerto, "with a big and brash first movement, songful second movement—similar to 'grade B' movie music, and a third movement of 'pure camp.'"

Bingham, Seth. "Recitals and Concerts." *American Organist* 45 (December 1962): 23-24.

> Hampton plays a recital of Franck and Bach at St. Thomas Church, New York, 4 November 1962; the review was favorable.

Brashier, Joe H. "Calvin Hampton's Variations on *Amazing Grace* for English Horn and Organ Transcribed for Wind Ensemble with English Horn Solo." D.M.A., University of Kansas, 1987. *Dissertation Abstracts* 49 (January 1989): 1614A.

Includes biographical information about Hampton, performance suggestions, bibliography, and the scores of the original and the transcribed version of *Amazing Grace*.

"Calvin Hampton." *Diapason* 54 (October 1963): 18.

Hampton is appointed organist-choirmaster of Calvary Episcopal Church, New York. Supplies educational history.

"Calvin Hampton Features Own Works in May." *Diapason* 62 (August 1971): 10.

Transformation of Despair, for organ and percussion, was commissioned by New Dimensions in Music; the work is very complex rhythmically and requires three percussionists to perform it; *God Plays Hide and Seek* is for a taped Moog synthesizer part and "live" organ. The works were performed throughout May at Hampton's church, Calvary Episcopal, New York.

"Calvin Hampton Goes to New York Post." *American Organist* 54 (August 1963): 22.

Announcement of Hampton assuming the post of organist-choirmaster at Calvary Episcopal Church, New York, 1 September 1963; gives educational history.

"Calvin Hampton, 1938-84." *Journal of Church Music* 27 (January 1985): 17.

A tribute to Hampton's life by Alec Wyton; how Hampton changed the musical life in Greenwich Village.

Hampton, Calvin, et al. "Approaches to Writing Hymn Tunes." *Hymn* 35/2 (1984): 86-93.

Hampton addresses the problems of composing hymn tunes and organ accompaniments, to be both succinct and significant.

Heindl, Christian. "Internationales Festival Orgelkunst 1989." *Österreichische Musik Zeitschrift* 44 (October/November 1989): 553.

Hampton's piece *Toccata for Organ* is a requirement for the international organ competition.

"Here and There." *Diapason* 74 (January 1983): 4.

Five Dances is premiered by David Higgs, 7 November 1982, at Park Avenue Christian Church, New York.

"Here and There." *Diapason* 76 (January 1985): 5.

Alexander Variations, Hampton's last major work for organ, receives its world premiere at Trinity Episcopal Church, Wall Street, New York, 11 December 1984. Written for two organs, Harry Huff and David Higgs perform the work.

King, Larry. "Calvin Hampton: A Twenty Year Ministry." *American Organist* 17 (October 1983): 28.

Tribute is paid to Hampton's service by a recital, choral vespers, and reflections on how Hampton built up the Greenwich community for receiving organ music.

Kratzenstein, Marilou, and Bruce Gustafson. "The Minneapolis/St. Paul AGO National Convention." *Diapason* 71 (August 1980): 4.

David Craighead performs Hampton's *Concerto in E Major* at the House of Hope Presbyterian Church, St. Paul; the new work was well received.

Nalle, Billy. "Calvin Hampton." *American Organist* 50 (March 1967): 11-12.

Lee Erwin and Hampton perform their combined effort entitled *Dialogue of the Organs*, at Calvary Church, New York, 5 February 1967.

[Obituary.] *American Organist* 8 (September 1984): 5.

Summary of Hampton's life.

[Obituary.] *Billboard* 96 (18 August 1984): 53.

Cites Hampton's death and provides career details.

[Obituary.] *Diapason* 75 (October 1984): 4.

Notice of Hampton's death and memorial service.

Owen, Barbara. "Calvin Hampton." *American Organist* 53 (June 1970): 10-11.

Hampton performs at Old South Church, Boston, Mass., 3 May 1970. The reviewer scolds Hampton for his verbal program notes, then admires him for his musical skill, for his transcription of Mussorgsky's *Pictures at an Exhibition*.

"Premieres." *American Organist* 19 (February 1985): 50-51.

Commissioned by San Francisco's Grace Cathedral, *Alexander Variations* are introduced 11 December 1984 at Trinity Church, New York.

"Premieres." *American Organist* 24 (July 1990): 54.

On 25 March 1990 at Jehovah Lutheran Church, St. Paul, Minn., Mark Seerup, English horn, and Allan Mahnke, organ, premiere *Variations on Amazing Grace*.

Westenburg, Richard, and Seth Bingham. "The Music of Olivier Messiaen." *American Organist* 49 (March 1966): 6, 8.

Hampton performs the music of Messiaen in two recitals in New York at Calvary Episcopal Church, 30 January and 6 February 1966; both recitals received high praise from the reviewers: "In a word, the performance was superb."

Eugene W. W. Hancock

B. St. Louis, Mo., 17 February 1929; d. New York City, 21 January 1994. B.M., University of Detroit, 1951; M.M., University of Michigan, 1956; S.M.D., Union Theological Seminary School of Sacred Music, 1967. Organ studies with William I. Green, Alle Zuideman, Robert Cato, Marilyn Mason, and Vernon De Tar. Assistant organist-choirmaster, Cathedral of St. John the Divine, 1963-66; organist-choirmaster, St. Philip Episcopal Church, New York, 1974-82; director of music, West End Presbyterian Church, New York, 1982-90. Music instructor at the Borough of Manhattan Community College, from 1970 until his death. ASCAP awards, Advancement for Musical Culture Award from the National Association of Negro Musicians. Organ music listed in Arnold's book.

ABD, CACA, IWW92, OL, OL95.

[Obituary.] *American Organist* 28 (November 1994): 52.

Obituary includes Hancock's education and career highlights.

Southern, Eileen. "Conversation with Clarence E. Whiteman: Organ-Music Collector." *Black Perspective in Music* 6/2 (fall 1978): 168-87.

Hancock's organ music is included in this collection of 14 black composers.

Gerre Hancock

B. Lubbock, Texas, 21 February 1934. B.M., University of Texas, 1955; organ study with E. William Doty. Rotary Foundation Fellowship for International Study, with Jean Langlais, Nadia Boulanger, and Marie-Claire Alain, at the Sorbonne, 1955-56. Student of Hugh Porter at Union Theological Seminary. Assistant organist, St. Bartholomew's Church, New York, 1960-62; organist-choirmaster, Christ Church, Cincinnati, 1962-71; organist-choirmaster, St. Thomas Church, New York, from 1971. Lecturer in organ and improvisation, Cincinnati Conservatory of Music, 1965-71; Juilliard School of Music, since 1971; Yale University, since 1974.

ABD, CACA, IWW92, OL, OL95, X74.

"Gerre Hancock." *American Organist* 43 (November 1960): 31.

Hancock is appointed assistant organist-choirmaster of St. Bartholomew's Church, New York; he will also assist Jack Ossewaarde and be director of music for the church school.

"Gerre Hancock." *Diapason* 51 (October 1960): 11.

Same information as in the item above.

"Gerre Hancock." *Diapason* 53 (July 1962): 28.

Hancock will begin duties October 1 as organist-choirmaster at Christ Church, Cincinnati.

"Gerre Hancock." *American Organist* 47 (April 1964): 28.

Hancock, organist-choirmaster of Christ Church, Cincinnati, is invited to represent the AGO at the Centenary Celebration of the Royal College of Organists in London, 28-31 July 1964, and will perform a recital there.

"Gerre Hancock." *Diapason* 62 (March 1971): 3.

St. Thomas Church, New York, hires Hancock as organist-choirmaster, effective September 1. Provides educational data.

"Here and There." *Diapason* 69 (October 1978): 9.

Trumpet Flourishes for Christmas is premiered by Fred Swann, 1 August 1978. The work was commissioned for the newly-installed organ stop Trompeta Majestatis.

"Here and There." *Diapason* 78 (August 1987): 3.

A Fancy for Two to Play was both commissioned and introduced by Elizabeth and Raymond Chenault. The premiere was performed 29 May 1987 in Grace Episcopal Cathedral, Charleston, S.C.

"Here and There." *Diapason* 85 (September 1994): 4.

Hancock will be awarded an honorary fellowship of the Royal College of Organists in London in October.

Humphreys, Henry S., and Eleanor Bell. "Cincinnati, Ohio." *Music & Artists* 1/2 (1968): 64.

A snapshot look at quotes from reviews of Hancock's recital performed on 29 March 1968.

"Organ & Church Music Notes." *Musical Opinion* 87 (September 1964): 737. *

"People at the Convention." *Musart* 18/2 (1966): 35.

A summary of Hancock's career.

Tufts, William O. "Recitals and Concerts." *American Organist* 48 (May 1965): 7.

On 8 March 1965, at the First Baptist Church of Clarendon, Arlington, Va., Hancock performs his *Air for Organ*. The reviewer writes, "A fine recital by a real organist."

Wells, Frederick. "Some Past Season Bay Area Concerts Feature Contemporary Music." *American Organist* 49 (October 1966): 12.

> Hancock performs a recital that includes contemporary music on the San Francisco AGO chapter's series.

"Workshop and Conference Reports." *American Organist* 21 (October 1987): 93.

> Hancock performs the premiere of his *Prelude on "Slane,"* 7 June 1987, at the Yale Institute of Sacred Music, New Haven. The work is inscribed to Robert Baker.

Ellen Harrison

B. Streator, Ill., 1956. Compositional studies with Thomas Frederickson and Paul Zonn, University of Illinois, Champaign-Urbana; continued work at the State Conservatory of Music and Theater in Stuttgart, Germany, with Milko Kelemen, Erhard Karkoschka, and Helmut Lachenmann. Completed her degree in Stuttgart, and moved to California to work on her Ph.D. in composition at the University of California, Berkeley. Student of Edwin Dugger, Richard Felciano, Andrew Imbrie, and Olly Wilson. Recipient of the D.A.A.D. grant, Jacob K. Javits fellowship, and Nicola De Lorenzo Prize in music composition. Winner of the 1991-92 Holtkamp-AGO Award for Organ Composition, for her work *that line which is earth's shadow.*

No biographical information located apart from the article below.

"Composer Ellen Harrison Wins Holtkamp-AGO Award." *American Organist* 25 (December 1991): 8.

> Harrison's educational background is provided; includes a description of the winning piece, *that line which is earth's shadow.* Karel Paukert will perform the work during the AGO National Convention in Atlanta, 28 June-2 July 1992.

Robert Christian Hebble

B. Orange, N.J., 14 February 1934. Assistant to Virgil Fox, 1950-63. B.M., with Quincy Porter, Yale University, 1955; studied with Nadia Boulanger, Paris, 1955-56; M.S., with Vittorio Giannini and Roger Sessions, Juilliard School of Music, 1966. Department chairman, Red Bank Catholic High School (N.J.), 1957-76; on the music faculty, Stevens

Institute of Technology, from 1968; organist in different churches in New Jersey and New York, from 1955.

ABD, CACA, OL, OL95.

"Premiere Performances." *Musical Courier* 156 (July 1957): 6.

Hebble's *Pastel* was premiered on Easter Sunday, 1957, at Riverside Church, New York, by organist Ted Alan Worth. The work is briefly described.

"Premieres." *American Organist* 20 (August 1986): 34.

Hebble performs the premiere of his *Symphony of Light* on 15 July 1986, Riverside Church, New York. Commission information included; it is a four-movement work, composed in Virgil Fox's memory; each movement has the word "light" taken from a biblical quotation. Hinshaw published the work.

David H. Hegarty

B. Mt. Clemens, Mich., 1 March 1945. B.A., Loma Linda University, 1968; M.M., Andrews University (Mich.), 1970; organ study with Warren Becker. Further study at Cincinnati Conservatory of Music with Wayne Fisher, 1972-73. Organist, Seventh Day Adventist Church, Kettering, Ohio, 1971-76; educational staff, Lorenz Publications, 1974-76; staff organist, Castro Theatre, San Francisco, since 1977. Also works as a free-lance composer and teacher.

OL, OL95.

"Here and There." *Diapason* 79 (April 1988): 3.

Kenrick S. Mervine presents three world premieres at Trinity Cathedral, Trenton, N.J., on February 7, including Hegarty's *Improvisation on Marian Themes*. The work is in the style of a French Romantic organ symphony.

"Premieres." *American Organist* 22 (June 1988): 44.

Same information as in the item above.

Adel Verna Heinrich

B. Cleveland, Ohio, 20 July 1926. B.A., *magna cum laude*, Flora Stone Mather College, 1951; M.S.M., Union Theological Seminary, 1954; and D.M.A., University of Wisconsin,

1976. Studied organ with Hugh Porter, John Harvey, E. Power Biggs, André Marchal, and Jean Langlais; conducting with Robert Shaw and Robert Fountain; composition with Harold Friedell and analysis with Julius Herford. Church organist in 1954-64; guest organist in New York under Margaret Hillis, and recitalist. Received the Clemens award in music and won two scholarships. In 1969 she received an award of merit from the National Federation of Music Clubs; Maximum Humanities travel grant to study and perform on historical organs in Europe, 1978-79; Mellon grant, 1978-79, to develop a course on Shakespeare and music; humanities grant in 1979-80 for further research on Shakespeare and music. Faculty member, Colby College (Maine), 1964-91. Authored *Bach's Die Kunst der Fuge: A Living Compendium of Fugal Procedures* (Lanham, Md.: University Press of America, 1983).

ABD, CACA, IWC, IWW92, WCH.

"Adel Heinrich at First Presbyterian, Auburn, N.Y." *Diapason* 46 (February 1955): 5.

Heinrich is appointed minister of music at First Presbyterian Church, Auburn, N.Y. Summary of her background provided.

"Adel Heinrich." *Diapason* 47 (November 1956): 16.

Heinrich moves to Holyoke, Mass., and is appointed organist-choir director of Second Congregational Church.

"Adel Heinrich." *Diapason* 52 (May 1961): 29.

Heinrich takes a leave of absence from Holyoke's Second Congregational Church to study for her doctorate.

"Retirements." *American Organist* 25 (July 1991): 36.

Heinrich retired from Colby College, Waterville, Maine, as professor emeritus of music. In addition to teaching classes, and organ and harpsichord students, she was organist and choirmaster of Lorimer Chapel.

Wilbur Held

B. Des Plaines, Ill., 20 August 1914. Attended the American Conservatory of Music, Chicago, where he received B.M. and M.M. degrees. Studied organ with Marcel Dupré and André Marchal; received his S.M.D., 1956, from Union Theological Seminary, New York; studied composition with Normand Lockwood and Wallingford Riegger. Professor,

1946-77, and head of organ and church music, Ohio State University, from 1965. Organist, Trinity Episcopal Church, Columbus, Ohio, since 1949. Dissertation is titled "Pentecost: A Cantata."

ABD, OL, OL95.

Bingham, Seth. "**Recital.**" *American Organist* 43 (August 1960): 14-15.

> Held performs a recital of the AGO's examination pieces at Detroit's Central Methodist Church as part of the AGO convention; the review is fairly favorable; the drawbacks of the instrument, however, are discussed rather than Held's playing.

"**Wilbur C. Held.**" *American Organist* 48 (April 1965): 27.

> Held wins the hymn-writing contest sponsored by the Festival of Church Music, Trinity Presbyterian Church, Atlanta, Ga.

Victor Hildner

B. 1917. Professor of music, Concordia Teachers College, River Forest, Ill. Organ music and biography listed in Arnold's book.

OL, OL95.

No bibliographical information located.

Jackson Hill

B. Birmingham, Ala., 23 May 1941. A.B., 1963, M.A., 1966, and Ph.D., 1970, University of North Carolina; studied with Iain Hamilton and Roger Hannay. Taught at Duke University, 1965-68; on the faculty of Bucknell University as assistant and associate professor, 1968-80, head of the music department, 1980-90, and associate dean of faculty, since 1990. Hays-Fulbright fellow to Japan, 1977; visiting fellow, Clare Hall, Cambridge, England, 1982-83. ASCAP awards and numerous composition prizes. Authored "The Music of Kees van Baaren: A Study of Transition in the Music of the Netherlands in the Second Third of the Twentieth Century," *Dissertation Abstracts* 31 (Feburary 1971): 4201A; and *The Harold E. Cook Collection of Musical Instruments: An Illustrated Catalogue* (Lewisburg, Penn.: Bucknell University Press, 1975).

ABD, ASUC, CACA, CACJ, IWW92, NGA, OL, OL95, X71, X74.

"American Composer Update." *Pan Pipes* 73/2 (1981): 30-31.

>Hill serves as acting head of the department of music at Bucknell University; also lectures on Buddhist music at the Society for Ethnomusicology.

Drone, Jeanette, comp. "American Composer Update." *Pan Pipes* 75/2 (1983): 29-30.

>Hill is named head of the music department at Bucknell; visiting fellow at Clare Hall, Cambridge University, England; ASCAP award.

"Here and There." *Diapason* 69 (April 1978): 19.

>Both choral and organ composition competitions sponsored by the New York City AGO are won by Hill. The organ work *Three Mysteries* is to be published by Hinshaw; its premiere was performed at the Church of St. Paul the Apostle, New York, February 27.

"Honors and Competition Winners." *Diapason* 70 (May 1979): 6.

>Hill is named winner of the $5,000 McCollin Prize, awarded by the Musical Fund Society of Philadelphia, for his *Fanfare and Alleluia*, for organ and brass quartet.

Kyle, Marguerite K. "AmerAllegro." *Pan Pipes* 66/2 (1974): 55.

>*Ave Maria* is first performed at Christ Church, Riverdale, New York, by organist Louise Basbas; *Fanfare* is premiered 8 June 1973 at Central Pennsylvania's Episcopal Diocesan Convention; on May 6 organist Charles Glandorf introduces the *Fugue on "Wie schön leuchtet der Morgenstern."*

>67/2 (1975): 58.

>Hill premieres his *Dark Litany for Organ and Tape*, 8 November 1973, at the University of North Carolina's Guest Composer Series; *Jam Christus astra* is premiered at Bucknell University by the composer.

>69/2 (1977): 51.

>Hill is cited as a regular reviewer of contemporary music for *Notes*.

>71/2 (1979): 34.

>Hill receives an ASCAP award, and is a dual winner in the New York City's AGO choral and organ composition competition.

Richard Hillert

B. Granton, Wisc., 14 March 1923. B.S.E., Concordia College (River Forest, Ill.), 1941; M.M., 1955, and Doctor of Music degree, 1968, Northwestern University. Student of Anthony Donato and Robert Delaney; music composition with Goffredo Petrassi,

Berkshire Music Festival. Won first prize, International Society of Contemporary Music, Chicago chapter, 1961. Helped prepare *Worship Supplement* (1969) and *Lutheran Book of Worship* (1978) for the Lutheran Church-Missouri Synod. Editor, with Hubert Gotsch, of the 42-volume series entitled *The Concordia Hymn Prelude Series* (St. Louis: Concordia, 1986). Taught in St. Louis, 1951-53; Wausau, Wisc., 1953-59; since 1959 on faculty at Concordia Teachers College, River Forest, Ill.; and in 1966-71 he was an instructor at Northwestern University.

ABD, CACA, DN72, DN77, OL, OL95.

"Richard Hillert." *Hymn* 34/4 (1983): 200.

A biographical sketch of Hillert.

Schalk, Carl. "Composers for the Church: Richard Hillert." *Church Music* (St. Louis) 1 (1972): 20-33.

An in-depth review of Hillert's works for the church: choral, organ, chamber, congregational, and liturgical. A selective listing of his music is included as well as biographical data.

Everett Jay Hilty

B. New York, 2 April 1910. M.B., with Hunter Johnson, University of Michigan, 1934; M.M., with Mark Wessel, University of Colorado, 1939; and with Seth Bingham and Normand Lockwood at Union Theological Seminary, while he was a visiting lecturer, 1956-57. Professor, University of Colorado, 1940-78; now emeritus. Authored *Principals of Organ Playing* (Boulder: Pruett, 1971).

ABD, CACA, OL, OL95.

"Everett Jay Hilty." *American Organist* 48 (January 1965): 23.

Hilty is honored by an anonymous gift of $25,000, presented to the organ-church music division of the University of Colorado College of Music. The gift will be used to "provide additional opportunities for cultural development to students, faculty, and townspeople."

"Everett Jay Hilty." *Diapason* 56 (March 1965): 3.

Same information as in the item above.

"Pedal Study on 'Ein' feste Burg.'" *Diapason* 42 (July 1951): 23.

Ein' feste Burg is published by H. W. Gray; "a stunt piece for pedals alone, in the virtuoso class."

Charles Kelso Hoag

B. Chicago, Ill., 14 November 1931. B.M., 1954, and Ph.D., 1962, University of Iowa; M.A., 1955, University of Redlands (Calif.). Associate professor of music, University of Oklahoma, 1963-68; professor of music theory and composition, University of Kansas, since 1968. Conductor of the Lawrence Symphony Orchestra, 1978-93. Received the Charles Wakefield Cadman Scholarship in composition, 1955; Aspen Award, 1966; University of Kansas Composers Forum prize, 1971; standard awards from ASCAP; National Endowment for the Arts grant, 1983; Composer Consortium grant, 1983; National Endowment for the Humanities grant. *Dark Tango* for organ and trombone was premiered in 1992; *Adoro Fantasy*, for organ, flute, trumpet, and oboe, was written and premiered in 1992. Authored *The New Scale Book: Foundation Studies in 20th-century Music for Double Bass* (Bryn Mawr, Penn.: Theodore Presser, 1991).

CACJ, OL95, WWAM-Cl.

"Composer Profile: Charles Hoag." *National Association of College Wind and Percussion Instructors* 38/3 (1990): 42-43.

> Selected list of compositions by Hoag, featuring wind and percussion instruments; provides his roster of positions held, grants received, and indicates residencies he has held at the Millay Colony for the Arts, Austerlitz, N.Y., and at the MacDowell Colony.

"Here and There." *Diapason* 84 (July 1993): 5.

> *Adoro Fancy*, for organ, flute, oboe, and trumpet, received its premiere on 12 September 1992, by the Deknatel Consort at Bethel College, North Newton, Kans.

Kyle, Marguerite K. "AmerAllegro." *Pan Pipes* 61/2 (1969): 58.

> Hoag is appointed to the University of Kansas music faculty, Lawrence.

"News and Honors." *ASCAP* 5/3 (1972): 31.

> Hoag wins 1971 Kansas Music Teachers Association composition contest.

"Premieres." *American Organist* 27 (July 1993): 46.

> Hoag's new work for organ, flute, oboe, and trumpet, entitled *Adoro Fancy*, received its premiere performance at Bethel College, North Newton, Kans., 12 September 1992, by the Deknatel Consort. The work was commissioned for the consort, which is in residence at Bethel College.

Alan Hovhaness

(*Né* Alan S. Chakmakjian.) B. Somerville, Mass., 7 March 1911. Private piano lessons with Adelaide Proctor and Heinrich Gebhard, Boston; academic studies at Tufts University, 1932; New England Conservatory, Boston, student of Frederick Converse; scholarship student of Martinů at Berkshire Music Center, Tanglewood. Faculty member of New England Conservatory of Music, 1948-51; awarded two Guggenheim fellowships, 1954 and 1958; Fulbright fellowship, 1959; composer-in-residence, University of Hawaii, 1962; traveled to Korea and later settled in Seattle.

ABD, AMH, BB65, BB71, BB78, BB92, BBCch, BBCpo, BDA, BMI, CA11, CACA, CC92, CCM, CPM, DCM, DN72, DN73, DN74, DN76, EDM, EMS, EVM, GD54, HHH, IMD, IWW92, JCN, KTL, LMD, MGG, MHHH, NG, NGA, OCM, OL, OL95, PC71, PCM, PET, REM, TCAC, TCH, WTM, X51, X52, X53, X54, X55, X56, X57, X58, X59, X60, X61, X62, X65, X66, X67, X68, X69, X70, X71, X74.

"Alan Hovhaness." *Composers of the Americas* 11 (1965): 47-68.
> A brief biography in Spanish and English; listing of works to date, with duration, notes, and publishers provided.

"Alan Hovhaness." *Pan Pipes* 45 (January 1953): 55. *

47 (January 1955): 50.
A second Guggenheim fellowship is received by Hovhaness.

Bozeman, George. "The OHS National Convention, Chicago." *Diapason* 75 (December 1984): 17.
> The premiere of *Organ Sonata No. 2, "Invisible Sun,"* was given at the convention; the work is briefly discussed. Commissioning information provided.

"The Composer Speaks." *Music Clubs Magazine* 39 (November 1959): 10.
> Hovhaness encourages the building of a musical culture that is creative, by encouraging not only composers and performers but also the listener.

Chou Wen-Chung. "Asian Concepts and 20th-Century Western Composers." *Music Quarterly* 57/2 (1971): 220-21.
> Hovhaness stands at the forefront of using Asian concepts in American music; he is highly influenced by Eastern and Southern Asian music: the use of figurative reiteration, sustained sonorities, and fluctuations in dynamics and pitch, bending the tones, and "slides."

"Composers in Focus." *BMI: The Many Worlds of Music,* winter 1976, 22-23.
> The article zeroes in on Hovhaness's life-story.

Daniel, Oliver. "Alan Hovhaness." *American Composers Alliance Bulletin* 2/3 (1952): 3-4.

Contemporaries of Hovhaness, i.e., Virgil Thomson, Olin Downes, Henry Cowell, and Peggy Glanville-Hicks, comment on his music and his influence on current and future composers.

————. **"Alan Hovhaness."** *BMI: The Many Worlds of Music*, May 1971, 18.

A summary of his background.

Holtz, John. "Southern New England Regional AGO Convention." *American Organist* 46 (September 1963): 39.

Sonata for 2 Oboes and Organ was premiered by organist Leonard Raver at the Southern New England Regional AGO Convention, Hartford, Conn. Commission information given; reviewer is disappointed in the work.

Kyle, Marguerite K. "AmerAllegro." *Pan Pipes* 46 (January 1954): 46.

Hovhaness receives a Guggenheim fellowship, 1953-54.

49 (January 1957): 53.

The past summer at Eastman School of Music provided Hovhaness an opportunity to teach composition.

50 (January 1958): 58.

Alleluia & Fugue, Triptych, Prelude & Quadruple Fugue, among others by Hovhaness, are published.

51 (January 1959): 68.

An honorary Doctor of Music degree is accorded Hovhaness by the University of Rochester.

54/2 (1962): 55.

Hovhaness is appointed the "East-West Center Visiting Scholar" and composer-in-residence, University of Hawaii, Honolulu, from February through June 1962.

56/2 (1964): 62.

Sonata for Two Oboes and Organ is premiered 23 June 1963, for the AGO in Hartford, Conn.; *Dawn Hymn* for organ and *Sonata for Trumpet and Organ* are published by C. F. Peters.

60/2 (1968): 76-77.

Hovhaness receives a Rockefeller grant to serve as composer-in-residence with the Seattle (Wash.) Symphony.

63/2 (1971): 63.

Hovhaness's *Hymn to Yerevan* and *I Will Lift Up Mine Eyes Sanahin* are published by Peters.

"Premieres." *American Organist* 18 (September 1984): 33.

> Hovhaness was commissioned to write his first major organ work, *Sonata for Organ*, for the 29th anniversary of the Organ Historical Society National Convention in Chicago. Douglas Reed performed the premiere.

Rangel-Ribeiro, Victor. "Another Passage to India." *New York Times* 108 (21 June 1959): Section 2, 9.

> Hovhaness and Howard Boatwright will travel to India to study its ancient system of classical music; discusses the difficulty of notating India's complex music.

Rosner, Arnold. "An Analytical Survey of the Music of Alan Hovhaness." Ph.D., State University of New York, Buffalo, 1972. *Dissertation Abstracts* 33 (August 1972): 779A.

> Works are divided into four style periods. A discussion regarding the roles of religion and mysticism with reference to the various periods is provided.

Sabin, Robert. "American in India." *Musical America* 80 (August 1960): 28-29.

> In August 1959, Hovhaness left the U.S. on a Fulbright Research Grant for study in India. His study there influenced his succeeding compositions, by using ragas and tonal systems hundreds of years old.

Wade, James. "Alan Hovhaness: Pilgrimage to the Orient." *Musical America* 83 (September 1963): 56.

> Hovhaness's trip to the Orient has a major impact on his compositional procedures, which are examined here.

Will, Ned E., Jr. "Alan Hovhaness; West Meets East." *Music Journal* 21 (April 1963): 30-31, 62, 74-75.

> Juxtaposing East and West in composing results in music that "sounds modern in a natural and uninhibited fashion." New ways to use archaic materials, such as modal sequences and poly-modality, are examined.

Richard Albert Hudson

B. Alma, Mich., 19 March 1924. B.M., Oberlin Conservatory, 1949; M.M., Syracuse University, 1951; Ph.D., University of California, Los Angeles, 1967. Fulbright grant to the Netherlands, 1952-53. Faculty member at Converse College, 1949-50; Oberlin Conservatory, 1953-55; and UCLA, from 1967. Authored *Passacaglio and Ciaccona: From*

Guitar Music to Italian Keyboard Variations in the 17th Century (Ann Arbor: UMI Research Press, 1981), and *The Allemande, the Balletto, and the Tanz*, vol. 1: *The History*; vol. 2: *The Music* (Cambridge: Cambridge University Press, 1986).

ABD, CACA, OL, OL95.

"Richard Hudson at New Studio Organ." *Diapason* 49 (February 1958): 32.

> Hudson purchases a new organ by Hunter Mead and Raymond Durant. After two years on staff at Oberlin, he opens his own studio in 1957. Provides biographical information.

David Hurd, Jr.

B. New York, 1950. Graduated from Oberlin Conservatory; studied at the University of North Carolina. Organist, Trinity Parish, Chapel of the Intercession. In 1985, became director of music, All Saints Church, New York City. Taught at Duke University, Yale Institute of Sacred Music, Manhattan School of Music; professor of church music/organist, General Theological Seminary, New York. Honorary doctorates from Church Divinity School of the Pacific, Seabury-Western Theological Seminary, Berkeley Divinity School, Yale University. Hope Publishing Co. Visiting Professor of Church Music, Westminster Choir College, 1993.

OL95.

"Here and There." *Diapason* 81 (September 1990): 3.

> Hurd premiered his *Three Fugues*, 7 June 1990, at St. Paul's Chapel, Trinity Parish, New York. The recital was played in honor of Clifford Dodds Maxwell for his many years of service to the noonday concert series here.

"Premieres." *American Organist* 25 (October 1991): 55.

> Hurd's *Toccata*, commissioned by Gerald Morton, music director of St. Philip's Church, New York, who premiered the work 16 July 1991 at Riverside Church in Manhattan.

"Westminster Choir College Visiting Professor of Church Music." *Hymn* 44/2 (1993): 4. *

Karel Husa

B. Prague, Czechoslovakia, 7 August 1921. Studied composition with Jarolsav Řidký at Prague Conservatory, 1941; Academy of Music, 1945-46; French government grant to study composition in Paris with Nadia Boulanger and Arthur Honegger, 1946, and conducting with Jean Fournet and André Cluytens. Emigrated to the United States in 1954; became a U.S. citizen in 1959. Joined Cornell University faculty in composition and conducting: assistant professor, 1954-56; associate professor, 1957-60; professor, 1961-72; Kappa Alpha professor of music, from 1973; now professor emeritus. Also on Ithaca College faculty, 1967-86. Received a Guggenheim fellowship, 1964, and the Pulitzer Prize in 1969, for his 3rd String Quartet. Elected to Royal Belgian Academy of Arts and Sciences, 1974; honorary doctorate of music degree, Ithaca College, 1986. Editor of music by Lully, Rameau, Herschel, and Lalande.

ABD, AMH, BB78, BB92, CA18, CACA, CACJ, DCM, DN73, DN74, DN76, DN77, DN78, JLN, KTL, MGGs, NG, OL95, X53, X54, X60, X61, X62, X69, X70, X71, X74.

"Awards and Appointments." *American Record Guide* 56/5 (1993): 36.

Husa is awarded the 1993 University of Louisville Award.

Brin, D. M. "Profile." *Strings* 7/6 (1993): 15.

An introduction to Husa.

Duff, John Andrew. "Three Works of Karel Husa: An Analytical Study of Form, Style, and Content." Ph.D., Michigan State University, 1982. *Dissertation Abstracts* 43 (June 1983): 3748A.

Includes biographical information about Husa and examines in detail three of his most popular compositions; information provided on his compositional style and musical philosophy.

"Here and There." *Diapason* 84 (October 1993): 3.

Husa is named winner of the Grawemeyer Award, presented by the University of Louisville. His *Concerto for Organ and Orchestra* was performed by Karel Paukert, 28 October 1987, at the Cleveland Institute of Music. Husa transcribed one movement of the *Concerto* for organ solo, "Frammenti."

Hitchens, Susan H. *Karel Husa: A Bio-Bibliography.* Westport, Conn.: Greenwood, 1991.

Includes biography, bibliography, discography, works and performances, and listing of works.

John Huston

B. Greenville, Texas, 13 August 1915; d. New York, 6 April 1975. B.M., University of Texas, 1947; M.S.M., School of Sacred Music, Union Theological Seminary, 1949. Organ student of Nita Akin, Hugh McAmis, E. William Doty, and Clarence Dickinson; composition with

Kent Kennan and Harold Friedell. Performed in England, 1957, at the International Congress of Organists, as one of four Americans invited to participate. Taught on the Union Theological Seminary School of Music faculty until it closed in 1973.

OL, OL95.

Bingham, Seth. "Organ Personalities." *American Organist* 46 (November 1963): 14.

> Huston's positions at New York's First Presbyterian Church and Temple Emanu-El, and as music faculty member at Union Theological Seminary are cited, and his performance at St. John's College for the London Organists Congress in 1957 is praised.

Grobe, Dalos W. "Huston in Minneapolis." *Diapason* 49 (April 1958): 6.

> A review of Huston's 25 February 1958 recital at St. Mark's Cathedral, Minneapolis. The programming was appreciated by the reviewer, and Huston's playing is praised.

"John Huston." *American Organist* 44 (November 1961): 35.

> Huston is appointed organist of Temple Emanu-El, New York. Lists additional posts and prior positions, and a brief biographical sketch.

"John Huston." *Diapason* 52 (November 1961): 4.

> Huston is appointed organist of Temple Emanu-El, New York.

"John Huston, Who Assumes New York Post." *Diapason* 48 (February 1957): 6.

> Huston is appointed organist-choir director at First Presbyterian Church, New York. Includes biography.

Kelsey, Howard. "John Huston Plays in St. Louis." *Diapason* 47 (March 1956): 15.

> A review of Huston's first recital in St. Louis, performed at Christ Church Cathedral on November 28; program included.

"Know Your Guild." *Diapason* 58 (March 1967): 10.

> Huston will serve as the chairman of the Board of Judges for the AGO anthology contest. Lists previous positions; background information included.

[Obituary.] *Diapason* 66 (May 1975): 19.

> Brief biography and career information; recital of Huston's music is given on 6 May 1979 as a remembrance of him.

[Obituary.] *American Organist* 13 (August 1979): 26.

> In memory of Huston, an afternoon of music provides an affectionate remembrance, 6 May 1979.

"Recitals and Concerts." *American Organist* 40 (May 1957): 162.

Huston performs a recital of Vivaldi, Kellner, Howells, Karam, Roger-Ducasse, and Langlais at Temple Emanu-El, New York, 16 March 1957. "His handling of the resources of the instrument was astute and agile."

"Recitals and Concerts." *American Organist* 42 (March 1959): 111.

A recital by Huston at St. Matthew's Cathedral, Washington, D.C., 11 November 1958, included his own *Civitas Dei* on the Gregorian chant text "Caelistis urbs Jerusalem, beata pacis visio." The reviewer spoke of the new work, stating "it was reminiscent of Reger in style at times. . . . A well balanced program, well worked out, very beautifully played, and not too long to be enjoyed."

"Recitals and Concerts." *American Organist* 42 (September 1959): 313-14.

Huston is commended on his "sensitivity and innate musicianship" that provide the basis for "pretty wonderful music making." His recital was performed 5 May 1959 at St. Paul's Chapel, Columbia University, New York.

Thomas Scott Huston, Jr.

B. Tacoma, Wash., 10 October 1916; d. Cincinnati, Ohio, 2 March 1991. Studied with Burrill Phillips, Bernard Rogers, and Howard Hanson at Eastman School of Music, B.M., 1941, M.M., 1942, and Ph.D., 1952. Taught at Redlands University, 1946-47; Kearney State Teachers College, 1947-50; and the University of Cincinnati College-Conservatory of Music, 1952-88.

AA73, ABD, BB78, BB92, CACA, CACJ, IWW92, JCN, NG, NGA, OL, OL95, TCH, X52, X55, X62, X66, X67, X68, X69, X70, X71, X74.

Drone, Jeanette, comp. "American Composer Update." *Pan Pipes* 75/2 (1983): 30.

The University of Cincinnati awards Huston the Mrs. A. B. (Dolly) Cohen Award for excellence in teaching.

"Huston Speaks." *BMI: The Many Worlds of Music*, May 1972, 38.

Recently Huston spoke to a reporter from the *Cincinnati Enquirer* about composition techniques, composers on college campuses, why compositions tend to be shorter in length, and influences on composition students. Excerpts are taken from that interview.

Koukios, Ann Marie. "In Memoriam Thomas Scott Huston: 1916-91." *Music Research Forum* 6 (1991): 1-14.

Article presents a biographical sketch and list of works, which includes nineteen works for organ. Commission, premiere, and dedicatory information about the works is provided.

Kushner, David Z. "A Profile of Scott Huston." *Music Journal* 30 (September 1972): 26-27, 52.

A look at the man, influences on his writing, his styles, and a list of major works, including *Diorama* for organ.

Kyle, Marguerite K. "AmerAllegro." *Pan Pipes* 52/2 (1960): 55.

Huston's commissioned work, *Sonata for Organ*, is completed.

54/2 (1962): 55.

Huston is professor of composition at Cincinnati College-Conservatory of Music.

55/2 (1963): 55.

Presents lectures on the techniques of contemporary organ composing for the AGO, November 5, in Cincinnati.

56/2 (1964): 63.

Sonata for Organ is premiered at the Conservatory of Music in Cincinnati by organist Karen Musser.

61/2 (1969): 58-59.

Holy God, We Praise Thy Name, an organ solo, is published by World Library.

62/2 (1970): 67.

Diorama is published.

63/2 (1971): 64.

Diorama is premiered 4 April 1970 by Robert Delcamp, University of Cincinnati; receives a grant to make thirteen broadcasts regarding the development of music and musical styles, for National Educational Radio Network.

66/2 (1974): 57-58.

Huston is winner of the Major Armstrong FM Radio Award for music.

"Premieres." *BMI: The Many Worlds of Music*, summer 1971, 27.

Organist Robert Delcamp introduces *Diorama*, 4 April 1970, at Corbett Auditorium, Cincinnati Conservatory of Music.

Jere Hutcheson

B. Marietta, Ga., 16 September 1938. B.M., Stetson University, 1960; M.M., Louisiana State University, 1963; Ph.D., Michigan State University, 1966. Composition teachers include Harry Bolza, Frances Buxton, Helen Gunderson, H. Owen Reed, Ernst Krenek, and Gunther Schuller. Since 1965, faculty member, and since 1975 chairman of composition, Michigan State University. Distinguished Composer of the Year, National Music Teachers Association, 1976; Martha Baird Rockefeller Fund grant, 1977; National Endowment for the Arts grant, 1978; fellowship, Berkshire Music Center, 1968; fellowship, Composers' Conference, 1979; Guggenheim fellowship, 1979; ASCAP awards. Authored *Music for the High School Chorus* (Boston: Allyn & Bacon, 1967) and *Musical Form and Analysis: A Programmed Course* (Boston: Allyn & Bacon, 1972).

ABD, CACA, CACJ, DN76, DN78, IWW92, OL, OL95.

"ABA Salutes Additional Compositions in 1974 ABA-Ostwald Contest." *School Musician* 46 (December 1974): 62-63.

Hutcheson's *Passacaglia profundis* is first runner-up in the contest; an overview of the work and the composer's biography are provided.

Kyle, Marguerite K. "AmerAllegro." *Pan Pipes* 68/2 (1976): 56.

Hutcheson is appointed chairman of graduate composition at Michigan State University.

69/2 (1977): 52.

Patterns, for trombone and organ, is premiered by Jeffrey Price, who commissioned it, December 1976, Wenhem, Mass.

70/2 (1978): 47.

Patterns is published by Seesaw Music.

Herbert Reynolds Inch

B. Missoula, Mont., 25 November 1904; d. La Jolla, Calif., 14 April 1988. Studied privately at the University of Montana-Missoula with Josephine Swenson and A. H. Weisberg; at the Eastman School of Music, with Howard Hanson and Edward Royce: B.M., 1925, M.M., 1928, and Ph.D., 1941. Fellow, American Academy in Rome, 1931-34. Taught several years at Eastman and then on faculty of Hunter College (New York), 1937-65. Received the Ernest Bloch Award, 1945.

ABD, BB58, BB78, BB92, BDA, CACA, EDM, EVM, HHH, KTL, LMD, MHHH, NGA, OL, OL95, PCM, REM, TCAC, WI62, WI69, X50, X55, X56.

Kyle, Marguerite K. "AmerAllegro." *Pan Pipes* 57/2 (1965): 64.

Inch's *Recessional* receives its premiere on 25 May 1964 by organist Lawrence Perry, at Montana State University.

[Obituary.] *American Organist* 22 (July 1988): 41.

> Inch's death on 14 April 1983 is reported; cause of death is Alzheimer's disease. After his retirement from Hunter College, he wrote *Study for Left Hand and Pedal*.

[Obituary.] *Notes* 45/4 (1989): 725.

> Indicates Inch died in La Jolla, Calif., 14 April 1988.

David Clark Isele

B. Harrisburg, Penn., 25 April 1946. B.M., Oberlin, 1968; M.M. and M.S.M., Southern Methodist University, 1970; D.M.A., Eastman School of Music, 1973. Composition studies with Samuel Adler; organ with Sue Seid, David Boe, and Robert Anderson. Assistant professor of music and composer-in-residence, Notre Dame, 1973-79; director of choral and vocal activities, Otterbein College, 1979-80; associate professor, composer-in-residence, University of Tampa, from 1980. Received a DANA Foundation grant for composition. Organ music listed in IWW92.

CACA, IWW92, OL, OL95.

"Here and There." *American Organist* 24 (July 1990): 53.

> Isele is promoted to full professor at the University of Tampa, where he teaches theory, composition and organ, and directs the Collegiate Chorale. Received a DANA Foundation faculty development grant, which will fund the composition of an orchestral work.

Dorothy E. James

B. Chicago, Ill., 1 December 1901; d. St. Petersburg, Fla., 1 December 1982. Studied composition with Louis Gruenberg and Adolf Weidig, B.M. and M.M., American Conservatory of Music; Howard Hanson at Eastman; Ernst Krenek at the University of Michigan; and Healey Willan in Toronto. Professor of theory and music literature at Eastern Michigan University, Ypsilanti, 1927-68. Received two music scholarships from Adolf Weidig and the Adolf Weidig Gold Medal for Composition. Won three first prizes in Mu Phi Epsilon contests and first prize in the Milliken University Choral Clinic contest and the Michigan Composer Club contest; received four MacDowell fellowships; in 1971, received an honorary doctorate of musical arts degree upon her retirement from Eastern Michigan University, as professor emeritus of music. Published *Music of Living Michigan Women Composers* (n.p., 1976).

ABD, ASUC, BB58, BB78, BB92, BDA, CACA, ED, EVM, IWC, KTL, LMD, MHHH, MLA, NG, NGA, WCH.

Doss, Carol B. "Ann Arbor Alumnae's Dorothy James." *Triangle* 67/3 (1973): 9-10.
  A tribute to Dorothy James's career.

[Obituary.] *Triangle* 77/3 (1983): 22.
  Announcement of James's death.

Thomas Janson

B. Racine, Wisc., 1947. Studied with Ross Lee Finney and Leslie Bassett, University of Michigan. Won Charles E. Ives Award from the American Academy of Arts and Letters, 1972. Was a faculty member of the music department, University of Pittsburgh; currently on faculty at Kent State University, where he teaches theory and composition. His dissertation is titled "Departures for Symphony Orchestra" (*Dissertation Abstracts* 36 [April 1976]: 6360A). Organ music and biography listed in Arnold's book.
OL, OL95.

No bibliographical information located.

Donald Charles Johns

B. Chicago, Ill., 9 June 1926. Studied with Frank Cookson, Anthony Donato, and Wallingford Riegger, B.M., 1951, M.M., 1952, Ph.D., 1960, Northwestern University. Fulbright grant to study with Karl Schiske, Vienna Academy of Music, 1952-54. Professor of music, University of California, Riverside, since 1957; associate professor, Creative Arts Institute, University of California, 1966-67; now emeritus. Authored "Johann Nepomuk David's 'Choralwerk': A Study in the Evolution of Contemporary Liturgical Organ Style" (*Dissertation Abstracts* 21 [March 1961]: 2738).
ABD, CACA, CACJ, IWW92, OL, OL95, PC71, X65, X67, X74.

"Biola College Sponsors American Music Series." *Diapason* 65 (May 1974): 13.
  Donald Johns's music will be featured along with other American composers in a series of twelve concerts, February through May, at Biola College, La Mirada, Calif. Johns's *Prelude, Aria, and Finale* for trumpet and organ will receive its premiere in one of the recitals.

David N. Johnson

B. San Antonio, Texas, 1922; d. Tempe, Ariz., 2 August 1987. Studied at the Curtis Institute, Philadelphia; graduate of Trinity University, San Antonio; M.M. and Ph.D., 1956, from Syracuse University, where he studied composition with Ernest Bacon and Rosario Scalero. Studied organ with Arthur Poister, Alexander McCurdy, and Donald Willing. Positions held include chairman, music department, Alfred University, 1956-60; St. Olaf College, 1960-65; professor of music, Syracuse University, 1967-69; Arizona State University, 1969-81. Organist-choirmaster, Trinity Episcopal Cathedral, Phoenix, 1970-87. Authored *Instruction Book for Beginning Organists* (Minneapolis: Augsburg, 1965) and *Organ Teacher's Guide* (Minneapolis: Augsburg, 1971).

ABD, CACA, DCM, OL, OL95, X58, X69, X70, X71.

Cassels-Brown, Alastair, et al. "*Wondrous Love*: 3 Settings with Composers' Commentaries." *Hymn* 33/4 (1982):206-11.

Johnson expresses his considerations in composing hymn tunes and re-harmonizations.

"David N. Johnson." *American Organist* 43 (November 1960): 34.

Johnson is appointed associate professor of music, St. Olaf College, Northfield, Minn., and will also serve as chapel organist.

"David N. Johnson." *Diapason* 51 (October 1960): 17.

Same information as in the item above.

"Dr. David N. Johnson." *Diapason* 58 (April 1967): 3.

Johnson becomes professor of music, university organist, and director of music for Hendricks Chapel, Syracuse University, effective September 1.

"Here and There." *Diapason* 72 (February 1981): 16.

Announcement of Johnson's retirement, effective in the summer, from Arizona State University, Tempe.

[Obituary.] *American Organist* 21 (November 1987): 57.

Johnson died on 2 August 1987 in Tempe, Arizona. Provides title of his book *Organ Teachers' Guide*.

[Obituary.] *Diapason* 78 (October 1987): 6.

Johnson is a drowning victim on 2 August 1987; career summary included.

[Obituary.] *Hymn* 38/4 (1987): 35-36.

[Obituary.] *Journal of Church Music* 30 (March 1988): 13.
Notice of death, with a brief career summary.

[Obituary.] *Notes* 44/4 (1988): 699.

"Olaf Christiansen Retires." *American Organist* 48 (June 1965): 21.
Johnson, at St. Olaf since 1960, fills the shoes of Olaf Christiansen, who recently retired.

"Promote Johnson at St. Olaf as Christiansen Retires." *Diapason* 56 (June 1965): 7.
Same information as in the item above.

"Peter Gray." *Diapason* 63 (May 1972): 12.
Kansas City, Mo.'s organist Peter Gray performs the premiere of Johnson's *Fugue for Organ in A Minor*, February 6, at Grand Avenue Methodist Church.

Wetzler, Robert P. "Contemporary Composers: David N. Johnson." *Journal of Church Music* 11 (September 1969): 12-13.
A discussion on Johnson's view of composition today and how to write for people of varying abilities while maintaining integrity.

Robert W. Jones

B. Oak Park, Ill., 16 December 1932. University of Redlands, B.M., 1959, and M.M., 1960. Studied with Wayne Bohrnstedt, but largely self-taught in composition. Awards from Chicago Club of Women Organists; NACWPI; Episcopal Diocese in Albany, N.Y., and Southwest Virginia; Premio Valle D'Aosta, Italy; Ford Foundation grants; and MacDowell fellowships. Composer-in-residence, Music Educators National Conference; Ford Foundation Contemporary Music Project, West Hartford, Conn., 1965-69; and Livonia, Mich., 1969-72; instructor in theory and history, Schoolcraft College, from 1972.
ABD, CACA, CACJ, OL, OL95, PC71, TCH, X69, X70, X74.

"Jones Proves Worthy Composer." *Music of the West* 15 (January 1960): 16.
Jones is awarded the Charles Wakefield Cadman Scholarship for Young American Composers for the second time; usually given only once, the judges found Jones's work so worthy that an exception was made to honor him a second time.

Alice Yost Jordan

B. Davenport, Iowa, 31 December 1916. B.M.E., Drake University, 1938, with Francis J. Pyle; M.S.M., Union Theological Seminary, 1965. First prize, Composers Press Competition; awarded the Orah Ashley Lamke Distinguished Alumni Award at the national convention of Mu Phi Epsilon, 1980.

ABD, CACA, IWC, OL, OL95, WCH.

"AGO Chapter News: Saginaw, Michigan." *American Organist* 24 (July 1990): 24.

Commissioned by Marilyn Mason, Jordan's *Suite on the Tune "Webb"* is featured in a workshop with other American composers.

"American Composer Update." *Pan Pipes* 73/2 (1980): 33.

Processional on a Traditional English Melody, for organ, is recorded by James W. Thrash at First Methodist Church, Des Moines, Iowa.

"Des Moines Alumni Chapter's Own Composer, Alice Jordan." *Triangle* 84/3 (1990): 7. *

Drone, Jeanette, comp. "American Composer Update." *Pan Pipes* 75/2 (1983): 32.

Jordan is recognized as a regular contributor to *Pedalpoint* (Broadman Press) and *The Organist's Companion* (McAfee-Belwin Mills).

"Here and There." *Diapason* 82 (November 1991): 4.

Suite for Organ on "Webb" has been issued in the Marilyn Mason Organ Series, published by Randall M. Egan.

Kyle, Marguerite K. "AmerAllegro." *Pan Pipes* 63/2 (1971): 64-65.

Jordan receives the Alumni's Distinguished Service Award, Drake University, Des Moines.

66/2 (1974): 58-59.

Two works are in preparation for publication by Sacred Music Press: *Cantabile on "Hyfrydol"* and *Meditation on "Penitentia."*

67/2 (1975): 60.

The premiere of *Adagio on "Blott en Dag"* occurred on 28 April 1974, First United Methodist Church, Des Moines, by organist Edna Raitt Hutton; the work is also in preparation for publication by Broadman.

68/2 (1976): 57.

New Sounds for Familiar Hymns is published by Broadman; the collection includes three of Jordan's arrangements.

69/2 (1977): 53-54.

Fantasy on an Early American Melody received its premiere by Jon Spong, June 12, at the Iowa Methodist Conference; on September 12, James W. Thrash premieres *Procession on an Old English Melody*, First United Methodist Church, Des Moines. Several works by Jordan are published: *Four Familiar Nativity Melodies, Terra Patris, All Hail the Power* (Broadman), and *Organ Variations for Hymn Singing* (Sacred Music).

70/2 (1978): 48.

Organ Variations for Hymn Singing is now published by Broadman, as well as *A Season and a Time* (12 pieces); Lorenz publishes *Meditation on "Penitentia."*

71/2 (1979): 36.

Jordan's *Fount of Blessing* is included in Jon Spong's organ collection, released by Arvon Publishing Company.

McNurlen, Bonnie. "Award of Distinction to Mu Phi Epsilon Composer." *Triangle* 64/4 (1970): 11.

Jordan receives the Alumni Distinguished Service Award from Drake University, 7 May 1970, "for outstanding personal achievement as a composer." Other honors and awards are listed.

Robert A. Karlén

B. Erie, Penn., 4 December 1923. B.M., New England Conservatory, 1950; studied at the Conservatoire Nationale, Paris, 1953; M.A., University of Minnesota, 1959; composition studies with Francis Judd Cooke, Nadia Boulanger, and Paul Fetler. Since 1959, he has been on the faculty and served as department chairman, Augsburg College. National Federation of Music Clubs award, 1960; American Symphony Orchestra League, 1961; and the American-Scandinavian Foundation grant, 1968-69. Organ music and biography listed in Arnold's book.
OL, OL95.

No bibliographical information located.

Ulysses Simpson Kay

B. Tucson, Ariz., 7 January 1917; d. Teaneck, N.J., 20 May 1995. Received B.M., University of Arizona, 1938; M.M., Eastman School of Music, as a student of Bernard Rogers and Howard Hanson, 1940; attended Hindemith's classes at Berkshire Music Center, Tanglewood, 1941-42. Studied composition with Otto Luening, Columbia University, 1946-49. Winner of the American Prix de Rome, 1949-50 and 1951-52; Fulbright Fellow to Italy, 1950-51; consultant to Broadcast Music, Inc., New York, 1953-68; faculty, Boston University, 1965; University of California, Los Angeles, 1966-67; appointed professor of music at Herbert H. Lehman College of the City University of New York, 1968-72; distinguished professor there since 1972; retired in 1988. Awarded several honorary doctorates. Received a Guggenheim fellowship, 1964-65, and a Julius Rosenwald fellowship.

AA73, ABD, ACA VII 1, AFR, AMH, BB58, BB65, BB71, BB78, BB92, BCS, BDA, BMI, CA7, CACA, CACJ, DCM, EMS, EVM, GD54, HHH, IMD, IWW92, KTL, LMD, MGGs, MHHH, MLSR, NG, NGA, OL, OL95, PCM, PET, REM, TCAC, WI69, X51, X55, X56, X57, X58, X59, X60, X62, X64, X65, X66, X67, X68, X69, X70, X71, X74.

Berry, Lemuel. Review of Shaylor L. James, "Contributions of Four Selected 20th-Century Afro-American Classical Composers: William Grant Still, Howard Swanson, Ulysses Simpson Kay, and Olly Wilson" (Ph.D. diss., Florida State University, 1988). *Council for Research in Music Education* 104 (spring 1990): 47-48.

Lemuel Berry reviews James's dissertation that explores the contributions of these four Afro-Americans; biographies, surveys of contributions and achievements; description and analysis of each composer's orchestral work, which provides a synthesis of each composer's style and technique; a comprehensive list of works, letters from research centers, and the composers' addresses are several of the items found in appendices.

"Classified Chronological Catalog of Works by the U.S. Composer Ulysses Kay." *Boletin interamerican de musica* 28 (March 1962): 41-49.

An annotated, chronological listing of Kay's works through 1960.

"Composers in Focus." *BMI: The Many Worlds of Music*, winter 1976, 24-25.

Summary of his life and awards; lists significant works.

Dower, Catherine. "Ulysses Kay: Distinguished American Composer." *Musart* 24/3 (January-February 1972): 9-10, 16-17.

Lists awards, honorary degrees, and some of his many commissions; includes brief biography, sketch of his compositional style, and bibliography.

Drone, Jeanette, comp. "American Composer Update." *Pan Pipes* 75/2 (1983): 32.

Kay receives an honorary Doctor of Humanities degree from the University of Missouri, Kansas City; composer-in-residence at Bellagio Study and Conference Center, Bellagio, Italy.

Hayes, Laurence Melton. "The Music of Ulysses Kay, 1939-63." Ph.D., University of Wisconsin, Madison, 1971. *Dissertation Abstracts* 32 (December 1971): 3351A.

A brief biographical sketch precedes a stylistic analysis of most of Kay's compositions.

Kyle, Marguerite K. "AmerAllegro." *Pan Pipes* 50 (January 1958): 59.

Two Meditations is premiered by Leonard Raver at Corpus Christi Church, New York, and by Peter M. Fyfe at St. Paul's Chapel, New York; notice that the *American Composers Alliance Bulletin* (fall 1957) features Kay's music and gives a complete list of works.

51 (January 1959): 70.

Kay recently completed *Organ Suite No. 1*, commissioned by Marilyn Mason.

52/2 (1960): 56.

Marilyn Mason, commissioner and organist, performs the premiere of Kay's *Organ Suite No. 1*, 30 December 1958.

56/2 (1964): 64.

Kay receives his Doctor of Music degree, Lincoln College, Lincoln, Ill., 26 May 1963.

59/2 (1967): 82.

Kay receives honorary doctorate of music from Bucknell University, 5 June 1966; named visiting professor to the University of California, Los Angeles, 1966-67.

63/2 (1971): 65.

Honorary Doctor of Human Letters degree awarded Kay by Illinois Wesleyan University, 18 March 1969; and an honorary Doctor of Music degree from the University of Arizona, Tucson, 1 June 1969.

Slonimsky, Nicolas. "Ulysses Kay." *American Composers Alliance Bulletin* 7 (fall 1957): 3-6.

Kay is a composer who eludes a label; his history reveals many influences which transcend his music.

Southern, Eileen. "America's Black Composers of Classical Music." *Music Educators Journal* 62 (November 1975): 51-54.

A "new generation" of black composers includes Thomas J. Anderson, Arthur Cunningham, Julia Perry, Hale Smith, George Walker, and Kay. Kay's style is discussed briefly, as is his use of color, energetic rhythms, and especially his renown lyrical melodies.

_____. **"Conversation with Clarence E. Whiteman: Organ-Music Collector."** *Black Perspective in Music* 6/2 (fall 1978): 168-87.

Portrait, facsimile, and list of works by Kay and thirteen other black organ composers.

Tibbs, Constance. *Ulysses Kay: A Bio-Bibliography.* Westport, Conn.: Greenwood, 1994. *

"Two Meditations." *Diapason* 43 (December 1951): 31.

Published by Gray, the meditations are fairly easy to play; for service use or "for padding in concert lists."

"Two Meditations." *Notes* 9 (December 1951): 170.

> Same information as in the item above.

"Ulysses Kay." *Composers of the Americas* 7 (1961): 34-45.

> A brief biography in Spanish and English is followed by an annotated list of Kay's works.

"Ulysses Kay." *Pan Pipes* 45 (January 1953): 57. *

Homer Keller

B. Oxnard, Calif., February 1915. Studied at Eastman with Howard Hanson and Bernard Rogers, B.M., 1937, and M.M., 1938; to Paris, on a Fulbright grant for study with Arthur Honegger and Nadia Boulanger, 1950-51. Taught at the University of Michigan, 1947-54; resided in Hawaii; taught at Palama Settlement and Punahou Music School, 1956-58; lecturer in music at the University of Hawaii; professor, University of Oregon, 1958-77. Taught instrumental composition, National Music Camp, Interlochen, Mich., 1948-76. Edited *80 Chorale Preludes for Organ by 20 German Masters of the 17th and 18th Centuries* (St. Louis: Concordia, 1967).

ABD, AMH, ASUC, BB92, CACA, CRI 134, OL, OL95, PC71, PCM, TCH, X52, X74.

"Fantasy and Fugue." *American Organist* 32 (April 1949): 104.

> A sardonic review of Keller's *Fantasy and Fugue.*

"Fantasie [*sic*] and Fugue." *Diapason* 40 (May 1949): 23.

> The reviewer writes: "Its rather bleak and inchoate subject matter is given equally stern treatment. There is little lyrical appeal . . . it is not service music, nor for the majority."

"Fantasy and Fugue." *Musical America* 69 (September 1949): 33-34.

> Keller's work is published by Gray; author annotates the characteristics of the work.

"Fantasy and Fugue." *Music News* 41 (December 1949): 15. *

"Fantasy and Fugue." *Notes* 7 (December 1949): 138-39.

> Gray published this work in 1949; the reviewer indicates that it "offers little of interest to either the church or recital organist."

Kyle, Marguerite K. **"AmerAllegro."** *Pan Pipes* 46 (January 1954): 47.

> *Sonata for Organ* is premiered by Robert Noehren at Hill Auditorium, University of Michigan; *Fantasie and Fugue* is published by Gray.

"Our Cover." *Music of the West* 14 (October 1958): 6.

> Announcement of Keller's appointment as associate professor of theory and composition at the University of Oregon, fall 1958. Includes recent jobs and the influence that Hawaiian culture has had on his compositions.

Gerald Kemner

B. Kansas City, Mo., 28 September 1932. Studied with Quincy Porter, Yale University; with Howard Hanson, Henry Cowell, and Bernard Rogers, D.M.A., Eastman School of Music. Winner of the Howard Hanson Prize, 1962. Taught at Augustana College, Sioux Falls, S.D., 1962-66; from 1966, University of Missouri, Kansas City.

ABD, CACA, CACJ, OL, OL95.

"1977 Convention Performers, Speakers, Composers." *Music Clubs Magazine* 56/4 (1977): 18. *

Kent Wheeler Kennan

B. Milwaukee, Wisc., 18 April 1913. Studied composition with Hunter Johnson, University of Michigan, 1930-32; with Howard Hanson and Bernard Rogers, B.M., 1934, and M.M, 1936, Eastman. Won American Prix de Rome and took lessons with Pizzetti in Rome. Taught at Kent State University, 1939-40; University of Texas, Austin, 1940-42, and there again from 1945-46, after serving as bandleader in the U.S. Army, 1942-45; Ohio State University, 1947-49; University of Texas, from 1949 until 1983, when he retired. Authored *Counterpoint* (Englewood Cliffs, N.J.: Prentice-Hall, 1956; 3rd ed., 1987); *Counterpoint Based on 18th-Century Practice* (Englewood Cliffs, N.J.: Prentice-Hall, 1959); *The Technique of Orchestration* (Englewood Cliffs, N.J.: Prentice-Hall, rev. ed., 1970).

ABD, AS66, BB58, BB78, BB92, BDA, CACA, CC92, DCM, EDM, IWW92, KDK, KTL, MHHH, NG, NGA, OL95, PCM, SML, TCAC, WI62, WI69, X56, X58, X64, X66, X70, X71.

Kyle, Marguerite K. "AmerAllegro." *Pan Pipes* 46 (January 1954): 47-48.

Theme with Variations, for organ, is premiered by Donald Willing in San Antonio.

58/2 (1966): 70.

Kennan serves as the chairman of the music department, University of Texas, during the leave of E. William Doty, and pending appointment of a permanent chairman.

Ann S. Ker

B. Warsaw, Ind., 10 November 1937. B.M.E., Indiana University, 1974. Studied for her M.A. at Notre Dame. Organist, First Presbyterian Church, Warsaw, Ind., 1969-79; conductor of Central Christian Church choir, 1980; music faculty, Huntington College, from 1976; director of music, Redeemer Lutheran Church, Huntington, Ind., since 1980. Received first prize, St. Francis College composition competition, 1974. Co-founder and director of the board for the Northern Indiana Opera Association, from 1978. Organ music listed in Cohen's book.

IWC, WWAM-Cl.

No bibliographical information located.

Eunice Lea Kettering

B. Savannah, Ohio, 4 April 1906. B.M. from Oberlin, 1929; M.S.M., School of Sacred Music-Union Theological Seminary, 1933. Studied composition with Normand Lockwood, Felix Labunski, Edwin J. Stringham, and Béla Bartók. Taught at Madison College, Harrisonburg, Va., 1929-32; lecturer, then professor of music and composer-in-residence, Ashland College (Ohio), 1935-58; moved to New Mexico in 1959 to compose. First prize from National Federation of Music Clubs, 1943; special individual award of merit, 1968; merit award for outstanding service to other composers, 1970 and 1972; first prizes by National League of American Pen Women for secular choral composition, piano and vocal solo-art song. In 1961, first prize and citation from the annual Institute for Education by Radio and Television.

AA73, ABD, CACA, IWC, OL, OL95, PCM, X51, X54, X57, X62, X64, X65, X66, X67, X68, X69, X70, X71.

"Eunice Kettering and Uncle." *Diapason* 45 (February 1954): 32.

Kettering's uncle presents Ashland College (Ohio) with a new Möller organ, in memory of his wife and as a tribute to his niece. Eunice Kettering helped in the design of the instrument, and also performed the first half of the dedicatory recital, playing her own works.

"Eunice Lea Kettering Music Is Heard in Four Concerts." *Diapason* 42 (June 1951): 12.

Four recitals in Ohio feature Kettering's music for various performing forces, from choral to organ to trumpet to harp.

Kyle, Marguerite K. "AmerAllegro." *Pan Pipes* 58/2 (1966): 70.

St. Francis, for organ and chamber orchestra, was premiered 10 October 1965, First Presbyterian Church, Albuquerque, N.M. Goodsell Slocum was organist.

62/2 (1970): 68-69.

Kettering's organ arrangement of *Four American Folk Hymns* is premiered 24 October 1969.

"Paraphrase on an American Folk Hymn." *Diapason* 42 (July 1951): 23.

St. Cecilia series publishes *Paraphrase on an American Folk Hymn*. The tune, "Kemath," is taken from the 1857 collection *Timbrel of Zion*. "The piece is a novelty—and of worthwhile musical values, too."

Larry Peyton King

B. Whittier, Calif., 16 February 1932; d. Fullerton, Calif., 12 April 1990. B.M., Redlands University; M.S.M., Union Theological Seminary. Associate, Royal College of Organists; Licentiate, Royal Academy of Music, London. Associate to organist and master of choristers, Westminster Abbey, London; organist-choirmaster, St. Paul's Episcopal Church, San Diego; organist-choirmaster, Trinity Church, New York, since 1968. Organ student of Roberta Bitgood, Clarence Mader, Leslie Pratt Spelman, C. H. Trevor, and Alec Wyton; choral conducting with J. William Jones and Margaret Hillis; and composition with Joseph Goodman.

OL, OL95.

"AGO National Convention, Washington, D.C., 1982." *Diapason* 73 (September 1982): 6.

Fanfare for the Tongues of Fire is introduced by Catharine Crozier at the convention; the work is described as "evocative in the style of Tournemire, very organistic."

Belt, Byron. "Music in the Churches." *Music* (AGO) 7 (July 1973): 20-23.

> Larry King, Alec Wyton, and James Litton head the conference on music in the churches that established an essential dialogue between composers and their interpreters: every possible means must be used to assure that "historical continuity and contemporary adventurousness of the art."

"A Capital Convention, Washington, D.C., June 28-July 2, 1982: Composers and Their Commissions." *American Organist* 16 (May 1982): 5.

> An introduction to Larry King and a brief discussion about his commissioned work for organ, *Resurrection*.

"Convention Event." *American Organist* 16 (April 1982): 106.

> Biographical information.

"Here and There." *Diapason* 69 (October 1978): 9.

> *Fanfare for the Tongues of Fire* is included in a series of summer recitals at Riverside Church, New York; it was commissioned to feature the recently-installed Trompeta Majestatis.

"Larry King." *Diapason* 49 (April 1958): 34.

> King is awarded the licentiate diploma in organ performance from the Royal Academy of Music, London, where he is studying on a Fulbright grant.

"Larry King." *Diapason* 53 (December 1961): 36.

> King is appointed organist-choirmaster of St. Clement's Episcopal Church, St. Paul, Minn.; brief background information.

"Larry King." *Diapason* 54 (November 1963): 3.

> King began his new duties as organist-choirmaster at St. Paul Episcopal Church, San Diego, Calif.

[Obituary.] *American Organist* 24 (June 1990): 59.

> A brief look at King's life and career.

[Obituary.] *Notes* 47/4 (1991): 1088.

> American organist and composer King dies at Fullerton, Calif., on 12 April 1990, at age 58.

"Round and About." *Music* (AGO) 5 (December 1971): 44-45.

> King discusses his approach to making recitals a time of fellowship, and how the age of the typical concert-goer has dropped.

"Succession at Trinity." *Diapason* 59 (July 1968): 2.
> Larry King succeeds Dr. George Mead at Trinity Church, New York.

"Tributes for Larry King (1932-90)." *American Organist* 24 (September 1990): 73-77.
> Several friends and colleagues speak about how King's life touched theirs.

Peter Ballard Klausmeyer

B. Cincinnati, Ohio, 28 November 1942. Studied with Scott Huston, University of Cincinnati; Leslie Bassett, Ross Lee Finney, George Cacioppo, and George Balch Wilson, University of Michigan. Tied for 1st place in the Second International Competition for Electronic Music, sponsored by the Dartmouth Arts Council. Faculty member, Meredith College (N.C.), 1973-78. His dissertation is titled "Partial Fulfillment, for Orchestra" (*Dissertation Abstracts* 34 [November 1973]: 2682A).

ABD, CACA, OL, OL95.

"Electronic Music Composition Winners Announced for 1969." *School Musician* 40 (June-July 1969): 28.
> Klausmeyer wins a $500 prize from the Dartmouth Arts Council for his work *Cambrian Sea*.

Ellis Bonoff Kohs

B. Chicago, Ill., 12 May 1916. Studied piano with Adelaide Belser, Institute of Musical Arts, New York, 1928; composition student of Carl Bricken, M.A., 1938, University of Chicago; entered Juilliard and studied composition, 1938-39; continued musical studies in composition at Harvard with Walter Piston and musicology with Hugo Leichtentritt, 1939-41; served as organist-chaplain's assistant in the U.S. Army, and in the Air Force as bandleader, 1941-46. Teaching posts: assistant professor, Wesleyan University, 1946-48; Kansas City Conservatory of Music, 1946-47; associate professor, College of the Pacific, 1948-50; Stanford University, 1950; and associate, then full professor, and chairman of the theory department at the University of Southern California, Los Angeles, 1950-85. Authored *Music Theory: A Syllabus for Teacher and Student*, in 2 vols. (New York: Oxford, 1961); *Musical Form: Studies in Analysis and Synthesis* (Boston: Houghton-Mifflin, 1976);

and *Musical Composition: Projects in Ways and Means* (Metuchen, N.J.: Scarecrow, 1980). Alice M. Ditson award, 1946; BMI Publication award, 1948; numerous commissions.

AA73, ABD, ACA VI 1, AMH, BB58, BB65, BB71, BB78, BB92, BBCch, BMI, CA15, CACA, CACJ, CPM, DCM, DN77, EDM, GD54, HHH, IWW92, KDK, KTL, LMD, MHHH, NG, NGA, OL, OL95, PC71, PCM, REM, TCAC, TCH, TSC, WI69, X50, X51, X52, X53, X54, X55, X56, X57, X58, X59, X61, X62, X64, X65, X66, X67, X68, X70, X71, X74.

"American Composer Update." *Pan Pipes* 75/2 (1983): 32.

> *Chorale Variation No. 2 on Hebrew Hymns* was recorded by Herman Berlinski on Musical Heritage Records.

"Capriccio." *Notes* 7 (June 1950): 447.

> Published by Mercury Music, 1949. "A convincing piece musically." Fresh ideas are presented in this piece that is not too technically demanding.

Daniel, Oliver. "Ellis B. Kohs." *BMI: The Many Worlds of Music,* November 1970, 8.

> Biographical information includes teaching posts, commissions, honors, and awards; cites his *Passacaglia for Organ and Strings.*

"Ellis B. Kohs." *Composers of the Americas* 15 (1969): 118-26.

> Brief biography in Spanish and English, followed by an annotated list of compositions to date.

"Ellis Bonoff Kohs." *Pan Pipes* 43 (December 1950): 124. *

"Ellis Bonoff Kohs." *Pan Pipes* 45 (January 1953): 58. *

"Ellis Bonoff Kohs." *Pan Pipes* 47 (January 1955): 53.

> *Passacaglia for Organ and Strings* was premiered in Stockton, Calif., with members from the Stockton Symphony and organist Fred Tulan.

Kyle, Marguerite K. "AmerAllegro." *Pan Pipes* 49 (January 1957): 56.

> *Chorale Variations on Hebrew Hymns* for organ solo was published by Mercury Music; *Syllabus in Music Theory* was published by the University of Southern California Bookstore.

50 (January 1958): 60.

Kohs is a MacDowell Colony resident, spring 1957; head of theory department at the University of Southern California School of Music.

52/2 (1960): 57-58.

Music Theory is published by Oxford University Press, 1960.

53/2 (1961): 63.

Kohs serves as acting dean at the University of Southern California's School of Music in Los Angeles, fall 1960.

54/2 (1962): 58.

In 1961, Oxford University Press published *Music Theory.*

60/2 (1968): 80.

Kohs is appointed director of the Institute for Music in Contemporary Education, an MENC Continuing Music Project.

64/2 (1972): 64-65.

Kohs's complete list of works is published in *Composers of the Americas*, volume 15.

70/2 (1978): 50.

Kohs is the recipient of the Helene Wurlitzer Foundation award, for a two-month residency in Taos, N.M.; he also is the U.S. representative to the International Rostrum of Composers in Paris, May 1978.

"Three Chorale Variations on Hebrew Hymns, for Organ." *Diapason* 45 (February 1954): 21.

Premiered at the San Francisco Guild convention in 1952 by Ludwig Altman, these pieces are now published by Mercury Music.

"Three Chorale Variations on Hebrew Hymns, for Organ." *Notes* 11 (September 1954): 604.

Mercury Music published the work in 1953; ideal for temple services or recitals. A description of each hymn is provided. The hymns are "Yigdal," "Mo' oz Zur," and "Kee Hinay kachomer."

Barbara Kolb

B. Hartford, Conn., 10 February 1939. Studied the visual arts and clarinet. Hartt College of Music, Hartford, Conn., studied composition with Arnold Franchetti, B.A., 1961, and M.M., 1964. Attended classes of Lukas Foss and Gunther Schuller at Berkshire Music Center, Tanglewood, 1960, 1964, and 1968. In 1969, she became the first American woman to win the American Prix de Rome in composition. Held two Guggenheim fellowships; Fulbright to Vienna; MacDowell Colony fellowships; ASCAP awards; Ford Foundation fellowship to study the Mills Electronic Studio (Oakland, Calif.); composer-in-residence at the Marlboro Music Festival; and received grants from the NEA, 1972-79. Taught at the American Academy in Rome; Brooklyn College, 1973-75.

ABD, BB92, CACA, CC92, DCM, DN74, IWC, IWW92, NGA, OL, OL95, WCH, X69, X70, X74.

"Another Distaff Victory." *Diapason* 50 (July 1969): 14.

> Kolb, recent winner of the American Prix de Rome, is a reminder of the "great strides women have made in our day toward equality of acceptance in all artistic fields."

"Barbara Kolb." *American Music Teacher* 25/2 (1975): 34.

> A brief biography recounts her awards; special note is made that Kolb was the first American woman to win the Rome Prize.

"Barbara Kolb Awarded Prix de Rome; First Woman to Win Coveted Prize." *Music Clubs Magazine* 49/2 (1969-70): 9.

> Kolb wins Prix de Rome; awards, education, and list of works composed.

"A Capital Convention, Washington, D.C., June 28-July 2, 1982: Composers and Their Commissions." *American Organist* 16 (May 1982): 4-5.

> An introduction to Barbara Kolb and a brief look at her commissioned work for organ, *the point that divides the wind.*

"Convention Event." *American Organist* 16 (April 1982): 96.

> Brief biography and information about Kolb's career.

Gagne, Cole, and Tracy Caras. *Soundpieces: Interviews with American Composers.* Metuchen, N.J.: Scarecrow, 1982.

> Biographical sketch, photograph, and list of works accompany an interview with Kolb regarding the current trends in American music.

"Here and There." *Diapason* 83 (April 1992): 3.

> *Cloudspin*, for brass quintet and organ, received its first performance at the Cleveland Museum of Art on 23 October 1991. It was commissioned by the Musart Society on the occasion of the museum's 75th anniversary. Fifteen minutes in length, it is divided into three movements, each of which denotes various cloud formations. Karel Paukert, organist, was joined by brass students from the Cleveland Institute of Music.

Kolodin, Irving. **"Composers Argento, Kolb, Tippett and Gluck."** *Saturday Review* 55/48 (1972): 82-83. *

LePage, Jane Weiner. *Women Composers, Conductors, and Musicians of the Twentieth Century: Selected Biographies.* Metuchen, N.J.: Scarecrow, 1980.

> Biography, list of works, and discography for Kolb are included in this book.

Matthei, Renate, and Brunhilde Sonntage, eds. *Annäherungen an sieben Komponistinnen: Mit Berichten, Interviews und Selbstdarstellungen* [Focus on Seven Women Composers: With Reports, Interviews, and Their Own Testimony]. Kassel: Furore, 1988.

Kolb is one of the seven women featured.

"A Salute to Women Composers." *Pan Pipes* 67/2 (1975): 6.

Biography, awards, honors, and professional memberships cited.

Gerhard Krapf

B. Meissenheim-bei-Lahr, Germany, 12 December 1924. Studied piano and organ in Karlsruhe. Church organist in Offenburg, 1939-42; drafted into the German army and taken prisoner of war in Russia; upon release, went to Karlsruhe to study organ, choral conducting, and composition in 1950. Emigrated to U.S. to study organ at the University of Redlands, and composition with Paul Pisk, 1951. Became a naturalized citizen. Taught music at Albion, Mich., 1953-54; Northwest Missouri State College, Maryville, 1954-58; University of Wyoming, 1958-61; and University of Iowa, 1961-77. Joined the faculty of the University of Alberta, Edmonton, 1977, where he became chair of the division of keyboard studies. Authored *Liturgical Organ Playing* (Minneapolis: Augsburg, 1964); *Organ Improvisation: A Practical Approach to Chorale Elaborations for the Service* (Minneapolis: Augsburg, 1967); and *Bach: Improvised Ornamentation and Keyboard Cadenzas: An Approach to Creative Performance* (Dayton, Ohio: Sacred Music Press, 1983). Translated Hans Klotz's *The Organ Handbook* (St. Louis: Concordia, 1969) and Werckmeister's 1698 *Orgelprobe* (Raleigh, N.C.: Sunbury, 1976).

ABD, BB65, BB71, BB78, BB92, CACA, IWW92, KTL, OL, OL95, PCM, TCH, X64, X65, X67, X68, X69, X70, X71, X74.

"Gerhard Krapf Appointed to University of Wyoming." *Diapason* 50 (January 1959): 32.

Krapf is appointed assistant professor of organ and music theory at the University of Wyoming; recent biographical information included.

"Here and There." *Diapason* 77 (February 1986): 3.

The premiere of *Partita on "Toulon"* was performed by Rudolf Zuiderveld at the dedicatory recital of the rebuilt Möller/Ott organ, for which it was commissioned, at the First Presbyterian Church, Jacksonville, Ill., 24 November 1985.

Johns, Daniel. **"Composers for the Church: Gerhard Krapf."** *Church Music* (St. Louis) 1 (1974): 40-49.

> A detailed discussion of Krapf: his education, imprisonment in a Soviet concentration camp, his organ and choral works, and a list of published works.

"Organ Music for Lent." *Notes* 43/4 (1987): 925.

> The work is published in Dayton, Ohio, by Roger Dean/Heritage Press, 1984. The music is conceived in the German Lutheran tradition, but it was written for a Lenten liturgy at the Methodist Theology School, Delaware, Ohio. An organ Passion is preceded by a prelude, and concluded with a fugue as postlude. In between are eleven short movements of the Passion, each preceded by scripture from St. Mark's gospel. Brief description of the movements.

Pine, Carol, and Susan Mundale. **"AGO '80 National Convention."** *American Organist* 14 (March 1980): 29.

> Krapf will lead a workshop dealing with contemporary church music practices and the responsibilities of the liturgical organist.

"Premieres." *American Organist* 20 (March 1986): 45.

> Krapf was commissioned by First Presbyterian Church, Jacksonville, Ill., to write *Partita on "Toulon,"* which was premiered on 24 November 1985, when the church rededicated its newly rebuilt organ. Rudolf Zuiderveld, church organist, performed the work.

"Who's Who?" *ISO* 3 (August 1970): 227-28.

> An introduction to Krapf, with a biography and a career chronology.

Rudolph Joseph Kremer

B. St. Louis, Mo., 11 June 1927. B.M., Curtis Institute, 1952; M.M., 1957, and Ph.D., 1963, Washington University, St. Louis. Organ student of Howard Kelsey, Alexander McCurdy, and Anton Heiller. University organist, Cornell University, Ithaca, N.Y., 1960-64; professor of music, University of North Carolina, Chapel Hill, since 1964. Fulbright scholarship to Vienna, 1952-53; National Endowment for the Humanities Younger Scholar, 1968. His dissertation is titled "The Organ Sonata Since 1845" (*Dissertation Abstracts* 24 [May 1964]: 4727-28).

OL, OL95.

"**Conclave in Charlotte.**" *Diapason* 57 (February 1966): 18.

> Kremer, a recitalist at the conclave, presents his new sonata to favorable reviews at First Presbyterian Church, Charlotte. His recital program is listed.

"**Dr. Rudolph Kremer.**" *Diapason* 55 (June 1964): 37.

> Kremer is appointed professor of music at the University of North Carolina, Chapel Hill.

"**Kremer Goes to Cornell.**" *Diapason* 51 (June 1960): 2.

> Kremer is appointed university organist at Cornell University, Ithaca, N.Y.; he will also teach organ, harpsichord, and music theory.

Tufts, William O. "**AGO Midwinter Conclave.**" *American Organist* 49 (February 1966): 10.

> Kremer's recital at First Presbyterian Church includes contemporary compositions by Persichetti, Koechlin, and himself.

William Kroeger

B. Davenport, Iowa, 1914. Associate professor of music, Valparaiso University (Ind.); organist in Chicago's Messiah Lutheran Church and Temple Emanuel.
OL, OL95.

"**William Kroeger.**" *Violins* 12 (May 1951): 127-28.

> A graduate of Chicago Musical College, Kroeger has toured as soloist and accompanist. Organist, Messiah Lutheran Church and Temple Emanuel, Chicago; on faculty at Valparaiso University.

Gail Kubik

B. South Coffeyville, Okla., 5 September 1914; d. Covina, Calif., 20 July 1984. B.M., Eastman School of Music; studied violin with Samuel Belov, composition with Bernard Rogers, Edward Royce, and theory with Allen I. McHose; M.M., American Conservatory of Music, with Leo Sowerby, 1936. Further study with Walter Piston at Harvard and Nadia Boulanger in Paris. Taught at Monmouth College (Ill.), 1934; Dakota Wesleyan University, Mitchell, S.D., 1936-67; Teachers College, Columbia University, 1938-40. Active as a concert violinist. Won two Guggenheim awards, 1944, 1956; American Prix de Rome, 1950, 1951;

Pulitzer Prize in music, 1952. Appointed composer-in-residence, Scripps College, Claremont, Calif., 1970; when asked to retire at 65 (1980), he brought an unsuccessful suit against the school claiming that productivity and not age should determine the time for retirement. He also made extensive travels to Africa as he had a great interest in that continent and the Diaspora. Awarded the Theodor Körner Foundation Prize twice, 1961 and 1985.

ABD, AMH, AS66, ASC, BB58, BB71, BB78, BB92, BBCch, BBCpo, BDA, CACA, CACJ, CPM, DCM, DN75, EDM, EVM, GD54, HHH, IMD, KTL, LMD, MHHH, NG, NGA, OL, OL95, PC71, PCM, REM, TCAC, TCH, WI62, WI69, X50, X51, X52, X54, X55, X56, X57, X58, X62, X64, X65, X66, X67, X68, X69, X70, X71, X74.

Drone, Jeanette. "American Composer Update." *Pan Pipes* 75/2 (1983): 33.

Prayer and Toccata, for organ and two pianos, is recorded by Leonard Raver, organ, and Leonid Hambro and Chet Swiatkowski, pianos, on Orion Master Recordings.

"Gail Kubik." *Pan Pipes* 42 (December 1950): 124. *

45 (January 1953): 58-59. *

"Gail Kubik." *London Music* 9 (May 1954): 22. *

Haskins, James. "Let's Check Our Record." *Kansas City Star*, 13 April 1969.

A discussion about new compositions, and the opportunity for audiences to hear new works in the midwest.

"Kubik Wins Pulitzer Prize." *Musical Courier* 145 (15 May 1952): 8.

Kubik was awarded the 1952 Pulitzer Prize for Distinguished Musical Composition. Includes thumbnail sketch of his background and honors.

Kyle, Marguerite K. "AmerAllegro." *Pan Pipes* 50 (January 1958): 60.

Kubik was a MacDowell Colony resident; he is head of the theory department, University of Southern California School of Music.

53/2 (1961): 64.

Kubik attended the UNESCO International Conference of Music and the Americas, 1959, representing ASCAP; he was the University of Kansas guest speaker at the American Composers' Symposium.

58/2 (1966): 72.

Guggenheim fellowship is renewed.

63/2 (1971): 67.

Kubik is visiting professor of music and composer-in-residence, Scripps College, Claremont, Calif.

65/2 (1973): 60.
Kubik is appointed as a permanent member of the faculty at Scripps College.

[Obituary.] *Variety* 316 (8 August 1984): 79.
Kubik's obituary indicates he was a Pulitzer Prize winner in music.

[Obituary.] *Central Opera Service* 26/2 (1985): 27.
Cites the highlights of Kubik's career.

"Pulitzer Prize Awarded to Kubik." *Musical America* 72 (May 1952): 5.
Kubik wins 1952 Pulitzer Prize for distinguished musical composition. Commission information provided.

"Quiet Piece." *Musical Times* 90 (June 1949): 196. *

Richter, Marion M. "Gail Kubik—A Profile." *Music Clubs Magazine* 48/4 (1969): 34-35.
Biography, awards, and works are included.

Lindsay Arthur Lafford

B. Gloucester, England, 27 October 1912. Became a U.S. citizen. His study was at the Royal College of Music, London, A.R.C.M., 1934; Royal Academy of Music, London, L.R.A.M., 1934; Fellow, Royal College of Organists, 1935; Trinity College of Music, London, F.T.C.L., 1947. Organist-choirmaster, St. John's Cathedral, Hong Kong, 1935-39; university organist, Princeton University, 1939-40; director of chorus and orchestra, Washington University, St. Louis, 1946-48; instructor of music history and theory, and director, Haverford and Swarthmore Colleges (Penn.), 1939-43; assistant professor of music history and organ, Middlebury College (Vt.); professor and chairman, music department, Hobart and William Smith Colleges (N.Y.), 1948-79; retired in 1979. Organist-choirmaster, St. Philip's Episcopal Church, Coral Gables, Fla., since 1979.
OL, OL95, WWAM-Cl.

"Appointments." *Diapason* 70 (December 1979): 12.
Retiring from his position at Hobart and William Smith Colleges in Geneva, N.Y., as organist, harpsichordist, and carillonneur, he has accepted the post as organist-choirmaster at St. Philip's Episcopal Church, Coral Gables, Fla.

John LaMontaine

B. Oak Park, Ill., 17 March 1920. Studied piano with Muriel Parker and Margaret Farr Wilson and received theory training in Chicago from Stella Roberts, 1935-38; courses in piano with Max Landow and in composition with Howard Hanson and Bernard Rogers, B.M., 1942, Eastman School of Music; further studies with Rudolph Ganz at Chicago Musical College, 1945; completed studies in composition with Bernard Wagenaar at Juilliard and with Nadia Boulanger at the American Conservatory in Fontainebleau. Guggenheim fellowship, 1959-60. Visiting professor of composition, Eastman, 1961; composer-in-residence at American Academy in Rome, 1962. Pulitzer Prize in music for his first piano concerto, 1959. In 1977, he was a Nixon Distinguished Scholar, Whittier College (Calif.). Founder and publisher of Fredonia Press-Discs, 1975.

ABD, AMH, ASH66, BB65, BB71, BB78, BB92, CA9, CACA, DCM, DN76, KTL, LMD, NG, NGA, OL95, PC71, PCM, TCAC, X52, X56, X57, X58, X59, X60, X61, X62, X64, X65, X66, X67, X68, X69, X70, X71, X74.

"Alla Breve." *American Organist* 27 (February 1993): 42.

> Four CDs from Fredonia Discs feature LaMontaine's works. *Wilderness Journal*, based on the writings of Henry David Thoreau, which was commissioned for the dedication of the Filene Organ at Kennedy Center, is featured on one of the discs, and is performed by Donald Gramm with the National Symphony under Antal Dorati's direction.

"Biographical Notes." *Hymn* 29/1 (1978): 40-44.

> John LaMontaine's biographical highlights are mentioned; three of his new hymn tunes, commissioned by the Hymn Society, are included in the journal.

"Here and There." *Diapason* 84 (February 1993): 3.

> Fredonia Discs released three compact discs of works by LaMontaine.

"John LaMontaine." *Pan Pipes* 44 (January 1952): 38. *

"John LaMontaine." *Showcase* 40/5 (1961): 16-17. *

"John LaMontaine." *American Organist* 53 (June 1970): 29.

> LaMontaine is commissioned to write a work for organ and orchestra for the opening season of the John F. Kennedy Center for the Performing Arts, Washington, D.C.

"John LaMontaine." *Composers of the Americas* 9 (1963): 79-85.

> Brief biography in Spanish and English is followed by an annotated listing of his works.

Kyle, Marguerite K. **"AmerAllegro."** *Pan Pipes* 53/2 (1961): 64-65.

Won Guggenheim award, 1959 and 1960; Pulitzer Prize in music, 1959.

54/2 (1962): 59-60.

LaMontaine is visiting professor of composition at Eastman School of Music, fall 1961; composer-in-residence, American Academy in Rome, 1962.

61/2 (1969): 64-65.

LaMontaine was visiting professor of music at the University of Utah, spring 1967.

"Large New American Work on Scene: LaMontaine—Thoreau." *Pan Pipes* 65/2 (1973): 2-3.

"Overwhelming" is how the reviewer described LaMontaine's *Wilderness Journal*, for bass-baritone, organ, and orchestra. The work was commissioned for the dedication of the Aeolian-Skinner organ in the Kennedy Center, and was premiered on October 10, 12, 13, and 14.

"News and Honors." *ASCAP* 5/3 (1972): 31.

LaMontaine's *Wilderness Journal*, for organ and orchestra, receives its world premiere 9 November 1972; Antal Dorati conducted the National Symphony at Kennedy Center, Washington. Commission information supplied. (This information does not agree with that found in *Pan Pipes* 65/2 [1973]: 2-3).

Simon, Geoffrey. **"New LaMontaine Work Premiered at Kennedy Center."** *Diapason* 64 (December 1972): 12.

Organist Paul Callaway is joined by the National Symphony Orchestra, Antal Dorati conducting, and Donald Gramm, bass-baritone, for the premiere of *Wilderness Journal*, 10 October 1972. The work is described and the recital is reviewed. Background information about the commission and the new organ at the hall is provided.

Tufts, Nancy Poore. **"Premiere of John LaMontaine's 'Wilderness Journal.'"** *Journal of Church Music* 15 (March 1973): 16-18.

The premiere occurs 10 October 1972 at Kennedy Center; the description of the work reveals that the speaker is as important as the organist.

Ward, L. P. **"—Something Inside Maybe, Not Just Notes."** *Music Clubs Magazine* 69/1 (1989): 14. *

Weintraub, Erica B. **"John LaMontaine—Life on the Edge."** *Music Educators Journal* 69 (March 1983): 41-43.

LaMontaine indicates that the study of an instrument is vital to a composer. As a composer, one should try to hear all the parts and read all the clefs. Oftentimes the contemporary composer is respected but rarely played; "if you're a composer, you'd better be a gambler."

Libby [Elizabeth Brown] Larsen

B. Wilmington, Del., 24 December 1950. B.A., 1971, M.A., 1975, and Ph.D., 1978, from the University of Minnesota. Composition studies with Paul Fetler, Dominick Argento, and Eric Stokes. Teaching associate, University of Minnesota, 1972-77; composer-in-residence for the Minnesota Orchestra, 1983-85; manager-composer of the Minnesota Composers' Forum, from 1973. Winner of many grants, awards, and commissions; Minnesota Woman of the Year in Arts, 1981; voted the Woman to Watch, 1983. National Endowment for the Arts Fellowship, 1982 and 1984; Minnesota State Arts Board Fellowship, 1980. Exxon, Rockefeller Foundation, and Meet the Composer grants, 1983-85. Dissertation is a one-act opera, *The Words upon the Windowpane*.

ABD, BB92, CACA, CC92, IWW92, NGA, OL95, WCH.

"Alla Breve." *American Organist* 28 (June 1994): 52.
> Notice that Oxford University Press now publishes Larsen's music.

Campbell, K. **"Meet the Composer."** *Ovation* 9 (September 1988): 24+. *

"The Composers Speak in Louisville." *Choral Journal* 29/5 (1988): 36-37.
> Norman Dello Joio and Larsen will speak in Louisville about their approach to composition. Biographies include awards and honors.

Larsen, Libby. **"A Composer and Her Public: A Mutual Seeking."** *Symphony Magazine* 35/6 (1984): 34-36, 78-79.
> The composer responds to the public by asking what it wants to hear. Basically the response is not against new music, but people want energy, beauty, and "spirit" in new compositions.

_____. **"Writing the Next Chapter."** *ASCAP*, winter 1987, 42.
> Larsen addresses how women, by understanding the business side of the arts, can more likely have their works performed.

Mary Jane Leach

B. St. Johnsbury, Vt., 12 June 1949. B.A. in theater and music, University of Vermont; post-graduate work in composition at Columbia University with Mark Zuckerman; vocal study with Jeanett Lovetri at the Voice Workshop, where she currently teaches voice.

Named Emerging Composer in 1987 by BACA Downtown; composer-in-residence at the Charles Ives Center in 1986.

IWW92, IWW94.

Demetz, B. "New Faces." *Ear* 12/6 (1987): 36. *

Mary Weldon Leahy

B. St. Louis, Mo., 20 August 1926. Studied composition at North Texas State University and privately with Carl Eppert, Normand Lockwood, and Gordon Jacob in England. First prize in Wisconsin's state contest for string quartet, and a song in 1949. Organ works listed in Cohen's book.

ABD, CCA, IWC, WCH.

No bibliographical information located.

Ludwig Lenel

B. Strasbourg, France, 20 May 1914. Became a U.S. citizen in 1955. Was an artist pupil of Albert Schweitzer, 1932. Holds diplomas from the Hochschule für Musik, Cologne Conservatory, and Basel Conservatory. Additional study at Oberlin, M.M., 1940. Worked at Oberlin, Monticello College, Westminster College, Elmhurst College, New School for Social Research, and since 1952 at Muhlenberg College. Various church positions have been held.

ABD, CACA, CACJ, OL, OL95.

Little, Jeanie R. "Serial, Aleatoric, and Electrical Techniques in American Organ Music Published between 1960 and 1972." Ph.D., University of Iowa, 1975. *Dissertation Abstracts* 36 (June 1978): 7722A.

This scholarly, in-depth work analyzes in detail Lenel's serial and chance works for organ, among other composers' works.

"Ludwig Lenel Is Organist of Allentown, Penn., Church." *Diapason* 42 (November 1951): 2.

> Lenel is appointed organist and director of music at Christ Lutheran Church, Allentown, Penn., effective November 4. Included is Lenel's music background.

Mullins, Terrence Y. **"Contemporary Composers."** *Journal of Church Music* 12 (November 1970): 5-6.

> A discussion with Lenel about "when music becomes sound"; also how one's cultural background influences composition, electronic music, and church music.

Stout, Alan. **"The Current Scene."** *Church Music* (St. Louis) 1 (1967): 64.

> A discussion of Lenel's organ works performed on 29 June 1966 at Grace Lutheran Church, River Forest, Ill. Based on hymn melodies, each work is described; "Lenel's music . . . is most effective in the service of the liturgy."

Dan S. Locklair

B. Charlotte, N.C., 7 August 1949. Study at Mars Hill College, B.M., *cum laude*; S.M.M., Union Theological Seminary. Teachers were Donna Robertson, Robert Baker, Eugenia Earle, Joseph Goodman, and Gerre Hancock in New York; Ezra Laderman, Binghamton, N.Y. Won the Crisp Award, 1971; AGO Washington, D.C., chapter first prize, 1972; Martha Baird Rockefeller grant, 1978. On faculty, Hartwick College, 1973-74; dean of Syracuse Catholic Diocese's organ training program, 1974-82; organist-director, First Presbyterian Church, Binghamton, 1973-82. D.M.A., Eastman School of Music, 1981. Assistant professor, Wake Forest University, 1982. Composer-in-residence, Ives Center of American Music, 1981 and 1984; Friend of the Arts, SAI award, 1982; Meet the Composer award, 1981-85; received his fifteenth ASCAP award in 1994.

ABD, CACA, IWW92, OL, OL95, WWAM-Cl.

"American Composer Update." *Pan Pipes* 87/2 (winter 1995): 32.

> Marilyn Keiser premiered Locklair's *A Spiritual Pair (Diptych for Organ)* at the dedication of Christ Church Cathedral's organ, New Orleans, in September 1994.

"Appointments." *Diapason* 73 (June 1982): 4.

> Locklair is appointed to the faculty of Wake Forest University, Winston-Salem, N.C., to teach music composition and theory; brief biographical data.

"Dan S. Locklair." *Diapason* 62 (August 1971): 6.

Locklair is named winner of the 1971 Elizabeth Utley Fletcher Scholarship, held in Raleigh, N.C.; the competition is open to all North Carolina organists who are entering an S.M.M. degree program; the winner receives a $200 prize.

"Dan S. Locklair Appointed." *Diapason* 64 (October 1973): 10.

Locklair goes to First Presbyterian Church, Binghamton, N.Y., to serve as organist-choirmaster.

"Here and There." *Diapason* 69 (July 1978): 10.

Locklair's *Sonata for Organ* is premiered by Leonard Raver at the First Presbyterian Church of Binghamton, N.Y., on April 9.

"Here and There." *Diapason* 72 (July 1981): 20.

Constellations, for percussion and organ, is premiered by the composer and percussionist Joe Roma, 31 May 1981, at the First Presbyterian Church, Binghamton, N.Y. The brief article indicates he was winner of the 1981 Eastman School of Music Howard Hanson Award and an ASCAP award for 1981-82.

"Here and There." *Diapason* 83 (April 1992): 3.

Ricordi published Locklair's organ work *Ayre for the Dance* in August 1991.

"Here and There." *Diapason* 83 (September 1992): 3.

Rubrics ("A Liturgical Suite for Organ" in five movements) has been published in a new engraved edition by E. C. Kerby, Ltd.

"Here and There." *Diapason* 84 (October 1993): 3.

H. W. Gray/CPP Belwin re-released Locklair's *Triptych for Manuals*, a set of miniatures that had been out of print for several years.

"Here and There." *Diapason* 85 (January 1994): 4.

Locklair's works receive recent performances: *Voyage—a Fantasy for Organ* was performed by Alan Morrison, Pasadena Presbyterian Church, October 10; *Rubrics*, by Marilyn Keiser, St. Andrews Presbyterian Church, Raleigh, N.C., October 23, and Trinity-by-the-Cove Episcopal Church, Naples, Fla., November 14; and *Constellations* (concerto for organ and percussion) by Delbert Disselhorst, University of Iowa, November 14.

"Here and There." *Diapason* 85 (December 1994): 3.

A Spiritual Pair (Diptych for Organ) received its premiere on September 18 by Marilyn Keiser at Christ Church Cathedral, New Orleans, at the dedication of the cathedral's new Goulding & Wood organ.

Page, Charles. "Hartt School of Music/University of Hartford: 10th Anniversary of the International Contemporary Organ Music Festival." *American Organist* 14 (October 1980): 51.

> An in-depth report on the Hartt Contemporary Organ Music Festival. The festival included the premiere of numerous works, including Locklair's *Inventions*.

"Pipings." *American Organist* 14 (June 1980): 38.

> An evening of music by Locklair was presented 14 February 1980; it included three movements of his *Inventions*. Earlier in February his *Phoenix Fanfare* for organ, brass, and timpani, commissioned by New York's Union Theological Seminary, was played at the ceremony marking the re-opening of Union's newly-reconstructed James Memorial Chapel.

"Pipings." *American Organist* 24 (September 1990): 50.

> Organist Barbara Harbach recorded *Rubrics*, *Ayre for the Dance*, *Pageant for Sally*, and *Inventions* on the Gasparo label.

"Premiered." *ASCAP*, spring 1981, 40.

> Locklair's *Inventions* is premiered at Trinity Chapel, Hartford, Conn., 21 June 1981.

"Premieres." *Music Educators Journal* 65 (November 1978): 73.

> *Sonata for Organ* is premiered on 4 April 1978 at the First Presbyterian Church, Binghamton, N.Y.

"Premieres." *American Organist* 23 (June 1989): 43.

> *Rubrics* was premiered on April 16 by Dallas organist Mary Preston on a program at East Liberty Presbyterian Church, Pittsburgh, Penn. Commission information supplied.

Normand Lockwood

B. New York, 19 March 1906. Studied at the University of Michigan; in 1925, went to Europe and took lessons with Ottorino Respighi in Rome and Boulanger in Paris; fellow at the American Academy in Rome, 1929-1931; upon his return to the U.S., he was instructor in music at Oberlin Conservatory, 1932-43; lecturer at Columbia University, 1945-53; Trinity University in San Antonio, 1953-55; taught at the Universities of Hawaii and Oregon, 1955-61; appointed faculty member, University of Denver, 1961; emeritus in 1974. Winner of a Guggenheim fellowship, 1942-44; World's Fair Prize, 1939; Ernest Bloch Award, 1947; and the Marjorie Peabody Waite award, 1981.

AA73, ABD, ACA, AMH, BB58, BB78, BB92, BBCch, BDAm, BMI, CACA, CACJ, CPM, DCM, EVM, HHH, IWW92, KTL, LMD, MHHH, NCE, NG, NGA, OL, OL95, PC71, PCM, REM, TCAC, WI62, WI69, X51, X53, X54, X56, X57, X58, X59, X60, X61, X62, X64, X65, X66, X67, X68, X69, X70, X71, X74.

"AmerAllegro." *Pan Pipes* 46 (January 1954): 50.

Concerto for Organ and Brasses was recorded by Marilyn Mason and members from the New York Philharmonic Symphony Orchestra, for Remington Records; became chairman of music department, Trinity University, San Antonio.

50 (January 1958): 61.

American Composers Alliance Bulletin (6/4, 1957) features Lockwood's music.

"American Composer Update." *Pan Pipes* 73/2 (1980): 34.

Six Organ Preludes is premiered by Phyllis Tremmel, Little Ivy Chapel, Denver, on 27 April 1980. *Canonic Toccata* for two organs was premiered by Austin Lovelace and Tremmel, Wellshire Presbyterian Church, 19 May 1980.

Bennett, Elsie M. "Normand Lockwood, a Composer Who Listens." *Music Journal* 27 (April 1969): 90.

Career summary of Lockwood; he listens to the requests of those who commission work from him.

Biggs, E. Power. "Concerto for Organ and Brasses." *American Organist* 34 (December 1951): 405.

Biggs performs the premiere of Lockwood's *Concerto for Organ and Brasses*, 6 January 1952, on CBS. Other upcoming premieres to be performed by Biggs are mentioned.

Daniel, Oliver. "New Recordings." *American Composers Alliance Bulletin* 4/2 (1954): 14-16.

Lockwood has two works recorded by organist Marilyn Mason on Remington Records: *Concerto for Organ and Brasses* and *Quiet Design*. Commission information supplied in addition to an overview of the works and basic biographical data.

"In the News." *BMI: The Many Worlds of Music*, October 1971, 6.

Lockwood is saluted at the University of Denver on May 16 for his contribution to the university and to the community. On July 1 he was honored with the Governor's Award.

Kyle, Marguerite K. "AmerAllegro." *Pan Pipes* 53/2 (1961): 65.

Lockwood is visiting professor of music, University of Hawaii, Honolulu.

54/2 (1962): 60.

Composer-in-residence, University of Denver, 1961-62.

57/2 (1965): 26.

Many works by Lockwood are published: *Toccata for World Communion*, *Fantasy for Reformation Sunday*, *Meditation on Lent*, *Easter Fanfare*, *Prelude for National Church Music Sunday*, *The Gospel and the Call*, *Hommage to Hassler*, *Veni sancte spiritus*, *Away in a Manger*, *Toccata for Advent*, and *A Mother's Day Remembrance*.

64/2 (1972): 66-67.

Continues as composer-in-residence, University of Denver, after ten years.

65/2 (1973): 61.

Lockwood's *Fantasy on Jesus, My Joy* is premiered by Alexander Boggs Ryan, 8 March 1972.

66/2 (1974): 61.

Processional Voluntary is published by Waterloo Music; *Eventide* is released by Standard Music.

67/2 (1975): 62-63.

Concerto for Organ and Orchestra is introduced on April 24 at Cleveland's Museum of Art, with organist Gerre Hancock; Walter Blodgett conducted the ensemble.

Lange, Stephen R. "An Analysis of Concerto for Brass, Organ and Percussion by Robert Elmore, Concerto for Brass and Organ by Seth Bingham, and Concerto for Organ and Brasses by Normand Lockwood." Ph.D., Michigan State University, 1978. *Dissertation Abstracts* 39 (September 1978): 1182A. *

Martin, Warren. "Three American Composers." *Repertoire* 1 (November 1951): 114-16.

Lockwood's approach to choral writing is praised; he has a facility to compose in many styles and for different voicings.

"Normand Lockwood." *Pan Pipes* 45 (January 1953): 59-60. *

47 (January 1955): 55-56.

Concerto for Organ and Brasses is in preparation with Associated Music Publishers; Remington issued a recording of the concerto, with organist Marilyn Mason and conductor Thor Johnson.

Norton, Kay. *Normand Lockwood: His Life and Music.* Metuchen, N.J.: Scarecrow, 1993.

A definitive study, based on the author's dissertation. Includes a catalog of his music, by category: choral, keyboard, chamber music, solo songs, instrumental music, opera and non-operatic theater music. Extensive biography.

"Premieres." *BMI: The Many Worlds of Music*, October 1967, 23.

Sonata for Organ, written for Phyllis Tremmel, was premiered by her on July 23 at Mackey Auditorium, University of Colorado, Boulder.

Tremmel, Phyllis. "Round & About." *Music* (AGO) 6 (October 1972): 18, 72.

> A tribute to Lockwood as he completes ten years as composer-in-residence at the University of Denver. Overviews on several of his organ works and a cantata are provided.

Ruth Lomon

B. Montreal, Canada, 7 November 1930. Became a U.S. citizen, 1965. Lives and teaches in Cambridge, Mass. Educated at McGill University and New England Conservatory; studied with Witold Lutosławski. Received numerous commissions; awarded Meet the Composer grants, 1981 and 1983; fellowships from Yaddo, 1977, MacDowell/Norlin, 1982, Ossabaw Island Project, and the Helene Wurlizter Institute at Taos, N.M.; awarded National League of Pen Women's scholarship for mature women, 1984, and a recording award from American Women Composers.

BB92, CACA, IWC, IWW92, WWAM-Cl.

"Seven Portals of Vision." *Notes* 42/4 (1986): 858-59.

> Published in Washington, by Arsis, 1984. The seven-movement difficult work was premiered by Joanne Vollendorf at the 1983 Conference on Women in Music, University of Michigan, Ann Arbor. A description of the work is included.

Page Long

B. Lima, Ohio, 7 April 1933. B.M., Oberlin College, 1955; M.A., University of Iowa, 1956. Instructor of music, University of Rhode Island, Kingston, 1956-57; Western Reserve Naval Academy, Hudson, Ohio, 1957-61. Organist, First Congregational Church, 1957-61; director of music, Rincon Congregational Church, Tucson, 1961-63. D.M.A., University of Arizona, 1963. Organ student of Fenner Douglass and Garth Peacock; composition with Richard Hudson and Andrew Buchhauser. Assistant professor of music, Sam Houston University, 1963-64. Minister of music, First Congregational Church, Saginaw, Mich., since 1964; instructor of organ, Saginaw Valley State College. Dissertation titled "Transformations of Harmony and Consistencies of Form in the Six Organ Symphonies of Louis Vierne" (*Dissertation Abstracts* 24 [November 1963]: 2071-72). Organ music listed in Arnold's book.

ABD, OL, OL95.

No bibliographical information located.

Austin Lovelace

B. Rutherfordton, N.C., 26 March 1919. A.B., 1939, and honorary doctorate of music, High Point College (N.C.); M.S.M., 1941, and D.S.M., 1950, Union Theological Seminary School of Sacred Music. Organist-choirmaster, Holy Trinity Episcopal Church, Lincoln, Neb., 1941-42; instructor, music department, University of Nebraska, 1941-42; organist-choirmaster, Myers Park Presbyterian Church and instructor, Queens College (N.C.), 1942-44; organist-choirmaster, First Presbyterian Church, Greensboro, N.C., 1946-52; organist-choirmaster, First Methodist Church and instructor, Garrett Theological Seminary, Evanston, Ill., 1952-62; organist-choirmaster, Christ Church Methodist, New York, 1962-64; adjunct teacher, School of Sacred Music, Union Theological Seminary, 1963; organist-choirmaster, 1964-70, Montview Boulevard Presbyterian Church, and faculty member, Temple Buell College, Denver, 1964-70; organist-choirmaster, Lovers Lane Methodist Church, Dallas, 1970-77; minister of music, Wellshire Presbyterian Church, and faculty member, Iliff School of Theology, Denver, 1977-86. Retired. With William C. Rice, authored *Music & Worship in the Church* (Nashville: Abingdon, 1960; rev. ed., 1976); and compiled *Wedding Music for the Church Organist and Soloist* (New York: Abingdon, 1961); *The Organist and Hymn Playing* (New York: Abingdon, 1962); *The Anatomy of Hymnody* (Nashville: Abingdon, 1965).

OL, OL95.

"American Composer Update." *Pan Pipes* 87/2 (winter 1995): 33-34.

> Lovelace's *Toccata on "A Mighty Fortress"* is published by Augsburg Fortress, and *Triptych and Pastorale on "Divinum Mysterium"* is published by Concordia Publishing House.

"Austin C. Lovelace." *Diapason* 43 (November 1952): 9.

> Lovelace is appointed minister of music at the First Methodist Church of Evanston, Ill., October 1952. Biographical data included.

"Austin C. Lovelace." *Pan Pipes* 47 (January 1955): 56.

> Lovelace is organist at First Methodist Church, Evanston, Ill.

"Contributing Editors." *Journal of Church Music* 4 (January 1968): 12. *

"Dr. Austin C. Lovelace." *Diapason* 53 (July 1962): 2.

> Lovelace assumes duties as minister of music at Christ Methodist Church, New York, September 1, succeeding Everett Tutchings.

"Dr. Austin C. Lovelace." *Diapason* 55 (June 1964): 27.

Lovelace will become minister of music at Montview Boulevard Presbyterian Church, Denver, on September 1.

Kyle, Marguerite K. "AmerAllegro." *Pan Pipes* 50 (January 1958): 61.

Lovelace releases an organ concert on Concertapes; he is associate professor of church music, Garrett Biblical Institute, Evanston.

51 (January 1959): 74.

By Waters Still, organ solo, was released by J. Fischer.

54/2 (1962): 61.

Abingdon publishes *Wedding Music for the Church Organist and Soloist.*

55/2 (1963): 59-60.

Abingdon publishes Lovelace's *Funeral Music.*

58/2 (1966): 73.

Lovelace is appointed lecturer in hymnology at Iliff School of Theology, Denver.

59/2 (1967): 86.

Iliff hires Lovelace onto the permanent faculty.

61/2 (1969): 65.

Gray publishes *What Is This Lovely Fragrance?*

66/2 (1974): 61-62.

Augsburg publishes the *Easter Concertata on "Llanfair"* for organ and trumpets.

67/2 (1975): 63.

Preludes and Postludes, volume 2, published by Augsburg, contains several works by Lovelace.

69/2 (1977): 58.

Early American Hymns, a collection published by AMSI, contains a work by Lovelace; a work for organ with brass, *Concertato on "Adeste Fidelis,"* is published by Augsburg.

70/2 (1978): 58.

Lovelace served on the editorial board with Alec Wyton and Erik Routley for the hymnal *Ecumenical Praise*, published in 1977.

71/2 (1979): 38.

Hymn Preludes and Free Accompaniments is published by Augsburg.

Lovelace, Austin C. "Exploring *Eight Hymn Preludes.***"** *Clavier* 20/6 (1981): 28-31.
 Lovelace annotates his work.

Williams, L. R. "More of Who's Who!" *Church Music* 15 (February 1964): 18. *

Dennis Michael Lovinfosse

B. Philadelphia, Penn., 13 January 1947. B.M., in organ, University of New Mexico, 1970; M.M. in theory and composition, 1973, and D.M.A., in composition, 1981, Northwestern University (Ill.). Organ pupil of Karel Paukert; composition with Alan Stout, James Hopkins, and Lyden DeYoung. Instructor, DePaul University, Chicago, 1976-78; instructor, assistant professor, University of Nebraska, Lincoln, since 1978.

OL, OL95.

Lawrence, Arthur. "The Organ and the Concert Hall." *Diapason* 73 (March 1982): 18.
 Lovinfosse, on a panel of composers, discusses the problems of writing for organ with other instruments at a conference on "The Organ and the Concert Hall," at the University of Nebraska, Lincoln. His *Studies in Colors and Textures*—a one-movement work "in fairly dissonant style," for organ, two pianos, and percussion—was featured in one of the concerts during the conference.

Kenneth D. Lowenberg

B. Chicago, Ill., 15 November 1939. B.M.E., Northwestern University, 1961. Taught at Lew Wallace High School, 1961-62; public school music teacher, Gary, Ind., and East Moline, Ill., 1963-67. M.M. in composition, University of Southern California, 1966. AAGO, 1968, FAGO, 1971. Fellow, College of Church Musicians, Washington, D.C., 1968. Organ student of Richard Enright and Irene Robertson; composition with Ellis Kohs, Halsey Stevens, Ingolf Dahl, Leo Sowerby, and Paul Callaway. Teacher of composition, Columbia Union College, Takoma Park, Md., 1974-75; organist-choirmaster, Chevy Chase Presbyterian Church in Maryland since 1968.

ABD, OL, OL95.

"Kenneth Lowenberg, Organ." *High Fidelity/Musical America* 26 (February 1976): MA23.

> Lowenberg's dedicatory recital of the Rieger organ at Chevy Chase Presbyterian Church, 2 November 1975, is panned. Details of the organ provided.

Donald McAfee

B. Roanoke, Va., 3 June 1935. Studied at Lynchburg College, B.A., 1956; M.S.M., Union Theological Seminary, 1958; studied with Nadia Boulanger, Robert Baker, and Elaine Brown. Music director, White Plains, N.Y., 1958-65; music editor and manager in publishing firms, 1965-71; president of McAfee Music Corporation since 1971.

ABD, CACA, OL, OL95.

No bibliographical information located.

Robert McBride

B. Tucson, Ariz., 20 February 1911. Played clarinet, saxophone, organ and piano; studied music theory at the University of Arizona, B.M., 1933, and M.M., 1935. Oboist, Tucson Symphony Orchestra, 1928-35; taught wind instruments at Bennington College (Vt.), 1935-46; music arranger for Triumph Films, New York, 1946-57; music faculty member of University of Arizona, 1957-78. Guggenheim fellowship, 1937; American Academy of Arts and Letters, 1942; Composers' Press award,1943.

ABD, ACA, AMH, BB58, BB78, BB92, BBCch, BDA, BMI, CA9, CACA, CPM, DCM, EVM, GD54, HHH, KTL, LMD, MHHH, NG, NGA, OL, OL95, PCM, PET, REM, TCAC, X51, X56, X57, X62, X69.

"The Composer Speaks." *Music Clubs Magazine* 39 (November 1959): 11.

> McBride questions the need to be "examining art under a microscope" and "Couldn't we just enjoy it or just hate it?"

"Four Composers Discuss Modern Music." *National Music Council Bulletin* 20 (fall 1959): 7-8.

> McBride questions the idea of analysis of music: Can't we just enjoy music? Or hate it?

Kyle, Marguerite K. "AmerAllegro." *Pan Pipes* 54/2 (1962): 62.

> McBride is awarded the University of Arizona's 75th Anniversary Medallion of Merit, 13 December 1960.

McKelvey, Nat. "Practical Music-Maker: Robert McBride." *American Composers Alliance Bulletin* 8/1 (1958): 7-13.

> An essay on the diverse compositions of McBride; list of works accompanies the piece.

"Robert McBride." *Composers of the Americas* 9 (1963): 90-99.

> A brief biography in Spanish and English is followed by an annotated catalog of his works.

Charles R. McHugh

B. Minneapolis, Minn., 5 August 1940. B.A., 1963, M.A., 1967, and Ph.D., 1970, from the University of Minnesota. Studied with Dominick Argento and Paul Fetler. Won first prize, 1968, in the University of Minnesota contest for composition. On the University of Minnesota faculty, 1965-70; Minnesota Metropolitan State College, since 1973. Co-editor of *Synthesis*, an electronic music magazine, 1970-71. His dissertation is "Symphony No. 2" (*Dissertation Abstracts* 32 [August 1971]: 1001A-02A).

ABD, CACA, OL, OL95.

No bibliographical information located.

Isa Roberta McIlwraith

B. Paterson, N.J., 17 May 1909. B.A., Barnard College; studied with Philip James, Daniel Gregory Mason, and Douglas Moore, M.A., Columbia University; with Seth Bingham at Union Theological Seminary; and with Albert Stoessel at Juilliard. Received fellowships at Columbia University and Juilliard. Organist, Brooklyn and New York, 1932-38; on faculty of Mt. Holyoke College, 1937-38; University of Tennessee, 1938-75.

CACA.

No bibliographical information located.

Mathilde McKinney

B. South Bend, Ind., 31 January 1904. Studied at Oberlin College and the Juilliard School of Music. Piano study with Lee Pattison and Josef and Rosina Lhevinne. Taught at the College of Wooster (Ohio) and Douglass College; private teacher in Pittsburgh, Oklahoma, New York, and Princeton, N.J. On faculty at Westminster Choir College, 1960-70.
ABD, BB78, CACA, IWC, OL95, WCH.

"Mathilde McKinney's Activities." *Musical Courier* 144 (July 1951): 21.
> A recitation of McKinney's activities as lecturer, composer, teacher, and pianist.

Marian McLaughlin

(Mrs. Thomas R. Ostrom.) B. Evanston, Ill., 26 November 1923; d. January 1982. B.M.E., Northwestern University; M.M. in composition, New England Conservatory. Clarinet study with Robert Lindeman of Chicago Symphony Orchestra; composition with Albert Noelte, Carl McKinley, Frances Judd Cooke, and Walter Piston. Taught theory and woodwind instruments at Evansville College (Ind.); first clarinet, Evansville Philharmonic Orchestra. Teaching fellowship in theory, New England Conservatory, 1947-48. Her *Three Fantasies* won the AGO Prize for composition, 1968.
ABD, CACA, IWC, WCH.

Kyle, Marguerite K. "AmerAllegro." *Pan Pipes* 61/2 (1969): 67.
> *Three Fantasies for Organ* was premiered by Nancy Reed, 2 June 1968, at Trinity Methodist Church, Alexandria, Va. It won first prize in the AGO composition competition.

Clarence V. Mader

B. Easton, Penn., 23 January 1904; d. Laguna Hills, Calif., 7 July 1971. By age eleven, he was organist in churches: St. Peter's Reformed Church, Easton, 1915; St. John's Lutheran Church, Easton; Holliston Ave. Methodist Church, Pasadena. Studied with Lynwood Farnam, New York, 1926; organist, Wilshire Presbyterian Church (formerly

Immanuel Presbyterian Church), Los Angeles, 1929-66; taught at Orange Coast College, Costa Mesa, Calif.; and at Occidental College, 1955-68.

ABD, AMG, CACA, DN70, OL, OL95, X54, X62, X70, X71, X74.

"Clarence Mader." *Diapason* 55 (April 1964): 49.

> Mader is honored on March 1 at ceremonies observing his 35th anniversary as organist of Immanuel Presbyterian Church, Los Angeles.

"Clarence Mader." *American Organist* 49 (March 1966): 22.

> Notice of Mader's retirement 16 January 1966 as organist of Immanuel Presbyterian Church, Los Angeles; he received the honorary title Organist Emeritus. Mader continues to teach privately and at Occidental College.

"Clarence Mader." *Diapason* 57 (March 1966): 3.

> Announcement of Mader's retirement from his post as organist of Immanuel Presbyterian Church, Los Angeles. He continues, however, his responsibility of teaching at Occidental College.

"Clarence Mader, Granted Leave on 30th Anniversary." *Diapason* 50 (June 1959): 1.

> Mader's leave provides him time for travel, study, and research in Europe.

Murray, Thomas. "Remembering Clarence Mader." *Music* (AGO) 5 (November 1971): 33.

> A tribute to the memory of Clarence Mader.

[Obituary.] *Diapason* 62 (August 1971): 8.

> The obituary notice provides a complete look at Mader's musical career.

Ochse, Orpha. "Mader Day at UCLA." *American Organist* 14 (August 1980): 41.

> On 27 April 1980, the dedication of the Clarence V. Mader Archive at the University of California, Los Angeles, occurred. The dedication was in three main sections: performances of representative compositions by Mader; the dedication of the Archive; and the premiere performance of a work for organ, Gordon Schuster's *Sonata for Organ*, played by Cherry Rhodes.

"Presenting Clarence Mader." *Music Ministry* 2 (June 1961): 9.

> A brief introduction to Mader; lists his current positions and his renown students.

"St. Bartholomew's Church." *American Organist* 39 (August 1956): 264.

> Mader's recital at the National AGO Convention is reviewed. He performed his own *Portrait Cycle* in addition to other contemporary works by composers Raphael, Micheelson, and Vaughan. Reviewer wished for "music more agreeable to listen to."

Tusler, Robert L. "Concerto—Dedication of the Clarence V. Mader Archive at the University of California, Los Angeles." *Diapason* 71 (September 1980): 10-11.

A thorough review of Mader's life and career, and an insight into the collection made available through the generous gift of the Mader family, the Clarence V. Mader Archive at the UCLA Music Library.

August Maekelberghe

B. Oostende, Belgium, 15 January 1909; d. Mt. Clemens, Mich., 8 August 1975. Studied at Notre Dame College, Oostende, and at the Royal Conservatory of Music, Ghent. Organ pupil of Leandre Villain. Emigrated to the U.S., 1930; accompanist for Father Leo DeGreeter; organist, Dominican Church, Detroit, Mich.; organist, St. Peter's Church, Mt. Clemens; organist, St. Vincent de Paul, Pontiac, Mich.; staff organist, radio station WWJ. M.M., Institute of Musical Arts, Detroit, 1941; FAGO, 1941. Organist, Church of the Messiah, Detroit, 1940-45; organist, St. John's Episcopal Church, Detroit, 1945-74.

ABD, AS66, CACA, OL, OL95, X56, X65, X66.

Bingham, Seth. "Maekelberghe Plays in New York." *Diapason* 46 (January 1955): 22.

The reviewer gave Maekelberghe high marks for his recital at St. Paul's Chapel, Columbia University, 30 November 1954.

"Flandria, for Organ." *Musical Courier* 154 (August 1956): 29.

Published by H. W. Gray, the reviewer indicates Maekelberghe's work, *Flandria*, is an important contribution to the concert organist's repertory. Brief overview of the work is given.

Gay, Harry. "Prelude Recital." *American Organist* 43 (August 1960): 20-21.

Playing at Christ Church Cranbrook, Bloomfield Hills, Mich., Maekelberghe's recital is given a banal review.

McDonald, Kent. "Recitals and Concerts." *American Organist* 43 (August 1960): 26.

St. John's Episcopal Church, Detroit, is the setting for Maekelberghe's recital, 25 March 1960. The reviewer lauded his playing, especially of the Weitz *Symphony for Organ*.

"Maekelberghe Broadcasts from Detroit to Europe." *Diapason* 46 (November 1955): 7.

On October 1, in what may have possibly been the first instance of an American organ recital being broadcast over a European network, Maekelberghe performed at the console of St. John's Episcopal Church, Detroit. Another recital on Christmas Eve will be broadcast by him.

"Maekelberghe in New York." *Diapason* 41 (March 1950): 10.

Riverside Church was the scene for Maekelberghe's recital on 12 February 1950. He opened the second half of his recital with his new work, *Theme and Variations*, which the reporter considered to be a "craftsman's work."

"Maekelberghe Is Praised by Newspapers in Detroit." *Diapason* 43 (May 1952): 33.

Reviewers applaud Maekelberghe's performances; several quotes are included in the article.

[Obituary.] *Diapason* 66 (September 1975): 10.

The obituary includes information about his music career, and his radio-announcer posts.

Paul O. Manz

B. Cleveland, Ohio, 10 May 1919. Graduated from college in 1941. Music director, Winnebago, Wisc., Lutheran High School and St. Peter's Lutheran Elementary School; principal for the grade school and music director of Emmanuel Lutheran Church, West St. Paul, 1943; director of Christian education and music, Mt. Olive Lutheran, Minneapolis, 1946. M.M. in organ and composition, Northwestern University, 1955; received a Fulbright to study with Flor Peeters and Helmut Walcha; first prize "with highest distinction" in organ and improvisation at the Royal Conservatory in Antwerp. On faculty, Concordia College, St. Paul, 1957-76; organ instructor, Macalester College, St. Paul, 1949-54; resigned from Concordia College in 1976 to become full-time musician at Mt. Olive Lutheran Church.
ABD, CACA, OL, OL95.

Gebauer, Victor. "Composers for the Church: Paul Manz." *Church Music* (St. Louis) (1979): 31-48.

A very detailed look at Manz's life: as a performing composer, his background, musical influences, choral works, organ works, a list of his music and recordings, and charts of composition categories employed in his *Ten Chorale Improvisations*, Sets I-VII.

"Here and There." *Diapason* 81 (December 1990): 3.

Manz was one of four recipients of the Gutenberg Award from the Chicago Bible Society at the society's 150th anniversary celebration on October 23. The award is presented to an individual who works to spread the good news of the Bible in the community.

Lodine, Robert. "Recitals and Concerts." *American Organist* 46 (May 1963): 5.

Manz performed a dedicatory recital on the Schlicker organ at the Evangelical Lutheran Church of St. Luke, 20 January 1963, playing three of his chorale preludes, which were favorably reviewed.

"Paul Manz." *Diapason* 57 (July 1966): 2.

> Manz was awarded the degree Doctor of Letters by the faculty of Concordia Teachers College, Seward, Neb., on the occasion of the dedication of the new fine arts facilities on the campus, 1 May 1966.

"Paul Manz Accepts Call to Faculty of Christ Seminary-Seminex." *Journal of Church Music* 25 (September 1983): 18.

> Manz establishes a music program at the Lutheran School of Theology, Chicago, and serves also as organist and artist-in-residence; he will work as cantor at the Evangelical Lutheran Church of St. Luke.

"Paul Manz Honored by Northwestern University." *Journal of Church Music* 29 (September 1987): 29.

> Manz is awarded Northwestern University's 1987 Merit Award from the School of Music on April 4.

"Paul Manz to Study with Flor Peeters in Belgium." *Diapason* 46 (September 1955): 26.

> A Fulbright award provides Manz the means to study with Peeters in Belgium. His primary areas of concentration will be organ and improvisation.

Pine, Carol, and Susan Mundale. "AGO National Convention." *American Organist* 14 (March 1980): 29.

> Manz to lead a workshop on hymn improvisation; focus on accompanying at the organ and improvising chorale preludes will occur in a workshop of personal demonstration and participation.

"Portrait." *Response* 17/1 (1977): 1.

> A photograph of Manz is accompanied by a dedication, that this issue of *Response* is dedicated to Manz for his service to the church and to his students.

"Profiles." *Sacred Music* 103/2 (1976): 42.

> Manz is profiled as the new reviewer of organ music for *Sacred Music*; career summary.

Ada Belle Gross Marcus

B. Chicago, 8 July 1929. Studied piano with Sergei Tarnowsky and theory and composition with Samuel Lieberson, on a five-year scholarship to De Paul University, graduating in 1944. Composition with Leo Sowerby, American Conservatory of Music and with Karel

B. Jirak, Chicago College of Music, Roosevelt University, 1954-59; electronic music with Alexander Tcherepnin until 1961, and Philip Winsor until 1974, De Paul University; and conducting with Milton Preves of the Chicago Symphony Orchestra. Concert pianist from 1942; piano teacher since 1959. Member of ASCAP.

ABD, CACA, IWC, IWW92, WCH.

"Here and There." *Diapason* 79 (September 1988): 6.

> *Highlights Suite* received its premiere by organist Emma Lou Diemer on June 27, for a joint centennial celebration of the National Council of Women of the United States, Inc., and the International Council of Women, Kennedy Center, Washington, D.C. *Toccata* for organ solo, performed by Sally Saley at Immaculate Heart of Mary Church, Chicago, was premiered 9 February 1986.

"New Nuggets." *International Musician* 71 (December 1972): 12.

> Marcus is listed in the 8th edition of *Who's Who of American Women.*

Henry J. Markworth

B. St. Joseph, Mich., 1900; d. Cleveland, Ohio, 1 December 1953. Graduated from Concordia Seminary, River Forest, Ill., 1921; taught at Trinity School in Cleveland. Music study with Edwin Arthur Kraft. Organist for 32 years, Trinity Evangelical Lutheran Church, Cleveland.

OL, OL95, and the article below.

"Henry Markworth, 32 Years at Cleveland Church, Dies." *Diapason* 45 (January 1954): 6.

> Markworth's death on 1 December 1953 is announced; biographical information included.

Gilbert Martin

B. Southbridge, Mass., 6 January 1941. Studied composition with James Waters and Warren Martin, Westminster Choir College, Princeton, N.J. Music director, Presbyterian Church, Dayton, Ohio; music director, United Methodist Church, Kettering, Ohio.

ABD, CACA, OL, OL95.

"Gilbert M. Martin Wins AGO Competition in Choral Composition." *American Organist*
18 (December 1984): 52.

> Martin wins the first AGO choral composition competition with his work *Let There Be Light!*
> Biographical information included.

Thomas Matthews

B. Utica, N.Y., 1 April 1915. Studied with Norman Coke-Jephcott, New York. Received
the Pi Kappa Lambda award. Honorary Doctor of Music degree, 1955, from Ripon
College (Wisc.). Posts: music staff, Cathedral of St. John the Divine, New York; organist-
choirmaster, St. Martin's-in-the-Fields, Philadelphia; director of music, Seabury-Western
Seminary, Northwestern University; organist, St. Luke's Episcopal Church, Evanston,
Ill.; and organist-choir director, Trinity Episcopal Church, Tulsa, Okla. On faculty,
University of Tulsa, since 1960.

ABD, CACA, OL, OL95.

Swann, Fred. "Thomas Matthews at 75." *American Organist* 24 (September 1990): 70-71.

> Matthews's life is reviewed in thanksgiving for all he has done, for his students and those
> he has served. A list of choral works is included.

"Thomas Matthews." *Pan Pipes* 43 (December 1950): 125. *

"Thomas Matthews." *Pan Pipes* 45 (January 1953): 61. *

"Thomas Matthews." *Diapason* 51 (May 1960): 3.

> Matthews resigns his post on the faculty of Northwestern University and as choirmaster and
> organist of St. Luke's Episcopal Church, Evanston, Ill., to assume his new duties as organist-
> choir director of Trinity Episcopal Church, Tulsa, Okla.; provides some background data.

"Thomas Matthews." *Diapason* 57 (May 1966): 7.

> Matthews will join the University of Tulsa faculty, June 1, as assistant professor of organ
> and theory.

"Thomas Matthews Becomes Assistant Professor at NU." *Diapason* 46 (November 1955): 1.

> Matthews is promoted from associate to assistant professor at the Northwestern University
> Music School.

Claude Means

B. Cincinnati, Ohio, 12 May 1912. Organ study with Karl O. Staps and David McK. Williams; theory with Frank Wright and Norman Coke-Jephcott. Served in the U.S. Army from October 1942-March 1946; appointed organist-director of Christ Church, Greenwich, Conn., 1934-72.

ABD, CACA, OL, OL95.

"Claude Means." *American Organist* 33 (February 1950): 72.

> An introduction to the composer. A list of compositions is provided.

"Claude Means." *Diapason* 55 (May 1964): 4.

> Means was honored April 30 at a celebration observing his 30 years as organist and choirmaster of Christ Episcopal Church, Greenwich.

"Claude Means Is Honored on Silver Anniversary." *Diapason* 51 (December 1959): 3.

> Means was honored October 18 on the occasion of his 25th anniversary as organist and choirmaster of Christ Episcopal Church, Greenwich.

James Melby

B. Fargo, N.D., 11 May 1947. B.M., St. Olaf College, 1971; studied composition with David N. Johnson and Paul Fetler, University of Minnesota. Director of music, First Lutheran Church, Albert Lea, Minn., 1969-72; director of music, Lake Harriet United Methodist Church, Minneapolis, 1972-85; organist and choirmaster, St. Paul's Episcopal Church, Milwaukee, Wisc., since 1985.

OL, OL95.

No bibliographical information located.

Gian-Carlo Menotti

B. Cadegliano, Italy, 7 July 1911. Studied at Milan Conservatory, 1924-27; Curtis Institute, 1927-33, with Rosario Scalero. Music director of Cornell Symphony Orchestra, 1957-75,

Cayhuga Chamber Orchestra, 1977-84. Received the Pulitzer Prize for his opera *The Consul*, 1950, and *The Saint of Bleecker Street*, 1955. Organized the Festival of Two Worlds (Spoleto, Italy and Charleston, S.C.), 1958.

ABD, AMH, BB78, BB92, BBCch, BDA, CACA, DCM, HLM, KTL, MLSR, NG, OL95, X50, X51, X52, X54, X55, X56, X57, X58, X59, X60, X61, X62, X69, X70, X71, X74.

"Appointments." *Opera* 44 (February 1993): 157.
  Menotti is the new artistic director of the Teatro dell' Opera, Rome.

Ardoin, John. *The Stages of Menotti.* Garden City, N.Y.: Doubleday, 1985.
  Includes bibliography and discography.

Belt, Byron. **"AGO National Convention, San Francisco 1984."** *American Organist* 18 (August 1984): 28-33.
  Menotti's *Ricercare for Organ* is presented by John Weaver, and is dedicated to Fred Tulan.

Gruen, John. *Menotti: A Biography.* New York: Macmillan, 1978.
  Includes bibliographical information.

Gustafson, Bruce. **"AGO San Francisco: Some Perspectives."** *Diapason* 75 (October 1984): 6, 8-9.
  Gustafson pronounces Menotti's *Ricercare for Organ* "unpretentiously pretty."

Ryan, Sylvia Watkins. **"The Solo Piano Music of Gian-Carlo Menotti: A Pedagogical and Performance Analysis."** D.M.A., University of Oklahoma, 1993. *Dissertation Abstracts* 54 (September 1993): 730A.
  A biographical sketch of Menotti, including an overview of his operatic, concert, keyboard, and literary works. Although this work concentrates on piano music, the keyboard aspect will be of interest to organists. Provides a list of Menotti's operatic, concert, keyboard, and literary works.

Daniel Moe

B. Minot, N.D., 2 November 1926. Studied with Paul Christiansen, Concordia College, Moorhead, Minn.; with Russell Harris, Hamline University; with George McKay and John Verrall, University of Washington; with Darius Milhaud, Aspen School; Karl F. Miller, Hannover, Germany; Ph.D., with Philip Bezanson, University of Iowa. First prize,

Seattle Centennial Composition contest. Received a Danforth Foundation grant. Choral director, University of Denver, 1953-59; University of Iowa, 1961-72; and Oberlin Conservatory of Music, 1972-92; artistic and music director of Tampa's Master Chorale, since 1992. Authored *Problems in Conducting* (Minneapolis: Augsburg, 1968) and *Basic Choral Concepts* (Minneapolis: Augsburg, 1972).

ABD, CACA, OL, OL95, X71, X74.

"Appointments." *American Organist* 28 (October 1994): 48.
> Moe is named conductor of the Concordia Choir, Concordia College, Moorhead, Minn., during the one-year sabbatical leave of René Clausen.

"Daniel Moe Named New Artistic and Music Director." *Voice of Chorus America* 15/4 (1992): 20.
> Moe is named artistic and music director of Tampa's Master Chorale.

"Daniel T. Moe Awarded the Canticum Novum Award." *Diapason* 65 (April 1974): 13.
> Moe is awarded Wittenberg University School of Music's highest honor. A list of his accomplishments at the university is summarized.

Kyle, Marguerite K. "AmerAllegro." *Pan Pipes* 50 (January 1958): 64.
> *Three Preludes for Organ* is premiered by John Moseley at St. John's Cathedral, Denver, in 1957.

54/2 (1962): 63.
> Moe is currently director of choral music at the State University of Iowa.

Robert W. Moevs

B. La Crosse, Wisc., 2 December 1920. Studied with Piston at Harvard, A.B., 1942; with Boulanger at Paris Conservatory, 1947-51; A.M., Harvard, 1952. From 1952-55, he was a Rome Prize Fellow in music at the American Academy in Rome; received a Guggenheim fellowship, 1963-64; taught at Harvard, 1955-63; composer-in-residence, 1964, at Rutgers University, where he was later professor, from 1968, and chair of the music department at its New Brunswick campus, 1974-81. He also performs as a pianist, often playing his own works. In 1978, he was awarded the Stockhausen International Prize for his *Concerto Grosso for Piano, Percussion, and Orchestra*. Received numerous ASCAP awards; inducted into the National Institute of Arts and Letters, 1956.

AA73, ABD, AMH, ASUC, BB65, BB71, BB78, BB92, CACA, CACJ, CRI 136, DCM, IWW92, KTL, LMD, NG, NGA, OL, OL95, PC71, PCM, X55, X56, X61, X65, X66, X67, X68, X69, X70, X71, X74.

"American Composer Update." *Pan Pipes* 73/2 (1980): 37.

Moevs is recipient of the Naumburg Award; he is commissioned by David Drinkwater to compose an organ postlude.

Archibald, Bruce. "Composers of Importance Today: Robert Moevs." *Music News* 2 (April 1971): 19-21.

A general introduction to Moevs's music; stresses the sense of tradition and the emotional power of his avant-garde style. Discography and selective list of published works is included.

Boros, James. "A Conversation with Robert Moevs." *Perspectives of New Music* 28/1 (1990): 324-35.

An in-depth look at the influences on Robert Moevs's music: especially Stravinsky, Piston, and Boulanger. He coined the phrase "systematic chromaticism"; a discussion of what that really means.

_____. "The Evolution of Robert Moevs's Compositional Methodology." *American Music* 8/4 (1990): 383-404.

"The characteristics of Moevs's mature works are three-fold: in general, they tend to begin with the exposition of basic, germinal material which are subsequently subjected to various developmental processes; they manifest a concern with the integrity of the interval, rather than successions of pitch classes; and they illustrate the necessity felt by Moevs for chromatic completion." The article reviews the evolution of these "preoccupations" by dividing his compositional time into four periods: a period of questing, the 1950s; a period of technical formalization, the early 1960s; a period of further expansion of the sound-world, the late 1960s; and in the 1970s, concentration on the "integrity of the interval."

_____. "The Systematic Chromaticism of Robert Moevs." *Perspectives of New Music* 28/1 (1990): 294-322.

How Moevs handles musical materials: "A modification of serial technique in which a pitch collection is systematically exhausted but not in a rigidly ordered way." Boros examines solo instrumental and chamber works, provides a chronological list of Moevs's works, a discography, and a bibliography.

Kyle, Marguerite K. "AmerAllegro." *Pan Pipes* 50 (January 1958): 64.

Moevs is named assistant professor of music at Harvard.

55/2 (1963): 62.

Guggenheim fellowship recipient.

63/2 (1971): 71.

Organist David Drinkwater, who commissioned the work, performed the premiere of Moevs's *B-A-C-H—Es ist genug* in May at Rutgers University, New Brunswick, N.J.

65/2 (1974): 63.

Moevs publishes an arrangement of Bach's *Est ist genug*, for organ.

66/2 (1974): 64.

Belwyn-Mills publishes *Es ist genug*.

67/2 (1975): 65.

Moevs is chairman of the Douglass College department of music, New Brunswick; he is commissioned to write a bicentennial work for double choir and two organs.

69/2 (1977): 60.

In May 1976, the commissioned work for the bicentennial, *The Aulos Player*, is premiered at Douglass College, New Brunswick. In October, *Interludium and Postludium*, for organ, was premiered by David Drinkwater at Voorhees Chapel, Rutgers.

70/2 (1978): 54.

Moevs is now chairman of Douglass College's department of music and graduate director, New Brunswick.

Carman LeRoy Moore

B. Lorain, Ohio, 8 October 1936. Studied horn with Martin Morris, cello with Peter Brown, and conducting with Cecil Isaacs at Oberlin; further studies at Ohio State, B.M., 1958; went to New York, where he studied at the Juilliard School with Vincent Persichetti and Luciano Berio, B.M., 1966; completed his studies with Stefan Wolpe in 1967. Helped launch the Society of Black Composers, 1968; taught at Manhattanville College, 1969-71, and Brooklyn College of the City University of New York, 1972-74. Presented concerts with his own group, Carman Moore and Ensemble, which he transformed into the Skymusic Ensemble in 1985. In addition to writing music criticism, he published a biography of Bessie Smith, *Somebody's Angel Child* (New York: Crowell, 1970); and a text on teaching popular music, *The Growth of Black Sound in America* (unpublished, 1980).

ABD, AFR, BB78, BB92, CACA, IWW92, NGA, OL, OL95.

Gann, K. "Music: A Neat Little House." *Village Voice* 33 (17 May 1988): 92.

Moore is praised for his tightly-written music, written to gratify the ear rather than mandates and theories. Gann said, "If more [people] wrote like him, the market for dead people's music would collapse."

Southern, Eileen. **"America's Black Composers of Classical Music."** *Music Educators Journal* 62 (November 1975): 46-59.

An overview of black composers in the twentieth century includes Carman Moore.

"Southern Music Publishing Company, Inc. Signs Carman L. Moore." *Wood World Brass* 16/6 (1977): 7.

Moore signs an exclusive publishing agreement with Southern Music; he is co-founder of the Society of Black Composers and has taught music at Brooklyn and Queens College, in addition to Yale University.

Tischler, Alice, and Carol Tomasic. *Fifteen Black American Composers: A Bibliography of Their Works.* Detroit: Information Coordinators, 1981.

Moore and his works are included in this bibliography.

Robert Daniel Morris

B. Chettenham, England, 19 October 1943, of American parents. Studied with LaMontaine and Rogers at Eastman, B.M., 1965; Ross Lee Finney, Leslie Bassett, and Eugene Kurtz at the University of Michigan, M.M., 1966, and D.M.A., 1969. Instructor, University of Hawaii, Honolulu, 1968-69; since 1969, assistant professor and later associate professor of composition, since 1972, director of the electronic music studio, 1973-76, chariman of the composition division, Yale University School of Music. Studied with Gunther Schuller at Tanglewood on a Crofts fellowship, 1967; BMI award, 1968; A. W. Griswold grant, 1975; NEA grant, 1978. In 1976 he left Yale for the University of Pittsburgh. Authored *Composition with Pitch-Classes: A Theory of Compositional Design* (New Haven: Yale University Press, 1987) and his dissertation is titled "Continua for Orchestra" (*Dissertation Abstracts* 31 [October 1970]: 1834A).

ABD, CACA, CACJ, OL, OL95.

Cohn, Richard. **"Properties and Generability of Transpositionally Invariant Sets."** *Journal of Music Theory* 35/1-2 (1991): 1-32.

Morris and Daniel Starr work on the generability of transpositional invariance collections from combinations of transposition cycles or interval cycles; a view of Morris's approach to composition.

Dembski, S. **"The Context of Composition: The Reception of Robert Morris' *Theory of Compositional Design*."** *Theory and Practice* 14-15 (1989-90): 187 + . *

Shirley Munger

B. Everett, Wash., 1925. B.A., 1946, M.A., 1951, University of Washington, with George F. McKay and John Verrall; D.M.A., 1963, University of Southern California, with Halsey Stevens and Ingolf Dahl. Fulbright grant, 1952-53, to study piano at Paris Conservatory. Associate professor, piano and theory, University of California, Santa Barbara, 1954-60; University of Minnesota, Duluth, 1963-68; professor of theory, West Chester University, since 1968; now emeritus. Member of ASCAP.

ABD, CACA, CACJ, IWC, WCH.

"Contest Judge Selections Made: Music Education Award." *Triangle* 70/2 (1976): 6-7.
> Munger serves as one of three judges for the Madge C. Gerke Music Education Award. Biographical notes are furnished.

"March Humoresque, for Organ." *Musical Courier* 154 (August 1956): 29.
> Galaxy Music publishes Munger's *March Humoresque*; a brief overview of the work is given; review states the work is suitable for recital use.

Gerald Near

B. St. Paul, Minn., 23 May 1942. Organ pupil of Rupert Sircom, Gerald Bales, and Robert Glasgow. M.M., University of Michigan; composition with Bales, Leo Sowerby, and Leslie Bassett; conducting with Gustav Meier; church music with Allan Wickes, Canterbury Cathedral. Served as organist in Illinois, Michigan, and Minnesota. Director of music, Calvary Church, Rochester, Minn.; since 1973, organist-choirmaster, Zumbro Lutheran Church, Rochester, Minn. Was on the faculty of Carleton College, Northfield, Minn.

ABD, CACA, OL, OL95, X69.

Bollinger, Edward T. "Denver." *Diapason* 56 (September 1965): 20.
> Marilyn Mason and Kathryn Eskey gave the world premiere of Near's *Concertino for Two Organs* at the Denver Convention, July 15-17.

"A Capital Convention! Washington, D.C., June 28-July 2, 1982." *American Organist* 16 (May 1982): 4-5.
> An introduction to Near and an overview of his two choral pieces commissioned for the convention.

"Concert Event." *American Organist* 16 (April 1982): 123.

A brief introduction to the composer.

Vaclav Nelhybel

B. Polanka, Czechoslovakia, 24 September 1919; d. Scranton, Penn., 22 March 1996. Studied composition and conducting with Ridký at the Conservatory, Prague, 1938-42; musicological studies at Prague University, 1938-42; medieval and Renaissance music studies at Fribourg University, Switzerland, 1942. Worked for the Swiss National Radio, 1947-50; music director of Radio Free Europe, 1950-57. Emigrated in 1957 to the U.S., and became a citizen in 1962. Organist, Church of St. Elizabeth of Hungary, N.Y., 1962-69. Honorary doctorate from Lebanon Valley College (Penn.) and Ohio Northern University. Guest lecturer and conductor at numerous universities. On the advisory board for Blue Lake Fine Arts Camp, Twin Lake, Mich. Retired to Newton, Conn., but was composer-in-residence at the University of Scranton when he died.

ABD, BB71, BB78, BB92, BBCch, CACA, IMD, KTL, NG, NGA, OL, OL95, X60, X66, X67, X68, X69, X70.

Blahnik, J. **"Vaclav Nelhybel: The Man and His Music."** *Music News from Prague* 7/8 (1992): 2-5. *

Blake, A. **"American Classical Releases."** *Metro* 78 (June 1961): 26. *

Boonshaft, Peter Loel. **"Vaclav Nelhybel: A Biographical Study and Survey of His Compositions with an Analysis for Performance of *Caucasian Passacaglia*."** D.M.A., University of Hartford, 1991. *Dissertation Abstracts* 53 (July 1992): 94A.

Included is a detailed biography about Nelhybel's early years and development, years before and during World War II, his conducting and composition career, his emigration to the United States, influence on his writing style, and his philosophy of composition. A catalog of compositions and a bibliography are also provided.

Knapp, Joel Davis. **"Vaclav Nelhybel: His Life, Influences on His Compositional Style, and a Review of His Published Choral Compositions."** D.M.A., University of Missouri-Kansas City, 1991. *Dissertation Abstracts* 52 (October 1991): 1125A.

Influences of gypsy music, Gregorian chant, and Nelhybel's own private study are important to his works. Brief biography. Review of Nelhybel's choral works.

"Meet the Composer: Vaclav Nelhybel." *Instrumentalist* 36 (July 1982): 19-20.

Nelhybel discusses his first writing experiences and how he writes now—without the assistance of a piano. He prefers to use modal scales and chant.

"Tomanek Plays New Works Written for Solemn Rite." *Diapason* 51 (May 1960): 38.

Nelhybel composed *Intrata pontificalis, Chorale & Ad multos annos* for the consecration and installation of Bishop Vincent J. Hines. The work was performed by a brass quartet from the Hartford Symphony and organist Godfrey Tomanek, the cathedral organist at St. Patrick's Cathedral, Norwich, Conn., where the premiere occurred.

Dika Newlin

B. Portland, Oreg., 22 November 1923. B.A., Michigan State University, 1939; studied composition privately under Roger Sessions and Arnold Schoenberg, 1938-41. M.A., University of California, Los Angeles, 1941; in 1945, she was awarded the first Ph.D. in musicology by Columbia University. Piano studies were with Ignace Hilsberg, Rudolf Serkin, and Artur Schnabel. Fulbright fellowship to Vienna, 1951-52. Taught at Western Maryland College, 1945-49, and Syracuse University, 1949-51; professor and chair of music department, Drew University, Madison, Wisc., 1952-65; North Texas State University, Denton, 1965-73; 1973-78, taught at Montclair State College, N.J.; in 1978, she was appointed professor at Virginia Commonwealth University, Richmond, where she was asked to develop a doctoral program in music. Yaddo Fellowship, 1960-66. Authored *Self-Revelation and the Law: Arnold Schoenberg in His Religious Work*, Studies of the Jewish Music Research Center (Jerusalem: Magnes Press, 1968); *Bruckner, Mahler, Schoenberg* (New York, 1947; rev. ed., New York: Norton, 1978); *The Schoenberg Diaries* (New York: Pendragon, 1978); *Schoenberg Remembered: Diaries and Recollections, 1938-76* (New York: Pendragon, 1980). Translated René Leibowitz's *Schoenberg and His School* (New York: Philosophical, 1949); Josef Rufer's *The Works of Arnold Schoenberg* (London and New York: Faber & Faber, 1962); Arnold Schoenberg's *Style and Idea* (New York & Toronto, 1950); and Eric Werner's *Felix Mendelssohn* (London and New York: Faber & Faber, 1963).

AA73, ABD, ACA X 4, BB58, BB78, BB92, BBCch, CACA, CACJ, DAS, IMD, IWC, IWW92, KTL, LMD, MHHH, NG, NGA, TCAC, WCH, X56, X60, X62, X64, X65, X66, X67, X68, X69, X70, X71, X74.

"Dika Newlin." *Pan Pipes* 45 (January 1953): 62. *

"Dika Newlin Joins Pan Pipes Staff." *Pan Pipes* 73/1 (1980): 7.

A brief biography accompanies the announcement that Newlin will be editor of the books column.

"Dika Newlin Receives Mahler Medal." *Pan Pipes* 50 (March 1958): 7 + . *

Kyle, Marguerite K. "AmerAllegro." *Pan Pipes* 51 (January 1959): 76-77.

Announcement that Newlin's biography will appear in the revised edition of *Directory of American Scholars, Baker's Biographical Dictionary*, and in the newly-planned *Who's Who of American Women*.

53/2 (1961): 69.

The translation of Josef Rufer's book *Das Werk A. Schönbergs* (London: Faber & Faber, 1961) is to be released.

57/2 (1965): 72-73.

Honorary Doctor of Humane Letters given to Newlin from Upsala College, East Orange, N.J.

58/2 (1966): 77-78.

Newlin is appointed professor of musicology, North Texas State University, Denton, Tex.

64/2 (1972): 72.

Elected president of the American Musicological Society, Southwest Chapter, for 1971-73; received a faculty research grant from North Texas State for creative work in multi-media composition.

66/2 (1974): 65.

Newlin is made chairman of the Electronic Music Studio, Montclair State College (N.J.), effective September 1.

70/2 (1978): 54-55.

Newlin joined the faculty of the New School for Social Research in New York, to teach music criticism and other topics; her book *Bruckner-Mahler-Schoenberg* is revised and enlarged (New York: Norton, 1978); Pendragon published *The Schoenberg Diaries*, 1978; her translation of Bauer-Lechner's *Recollections of Gustav Mahler* is released by Faber & Faber, with additional material by Donald Mitchell.

71/2 (1979): 40.

Announcement that Newlin's music is published by American Composers Alliance; in August, she became professor of music at Virginia Commonwealth University, Richmond. Correction is made that the *Schoenberg Diaries* and *Recollections* will be published in the spring of 1979.

73/2 (1981): 37-38.

Newlin's *Schoenberg Remembered* was published by Pendragon, 1980; she works as a music critic for the *Richmond Times-Dispatch*.

"A Salute to Women Composers." *Pan Pipes* 67/2 (1975): 4.

A brief note about Newlin's activities in the past year.

Wolff, Konrad. "Dika Newlin." *American Composers Alliance* 10/4 (1962): 1-6.

> A thorough examination of Newlin's compositional procedures, influences on her works, and a list of compositions is supplied; *Sonata da chiesa*, for organ, is discussed.

Anthony Newman

B. Los Angeles, Calif., 12 May 1941. Studied at the École Normale de Musique, Paris, diploma, 1960; B.S. in organ from Mannes School, New York, 1963; M.A., in composition, Harvard; D.M.A., Boston University. Taught organ, Juilliard, 1967-74; associate professor of organ and harpsichord, Dartmouth, 1973-74; associate professor of music history, Indiana University, 1979-82; associate professor of music history and composition, SUNY, Purchase, since 1983. Recipient of the Medaille d'Or from the French government, 1963; Cortot Award, Paris, 1963; a ten-time winner of the composition award from ASCAP, 1974-85. Authored *Bach and the Baroque: A Performing Guide to Baroque Music with Special Emphasis on the Music of Johann Sebastian Bach* (New York: Pendragon, 1985); ed. *Anthology of English Harpsichord Music* (New York: G. Schirmer, 1984).

ABD, BB92, CACA, IWW92, NGA, OL, OL95, TCH, WWAM-Cl, X67, X68, X70, X71, X74.

Brady, Owen. "Recitals and Concerts." *American Organist* 46 (November 1963): 5-6.

> Newman performs an all-Bach recital at St. Paul the Apostle Church, Westwood, Calif., 25 August 1963; a rave review.

Ferris, Timothy. "Anthony Newman, of Karma & Bach." *Rolling Stone* 89 (19 August 1971): 20.

> Newman talks about "leaping the gap" in interpreting music. Criticized for his performance practice approach to playing Bach, he feels that if you don't take the jump, the music and the playing will never be interesting.

"ICO, '67." *Diapason* 58 (October 1967): 34.

> Newman's recital was termed "a thoroughly unenjoyable recital . . . one comes to the grudging conclusion that this young man is ploughing ahead along a dangerous and musically unwholesome tangent. His attempts to overlay theories of French ornamentation on his Bach divided his audience between derision and shock; certainly no music was communicated." Even his own music, *Fantasie on La Fa Fis*, was panned; it was "both unnecessarily complex and consistently exhibitionist."

McDonald, Kent. **"Recitals and Concerts."** *American Organist* 46 (August 1963): 5.

Newman's performance, 23 June 1963, at St. Raymond's Roman Catholic Church, Detroit, was given an outstanding review.

Polkow, Dennis. **"Anthony Newman Comes of Age."** *Clavier* 27/2 (1988): 8-13.

Biographical information accompanies this interview with Newman. The discussion reveals interesting details about his interpretations, especially regarding his controversial fast tempos, original instrumentation, and religious influences.

"Premieres." *American Organist* 23 (March 1989): 50.

Newman's *Concert Etude* (largely for pedals) was premiered by Fred Tulan on 4 December 1988 at St. Paul's Cathedral, London.

"Recital, Boston." *American Organist* 48 (January 1965): 8.

Newman's recital on 19 November 1964 at King's Chapel, Boston, Mass., includes Bach, Hindemith, and Mozart. Reviewer praises Newman's imagination, desire to communicate, and his musicianship.

"Recital, Boston." *American Organist* 49 (February 1966): 7-8.

Newman plays a marathon of all-Bach recitals, King's Chapel, Boston, Mass. The organizational plan of his recitals is presented; and the recognition of a new performance practice is apparent to the reviewer who cites this.

"Recital, Newton, Mass." *American Organist* 49 (December 1966): 10-11.

Newman presents an all-Bach recital at Chapel of Newton College of the Sacred Heart, Newton, Mass., 19 October 1966. Reviewer is impressed with Newman's new approach to performance practices that allow the pieces to be heard anew.

"Recitals and Concerts." *American Organist* 51 (December 1968): 26.

Messiaen, Berio, and Newman compositions were played in Newman's performance at Methuen Memorial Music Hall, Methuen, Mass., 25 September 1968. Reviewer felt the program was "aurally offensive, and spiritually debasing and depressing."

Rimmer, Frederick. **"Adventurous Attitudes: Some Recent Organ Music."** *Organists Review* 60/241 (1976): 15.

Newman's work *Bhajebochstiannanas* is discussed as one of the new adventurous organ works by an American. Matthias Bamert's *Organism* and Richard Felciano's *Ekāgrata* are the other American works discussed and outlined; some Scandinavian, Polish, and British composers are also included.

Satz, Arthur. "Musician of the Month—Anthony Newman." *High Fidelity/Musical America* 22 (April 1972): MA4-5.

Newman's biography, with educational information, is presented; addresses Newman the man, artist, and composer.

Sly, Allan. "A New England Report." *American Organist* 48 (February 1965): 20-21.

Kudos for Newman, a young, gifted musician, who has played many recitals in recent months.

James Niblock

B. Scappoose, Oreg., 1 November 1917. Studied at Washington State University, B.A., 1942; Colorado College, M.A., 1948; University of Iowa, Ph.D., 1952. Professor of theory, composition, and music literature, Michigan State University, from 1948 until his retirement, 1992. Continues to reside in East Lansing, Mich. MacDowell fellow, 1960; NEA grant, 1978; and an All-University Research Grant, Michigan State University, 1982.

ABD, AS66, ASUC, CACA, CACJ, OL, OL95, PCM, WWAM-Cl, X62, X64, X65, X66, X67, X70.

Kyle, Marguerite K. "AmerAllegro." *Pan Pipes* 52/2 (1960): 63-64.

Niblock teaches theory and composition at Michigan State University; he is also violinist in a faculty string quartet.

56/2 (1964): 73.

Niblock is appointed head of the music department, Michigan State University, September 1.

Robert Noehren

B. Buffalo, N.Y., 16 December 1910. Studied with Gaston Dethier at Institute of Musical Art, New York, and Lynnwood Farnam at Curtis Institute of Music, 1930-31; B.Mus., University of Michigan, 1948, and D.Mus. (hon.), Davidson College, 1957. Taught at Davidson College (N.C.), 1946-49; professor of music and university organist, University of Michigan, 1949-77, then emeritus; now resides in San Diego. Researched 17-18th century European organs; organ builder, beginning 1954; important recordings, one of which was awarded the Grande Prix du Disque.

ABD, BB92, CACA, NG, NGA, OL, OL95, WWAM-Cl.

Angel, Clark B. "Organ and Choral Festival in Honor of the 90th Birthday of Albert Schweitzer." *American Organist* 48 (September 1965): 8-9.

Noehren's playing of an all-Bach recital is commended.

"Atlanta Plays Gracious Host to Its First National." *Diapason* 57 (August 1966): 35.

Robert Noehren plays the opening recital of the convention. "His modest, unassuming personality, his breathtaking accuracy, his inner glow of musicianship, left everyone in exactly the right frame of mind for the week to come."

Barnes, William H. "Recitals and Concerts." *American Organist* 43 (December 1960): 20.

Performing at Hill Auditorium, University of Michigan, Ann Arbor, Noehren performs an all-Bach recital, identical to the one Mendelssohn played in St. Thomas Church, Leipzig, 6 August 1840; Noehren's playing is applauded.

Bingham, Seth. "Organ Personalities." *American Organist* 46 (November 1963): 16.

Announcement that Noehren is chosen one of three judges of the International Improvisation Competition in Haarlem, Holland; recognition for his Prix du Disque and for his willingness to travel abroad to examine earlier instruments and report on his findings.

"Church Musicians at N.W.U. Field Day." *Diapason* 43 (March 1952): 2.

Noehren performs a recital at Northwestern University, Evanston, Ill., during the midwinter conference on church music, February 18 and 19; the recital is reviewed. Noehren also lectured on European organs.

Craighead, David, et al. "Robert Noehren at 80: A Tribute." *Diapason* 81 (December 1990): 12-14.

Congratulations to Noehren on his 80th birthday come from a variety of colleagues, from Craighead to George Faxon to Beverly Howerton to Ed Gress.

"The Discography of Robert Noehren." *Diapason* 81 (March 1990): 12-13.

Included in this discography is Noehren's perspective of the organ, and he speaks of those concerns in the first half of the article.

"Here and There." *Diapason* 82 (February 1991): 4.

Noehren's 80th birthday is celebrated in Cleveland on December 14-15, with a lecture by Noehren at the Cleveland Museum of Art, followed by a dinner, and a recital by Noehren the following afternoon.

"Here and There." *Diapason* 83 (May 1992): 4.

Noehren is featured on a new CD recording, *A Temple of Tone*, recorded on the Reuter organ at the University of Denver on the Pro Organo label. Includes works by Messiaen, Langlais, Balbastre, Schumann, and others.

Holtz, John. "Recitals and Concerts." *American Organist* 45 (May 1962): 24.

> Hill Auditorium, University of Michigan, was the site for Noehren's all-Bach recital, 11 March 1962. A laudatory review was given.

"I.C.O. Canada—1967." *Musical Opinion* 91 (December 1967): 134. *

Nalle, Billy. "Recitals and Concerts." *American Organist* 47 (January 1964): 11, 30.

> An extremely fine, rave view.

"Noehren Appointed to Post in Ann Arbor." *Diapason* 40 (September 1949): 4.

> Noehren is appointed to the position of University Organist at the University of Michigan, effective September 1. An overview of his summer's study in the Netherlands is provided.

"Noehren at Moody." *Diapason* 50 (April 1959): 28.

> A nearly unpublicized recital by Noehren attracted only a small crowd from the Moody Bible Institute on 27 February 1959. Noehren was "slow in getting warmed up" and yet his ability "to achieve personal penetration into various styles" and "a genuine . . . eclecticism seem to us the keys to [his] special quality."

"Noehren in Chicago." *Diapason* 51 (March 1960): 20.

> Noehren appeared in recital at St. Paul's United Church of Christ, 25 January 1960. The recital program is printed.

"Noehren Completes School Instrument." *Diapason* 48 (November 1957): 19.

> Noehren completed a three-manual organ, and installed it in the Carr Memorial Room at the New England Conservatory of Music, Boston.

"Noehren Receives Patent for Combination Action." *Diapason* 60 (March 1969): 1.

> The U.S. Patent Office gives Noehren's combination action a patent. His combination action allows the performer to set combinations in advance by punching a data processing card; when the punched card is inserted in the action, all the combination pistons are set at once. Three churches already use this particular action in organs he has built.

"Organist Named Performer of the Year." *Clavier* 17/9 (1978): 12.

> Noehren was named the International Performer of the Year by the New York City AGO. He received the honor from Miss Alice Tully at Alice Tully Hall, New York.

"Recitals and Concerts." *American Organist* 41 (January 1958): 40.

> Noehren plays at St. James's Church, New York, November 11. Congratulations were accorded Noehren for "conquering the environment at the church."

"Recitals and Concerts." *American Organist* 41 (February 1958): 80.

A performance by Noehren at Methuen Memorial Music Hall (Mass.) on November 13. Reviewer Allan Sly felt Noehren "communicated, in purely musical terms, the essence of the composer's intention. . . ."

"Recitals and Concerts." *American Organist* 51 (May 1968): 10.

Noehren plays at Concordia Lutheran Seminary, St. Louis, Mo., on 19 March 1968; the reviewer enjoyed the eclectic recital.

"Robert Noehren." *Diapason* 66 (September 1975): 18.

Noehren is appointed Rose Morgan Professor of Organ for the fall semester of 1975 at the University of Kansas School of Fine Arts.

"Robert Noehren Is Winner of Prize for His Recording." *Diapason* 44 (November 1953): 1.

Noehren wins the French Grand Prix du Disque for the best organ recording of 1953. This honor was won for his performance of two Bach trio sonatas issued by Allegro Records.

"Robert Noehren on 4th Tour of Recitals in Europe." *Diapason* 44 (September 1953): 17.

During August and September 1953, Noehren will give recitals and make radio broadcasts in Holland, Denmark, Norway, and Germany. Biographical data included.

"Robert Noehren to Play in Düsseldorf." *Diapason* 45 (June 1954): 1.

Noehren is invited to perform two recitals at the International Organ Congress in Düsseldorf, Germany, October 10-15.

"Robert Noehren to Play at International Congress." *Diapason* 45 (October 1954): 2.

Includes the same information as in the item above, and indicates the first recital will be devoted to American composers and the second will feature music by early composers.

"1960 AGO National Convention." *American Organist* 49 (August 1966):11.

Noehren performs music he enjoys: Buxtehude, Vierne, Hindemith, and a new toccata by Henk Badings.

Gladys Nordenstrom

(Mrs. Ernst Krenek.) B. Pokegama, Minn., 23 May 1924. Studied music and philosophy at Hamline University (Minn.), B.A., 1946, and the University of Minnesota, M.A., 1947; studied with Ernst Krenek.

ABD, CACA, IMD, IWC, KTL, WCH, X69, X70.

Szmolyan, Walter. "Die Komponistin Gladys Nordenstrom-Krenek." *Österreichische Musikzeitschrift* 35 (September 1980): 445.

> In German; a brief biography includes how she met her husband, Ernst Krenek; relates her compositional style: use of 12-tone technique and serial composition, and her interest in electronic music; her composition for organ and tape, *Signals from Nowhere*, is included in the discussion.

Kevin Edward Norris

B. New York, 12 April 1939. B.M., 1962, with Leo Sowerby, American Conservatory of Music; studied with Bernard Rogers at Eastman School of Music. Organist-choir director, Assumption Church, Morristown, N.J., from 1972.

CACA, OL, OL95.

"TAO Report on AGO Biennial Convention, Philadelphia, June 22-26." *American Organist* 47 (August 1964): 19.

> Marilyn Mason premieres Norris's *Concert Music* for organ, strings, and kettledrums on the first night of the AGO convention. The work incorporates off-beat rhythms, "shifting accents, alternating duple and triple meters adding to the exhilarating effect. . . ."

Orpha Ochse

B. St. Joseph, Mo., 6 May 1925. B.M., 1947, Central College, Fayette, Mo.; M.M., 1948, and Ph.D., 1953, in music education, Eastman School of Music. Student of Luther Spayde, Harold Gleason, Catharine Crozier, and Clarence Mader. Instructor, Central College, 1948-50; Western Illinois State College, Macomb, 1950-51; Phoenix College, 1952-57. Director of music at First Congregational Church, Pasadena; lecturer, California Institute of Technology, 1960-76; assistant professor, Whittier College (Calif.), 1970, and promoted to professor, 1977; professor emerita, 1993. Since 1980, organist, Hillcrest Congregational Church, Whittier. Authored *The History of the Organ in the United States* (Bloomington: Indiana University Press, 1975); with James Duncan, *Fundamentals of Music Theory* (New York: Holt, Rinehart & Winston, 1983).

ABD, CACA, IWC, OL, OL95, WWAM-Cl.

"Orpha Ochse." *Diapason* 57 (November 1966): 2.

> An overview of Ochse's seven-week European recital itinerary.

Madra Emogene Oliver

B. Three Rivers, Mich., 28 October 1905. Studied at the University of Michigan, B.S.M.; M.A., Claremont College. Organ music listed in Cohen's book.
IWC.

No bibliographical information located.

Alma Oncley

B. Parma, N.Y., 8 December 1904. B.Mus. (piano), 1931; B.Mus. (organ), 1932; M.M. (composition), 1933, Eastman School of Music; Doctor of Sacred Music, Union Theological Seminary, 1963; organist, Lake Avenue Baptist Church, Rochester, 1927-37; organist-associate director, Trinity Methodist Church, Staten Island, 1936-38; instructor (piano-organ), Woman's College, University of North Carolina, Greensboro, 1938-44; organist, First Presbyterian Church, Greensboro, N.C., 1940-42; organist-director, Trinity Methodist Church, Durham, N.C., 1944-45; organist-associate director, Presbyterian Church, Basking Ridge, N.J., 1945-56; organist-associate director, Methodist Church, Summit, N.J., 1946-58; organist, Temple B'nai Israel, Elizabeth, N.J., 1948-58; organist, First Presbyterian Church, Tacoma, Wash., 1958-62; professor of organ, piano, theory, University of Puget Sound, Tacoma, Wash., 1959-72; organist, Phinney Ridge Lutheran Church, Seattle, 1964-86. Organ music and biography listed in Arnold's book.
OL, OL95.

No bibliographical information located.

Charles William Ore

B. Winfield, Kans., 18 December 1936. B.S. with Theodore Beck, Concordia College, Seward, Nebr.; studied composition with Myron Roberts, University of Nebraska; organ study with Thomas Matthews, Northwestern University, M.M., 1960; D.M.A., University of Nebraska at Lincoln, 1986. Faculty member, Concordia Teachers College, River Forest, Ill., 1961-66; director of music, First St. Paul's Lutheran Church, Chicago; professor and chairman, Church Music & Organ, Concordia Teachers College, 1966-93; director of music and cantor, Pacific Hills Lutheran Church, Omaha, Nebr., 1975-93. Authored "Numbers and Number Correspondences in Opus 40 by Arnold Schoenberg: Pythagoras and the Quadrivium Revisited" (*Dissertation Abstracts* 47 [October 1986]: 1109A).

ABD, CACA, DN73, OL, OL95.

No bibliographical information located.

Jack Herman Ossewaarde

B. Kalamazoo, Mich., 15 November 1918. B.M., 1940, M.M., 1941, University of Michigan. Pupil of Palmer Christian and Percival Price. Further study at Union Theological Seminary with David McK. Williams, Harold Friedell, and Normand Lockwood; and at Columbia University. Additional study in composition with Leo Sowerby. Organist-choirmaster, Calvary Episcopal Church, New York, 1947-53; Christ Church Cathedral, Houston, Tex., 1953-58; St. Bartholomew's Episcopal Church, New York, 1958-82.

ABD, OL, OL95, and *American Organist* 22 (November 1988): 74-76.

"Jack Ossewaarde Will Go to Cathedral in Houston." *Diapason* 44 (August 1953): 1.

Ossewaarde accepts the position of organist and choirmaster at Christ Church Cathedral in Houston, Tex., effective September 15.

"Jack H. Ossewaarde Returns to New York City." *Diapason* 49 (June 1958): 7.

Ossewaarde succeeds the late Harold Friedell at St. Bartholomew's Episcopal Church, New York; biographical data included.

"Ossewaarde Appointed to St. Bartholomew's." *American Organist* 41 (July 1958): 254.

Ossewaarde's appointment to St. Bartholomew's Episcopal Church, New York, is announced. Biographical information included.

"Recitals and Concerts." *American Organist* 43 (April 1960): 23.

Ossewaarde plays at St. Bartholomew's Church, New York, 24 January 1960. Included on this program is his work *Litanies*, for organ, choir and soloists.

Tufts, William O. "Recital." *American Organist* 47 (February 1964): 26.

Ossewaarde performed at George Washington Memorial Masonic Auditorium, Alexandria, Va., 12 November 1963, for the Alexandria AGO chapter. The program consisted of works by Handel, Bach, Franck, Hurford, Friedell, Ives, Gerre Hancock, and an improvisation on a submitted theme.

Walters, Kevin. "Jack H. Ossewaarde at 70." *American Organist* 22 (November 1988): 74-76.

> A tribute to Ossewaarde on his birthday, and recollections of his contribution to church music. Biography included; a list of published and unpublished works for choir and for organ is provided.

Sam Batt Owens

B. Ashland, Ala., 14 February 1928. B.A., Birmingham Conservatory of Music, 1950; M.M., Birmingham Southern College, 1956; D.M.A., Peabody College of Vanderbilt University, Nashville, 1976. For five summers, Peters Corporation scholar; studied organ at the Organ Institute, Methuen, Mass. Organ study with Thomas H. Webber, Minnie McNeil Carr, Arthur Poister, Carl Weinrich, Catharine Crozier, Ernest White, Finn Viderø, E. Power Biggs, and Arthur Howes. Associate professor, Birmingham Southern College, 1950-67, and St. Mary's-on-the-Highlands; director of choral music, Vanderbilt University, 1967-68; director of choral activities, Fisk University, 1968-75; organist-choirmaster, St. George's Church, Nashville. In 1973 and 1974, he was elected Outstanding Professor at Fisk University. Since 1975, director of music and fine arts, Grace Episcopal Church and School, Memphis. Authored "The Organ Mass and Girolamo Frescobaldi's *Fiore Musicale* of 1635; Music for 2 organs; 4 Lenten Motets of Alessandro Scarlatti" (*Dissertation Abstracts* 35 [January 1975]: 4597A-98A).

OL, OL95.

"Pipings." *American Organist* 27 (January 1993): 51.

> In 1992, Owens was commissioned to compose *Two Preludes for Organ on Sacred Harp Hymn Tunes*, commissioned by Dorree and James Brinson, Memphis, Tenn., and *Two Preludes for Organ on Early American Melodies*, commissioned by Marie Pettet, among other commissions for choirs.

"Sam Batt Owens." *Diapason* 55 (October 1964): 33.

> Owens assumed the post of director of music and organist on September 1 at the First Methodist Church, Birmingham, Ala. He is also head of the organ department of Birmingham-Southern Conservatory of Music and associate choral director for the college.

Alice Parker

(Mrs. Thomas Pyle.) B. Boston, Mass., 16 December 1925. Studied with Ross Lee Finney and Werner Josten at Smith College, B.A., 1947; and with Vincent Persichetti, Shaw, and

Julius Herford at Juilliard, M.S., 1949. Arranger for Robert Shaw Chorale, 1948-67; composer and artistic director of Melodious Accord, since 1955; lectured at several schools, including Yale and Northwestern, 1958-73. Honorary doctorate from Hamilton College, 1979; ASCAP awards, since 1968; National Endowment for the Arts composer award, 1974; American Music Center Fellow of MacDowell and Millay Colonies award. Composes only on commission for performance. Authored *Dictionary of Music* (New York: Doubleday, 1964); *Music Pocket Crammer* (New York: Doubleday, 1964); and *Creative Hymn Singing* (Chapel Hill: Hinshaw, 1976).

ABD, CACA, IWC, IWW92, WCH, WWAM-Cl, X70.

"**Introducing a Person of Note.**" *Pastoral Music* 6/1 (1981): 45.

A career summary.

"**Introducing a Person of Note.**" *Pastoral Music* 12/2 (1987-88): 60. *

Loesch, Robert K. "**Alice Parker: Composer, Teacher, Arranger.**" *Music* (AGO) 9 (February 1975): 26-27.

A glimpse into Parker's method of composing and arranging.

Meier, Ann. "**Alice Parker: Working toward a Musical Society.**" *Music Educators Journal* 73 (January 1987): 36-41.

Biography; influences on her music; a woman's perspective of composing; and Parker's approach to arranging. She states, "Music reading should be taught with music writing"—a marriage that often does not happen.

Mussulman, Joseph A. "**Alice Parker: Riding a Surfboard.**" *Music Educators Journal* 66 (March 1980): 42-45, 90-91.

Parker states: "Study and performance are two sides of the same thing. They must not be separated." She feels music is like a surfboarder—it is conditioned by the currents down deep. "Attune yourself to what the music is doing" and your compositions will have a sense of balance and weight to them. She strongly advocates all performers to be in a constant state of learning about their art, the music, and the historical implications of the work, or relating to the work.

Robert Parris

B. Philadelphia, 21 May 1924. B.S., 1945, and M.S., 1946, University of Pennsylvania; studied with Peter Mennin, Juilliard, B.S., 1948; studied with Copland at Tanglewood,

1950; and with Arthur Honneger, at the École Normale de Musique, Paris, 1952-53. NEA grants in 1975, 1978, and 1983. On faculty at George Washington University, Washington, D.C., since 1963.

ABD, BB65, BB71, BB78, BB92, BMI, CA10, CACA, CACJ, DCM, LMD, NGA, OL, OL95, PC71, PCM, PET, TCH, X58, X60, X61, X62, X64, X66, X67, X69, X70, X71.

"Here and There." *Diapason* 69 (December 1977): 16.

Parris played the first performance of his *Sonata No. 1 for Organ* (1976) on a May 2 recital in Hendricks Chapel, Syracuse University; the work is published by Hinshaw Music in the Contemporary Organ Series.

"Robert Parris." *Composers of the Americas* 10 (1964): 79-84.

A brief biography in both English and Spanish is followed by an annotated catalog of his works.

Carl Parrish

B. Plymouth, Penn., 9 October 1904; d. Valhalla, N.Y., 27 November 1965. Studied at the American Conservatory in Fontainebleau, 1932; MacPhail School of Music, B.M., 1933; Cornell University, M.A., 1936; and Harvard University, Ph.D., 1939. Taught at Wells College, 1929-43; Fisk University, 1943-46; Westminster Choir College, 1946-49; Pomona College, 1949-53; and professor at Vassar College, 1953-65. Wrote *The Notation of Medieval Music* (New York: Norton, 1957; 2nd ed., 1959); and edited *A Treasury of Early Music* (New York: Norton, 1959), and, with John Ohl, *Masterpieces of Music before 1750* (New York: Norton, 1951). Translated Tinctoris's *Dictionary of Musical Terms* (New York: Free Press of Glencoe, 1963; London: Collier-Macmillan, 1963).

ABD, BB58, BB71, BB78, BB92, CACA, KTL, LMD, MHHH, NG, NGA, OL, OL95, REM, WI62, X52, X58, X64, X65, X66, X67, X68.

Haydon, Glen. **"Carl Parrish (1904-65)."** *American Musicological Society* 19/3 (1966): 434.

The obituary includes a summary of Parrish's life and career.

[Obituary.] *High Fidelity/Musical America* 16 (February 1966): 141.

Announcement of Parrish's death: he was killed in an automobile accident, 26 November 1965, at 61 years of age.

Stephen Paulus

B. Summit, N.J., 24 August 1949. Studied with Paul Fetler and Dominick Argento, University of Minnesota, B.M., 1971, M.M., 1974, and Ph.D., 1978. Founded the Minnesota Composers Forum in Minneapolis, with Libby Larsen, 1973; served as managing composer, 1973-84. Composer-in-residence: Minnesota Orchestra, 1983-87; St. Louis Symphony Orchestra, since 1983; Santa Fe Music Festival, 1986; Atlanta Orchestra, since 1988. Also served as composer-in-residence for Dale Warland Singers, Tanglewood, Santa Fe, and Oregon Bach Festival. Received a Guggenheim fellowship in 1982-83, and a National Endowment for the Arts grant, 1978.

ABD, CACA, OL95.

"Here and There." *Diapason* 85 (September 1994): 3.
> *The Triumph of the Saint*, a new duet written for Elizabeth and Raymond Chenault, is premiered by them, 14 June 1994, Christ and St. Luke Episcopal Church, Norfolk, Va. The work was inspired by a Heironymous Bosch triptych.

"Premieres." *American Organist* 28 (October 1994): 52.
> Same information as above.

Russell James Peck

B. Detroit, Mich., 25 January 1945. Studied at the Eastman School of Music, 1962-63; B.M., 1966, M.M., 1967, and D.M.A., 1972, University of Michigan. Composition study with Leslie Bassett and Ross Lee Finney; studied with Gunther Schuller and Aaron Copland, Tanglewood. Won many composition prizes and fellowships including the BMI Student Award, 1965, 1967, 1969, and the Koussevitzky Award, 1965. Resource person, 1967-69, Lincoln Center, New York; Ford Foundation composer-in-residence, public schools, Merrick, N.Y., 1967-69; since 1971, associated with the Indianapolis Symphony Orchestra and the city of Indianapolis. His dissertation is entitled "The Emperor's New 'Concerto'" (*Dissertation Abstracts* 36 [August 1975]: 591A-92A). Organ music listed in Arnold's book.

ABD, CACA, DN78, OL, OL95, X70, X74.

"1964 SCA winners." *BMI: The Many Worlds of Music*, July 1965, 5. *

Richard Peek

B. Mason, Wisc., 17 May 1927. B.M., 1950, Michigan State University, with H. Owen Reed; M.S.M., 1952, S.M.D., 1958, Union Theological Seminary, New York. Organ pupil of Helen Roberts Sholl, Richard Ross, Vernon De Tar, and Arthur Poister. Composition with Harold Friedell and Normand Lockwood. Organist-choirmaster, Grace Episcopal Church, Plainfield, N.J., 1950-52; since 1952, organist-choirmaster, Covenant Presbyterian Church, Charlotte, N.C. In 1975, Peek was named Composer of the Year by the North Carolina Federation of Music Clubs.

ABD, CACA, OL, OL95.

"Here and There." *Diapason* 81 (September 1990): 3-4.
> *Metamorphosis*, a work for organ and percussion by Peek, received its first performance on 10 June 1990 at Covenant Presbyterian Church, Charlotte, N.C. Performers were Peek, organist, and Harvey Warner, percussionist.

"Performance Reviews." *Choral Guide* 7 (October 1954): 26. *
> Includes Peek's *Scherzo and Fugue*.

"Richard M. Peek." *Diapason* 43 (September 1952): 38.
> Peek is named organist-choirmaster at Covenant Presbyterian Church, Charlotte, N.C. Biographical data included.

"Richard M. Peek." *Diapason* 49 (August 1958): 19.
> Peek resumes his duties as organist-choirmaster at Covenant Presbyterian Church, Charlotte, N.C., after a year's absence during which he completed his doctoral work at the School of Sacred Music, Union Theological Seminary, New York.

C. Alexander Peloquin

B. 1918; d. Providence, R.I., 27 February 1997. Music director, Cathedral of Sts. Peter and Paul, Providence, R.I.; composer-in-residence, Boston College. Recipient of an honorary doctorate of music, Brown University.

ABD, CACA, OL, OL95.

"Commentary: Alexander Peloquin on Prayer and Music." *Pastoral Musician* 1/2 (1976-77): 44-45.
> Peloquin discusses how God, the supreme artist, works through his people as they perform.

Lind, L. J. **"Liturgical Pied Piper."** *Catholic Choirmaster* 50/3 (1964): 137-39. *

McKenna, Edward J. **"Major Catholic Composers: A Critical Evaluation."** *American Organist* 18 (June 1984): 43.

> Peloquin succeeds as important composer in the Catholic Church with music that has an undeniable popular appeal.

Walter L. Pelz

B. Chicago, Ill., 30 December 1926. B.M., Northwestern University, M.M., Concordia Teachers College, River Forest, Ill.; Ph.D. study with Paul Fetler and Dominick Argento, University of Minnesota. Public school teacher, Indiana and Michigan, 1948-62; CAGO, 1960; minister of music, Christ Church Lutheran, Minneapolis, 1962-67; taught at the University of Minnesota, 1962-67; since 1969, faculty member, composer-in-residence, Bethany College, Lindsborg, Kans., now emeritus; organist, Messiah Lutheran Church, Lindsborg, now retired.

ABD, CACA, OL, OL95.

"American Composer Update." *Pan Pipes* 73/2 (1980): 39.

> Concordia publishes volume 3 of Pelz's *Hymns for Communion: Four Hymn Alternations.*

"American Composer Update." *Pan Pipes* 87/2 (winter 1995): 35.

> *Hymn Settings for Organ and Brass*, vols. 3-4, is published by Augsburg Fortress.

Drone, Jeanette, comp. **"American Composer Update."** *Pan Pipes* 75/2 (1983): 37.

> Pelz presents organ clinics throughout the United States.

Ronald Christopher Perera

B. Boston, Mass., 25 December 1941. Studied composition with Leon Kirchner, Harvard, B.A., 1963, and M.A., 1967; then traveled on a John Knowles Paine Traveling Fellowship to study electronic music and computer composition with Gottfried Michael Koening at the University of Utrecht, 1967-68; courses in the U.S. in choral music with Randall Thompson and in electronic music with Mario Davidovsky. Taught at Syracuse University, 1968-70;

director of the Dartmouth College Electronic Music Studio, 1970-71; taught theory, composition, and electronic music, Smith College, Northampton, Mass., from 1971; visiting scholar at the Columbia-Princeton Electronic Music Center, 1975-76. With J. H. Appleton, he edited *The Development and Practice of Electronic Music* (Englewood Cliffs, N.J.: Prentice-Hall, 1975). Received annual ASCAP awards from 1972; NEA grants in 1978 and 1988; and was a MacDowell Colony resident, 1978.

ABD, CACA, CACJ, DN72, IWW92, NGA, OL, OL95, X74.

Little, Jeanie R. "Serial, Aleatoric, and Electrical Techniques in American Organ Music Published between 1960 and 1972." Ph.D., University of Iowa, 1975. *Dissertation Abstracts* 36 (June 1978): 7722A.

This scholarly, in-depth work analyzes in detail Perera's works for organ and electronic tape, among other composers' works.

Zenobia Powell Perry

B. Boley, Okla., 3 October 1914. B.S., 1938, Tuskegee Institute, Ala.; M.A., 1945, Northern Colorado University; piano and composition with Alan Willman and Darius Milhaud, M.A., University of Wyoming. Piano study also with R. Nathaniel Dett, Gunnar Johansen, and Cortez Reece, and composition with Charles Jones. Faculty member, Arkansas Agricultural, Mechanical and Normal College, 1946-55; from 1955, lecturer and composer-in-residence, Central State University; composer-in-residence, Central State University; composer emeritus, Wilberforce University (Ohio).

ABD, CACA, IWC.

"Two of Perry's Works Heard." *Triangle* 81/3 (1987): 17. *

Vincent Persichetti

B. Philadelphia, 6 June 1915; d. there, 13 August 1987. B.M., Combs Conservatory, Philadelphia, 1936; was head of theory and composition departments at Combs Conservatory while studying piano with Olga Samaroff and composition with Nordoff at Philadelphia Conservatory, M.M., 1941, and D.M.A., 1945; conducting with Fritz Reiner at the Curtis Institute; composition study with Roy Harris at Colorado College. Head of theory and composition departments, Philadelphia Conservatory, 1941-47; joined faculty of the Juilliard School, 1947, where he became chairman of the composition department in 1963, and chairman of the literature and materials department, 1970. From 1952, he was director of publications for Elkan-Vogel. Organist-choirmaster, Arch St. Presbyterian Church, Philadelphia, 1932-49. With Flora Rheta Schrieber, he wrote the monograph *William Schuman* (New York: G. Schirmer, 1954), and is the author of *Twentieth Century Harmony* (New York: Norton, 1961). Recipient of two Guggenheim fellowships and many composition awards. Honorary doctorates from Combs College, Bucknell University, Baldwin-Wallace College, Millikin University, and Peabody Conservatory.

ABD, AMH, AS66, ASC, BB58, BB65, BB78, BB92, BBCch, BDA, CA14, CACA, CACJ, DCM, DDM, DN74, DN75, DN77, DN78, EDM, GD54, HHH, JCN, KTL, MEH, MGG, MHHH, NG, NGA, OL, OL95, PC71, PCM, REM, TCAC, TCH, WTM, X50, X51, X53, X54, X55, X56, X57, X58, X59, X60, X61, X62, X64, X65, X66, X67, X68, X69, X70, X71, X74.

"Afternoon at Lincoln Center." *Diapason* 54 (February 1963): 23.

Virgil Fox performs *Shimah B'koli* at Lincoln Center, 15 December 1962.

"American Composer Update." *Pan Pipes* 73/2 (1981): 37.

Persichetti received an honorary doctorate from Arizona State University, May 1980; Marilyn Mason premiered his *Dryden Liturgical Suite* on 17 June 1980 at the AGO convention in Minneapolis.

75/2 (1983): 37.

Song of David, for organ, is published by Elkan-Vogel.

Bullat, G. Nicholas. "Detroit, June 30-July 4." *Diapason* 77 (October 1986): 13.

Chorale Prelude on "Ann Arbor" is premiered by Donald Williams. "It proved to be quite a dramatic, freely virtuosic piece (with a stormy pedal cadenza) concluding in a mysterious calm. . . ."

Evett, Robert. "The Music of Vincent Persichetti." *Juilliard Review* 2 (spring 1955): 15-30.

Persichetti's music is "the music of extremes." An overview of his styles, examples of his works for various instrumentations, and a list of annotated works, through opus 66, are provided.

Kratzenstein, Marilou, and Bruce Gustafson. "The Minneapolis-St. Paul AGO National Convention." *Diapason* 71 (August 1980): 4.

The newly-commissioned work *Dryden Liturgical Suite* is performed by Marilyn Mason at Central Lutheran Church, Minneapolis.

Kremer, Rudolph. "First Performer Views *Sonata* by Persichetti." *Diapason* 52 (March 1961): 35.

Kremer discusses the commissioning of the new work, Persichetti's previous organ music, and some details about the sonata. The work will be published by Elkan-Vogel.

Little, Jeanie R. "Serial, Aleatoric, and Electrical Techniques in American Organ Music Published between 1960 and 1972." Ph.D., University of Iowa, 1975. *Dissertation Abstracts* 36 (June 1978): 7722A.

This scholarly, in-depth work analyzes in detail Persichetti's serial and chance works for organ, among other composers' works.

"New Works." *Music Journal* 21 (February 1963): 98.

Includes a brief description of *Shimah B'koli*.

[Obituary.] *American Organist* 21 (November 1987): 57.

A biography and summary of Persichetti's career is given.

[Obituary.] *Diapason* 78 (October 1987): 6.

Death date for Persichetti is August 14. Gives brief biography, lists his ten works for organ, and his eight sonatas for harpsichord.

Patterson, Donald L., and Janet L. Patterson. *Vincent Persichetti: A Bio-Bibliography.* Westport, Conn.: Greenwood, 1988.

Includes chronology, bibliography, works and performances, and discography.

"Persichetti's 'Shimah B'koli, Psalm 130' for Organ." *Pan Pipes* 55/2 (1963): 6.

Virgil Fox premieres the work, 15 December 1962, at Lincoln Center, New York; the work will be published by Elkan-Vogel.

Ramsey, Mark Deneen. "Vincent Persichetti's Final Three Organ Works: Analyses and Pedagogical Suggestions." D.M.A., Arizona State University, 1990. *Dissertation Abstracts* 51 (February 1991): 2561A.

An analysis of *Dryden Liturgical Suite*, *Song of David*, and *Give Peace, O God*; provides pedagogical suggestions for these three works.

Raver, Leonard. "Lincoln Center Inaugural Recital." *American Organist* 46 (February 1963): 14-18.

On December 15 Virgil Fox performed the premiere of Persichetti's *Shimah B'koli* (Psalm 130) at Lincoln Center; it will be published by Elkan-Vogel. The event is described as "the most challenging and stimulating musical experience. . . ."

Shackelford, Rudy. "Conversation with Vincent Persichetti." *Perspectives of New Music* 20/1 (1981-82): 104-33.

An extensive interview with Persichetti; biographical information; questions about his music, influences, his works, and religion are addressed.

————. "Correction." *Diapason* 68 (February 1977): 2.

One paragraph from the *Diapason* 67 (November 1976) article was omitted; the paragraph and place of insertion is indicated.

————. **"Notes on the Recent Organ Music of Vincent Persichetti."** *Diapason* 67 (November 1976): 5-9.

In excerpts from a 1972 radio interview "Composer's Forum," Persichetti discusses with critic Martin Bookspan the genesis of his interest in the organ and the meaning of the title *Parable*; after the main interview, the discussion encompasses his other works for organ: *Do Not Go Gentle*, *Shimah B'koli*, and *Sonata*, and the use of symbolism.

————. **"Vincent Persichetti's 'Auden Variations'—An Analysis."** *Diapason* 70 (October 1979): 12-16, 18-19.

A detailed analysis of the chorale is followed by more in-depth analyses of the variations.

————. **"Vincent Persichetti's Hymn and Chorale Prelude 'Drop, Drop Slow Tears'—An Analysis."** *Diapason* 64 (September 1973): 3-6.

A detailed analysis of *Drop, Drop Show Tears*, as shown through harmony, melody, and form. Musical examples are extracted from the work.

————. **"Vincent Persichetti's 'Shima B'koli' for Organ—An Analysis."** *Diapason* 66 (September 1975): 3-8, 12-13.

A detailed analysis. The Psalm is in Hebrew and an English translation is provided, as is commissioning information. The form, structure of the work, the series and derivation of motives from the series, and harmonic and rhythmic aspects of the work are discussed.

————. **"Vincent Perischetti's 'Sonata for Organ' and 'Sonatine for Organ, Pedals Alone'—An Analysis."** *Diapason* 65 (May 1974): 4-7.

A very detailed, scholarly analysis of the *Sonata*, the first movement.

65 (June 1974): 4-7.

The conclusion of the above article, analyzing the second and third movements of the *Sonata* and the *Sonatine*, for pedals only.

"Vincent Persichetti." *Pan Pipes* 44 (January 1952): 41. *

"Vincent Persichetti." *Pan Pipes* 45 (January 1953): 63. *

Lloyd Pfautsch

B. Washington, Mo., 14 September 1921. B.A., Elmhurst College, 1943; M.Th., M.S.M., Union Theological Seminary, 1948; composition with Harold Friedell and Burrill Phillips; D.Mus. in composition, Florida State University, 1969. Visiting professor, University of Illinois, 1946-47; professor of voice and choral director, Illinois Wesleyan, 1948-58; since 1958, professor and conductor of choirs, Southern Methodist University, Dallas; retired 1992. Honorary doctorate from Elmhurst College, 1959, and Illinois Wesleyan University, 1978. Author of *English Diction for the Singer* (New York: Lawson-Gould, 1971) and *Mental Warmups for the Choral Director* (New York: Lawson-Gould, 1971).

ABD, CACA, OL, OL95, PC71, PCM, X56, X64, X65, X70, X74.

Kyle, Marguerite K. "AmerAllegro." *Pan Pipes* 49 (January 1957): 63.

If Thou but Suffer God to Guide Thee, for organ, is published.

51 (January 1959): 78.

Pfautsch is now on the faculties of both the School of Music and the School of Theology at Southern Methodist University as associate professor of sacred music and director of choral activities.

52/2 (1960): 65.

Pfautsch receives an honorary doctorate degree from his alma mater, Elmhurst College.

55/2 (1963): 65.

If Thou but Suffer, for organ and brass, is published by Robert King.

62/2 (1970): 75-76.

Pfautsch receives his Doctor of Music degree in music composition from Florida State University, June 1969.

66/2 (1974): 66.

Pfautsch receives the Sigma Alpha Iota "Service to Music in Dallas Award" for 1972.

71/2 (1979): 41.

Southern Methodist University awards Pfautsch the Outstanding Professor Award, 1977-78; Illinois Wesleyan University grants him an honorary L.L.D. degree.

"Lloyd Pfautsch." *Pan Pipes* 47 (January 1955): 60.

If Thou but Suffer was premiered at the Los Angeles Church Federation program of contemporary church music.

Vivian Daphne Phillips

B. Colby, Kans., 9 March 1917. Studied organ, piano, violin, and composition, Ottawa University, Kans., 1934-36, with Harry Cooper; with Hagvard Brase, Bethany College, Lindsborg, Kans., 1936-39. Further studies at Oklahoma Baptist University, Shawnee, 1982-84. Organ music listed in Cohen's book.

ABD, CACA, IWC, WCH.

No bibliographical information located.

Boris William Pillin

B. Chicago, 31 May 1940. Studied with John Vincent, University of California, Los Angeles, B.A., 1964; with Robert Linn, University of Southern California, M.A., 1967; privately with Leon Stein. Woodrow Wilson fellowship, 1964-65; ASCAP awards, 1971-74. Private teacher, from 1967. Self-employed music engraver from 1968; staff member, Western International Music, since 1968. Arnold lists his organ music.

ABD, CACA, DN70, DN73, DN76, OL, OL95, PC71.

No bibliographical information located.

Daniel Rogers Pinkham

B. Lynn, Mass., 5 June 1923. B.A., 1943, and M.A., 1944, Harvard University, with A. Tillman Merritt, Walter Piston, Archibald Davison, and Aaron Copland; also studied at the Berkshire Music Center with Arthur Honegger and Samuel Barber, and privately with Nadia Boulanger. Harpsichord study with Putnam Aldrich and Wanda Landowska; organ with E. Power Biggs. Worked on the faculties of Simmons College, Boston University, and Harvard; lecturer on composition and chairman of the department of performance of early music, New England Conservatory, from 1959; music director of King's Chapel, Boston. Fulbright scholarship, 1950; Ford Foundation fellowship, 1962; fellow of the American Academy of Arts and Sciences.

AA73, ABD, ACA, AMH, BB58, BB65, BB71, BB78, BB92, BMI, CA12, CACA, CC92, DCM, DN72, DN73, IWW92, KTL, LMD, MHHH, NG, NGA, OL, OL95, PC71, PCM, PET, TCAC, TCH, X55, X56, X57, X58, X60, X61, X62, X64, X65, X66, X67, X68, X69, X70, X71, X74.

"AGO Convention Reports, 1989." *American Organist* 23 (October 1979): 79-80.

The Chenaults—Raymond and Elizabeth—perform the premiere of Pinkham's *Requiem Collects*, an organ duet.

Albright, William. "Fourth Festival of Contemporary Organ Music; Hartt College." *Music (AGO)* 8 (September 1974): 23.

Pinkham's *Liturgies* for organ, timpani, and tape premiered by Leonard Raver, demonstrates his wit and skill. "Most attractive was the first movement with its concentration on a few rhythmic and melodic cells."

"American Guild of Organists." *Music Journal* 26 (September 1968): 94.

Pinkham's *Signs in the Sun* is premiered at the convention in Denver.

Bingham, Seth. "Recitals and Concerts." *American Organist* 47 (July 1964): 9.

Pinkham's *Concertante: Aria, Scherzo, Elegy* (organ, celesta, and percussion), commissioned by Boston's AGO chapter, receives its second performance. A brief description of the work is supplied.

Black, George. "Hartt College Annual Contemporary Organ Music Fest—A Review." *Diapason* 64 (August 1973): 17.

Pinkham's *Revelations—Toccata* and *For Evening Draws On* (1973, premiere) for organ, English horn, and electronic tape, are featured in a recital of contemporary music for organ.

Burkett, John Morris. "Music for Two or More Players at One or More Organs." D.M.A., University of Illinois at Urbana-Champaign, 1973.

This dissertation traces the history of ensemble organ playing and music from the 15th century to the present. Pinkham is included.

"Composers in Focus." *BMI: The Many Worlds of Music*, winter 1976, 25-26.

Summary of Pinkham's career; awards and honors are listed; and a brief comment from him regarding composition with electronic tape.

"Concert Hall." *American Composer Alliance Bulletin* 12/1 (1964): 21.

Pinkham's *Concerto for Organ and Brass* is premiered at King's Chapel, Boston, 2 February 1964, with the composer conducting. His *Concertante for Organ, Celesta*, and *Percussion* is performed at Symphony Hall, Boston, by Boston Symphony Orchestra members and organist John Ferris on 26 January 1964, Pinkham conducting.

Corzine, Michael Lloyd. "The Organ Works of Daniel Pinkham." D.M.A., University of Rochester, Eastman School of Music, 1979. *Dissertation Abstracts* 40 (May 1980): 5641A.

Discusses Pinkham's organ works of 1943-79. Works are grouped according to performance medium.

"Daniel Pinkham." *Pan Pipes* 47 (January 1955): 60.

> *Sonata No. 2*, for organ and strings, is premiered on May 16 by the Juilliard String Quartet and Daniel Pinkham; it is published by the American Composers Alliance. Pinkham is appointed to Boston University as a teaching associate in harpsichord.

"Daniel Pinkham." *Diapason* 50 (December 1958): 2.

> Pinkham is appointed organist and choirmaster of King's Chapel, Boston. Brief career summary.

"Daniel Pinkham." *Composers of the Americas* 12 (1966): 118-24.

> A brief biography in Spanish and English is followed by a chronological catalog of Pinkham's compositions.

DeBoer, Kee, and John B. Ahouse. *Daniel Pinkham: A Bio-Bibliography.* Westport, Conn.: Greenwood, 1988.

> Includes a biography, bibliography, works and performances, and discography.

Devine, George. "Chamber Music." *Notes* 27/4 (June 1971): 805-06.

> Reviews Pinkham's *Concertante for Organ, Celesta, and Percussion*.

"Faculty Appointments." *Musical Courier* 150 (October 1954): 33.

> Pinkham is appointed teaching associate in harpsichord at Boston University.

Haller, William. "Organ Works of the Avante-Garde [*sic*]**."** *Clavier* 13/4 (1974): 33-36.

> A discussion of influential American composers on avant-garde works; includes a brief discussion on Pinkham's *When the Morning Stars Sang Together*.

Henderson, Charles. "Daniel Pinkham." *Music* (AGO) 8 (December 1974): 20-23.

> A biography; an interview with Pinkham about his overall compositional approach and then narrowing to organ, the use of tape, and synthesizer.

"Here and There." *Diapason* 79 (June 1988): 3.

> Several new works by Pinkham have received premieres recently; among them are two for organ: *Sonata da chiesa*, for viola and organ, April 24, Plymouth Church, Belmont, Mass.; and *Petitions*, by organists James David Christie and John Finney, Church of the Advent, Boston, on May 1.

"Here and There." *Diapason* 80 (July 1989): 3.

> Commissioned by Raymond and Elizabeth Chenault, *Requiem Collects* was premiered by them on June 13 at Oklahoma City's Westminster Presbyterian Church, during the regional AGO convention.

"Here and There." *Diapason* 83 (October 1992): 3-4.

The world premiere of *Overture Concertante* will take place October 27 at Symphony Hall, Boston. The 10-minute work is scored for organ and large orchestra, and will be performed by the Boston Philharmonic Orchestra (conducted by Benjamin Zander), with James David Christie, for whom the work was written, at the organ.

"Here and There." *Diapason* 84 (July 1993): 4.

Pinkham's 70th birthday was celebrated by a gala concert on June 4 in Faneuil Hall, Boston. The New England Composers Recording Project sponsored the event. In addition, Thorpe Music Publishing Co. released two new works; *Wondrous Love*, a set of five easy variations for organ; and *Three Introits for Christmastide*, a set of short pieces for two-part chorus. New England Conservatory of Music presented Pinkham with his fourth honorary doctorate on May 23.

Jones, Bruce. "Florida Conclave." *Music* (AGO) 8 (February 1974): 32-35, 53.

Pinkham's work *Mourn for the Eclipse of His Light* is premiered by organist V. Earl Copes and his son, violinist Ronald Copes, along with pre-recorded tape. An overview of the work is included.

Kyle, Marguerite K. "AmerAllegro." *Pan Pipes* 55/2 (1963): 65-66.

Leonard Raver, organ, and members of the New England Conservatory performed the premiere of *Concertante for Organ and Percussion* at the Church of the Advent, Boston, on April 8. Commission information is provided; the work will be published by C. F. Peters. Pinkham is named recipient of a Ford Foundation grant.

65/2 (1973): 67.

Publication of *Toccatas for the Vault of Heaven* (organ and tape) is announced.

68/2 (1976): 66.

Nebulae, for organ, band, and tape, was premiered in May; *Liturgies* (timpani, organ, and tape), *For Evening Draws On* (English horn, organ, tape), and *Toccata for the Vault of Heaven* (organ and tape) will soon be released by Golden Crest on an LP.

Little, Jeanie R. "Serial, Aleatoric, and Electrical Techniques in American Organ Music Published between 1960 and 1972." Ph.D., University of Iowa, 1975. *Dissertation Abstracts* 36 (June 1978): 7722A.

This scholarly, in-depth work analyzes in detail Pinkham's serial and chance works and pieces with electronic tape for organ, among other composers' works.

"Pipings." *American Organist* 15 (July 1981): 35.

Recently premiered works by Pinkham: *Diversions for Organ and Harp*, commissioned by Elizabeth Sollenberger and played by Leonard Raver and Carol Baum, AGO Regional Convention in Portland, Maine; *Man's Days Are Like the Grass*, a commissioned solo work performed by Richard Shirey at Westminster United Presbyterian Church, Akron, Ohio. James David Christie will record Pinkham's *Proverbs* later in the year.

"Premieres." *American Organist* 21 (May 1987): 52.

Organist Richard Benefield was assisted by a string ensemble in the first performance of Pinkham's *Sonata No. 3*, for organ and strings, on April 27 at St. Peter's Church in Osterville, Mass. Commission information supplied.

"Premieres." *American Organist* 22 (August 1988): 33.

Pinkham's *Sonata da chiesa* was introduced at the dedication of the Wissinger organ at Plymouth Church in Belmont, Mass., 24 April 1988 by violist Patricia McCarty and organist James David Christie. Christie and John Finney were the duo organists for the initial performance of Pinkham's *Petitions* at the Church of the Advent, Boston, 1 May 1988.

"Premieres." *American Organist* 22 (October 1988): 51.

Daniel Pinkham's *Pedals: A Prelude, Plaint and Strut for Organ Pedals and Four Pedal Timpani* was premiered by Fred Tulan, to whom it is dedicated, in Central United Methodist Church, Stockton, Calif., 8 July 1988. Brief overview of the work.

"Premieres." *American Organist* 23 (August 1989): 37.

Elizabeth and Raymond Chenault commissioned and performed the premiere of Pinkham's *Requiem Collects*, an organ duet, for the Oklahoma City Region VII AGO Convention at Westminster Presbyterian Church, 13 June 1989.

"Premieres." *Music Journal* 32 (September 1974): 19.

Liturgies is premiered at the fourth annual Contemporary Music Festival at the Hartt College of Music.

Raver, Leonard. **"The Solo Organ Music of Daniel Pinkham."** *American Organist* 17 (June 1983): 35-37.

Biography; annotated bibliography of Pinkham's organ works.

————. **"Daniel Pinkham, AGO Composer of the Year."** *American Organist* 24 (December 1990): 28, 30, 32, 34, 36, 38, 40-44.

Biography; a thoroughly annotated chronological bibliography of his organ music.

Rudd, Michael. **"Stylistic Features and Compositional Activities in Organ Literature Since World War II."** *Diapason* 59 (June 1968): 12.

Pinkham's *Suite* (1952) is included in the discussion. His use of colors, harmonic changes, tonal changes, and other factors are important in this well-written work.

Schuneman, Robert. **"Charles Benton Fisk: An Affectionate Remembrance."** *Diapason* 75 (April 1984): 4-5.

At a memorial service held for Fisk at King's Chapel on Sunday, January 22, Pinkham's *A Proclamation*, a solo work for organ in memory of Fisk, was introduced by Leonard Raver.

Smith, Warren S. "Daniel Pinkham." *American Composer Alliance Bulletin* 10/1 (1961): 9-14.

Pinkham's epicurean taste in instrumental sonorities and his eclecticism are discussed. Missing are comments on melody and harmony. A list of works follows the article.

Newman Powell

B. David, Panama, 27 September 1919. B.Mus., Ohio University, 1942; M.Mus., American Conservatory (n.d.), studied with Sowerby; M.A., Stanford, 1955; Ph.D., 1959; fellow, Newberry Library, Chicago, 1956; professor of music, Valparaiso University (Ind.), 1943-85; now emeritus. His 1958 Ph.D. dissertation at Stanford University is entitled "Rhythmic Freedom in the Performance of French Music from 1650-1735." Editor of *Festschrift Theodore Hoelty-Nickel: A Collection of Essays on Church Music* (Valparaiso: Valparaiso University Press, 1967); with Herbert Lindemann, *The Sunday Psalter* (St. Louis: Concordia, 1961). Organ music listed in Arnold's book.

OL, OL95.

No bibliographical information located.

Robert Jennings Powell

B. Benoit, Miss., 22 July 1932. Undergraduate degree, Louisiana State University, 1954, with Helen Gunderson; and M.M. at Union Theological Seminary, New York, 1958, with Alec Wyton, Harold Friedell, and Seth Bingham. FAGO. Assistant organist at the Cathedral of St. John the Divine, New York, 1957-58; organist-choirmaster at St. Paul's Episcopal Church, Meridian, Miss., 1958-64; organist-choirmaster, St. Paul's School, Concord, N.H., 1965-68; organist-choirmaster, Christ Church, Greenville, S.C., since 1968.

ABD, CACA, OL, OL95.

"American Guild of Organists." *Music Journal* 26 (September 1968): 94.

Powell's *Suite for Two Organs and Brass* was premiered by Kathleen Thomerson and Carl Staplin.

"Appointments." *American Organist* 51 (June 1968): 21.

Powell is appointed organist-choirmaster of Christ Church, Episcopal, Greenville, S.C.

Jones, Bruce. "Florida Conclave." *Music* (AGO) 8 (February 1974): 32-35, 53.

Commissioned by the Clearwater chapter of the AGO, Powell's *Sonatine for Violin and Organ* was premiered by organist V. Earl Copes and his son Ronald, violinist. The work is essentially a violin solo with organ accompaniment. "On the whole, the feeling [of the work] is somewhat noncommittal, no destination and no arrival."

"Premieres." *American Organist* 29 (February 1995): 52.

Duo-organists Elizabeth and Raymond Chenault played the world premiere of *Angels Among Us* by Powell on 11 December 1994. The performance was at Clayton State College's Spivey Hall in Morrow, Ga., and featured another premiere, Charles Callahan's *Christmas Fantasy.*

"Robert J. Powell." *Diapason* 50 (May 1959): 23.

Powell leaves the Cathedral of St. John the Divine for St. Paul's Episcopal Church, Meridian, Miss., where he will be organist-choirmaster. Brief biography.

"Robert J. Powell." *American Organist* 48 (June 1965): 21.

Powell is appointed organist-choirmaster and director of music at St. Paul's School, Concord, N.H., effective September 1956.

"Robert J. Powell." *Diapason* 56 (June 1965): 3.

Same information as in the item above.

"Robert J. Powell." *Diapason* 59 (June 1968): 2.

Powell has been appointed organist-choir director of Christ Church, Episcopal, Greenville, S.C.

Vera Nicolaevena Preobrajenska

B. San Francisco, Calif., 27 April 1926. B.A., San Francisco State University, 1953; M.A., 1972, and Ph.D., 1973, Bernadean University, Las Vegas. Studied with Milhaud at Mills College, 1945-47; with Ernest Bloch, Roger Sessions, and Frederick Jacobi, University of California, Berkeley; with Alexander Tcherepnin, San Francisco Institute of Music; and with Dmitri Shostakovich, by correspondence. Concert manager of Musical Artists of America, 1956-61; lecturer, University of California, Berkeley, 1965-68; chairman, department of music, Bernadean University, 1972-73; honorary director of music, Santa Cruz Academy of Music, 1974-75. Won two composition prizes from National League of Pen Women. Organ music listed in Cohen's book.

ABD, CACA, CACJ, IWC, WCH.

No bibliographical information located.

Richard Proulx

B. St. Paul, Minn., 3 April 1937. Studied at McPhail College of Music, Minneapolis; with Dominick Argento,University of Minnesota; and at the Columbus Boy Choir School. Music director-organist at St. Thomas Episcopal Church and Temple de Hirsch-Sinai, Seattle, Wash., in 1971-80; organist-choirmaster, Church of St. Bernadette, Seattle, Wash.; on the faculties of St. Thomas Day School and the Cornish Institute; appointed in 1980 as director of music and organist, Holy Name Cathedral, Chicago. Author of *Tintinnabulum: The Liturgical Use of Handbells* (Chicago: GIA, 1980); editor for *Worship II* (Chicago: GIA, 1977). ABD, CACA, OL, OL95.

"Appointments." *Diapason* 71 (August 1980): 17.
> Proulx has been appointed music director and organist at Holy Name Cathedral, Chicago, effective August 1. An overview of his music career is presented.

"Appointments." *American Organist* 26 (March 1992): 60.
> Proulx, music director for the Cathedral of the Holy Name, Chicago, since 1980, is on sabbatical leave and will teach in Australia and New Zealand for the Royal School of Church Music, followed by study and research in Europe. He will return to the cathedral in July 1992.

Richard Purvis

B. San Francisco, Calif., 25 August 1917; d. San Francisco, 25 December 1994. Studied at Peabody Conservatory; Curtis Institute; Royal School of Music, London. Organist-choirmaster in Philadelphia; bandmaster, U.S. Army, World War II. Organist, Calvary Presbyterian Church, San Francisco, 1931-34; organist, St. James Church, Philadelphia, 1937-39; head, department of music, Episcopal Academy, Overbrook, Penn., 1939-40. Pupil of Joseph Lhevinne, Edward Bairstow, Charles Courboin, Alexander McCurdy, David McK. Williams, and Marcel Dupré. Recitalist, California Palace of the Legion of Honor, 1939-69; organist-master of the choristers, Grace Cathedral, San Francisco, 1947-71, and head, music department, Cathedral School for Boys, San Francisco, 1959-68.
ABD, CACA, OL, OL95, PC71, X52, X54, X58, X66, X67, X71.

"An American Organ Mass." *Diapason* 45 (February 1954): 21.
> Purvis's *An American Organ Mass* is published by Flammer and provides organ music for a complete communion service based on well-known tunes; the individual movements are short and are in his "ingratiating style, so well known to the American organ world."

Bingham, Seth. "Organ Personalities." *American Organist* 46 (November 1963): 16.

Acknowledges Purvis's organ works as effective pieces.

Burkett, John Morris. "Music for Two or More Players at One or More Organs." D.M.A., University of Illinois at Urbana-Champaign, 1973.

Traces the history of ensemble organ playing and music from the 15th century to the present; includes Richard Purvis's work.

"Convention Personalities." *American Organist* 18 (April 1984): 127.

A brief introduction to Purvis.

"Four Players in Tone." *Diapason* 43 (May 1952): 34.

A set of four chorale fantasias, instrumental meditations on hymn-tunes, all of high quality, is published by M. Witmark & Sons. Brief description of the pieces; not too difficult for the average organist.

"Here and There." *Diapason* 84 (July 1993): 3.

Grace Cathedral and the San Francisco AGO Chapter will honor Purvis on his 80th birthday, August 15. Evensong will be followed by a recital of his works.

Herrenschwand, Franz. "Recitals and Concerts." *American Organist* 43 (November 1960): 27.

Purvis performs an all-Purvis recital at Grace Cathedral, San Francisco, 8 May 1960. The reviewer raved about this recital and called it "a true experience."

"The Music of Richard Purvis." *Caecilia* 85 (spring 1958): 253-54.

A review of his performance recorded on the Aeolian-Skinner in Grace Cathedral, San Francisco, and featuring his own works, is lukewarm.

[Obituary.] *American Organist* 29 (April 1995): 54.

Provides biographical and career information.

"On the Cover." *Choral Guide* 5 (January 1953): 13. *

Parton, Kenneth. "Recitals and Concerts." *American Organist* 46 (February 1963): 22.

A favorable review for Purvis's recital on 23 October 1962 at St. Michael and All Angels Episcopal Church, Dallas.

"Pipings." *American Organist* 27 (September 1993): 51.

Purvis celebrates his 80th birthday with a "Gala Celebration in Honor of Richard Purvis." A festival Evensong featuring his choral music was preceded by an organ recital of his compositions played by former students.

"Prayer for Peace, Elegy & Cappriccio on the Notes of the Cuckoo." *Diapason* 46 (December 1954): 37.

A brief description of the work accompanies the announcement that this piece is published by J. Fischer.

"Purvis Works to Open Organ Dedication." *American Organist* 49 (October 1966): 32.

Purvis's *Rondo for Pedals Alone (Homage à Moscheles)*, commissioned for the inauguration of the new Ruffatti organ, and a choral work, *Laudate Dominum*, scored for choir, brass, timpani, and finger cymbals, will be performed on 13 November 1966.

"Recitals and Concerts." *American Organist* 40 (April 1957): 125.

Purvis performs at Grace Cathedral, San Francisco, February 10. The review of his all-German "Masterpieces of Organ Literature" was one of resounding approval.

"Recitals and Concerts." *American Organist* 41 (September 1958): 345.

A recital by Purvis at Grace Cathedral, San Francisco, on May 11 includes his own *Supplication* and *Toccata Festiva "In Babilone."* The reviewer thoroughly enjoyed the recital and praised Purvis's playing.

"Recitals and Concerts." *American Organist* 48 (April 1965): 7.

Earl Ness and William Whitehead perform a recital of music for two organs at First Baptist Church, Philadelphia, on March 7. Purvis's *Dialogue monastique* is one of only two works on the program that is originally written for two organs. Wesley A. Day, the reviewer, encouraged more artists and composers to arrange and write for two organs.

"Richard Purvis." *American Organist* 33 (May 1950): 178.

A brief introduction to the composer.

"Richard Purvis." *Choral Guide* 6 (April 1953): 18. *

"Richard Purvis." *American Organist* 37 (March 1954): 91.

Purvis's *Four Dubious Conceits*, for organ, continues to receive high praise from many players.

"Richard Purvis Recital." *American Organist* 34 (February 1951): 56.

Central Presbyterian, New York, was the site of Purvis's recital on 20 February 1951. The program consisted of Handel, Franck, Bach, and four Purvis works: *Repentance, Thankgiving, Supplication, Toccata Festiva "In Babilone"*; a very favorable review.

"Richard Purvis' New Opus." *Diapason* 43 (February 1952): 20.

For his monthly recital at Grace Cathedral, San Francisco, Purvis gave his newly-composed chorale partita *Christ ist erstanden* its west coast premiere. The work is described.

"Seven Chorale Preludes." *Music Courier* 140 (July 1949): 15.

Purvis's *Seven Chorales* is published by Carl Fischer; Hammond registration is provided.

David Raksin

B. Philadelphia, 4 August 1912. Studied at the University of Pennsylvania; studied composition with Arnold Schoenberg and Isadore Freed. Taught theory and composition at the University of North Carolina, Southern Methodist University, University of New Mexico, Pomona College, and the University of Michigan. Currently on the faculties of the University of Southern California, lecturer-professor (1995-96, CMS director), and the University of California at Los Angeles. Documentaries have been made about his life by the BBC, Danish, Canadian, and West German radio networks.

ABD, BB78, BB92, CACA, CACJ [Raskin], KTL.

Belt, Byron. "AGO National Convention, San Francisco 1984." *American Organist* 18 (August 1984): 28-33.

Raksin's commissioned work, *A Song After Sundown* is presented at the convention; the work is written for organ and orchestra. Keith Chapman was soloist for this "rerun of some of his earlier tunes. . . ." Another Raksin piece, *Fanfare for Organ, Brass and Percussion* was "very exciting."

"Convention Personalities." *American Organist* 18 (April 1984): 127.

David Raksin is currently on the faculties of the University of Southern California and the University of California at Los Angeles, plus the biographical information given above.

Gustafson, Bruce. "AGO San Francisco: Some Perspective." *Diapason* 75 (October 1984): 6, 8-9.

The reviewer calls Raksin's *A Song After Sundown* "a sort of theater organ reverie with orchestra."

Gardner Read

B. Evanston, Ill., 2 January 1913. Studied theory, Northwestern University; conducting with Bakaleinikoff; composition with Paul White, Bernard Rogers, and Howard Hanson at the Eastman School of Music, B.M., 1936, M.M., 1937; further studies with Pizzetti in Rome on a Cromwell Traveling Fellowship, 1938-39; completed his training with Copland at Berkshire Music Center, Tanglewood, 1941. Studied briefly with Sibelius. Taught composition, St. Louis Institute of Music, 1941-43; Kansas City Conservatory of Music, 1943-45; and at the Cleveland Institute of Music, 1945-48; appointed composer-in-residence and professor of composition at Boston University School for the Arts in 1948; retired in 1978. Author of *Thesaurus of Orchestral Devices* (New York: Pittman, 1953); *Music Notation: A Manual of Modern Practice* (Boston: Allyn & Bacon, 1964); *Contemporary Instrumental Techniques* (New York: Schirmer Books, 1976); *Modern Rhythmic Notation* (Bloomington: Indiana University Press, 1978); *Style and Orchestrations* (New York: Schirmer, 1979); *Source Book of Proposed Music Notation Reforms* (Westport, Conn.: Greenwood, 1987); *20th-Century Microtonal Notation* (Westport: Greenwood, 1989) and *Compendium of Modern Instrumental Techniques* (Westport: Greenwood, 1993). MacDowell Colony fellow; Huntington-Hartford fellowship recipient.

AA73, ABD, AMH, AS66, BB58, BB65, BB71, BB78, BB92, BDA, BMI, CA8, CACA, CACJ, CPM, DCM, DN72, DN75, EDM, EVM, HHH, IWW92, JCN, KTL, LMD, MHHH, NCE, NG, NGA, OL, OL95, PC71, PCM, PET, REM, TCAC, TCH, WI62, WI69, WTM, X50, X51, X52, X53, X54, X55, X58, X60, X61, X62, X64, X65, X66, X67, X69, X70, X71, X74.

"American Composer Update." *Pan Pipes* 73/2 (1980): 39.

Galactic novae, for organ and percussion, will be premiered by Leonard Raver, who commissioned the work, at Alice Tully Hall, New York, on 12 March 1981. *Modern Rhythmic Notation* was published by Victor Gollancz, London.

"American Composer Update." *Pan Pipes* 87/2 (winter 1995): 36-37.

Read's *Chorale-Fantasia on "Good King Wenceslas,"* for organ, is published by CPP/Belwin; Greenwood Press will be publishing *Gardner Read: A Bio-Bibliography*, by Mary Ann Dodd.

"Composers World." *Musical America* 81 (November 1961): 61.

Gardner Read's second set of *Preludes on Old Southern Hymns for Organ* received its premiere performance on 8 October 1961 by David Craighead at Pasadena Presbyterian Church.

Drone, Jeanette. "American Composer Update." *Pan Pipes* 75/2 (1983): 38.

Eastman honors Read with the Music Alumni Achievement Award; a research grant is awarded him from the Ingram Merrill Foundation of New York for a monograph on the proposed reforms of music notation since 1700.

"Gardner Read." *American Organist* 32 (April 1949): 136.

A concentrated biography and list of published organ works provided. "His is music for the professional," says the author of this sketch on American composers.

"Gardner Read." *Diapason* 43 (December 1951): 16.

Organist Samuel Walter presents Read's most recent work for organ, *Eight Preludes on Old Southern Hymns*, op. 90, in a recital on October 29 in Marsh Chapel, Boston University.

"Gardner Read." *Pan Pipes* 43 (December 1950): 127. *

> 44 (January 1952): 42-43. *

> 45 (January 1953): 64-65. *

"Gardner Read." *Composers of the Americas* 8 (1962): 124-39.
> A brief biography in Spanish and English is followed by a chronological listing of his works, according to medium.

"Gardner Read." *American Organist* 46 (March 1963): 25.
> Read will be honored on his 50th birthday with a festival of his works by groups from Boston University, where he is composer-in-residence and professor of composition and theory.

"Here and There." *Diapason* 69 (June 1978): 14-15.
> George Faxon performed a recital of Gardner Read's works; included was the world premiere of *Invocation*, op. 135, for trombone and organ.

"Here and There." *Diapason* 84 (September 1993): 4.
> Greenwood Press announces the release of *Compendium of Modern Instrumental Techniques* by Read, with a foreword by Gunther Schuller.

Johns, Donald. "Solo and Ensemble Music." *Notes* 30/3 (March 1974): 611-12.
> Reviews Read's *Sinfonia da chiesa* for brass quintet and organ.

Kyle, Marguerite K. "AmerAllegro." *Pan Pipes* 48 (January 1956): 68.
> Samuel Walter premiered *Quiet Music for Organ* at Marsh Chapel, Boston University, 6 December 1954.

> 50 (January 1958): 69.
> *Little Pastorale* is published. Read is also a participant in an International Education Exchange for the State Department, to Mexico.

> 51 (January 1959): 80.
> Robert King Music published *De profundis*, op. 71, for horn and organ.

> 54/2 (1962): 68.
> David Craighead performed the premiere of *Preludes on Old Southern Hymns*, op. 122, on October 8, at Pasadena Presbyterian Church; Read also completed a book on orchestral style.

> 55/2 (1963): 67.
> Abingdon published *Quiet Music for Organ*; Gray published *Six Preludes on Old Southern Hymns*; and Doane College, Crete, Nebr., awarded Read an honorary Doctor of Music degree.

56/2 (1964): 76-77.

Repeat information about the *Six Preludes* is given.

57/2 (1965): 75.

Premiere of *Elegiac Aria*, op. 91a, is performed by Leonard Raver, 7 August 1964, at St. Thomas Church, New York.

58/2 (1966): 80-81.

Philip Gehring recorded "Toccata" from the *Suite for Organ*, op. 81, on the Valparaiso University Recording label; Read was a Huntington-Hartford Foundation fellow.

59/2 (1967): 92.

Announces the January 1967 premiere of Read's *Variations on a Chromatic Ground*, op. 121, performed by Arthur Newman at the MIT Chapel.

60/2 (1968): 77-78.

Announces the publication of *Elegiac Aria*, op. 91a.

62/2 (1970): 77-78.

Same information as the item above, with the addition of J. Fischer as publisher.

63/2 (1971): 74.

Sinfonia da chiesa, op. 61b, was premiered by organist George Faxon at Trinity Church, Boston, on February 3, with the Boston University Brass Quintet.

64/2 (1972): 75.

Suite for Organ is published by Transcontinental; Fred Swann records *Three Preludes on Old Southern Hymns*, op. 90, on Riverside Church Recordings.

66/2 (1974): 68.

Fourteenth year as an ASCAP award recipient.

67/2 (1975): 69.

Read receives his fifteenth consecutive ASCAP award.

68/2 (1976): 68.

Several organ works are in progress; *Contemporary Instrumental Techniques* was published by Schirmer Books.

69/2 (1977): 65.

Sonoric Fantasia, for organ and percussion, was premiered by organist Elizabeth Sollenberger and percussionist Neil Grover at Trinity Church, Boston. A list of biographical sources is provided.

70/2 (1978): 58.

Leonard Raver introduced *And There Appeared unto Them Tongues as of Fire* at the AGO Convention, June 28, during his recital at St. Joseph's Cathedral, Hartford, Conn.

"Meditation on 'Jesu, meine Freude.'" *Musical Courier* 154 (August 1956): 29.

H. W. Gray published *Meditation on "Jesu, meine Freude."* A reviewer states that it is good service music for the average organist.

"Music Journal's Gallery of Living Composers." *Music Journal* 32 (March 1974): 44.

Biographical information and a list of major works and publications is provided.

"News and Honors." *ASCAP* 9/1 (1978): 41.

David Craighead gave the premiere performance of Read's *And There Appeared unto Them Tongues as of Fire* at the regional AGO Convention in Hartford, Conn., 28 July 1977.

"Passacaglia and Fugue in D Minor for Organ." *Notes* 6 (March 1949): 331.

A brief review of the piece published by H. W. Gray indicates that it is difficult.

"Premiered." *ASCAP*, fall 1988, 67.

Read's *Phantasmagoria*, for organ and English horn, was premiered 15 March 1988 by Leonard Raver and Thomas Stacy at the Juilliard School, New York.

"Recitals." *American Organist* 22 (August 1988): 61.

Leonard Raver performs the premieres of Read's *Phantasmagoria* and David Diamond's *Symphony for Organ*.

"Suite for Organ: Preamble, Scherzo, Aria, Toccata, op. 81." *Notes* 8 (June 1951): 563-64.

This work won the top award in a recent competition sponsored by the Pennsylvania College for Women. "The *Suite* is done in the grand manner . . . with an opportunity for all-out attack. . . . A display piece." Basic description of the work is included.

"8 Preludes on Old Southern Hymns for Organ." *Diapason* 45 (March 1954): 30.

Read's preludes are published by Gray; the works are based on the hymn-tunes found in the 1902 edition of *The Sacred Harp*. "The music is interesting and vital, creative workmanship is of high order and the total result is intriguing."

"8 Preludes on Old Southern Hymns for Organ." *Notes* 11 (March 1954): 282.

Published by H. W. Gray, these preludes are "worth the attention of both the recitalist and the church organist."

Thomas Richner

B. Penn., 19—. M.M. and doctor of music degrees from Columbia University, New York. Concert pianist, interpreter of Mozart's keyboard music. Professor of music, Douglass College, Rutgers University, and organist, First Church of Christ, Scientist, the Mother Church, Boston, Mass. At Columbia University's Teachers College, he founded the organ department. Founder of the annual Colby Institute of Church Music, and since 1967 he has been its director. Author of *Orientation for Interpreting Mozart's Piano Sonatas* (Rexburg, Idaho: Ricks College Press, 1972). His New York recital debut as a pianist occurred in 1941 at the Town Hall, which was part of his prize as co-winner of the 1940 Naumburg Competition.

OL, OL95 and *American Organist* 51 (August 1968): 21.

"Appointments." *American Organist* 51 (August 1968): 21.

> Richner is appointed to full professorship at Douglass College, Rutgers University; resigned from Teachers College, Columbia University, where he founded the organ department.

"Here and There." *Diapason* 80 (November 1989): 4.

> Richner is featured on a new compact disc recording, *Thomas Richner Plays the Mother Church Organ*. The recording was made on the Aeolian-Skinner organ in First Church of Christ, Scientist, Boston.

"Workshop Leaders." *American Organist* 16 (April 1982): 158.

> Richner's biography in miniature is posted.

Marga Richter

B. Reedsburg, Wisc., 21 October 1926. B.S., 1949, and M.S., 1951, Juilliard; studied composition with William Bergsma and Vincent Persichetti and piano with Rosalyn Tureck. Instructor, Nassau Community College, New York, 1971-73. In 1972, co-founded and is co-director, with Herbert Deutsch, of the Long Island Composers' Alliance. Received awards, grants, and commissions from the National Endowment for the Arts, Martha Baird Rockefeller Fund for Music grant, 1975; NEA fellowship, 1979; National Federation of Music Clubs, Meet the Composer, and ASCAP awards. Founder of the League of Women Composers.

ABD, AS66, BB92, CACA, CACJ, DN78, IWC, NGA, OL, OL95, PCM, TCH, WCH, X69.

Ammer, Christine. *Unsung: A History of Women in American Music.* Westport, Conn.: Greenwood, 1980.

Includes Richter's biography.

Fuerst-Heidtmann, Monika. "Kompieren als emotionelle Notwendigkeit; ein Porträt der amerikanischen Komponistin Marga Richter." *Neuland* 4 (1983-84): 268-76.

Includes musical examples, bibliography, and list of works. In German.

"Here and There." *Diapason* 67 (September 1976): 18.

Richter's new work, *Variations on a Theme by Neihart von Reuenthal*, was premiered by Leonard Raver in the Summergarden of the Museum of Modern Art in New York, July 9 and 10; the work is published by Carl Fischer.

Kyle, Marguerite K. **"AmerAllegro."** *Pan Pipes* 67/2 (1975): 70.

Richter is an ASCAP Standard Award winner since 1966.

68/2 (1976): 69.

Recipient of grants from Meet the Composer and the Martha Baird Rockefeller Foundation; co-founded the League of Women Composers; Carl Fischer published *Variations on a Theme by Neihart von Reuenthal*, for organ.

69/2 (1977): 66.

Leonard Raver performs the premiere of the *Variations on a Theme by Neihart von Reuenthal* on July 9 and 10 at the Museum of Modern Art, New York.

70/2 (1978): 59.

Richter received a grant from the National Endowment for the Arts.

LePage, Jane Weiner. *Women Composers, Conductors, and Musicians of the Twentieth Century: Selected Biographies.* Metuchen, N.J.: Scarecrow, 1980.

Includes Richter's biography, discography, and list of works.

"Presenting the Composers of NFMC's Commissioned Works (1979)." *Music Clubs Magazine* 58/4 (1979): 15+. *

Myron J. Roberts

B. San Diego, Calif., 30 January 1912. Studied at the University of the Pacific, B.M., 1935; School of Sacred Music, Union Theological Seminary, M.S.M., 1937. Organ pupil of

Warren Allen, Allan Bacon, and Clarence Dickinson; composition with Edwin Stringham and Roger Sessions. Professor, University of Nebraska, 1940-74. Organist, First Plymouth Congregational Church, Lincoln, Nebr., 1940-56; organist, Holy Trinity Episcopal Church, Lincoln, 1957-67; since 1969, organist, Cathedral of the Risen Christ, Lincoln; retired, 1974.

ABD, CACA, OL, OL95.

"AGO Regional Convention Reports 1989." *American Organist* 23 (October 1989): 81.

Marilyn Keiser played Myron Roberts's *Church Sonata* in its premiere performance. The work was one of three commissioned pieces for the convention in San Jose.

Baker, Robert. "A Myron Roberts Festival." *Music* (AGO) 10 (August 1976): 19.

A festival recital to honor recently-retired Myron Roberts occurred 28 March 1976 at the First Plymouth Congregational Church of Lincoln, Nebr., under the guidance of John Levick. An autobiographical statement accompanies the article.

"Contemporary Composers: Myron J. Roberts." *Journal of Church Music* 16 (June 1974): 7-8.

Biography, list of published organ works, choral works, and works for organ with instruments are included; some works are described.

"Here and There." *Diapason* 81 (April 1990): 3.

Raymond and Elizabeth Chenault, duo-organists, perform the premiere of Roberts's *Fanfares*, February 25, at the Cathedral Church of the Advent, Birmingham, Ala.

"Here and There." *Diapason* 84 (October 1993): 3.

Raymond and Elizabeth Chenault gave the world premiere of *The Juggler*, written for them by Roberts, at the Cathedral of Christ the King in Atlanta, Ga., on June 25.

"Homage to Perotin." *Musical Courier* 155 (1 January 1957): 34.

H. W. Gray publishes Roberts's *Homage to Perotin*; brief sketch of the music is given.

Kyle, Marguerite K. "AmerAllegro." *Pan Pipes* 60/2 (1968): 90.

Claire Coci premieres *Improvisation for Pedals*, 20 August 1967, Boys Town, Nebr.; *Dialogue* is premiered by Robert Baker, 1 November 1966, Westminster Abbey, London, and the work is published by Oxford University Press.

62/2 (1970): 78-79.

Nova is premiered by Jon Spong at the June Regional AGO meeting in Kansas City, Mo.; *Pastorale* and *Aviary* are published.

64/2 (1972): 76.

Three Pieces for Organ and Marimba is premiered by Wilma Jensen and K. Dean Walker on June 9 at the AGO Convention, University of Nebraska, Lincoln; on May 9, Robert Baker introduced *Fanfare for a New Organ* at Kimball Hall, University of Nebraska.

66/2 (1974): 69.

Three Pieces for Organ and Two Horns was premiered by John Bucks, organ, and Susan Schmidt and Lou Stout, horns; *Nova* was published by Gray; and C. Fischer published *Four for Organ and Marimba.*

67/2 (1975): 71.

Five for Organ and Marimba is published by C. Fischer; Roberts retires from the University of Nebraska.

68/2 (1976): 70.

George Baker recorded *Prelude and Trumpetings* on the Cavaillé-Coll organ at the Basilica of St Sernin, Toulouse, on the Delos-Pi label.

69/2 (1977): 67.

David Drinkwater both commissioned and introduced *Blessed Assurance*, variations for organ, at Rutgers University; the work is published by Gray.

70/2 (1978): 60.

Nova is recorded by Robert Baker on Sonar, tape and disc.

71/2 (1979): 43.

Pastorella and *Invention for Two Organs* will be premiered by Austin Lovelace and Phyllis Tremmel in January 1979. In November 1978, Thomas K. Brown premiered the Roberts work he commissioned, *Four Short Pieces for Organ*, at Texas Women's University, Denton.

Lawrence, Arthur. **"The Organ and the Concert Hall: Perspectives on the Use of the Organ with Other Instruments."** *Diapason* 73 (March 1982): 18.

The author finds Roberts's *Three for Organ, Clarinet and Bassoon* "a carefully-crafted and registered piece with imitative lines . . . very gratifying."

"Myron J. Roberts Opens Large Reuter in Lincoln." *Diapason* 42 (April 1951): 7.

Roberts performs the dedicatory recital on the new four-manual Reuter organ installed at St. Paul's Methodist Church, Lincoln, Nebr., on 11 February 1951.

"Premieres." *American Organist* 24 (April 1990): 69-70.

Myron Roberts's *Fanfares*, an organ duet, was premiered by Elizabeth and Raymond Chenault in a recital on February 25 at the Cathedral Church of the Advent in Birmingham, Ala. Other commissioned works were on the program.

McNeil Robinson

B. Birmingham, Ala., 1943. Graduated from Juilliard; composition studies with Charles Wuorinen and Vincent Persichetti; advanced theory with Allen Forte; organ student of Clarence Watters, George Faxon, and Russell Saunders. Teaches on the faculties of Queens College, Manhattan School of Music, and Mannes College of Music; music director, Park Avenue Christian Church and Park Avenue Synagogue, New York. OL95.

Cantrell, Scott. "AGO National Convention, Boston." *American Organist* 24 (August 1990): 48.

Robinson's commission, *Sonata*, is in two movements. The first movement was a "maladroit stringing of lines over odd bleeps, bloops and oom-pah-pahs. The succeeding Allegro e furioso was a sassy *danse macabre*."

"Convention Personalities." *American Organist* 18 (April 1984): 129.

The recipient of many commissions, Robinson's works are published mostly by Theodore Presser. He graduated from the Juilliard School and the Mannes School. Composition study was with Anthony Newman, George Faxon, and Charles Wuorinen. Robinson served as organist at United Nations Church of the Holy Family, Park Avenue Synagogue, and Church of St. Mary the Virgin, New York.

Gustafson, Bruce. "AGO San Francisco: Some Perspectives." *Diapason* 75 (October 1984): 6, 8-9.

Concerto for Organ is one large movement that "relied heavily on orchestral colors similar to Ravel."

"Here and There." *Diapason* 81 (July 1990): 3.

McNeil Robinson premiered his own chorale prelude on "Douglass," and his chorale prelude and hymn for Fred Pratt Green's "When in Our Music, God Is Glorified" on April 30, during the 1990 Festival of the Arts at Douglass Boulevard Christian Church.

"Premieres." *American Organist* 21 (April 1987): 57.

David Higgs performed the premiere of Robinson's *Angels*, for organ and orchestra. The composer conducted the seven-movement work, commissioned by the Cleveland AGO chapter, at St. Paul's Episcopal Church, Cleveland Heights, Ohio, 24 November 1986.

Joseph Roff

(*Né* Roffinella.) B. Turin, Italy, 26 December 1910; d. 12 July 1993, n.p. B.M., M.A., D.M.A., 1948, University of Toronto; studied with Healey Willan, Leo Smith, and Ernest MacMillan. Fellow of Trinity College, London. Received ASCAP awards in 1972 and 1973. Composer-in-residence and lecturer, St. Joseph's College, Brooklyn, N.Y. Organ music listed in Arnold's book.

ABD, CACA, CCC, CLA, MIC, OL, OL95, X51, X53, X55.

No bibliographical information located.

Harald Rohlig

B. Aurich, Germany, 6 October 1926. Organist, Christuskirche, 1941-43 and 1948-51, Osnabrück, Germany. Studied at the Royal Academy of Music, London, 1948; graduated in 1951 from the Conservatory, Osnabrück; organ pupil of Günter de Witt and Fritz Heitman; composition pupil of Karl Schaefer and Wolfgang Fortner. Organist, Katharinenkirche, and professor of organ and piano, Conservatory, Osnabrück, 1951-53. Emigrated to the U.S., 1954. Organist, Memorial Presbyterian Church, Montgomery, Ala., 1955-61; since 1961, organist, St. John's Episcopal Church, Montgomery. Organ music listed in Arnold's book.

ABD, OL, OL95.

No bibliographical information located.

Ned Rorem

B. Richmond, Ind., 23 October 1923. Studied at the American Conservatory of Music, Chicago, with Leo Sowerby, 1938-39; Northwestern University, 1940-42; with Rosario Scalero, Curtis Institute; with Bernard Wagenaar, Juilliard School, B.S., 1946, and M.S., 1948; private studies with Virgil Thomson and Aaron Copland. Lived in Morocco, 1949-51, and in France, 1951-57. Won Gershwin Memorial Award, two Guggenheim fellowships, 1956-57 and 1978-79; in 1976, he was the recipient of the Pulitzer Prize in music. Composer-in-residence, University of Buffalo, 1959-61; University of Utah, 1966-67; Curtis Institute, 1980-86. Author of *Diary of a Composer* (New York: Braziller, 1966); *The Paris Diary of Ned Rorem with a Portrait of the Diarist by R. Phelps* (New York: Braziller, 1966); *Music from Inside Out* (New York: Braziller, 1967); *The New York Diary* (New York: Braziller, 1967); *Music and People* (New York: Braziller, 1968); *Critical Affairs: A Composer's Journal* (New York: Braziller, 1970); *Pure Contraption—A Composer's Essays* (New York: Holt, Rinehart & Winston, 1974); *The Final Diary* (New York: Holt, Rinehart & Winston, 1975); *An Absolute Gift: A New Diary* (New York: Simon & Schuster, 1978); *Setting the Tone—Essays and a Diary* (New York: Coward-McCann, 1983); *The Nantucket Diary of Ned Rorem*, 1973-85 (San Francisco: North Point, 1987); *Settling the Score* (New York: Harcourt Brace Jovanovich, 1988); and *Knowing When to Stop* (New York: Simon & Schuster, 1994).

AA73, ABD, AMH, AS66, BB58, BB65, BB71, BB92, BBCh, BDA, CA12, CACA, CC92, DCM, DN73, HHH, IMD, IWW92, JCN, KTL, MGGs, MHHH, NG, NGA, OL, OL95, PC71, PCM, PET, REM, TCAC, TCH, X50, X51, X52, X53, X54, X55, X56, X57, X58, X59, X60, X61, X62, X64, X65, X66, X67, X68, X69, X70, X71, X74.

"AGO National Convention, Washington, D.C., 1982." *Diapason* 73 (September 1982): 6.

John Obetz premieres the commissioned work by Ned Rorem, *Views from the Oldest House.* Performed at All Souls' Unitarian Church, Obetz is applauded for his command of the work. The movements are described in capsulated form.

"Alla Breve." *American Organist* 28 (November 1994): 50.

Knowing When to Stop, a memoir by Rorem, has been published by Simon & Schuster.

"American Composer Update." *Pan Pipes* 73/2 (1981): 41.

As of September 1980, Rorem has been teaching at the Curtis Institute, Philadelphia.

Anderson, Garland. "The Music of Ned Rorem." *Music Journal* 21 (April 1963): 34, 71-72.

Rorem's gift is the ability to write for a variety of media; list of published works and discography included.

Brinson, Doris Parker. "A Style Critical Study of the Solo Organ Works of Ned Rorem." D.M.A., Memphis State University, 1988. *Dissertation Abstracts* 49 (April 1989): 2856A.

The purpose of the work is to analyze Rorem's organ works and emphasize how they contribute to organ literature of the 20th century. Brief biography; comprehensive analysis of *A Quaker Reader* and *Views from the Oldest House.*

"A Capital Convention, Washington, D.C., June 28-July 2, 1982: Composers and Their Commissions." *American Organist* 16 (May 1982): 4.

An introduction to Rorem and his commissioned work, *Views from the Oldest House.*

"Clips on Composers." *Clavier* 24/5 (1985): 38.

Concerto for Organ received its world premiere by organist Leonard Raver, with the Portland (Maine) Symphony under the direction of Bruce Hangen, 19 March 1985.

Covington, Kate. "Music Reviews." *Notes* 48/3 (1992): 1102-04.

Rorem's *Organbook I*, *Organbook II*, and *Organbook III* are reviewed. An overview indicates that these pieces are less technically demanding than other works by Rorem, and may be used in recital or for worship services.

Drone, Jeanette. "American Composer Update." *Pan Pipes* 75/2 (1983): 39.

John Obetz premiered *Views from the Oldest House*, 29 and 30 June 1982, at the AGO Convention in Washington, D.C. Rorem authored *Setting the Tone* and *Diaries of Ned Rorem*, both published in 1982.

"Here and There." *Diapason* 76 (September 1985): 3.

The premiere of the *Organ Concerto* by Rorem took place in March with soloist Leonard Raver and the Portland (Maine) Symphony Orchestra, Bruce Hangen conducting.

Hinson, Maurice. "Great Composers in Our Time: Ned Rorem." *Piano Quarterly* 28/110 (summer 1980): 6-7, 9-11, 13-16.

The interview takes place via letters; a thorough examination of the composer's approach to writing. An addendum includes annotations by Rorem on his keyboard works.

Kolodin, Irving. "Carmelites and Quakers: Gilels, Père et Fille." *Saturday Review* 4 (19 March 1977): 47-48. *

Kyle, Marguerite K. "AmerAllegro." *Pan Pipes* 50 (January 1958): 70.

Rorem wins Guggenheim award, 1957-58.

55/2 (1963): 68.

Ford Foundation grant recipient.

58/2 (1966): 82.

Rorem was composer-in-residence, University of Utah, 1966.

70/2 (1978): 60.

A Quaker Reader, for organ solo, is published by Boosey & Hawkes; Rorem received an honorary doctorate from Northwestern University in Evanston, Ill. His eighth book, *An Absolute Gift*, will be published in March 1978.

"Leonard Raver, Organ." *High Fidelity/Musical America* 27 (May 1977): MA25.

> Dedicated to and premiered by Leonard Raver, Rorem's *A Quaker Reader*'s 11 movements are outlined and an overall concept of the work is presented.

McDonald, Arlys L. *Ned Rorem: A Bio-Bibliography.* New York: Greenwood, 1989.

> Biography, works and performances, discography, and bibliography.

McLelland, Jeffrey Randal. **"The Development of an Interpretational Scheme for the Performance of *A Quaker Reader* by Ned Rorem."** D.M.A., University of Alabama, 1993.

> The author considers four areas of investigation regarding the work: the initial study of the piece, the historical context of the composer and the work, Quakerism, and the association of Quakerism to the titles and epigraphs of the *Quaker Reader.*

"Ned Rorem." *Pan Pipes* 43 (December 1950): 128. *

"Ned Rorem." *Composers of the Americas* 12 (1966): 136-45.

> A biography in Spanish and English is followed by an annotated, chronological catalog of Rorem's works.

"Ned Rorem as Teacher." *Saturday Review* 7 (October 1980): 105-06.

> Rorem discusses the teacher's most important attribute: to understand the other, the student.

"News Section: Composers." *Tempo* 167 (December 1988): 62.

> *A Quaker Reader*, originally for organ, was transcribed by the composer for chamber orchestra. The premiere of this version was presented by Gerard Schwarz conducting the New York Chamber Symphony on 7 October 1988 at the 92nd Street Y, New York.

"News Section: Composers." *Tempo* 174 (September 1990): 71.

> *Organbook I* and *Organbook II* are premiered by Eileen Hunt, July 7, Nantucket, Mass.

"News and Honors." *ASCAP* 9/1 (1978): 41.

> World premiere of Rorem's commissioned work, *A Quaker Reader*, is performed by Leonard Raver at Lincoln Center's Alice Tully Hall.

"Pastorale for Organ." *Notes* 10 (September 1953): 686.

> Published by Southern Music, 1953, the "Andantino" from *Symphony No. 1* was transcribed by the composer for organ. The reviewer concluded the piece was too long.

"Potpourri—Rorem Organ Music Premiere." *Clavier* 29/8 (1990): 45.

Organist Eileen Hunt gives the premiere of *Organbook II* and *Organbook III* on July 7.

"Premieres." *Clavier* 16/7 (1977): 39.

A Quaker Reader is performed by organist Leonard Raver.

"Programs." *American Organist* 24 (April 1990): 94.

Leonard Raver premieres Rorem's *Organbook I* in a recital on 10 December 1989 at the Church of the Ascension, New York.

Raver, Leonard. "Ned Rorem, 1989 AGO Composer of the Year." *American Organist* 23 (March 1989): 56-57.

An overview of Rorem's life and his organ works; special attention to his *Organ Concerto* and his latest work, *Fanfare and Flourish*, for organ and brass.

————. **"The Solo Organ Music of Ned Rorem."** *American Organist* 17 (October 1983): 67-71.

Detailed observations of Rorem's *Quaker Reader* and *Views from the Oldest House*, movement by movement.

"Recitals and Concerts." *American Organist* 40 (April 1957): 126. *

"Rorem at Buffalo U." *Musical Courier* 160 (October 1959): 29.

Rorem is appointed Slee Professor at the University of Buffalo for the 1959-60 academic year.

"Rorem Wins Pulitzer." *Clavier* 15/6 (1976): 62.

The Pulitzer Prize in music is awarded to Rorem for his orchestral work entitled *Air Music*.

Satz, Arthur. "Ned Rorem: Musician of the Month." *High Fidelity/Musical America* 26 (August 1976): MA4-5.

Recognition of Rorem's work, especially in regard to his recent achievement, being awarded the Pulitzer Prize in music.

Olive Nelson Russell

B. Albert Lea, Minn., 28 September 1905; d. Aurora, Colo., 30 March 1989. On faculty, University of Missouri Conservatory of Music, Kansas City, 1966; organist, Countryside Christian Church, 1966. Organ music listed in Cohen's book.

IWC.

"Best of the Year 1966." *Piano Quarterly* 15/59 (1967): 19-20.

> Award-winner Russell lives in Shawnee Mission, Kans., teaches on the faculty of the University of Missouri's Conservatory of Music, and is organist at Countryside Christian Church. Sketchy background details.

"Recital Program." *Diapason* 72 (May 1982): 16.

> Organist Carlene Neihart performs the world premiere of Olive Nelson Russell's *Transformation*, February 5, at Asbury United Methodist Church, El Paso, Texas.

Peter Sandloff

B. New York, 3 July 1924. Studied piano, conducting, and composition with Jarnach at the Musikhochschule, Cologne. Kapellmeister, Bamberg, Munich, and Freiburg-im-Breisgau, 1947-53; since 1953, free-lance composer, Berlin.

EMC, KTL, OL, OL95, X57, X68, X71.

Koeser, W. "Uraufführung in der Stadt Jugendmusikschule Winnenden *Perspektiven* **von Peter Sandloff."** *Musik und Bildung* 14 (September 1982): 583. *

"Uraufführungen." *Orchester* 34 (February 1986): 232.

> Sandloff's *Fantasia* (1985) for clarinet and organ was premiered 16 February 1986 by clarinetist Hans Hartmann and organist Klaus Nothdurft.

Margaret Vardell Sandresky

B. Macon, Ga., 28 April 1921. B.M. in organ, Salem College, 1942; continued study of organ with Harold Gleason and Helmut Walcha, 1942; M.M. in composition, Eastman School of Music, 1944, with Charles Vardell, Howard Hanson, and Bernard Rogers; Fulbright scholar to Hochschule für Musik, Frankfurt, 1956, for organ, harpsichord, and composition. Lecturer, Oberlin, 1944-46; University of Texas, 1946-50; Salem College, 1950-55; North Carolina School of the Arts, founder and head of organ department, 1965-67; and again at Salem College, professor of theory and composition, 1968-86.

ABD, CACA, CACJ, IWC, TCH, WCH.

Drone, Jeanette, comp. "American Composer Update." *Pan Pipes* 75/2 (1983): 40.

> *Two Chorale Preludes on Moravian Tunes* and *Wedding March for Drewry and Christof*, both for organ, were premiered during the past year.

Leland B. Sateren

B. Everett, Wash., 13 October 1913. B.A., Augsburg College; studied with Donald Ferguson, M.A., University of Minnesota. School music director, 1935-38; research in choral music and techniques in Europe, 1937, 1966, 1970; honorary doctorates from Lakeland College and Gettysburg College, 1965; director of music, radio station KUOM, 1940-43; choir director-chairman of the music department, Augsburg College, since 1950. Author of *The New Song: A Guide to Modern Music for Use in the Church Choir* (Minneapolis: Augsburg, 1958).

CACA, OL, OL95.

Wetzler, Robert P. "Contemporary Composers: Leland B. Sateren." *Journal of Church Music* 12 (January 1970): 9-10.

An introduction to Sateren; background and brief career summary.

Stanley Saxton

B. Fort Plain, N.Y., 5 August 1904. B.M., 1927, and M.M., 1942, Syracuse University; studied at the American Conservatory and in Fontainebleau, France. AAGO. Pupil of Dupré and Widor for organ, and Boulanger for composition. Theater organist, Syracuse, 1923-28; organist-choirmaster, Union Presbyterian Church, Schenectady; pianist, the Collegians with Paul Whitman, 1927; organist and professor of music, Skidmore College, Saratoga Springs, N.Y., 1928-68.

ABDad, AS66, CACA, OL, OL95.

"A Mohawk Legend." *Music Clubs Magazine* 33 (March 1954): 43.

Galaxy Music publishes Saxton's *A Mohawk Legend*, a "tone picture" for organ based on a Mohawk Valley folk melody.

"Rejoice! The Lord Cometh—Fantasy for Organ on Veni, Emmanuel." *Diapason* 40 (November 1949): 28.

Published by Galaxy Music, Saxton's *Rejoice!* "will provide the service player with a virile, joyous prelude or postlude."

David A. Schack

B. Fort Wayne, Ind., 16 September 1947. B.M., studied with Richard Wienhorst at Valparaiso University, 1969; studied electronic music with Raymond Haggh, University of Nebraska, 1972. Faculty member, Concordia Teachers College, Seward, Nebr., 1970-77; minister of music, First Lutheran Church, Omaha, Nebr. Organ music listed in Arnold's book.

ABD, CACA, OL, OL95.

No bibliographical information located.

Carl Schalk

B. Des Plaines, Ill., 26 September 1929. Attended Northwestern University, 1950; B.S.Ed., Concordia Teachers College, River Forest, Ill., 1952; organ study with Victor Hildner, Carl Halter, and Harold Gleason; M.M., Eastman School of Music, 1957; M.A., Religion, Concordia Theological Seminary, St. Louis, 1965. Director of music, Zion Lutheran Church, Wausau, Wisc., 1952-58; director of music, the Lutheran Hour, 1958-65; instructor, 1950-51, assistant professor, 1965-68, and appointed associate professor of music, since 1968, Concordia Teachers College, River Forest, Ill.; editor, *Church Music*, 1966; president, Lutheran Society for Worship, Music, and the Arts, 1976-78. Author of *The Roots of Hymnody in the Lutheran Church-Missouri Synod* (St. Louis: Concordia, 1965); *Hymnals and Chorale Books of the Klinck Memorial Library* (River Forest: Concordia Teachers College, 1975); ed. *Key Words in Church Music: Definition Essays on Concepts, Practices, and Movements of Thought in Church Music* (St. Louis: Concordia, 1978); ed., with Carl Halter, *A Handbook of Church Music* (St. Louis: Concordia, 1978); *Luther on Music—Paradigms of Praise* (St. Louis: Concordia, 1988); *The Carl Schalk Hymnary* (Chicago: GIA, 1989); and *Psalmody in the Life of the Parish* (St. Louis: Morning Star Music, 1992). Organ music listed in Arnold's book.

OL, OL95.

"Here and There." *Diapason* 83 (July 1992): 4.

> The Association of Lutheran Church Musicians has released a new Parish Study Series published by Morning Star Music which includes Schalk's *Psalmody in the Life of the Parish*; it covers the Book of Psalms, psalms in hymnals, and ways of singing psalms.

William Schmidt, Jr.

B. Chicago, Ill., 6 March 1926. Studied with Max Wald, Chicago Musical College; studied with Halsey Stevens and Ingolf Dahl, University of Southern California, B.M., 1955, and M.M., 1959. President, Western International Music, Inc., and WIM Records.

ABD, BB65, BB71, BB78, CACA, DN70, DN75, DN76, DN77, DN78, KTL, LMD, OL, OL95, PC71, PCM, X62, X70.

"Composer William Schmidt Accepts ITG Commission." *International Trumpet Guild* 9/4 (1985): 4.

> This prominent composer of trumpet music is profiled. Biography; awards and honors mentioned, including his nomination for a Pulitzer prize in 1981.

William John Schneider

B. Lansing, Mich., 17 May 1949. B.M., Michigan State University, 1973; studied organ with Corliss Arnold and composition with Paul Harder. Piano and organ technician. Organ music listed in Arnold's book.

OL, OL95.

No bibliographical information located.

Brian Schober

B. 1951. Graduate of the Eastman School of Music; studied composition with Olivier Messiaen, and organ with Jean Guillou and André Isoir.

BS72, OL, OL95.

"Recitals." *American Organist* 21 (June 1987): 61.

> Brian Schober introduces his own *Toccatas and Fantasias*, 10 February 1987, Grace Church, New York.

Sanders, L. "Music: Medium Hip." *Village Voice* 31 (27 May 1986): 88.

> Schober performed his own "somewhat desultory *Arabesques*" at the Composers' Forum on April 26 at the Cathedral of St. John the Divine.

Ruth Esther Schonthal-Seckel

B. Hamburg, Germany, 27 June 1924. Studied at Stern Conservatory, 1929-36; with Etthoven at the Royal Academy, Stockholm, 1942-45; with Manuel Ponce in Mexico; and with Paul Hindemith at Yale, B.M., 1948. Awarded Delta Omicron's third international award, 1947. Taught at Adelphi University, 1973-76; and from 1974 at Westchester Conservatory. Won ASCAP and Meet the Composer awards; finalist in the New York City Opera competition and finalist in the Kennedy-Friedheim Competition.

ABD, CACA, IWC, DN77, DN78, WCH.

LePage, Jane Weiner. *Women Composers, Conductors, and Musicians of the Twentieth Century,* vol. 3: *Selected Biographies.* Metuchen, N.J.: Scarecrow, 1988.

Schonthal-Seckel's biography is included.

"Commissions." *American Organist* 24 (April 1990): 70.

Schonthal was commissioned by First Presbyterian Church, Greenwich, Conn., to write a 17-minute work for organ, *The Temptation of Saint Anthony,* for the dedication recital of its new Möller organ. Richard Bouchett, organist and director of music at the church, will play. The work is loosely based on a painting of the same name by Hieronymus Bosch and is divided into eight movements.

"Premieres." *Music Educators Journal* 65 (December 1978): 16.

In Homage, 24 preludes, is premiered in New York, 24 September 1978.

Sonntag, B., and R. Matthei, eds. **"Annährung I—an sieben Komponistinen: mit Berichten, Interviews und Selbstdarstellungen (Kassel, Fuore)."** *Musikhandel* 40/1 (1989): 78. *

Alexander Schreiner

B. Nuremburg, Germany, 31 July 1901; d. 15 September 1987. Emigrated to the U.S. in 1912, to Salt Lake City. Became a U.S. citizen, 1920. Originally he planned to become an electrical engineer; to subsidize his education, he was a theater organist for silent movies. Studied with Vierne, Widor, and Libert in Paris. Took time to study classical organ in Europe; joined the organ staff, 1924, at the Mormon Tabernacle, Salt Lake City, from 1939-77, he served as senior organist at the Tabernacle; organist and lecturer, University of California at Los Angeles, 1930-39. Ph.D. granted by the University of Utah, 1954. Also has several honorary doctorates. Author of *Alexander Schreiner Reminisces* (Salt Lake City: Publisher's Press, 1984).

NGA, OL, OL95.

"Alexander Schreiner." *Choral Guide* 6 (April 1953): 18. *

"Alexander Schreiner." *Music Clubs Magazine* 30 (January 1951): 41. *

"Alexander Schreiner Retires as Tabernacle Organist." *Clavier* 17/3 (1978): 8.

Schreiner discusses the importance of memorizing works, and stresses how it can free one to be able to concentrate on changing the registration colors.

Banta, Lorene. "Recitals and Concerts." *American Organist* 42 (September 1959): 313.

Schreiner's recital at Methuen Memorial Music Hall, Methuen, Mass., on 22 April 1959, is given a fair review. Schreiner gave oral program notes in the second half before he performed works by his colleagues.

Bingham, Seth. "Organ Personalities." *American Organist* 46 (November 1963): 17.

States that organist Schreiner has served with distinction over a long period at Salt Lake City's Mormon Tabernacle.

"Changes at Salt Lake." *Diapason* 56 (September 1965): 4.

Schreiner, who had served as a Tabernacle organist since 1924 and senior organist since 1937, was named chief Tabernacle organist.

"Chicago Goes Recital Happy." *Diapason* 51 (December 1959): 49.

Numerous recitals occur in the autumn of 1959 in Chicago, one of which is played by Schreiner at Rockefeller Chapel on November 2. The reviewer thought Schreiner's playing sounded "a bit tired."

"Dr. Alexander Schreiner." *American Organist* 51 (August 1968): 23.

Schreiner is awarded the degree Doctor of Humane Letters, *honoris causa*, at commencement 1968, University of Utah.

Haines, Aubrey B. "Church Organist or Concert Player?" *Etude* 74 (September 1956): 48-49.

An interview with Schreiner reveals his thoughts on the role of the organist in the church and in the recital hall.

Lundstrom, Harold. "Alexander Schreiner Retires after Half-Century as Mormon Tabernacle Organist." *Music* (AGO) 12 (February 1978): 28-29.

A reflection on Schreiner's long musical career. Biographical data included.

"Musical Happenings: Golden Anniversary." *Music* (AGO) 8 (June 1974): 40.

Schreiner marked his 65th year as an organist of the Church of Jesus Christ of Latter Day Saints and his 50th anniversary as organist of the Tabernacle in Salt Lake City in April 1980. Indicates that his dissertation was titled "Concerto in B Minor for Organ and Orchestra," and it was premiered at the Tabernacle in 1955 with the Utah Symphony.

[Obituary.] *American Organist* 22 (January 1988): 53.

Brief notice of Schreiner's death, 15 September 1987.

[Obituary.] *Diapason* 79 (April 1988): 5.

Schreiner's passing on 15 September 1987 is announced. Summary of his music education and career included.

[Obituary.] *Notes* 45/4 (1989): 731.

Death date, 15 September 1988; cites other obituary notices; his biography is located in the *New Grove Dictionary of American Music*.

Packard, Dorothy R. "Add Salt to Taste." *Clavier* 1/4 (1962): 24-27.

An interview with Schreiner gives insights to the man, performer, and teacher.

"Recitals and Concerts." *American Organist* 40 (May 1957): 162-63.

Schreiner presents a recital at Central Presbyterian Church on March 18 that includes Bach, Mendelssohn, Richard Keys Biggs, Dillon, van Hulse, and Vierne. His "technical accomplishments are great, but musicianship reigns foremost."

"St. James Church." *American Organist* 39 (August 1956): 258.

Schreiner is congratulated on his technique and musicality in his recital at St. James Church, New York.

Stoddard, Hope. "Music in Utah." *International Musician* 53 (April 1955): 24.

Briefly mentions Schreiner and his work at the Tabernacle; thumbnail biographical sketch provided.

Udy, Kenneth. "The California Years of American Organist Alexander Schreiner." In *Music in Performance and Society: Essays in Honor of Roland Jackson*, ed. Malcolm Cole and John Koegel. This publisher, 1997.

"Utah University Grants Doctorate to Alexander Schreiner." *Diapason* 45 (October 1954): 1.

Schreiner is awarded his Ph.D. from the University of Utah, August 27. His thesis is titled "Concerto in B Minor for Organ and Orchestra." Biographical data summarized.

VanBronkhorst, Charles. "Recitals and Concerts." *American Organist* 42 (November 1959): 398.

Schreiner performs a recital at Memorial Auditorium, Sacramento, Calif., on 18 June 1959 that appealed to the professional and the "man in the street."

Wolford, Darwin, Clay Christiansen, and James B. Welch. "Alexander Schreiner: Tabernacle Organist." *American Organist* 22 (December 1988): 63-66.

Three men look at Schreiner's life and career history, insights to him as a teacher, and fond reminiscences.

Gunther Schuller

B. New York, 22 November 1925. Began his study as a boy soprano at St. Thomas Choir School and soon added the study of composition, flute, and French horn. Played in the New York City Ballet Orchestra, 1943; 1st horn in Cincinnati Symphony Orchestra, 1943-45; horn, Metropolitan Opera Orchestra, New York, 1945-49. Played horn in Miles Davis's jazz combo, 1949-50. Taught at the Manhattan School of Music, 1950-63; Yale University School of Music, 1946-47; taught and was president, New England Conservatory of Music, 1967-77. Teacher of composition, Berkshire Music Center, Tanglewood, 1963-84, head of contemporary music activities, 1965-84, artistic co-director, 1969-74, and director, 1974-84; interim music director, Spokane (Wash.) Symphony Orchestra, 1984-85; then director of its Sandpoint (Idaho) Festival; founded the Boston Composers' Orchestra, 1986. Awarded the first Elise L. Stoeger Composer's Chair of the Chamber Music Society of Lincoln Center, 1988. Organized Margun Music to make available unpublished American music, 1975; founded GunMar Music, 1979, and organized GM Recordings the following year. Honorary doctorates from Northwestern University, University of Illinois, Williams College, New England Conservatory of Music, and Rutgers University. In 1967, he was elected to membership in the National Institute of Arts and Letters, and in 1980 to the American Academy and Institute of Arts and Letters. Awarded two Guggenheim fellowships, the Darius Milhaud award, and the Brandeis University Creative Arts award. Received the William Schuman Award from Columbia University, 1989, and in 1991 was awarded a MacArthur Foundation grant. Author of *Horn Technique* (New York: Oxford University Press, 1962); *Early Jazz: Its Roots and Musical Development* (New York: Oxford University Press, 1968); *Musings: The Musical Worlds of Gunther Schuller* (New York: Oxford University Press, 1986); and *The Swing Era: The Development of Jazz, 1933-45* (New York: Oxford University Press, 1989).

ABD, AMH, BB58, BB65, BB71, BB92, BDA, BMI, CA10, CACA, CACJ, CC92, CME, DCM, DN70, DN77, DN78, EDM, GD54s, IMD, IMD2, JCN, KTL, LMD, MEH, MGGs, MHHH, MNG, NG, NGA, OCM, OL, OL95, PC71, PCM, REM, TCAC, WTM, X54, X56, X57, X58, X59, X60, X61, X62, X64, X65, X66, X67, X68, X69, X70, X71, X74.

Bowen, Meirion. **"Gunther Schuller."** *Music & Musicians* 15 (February 1967): 26-30, 62-63.

A thorough examination of Schuller's approach to composition.

Cantrell, Scott. **"Canadian Cowtown's Classical Charms Are Nothing to Beef About."** *Kansas City Star*, 23 October 1994, J-4.

Schuller's *Concerto for Organ* is premiered during the Calgary International Organ Festival in Calgary, Alberta, Canada. In three movements, the somewhat atonal piece was presented six times over the course of the Organ Festival.

Carnovale, Norbert. *Gunther Schuller: A Bio-Bibliography.* New York: Greenwood, 1987.

Biography, bibliography, works and performances, and discography included.

"The Composer Speaks." *Music Clubs Magazine* 39 (November 1959): 10.

Schuller promotes increasing musical tolerance among audiences.

"Composers in Focus." *BMI: The Many Worlds of Music*, winter 1976, 28-29.

Biography, honors and awards, books, and jazz are covered briefly.

Copland, Aaron. **"America's Young Men of Music."** *Music & Musicians* 9 (December 1960): 11+. *

"Gunther Schuller." *Composers of the Americas* 10 (1964): 110-16.

A brief biography in Spanish and English is followed by an annotated catalog of his works.

Helm, Everett. **"Experimentelle Musik in den USA."** *Melos* 31 (April 1964): 125.

The works of American composers span a broad spectrum of styles, ranging from old-style romanticism to progressive forms of experimental music. A discussion of American composers' influence upon European composition, and the difference between American and European movements. Lukas Foss and Gunther Schuller are among composers who, in common with others, do not limit themselves to or specialize in a certain system of composition or in a single theory or system of aesthetics.

Hentoff, Nat. **"Counterpoint."** *Downbeat* 22 (23 February 1955): 6. *

————. **"Gunther Schuller."** *BMI: The Many Worlds of Music*, October 1967, 19.

Brief biography includes awards, honors, and teaching posts.

Hoffmann, James A., and Joseph G. Maneri. **"A Conversation with Gunther Schuller."** *Perspectives of New Music* 24/2 (spring-summer 1986): 242-49.

Schuller answers questions about the attitude of musicians and audiences toward new music, his teaching, his music, and influences on his music and musical life.

Kratzenstein, Marilou, and Arthur Lawrence. "AGO '76 Boston: A Review of the Biennial Convention of the AGO Boston, Mass., June 21-June 25, 1976." *Diapason* 67 (August 1976): 4-5.

> Yuko Hayashi introduced Schuller's new work *Triptych*, commissioned for the convention. *Triptych* is described as basically dodecaphonic, in three movements, and performed without pause. Hayashi was given many kudos for learning this lengthy and difficult work in only eight days.

"Music Journal's 1972 Gallery of Living Composers." *Music Journal* 30 (annual 1972): 56.

> Brief biography; honors and major works listed.

"New from the World of Music." *Music Clubs Magazine* 71/3 (1992): 24.

> Schuller is named a MacArthur Fellow.

"Prizes and Premieres." *Musical America* 84 (July 1964): 60.

> Schuller is appointed to the Yale School of Music faculty as a teacher of composition, beginning September 1964.

Rich, Alan. "Musician of the Month: Gunther Schuller." *High Fidelity/Musical America* 26 (April 1976): MA6-7.

> Schuller espouses diversity in the education of music students, and the ability to perform music in all styles and from all eras is of importance to him.

Tassel, Janet. "Gunther Schuller: Composer, Conductor, and Musical Conscience." *Ovation* 6 (November 1985): 22-26.

> Schuller's influence on music making, as composer, conductor, and author; and a discussion on the process of music's deterioration.

Ralph C. Schultz

B. Dolton, Ill., 23 June 1932. Studied with Herman Spies and Rossetter Cole in Chicago; with Ross Lee Finney, University of Michigan; with Marcel Dick, Cleveland Institute of Music; and with Seth Bingham, S.M.D., 1967, Union Theological Seminary, New York. His dissertation is titled "Lutheran Chorale Mass." Church music director in Cleveland, 1954-61; from 1961 faculty member, Concordia College, Bronxville, N.Y., and music director, Village Lutheran Church.

ABD, CACA, OL, OL95.

No bibliographical information located.

Joseph Schwantner

B. Chicago, Ill., 22 March 1943. Composition with Bernard Dieter, Chicago American Conservatory, B.M., 1964; with Anthony Donato and Alan Stout, Northwestern University, M.M., 1966, and D.M., 1968. Won three BMI Student Composer awards; Berns prize; Charles Ives scholarship; National Institute of Arts and Letters, 1970; Rockefeller grant, 1978; NEA grants, 1974, 1975, 1977; Guggenheim, 1978-79; won the Pulitzer Prize in music, 1979. On faculty, Pacific Lutheran University, 1968-69; Ball State University, 1969-70; Eastman School of Music, 1970, and became professor of composition, 1980; composer-in-residence, St. Louis Symphony Orchestra, 1982-85; returned to Eastman in 1985.

ABD, ASUC, BB92, CACA, DN77, KTL, NGA, OL, OL95, X69, X71, X74.

Briggs, Jeffrey L. **"The Recent Music of Joseph Schwantner: Unique and Essential Elements."** D.M.A., University of Illinois, Champaign-Urbana, 1984. *Dissertation Abstracts* 45 (May 1985): 3235A.

Explores various compositional techniques in his recent works, biography, and his relation to various trends which are manifest in "new American music" is discussed.

Chute, James E. **"The Reemergence of Tonality in Contemporary Music as Shown in the Works of David Del Tredici, Joseph Schwantner, and John Adams."** D.M.A., University of Cincinnati, 1991.

The thesis shows how contemporary composers are turning toward tonality, in a movement called "The New Romanticism."

"Composers in Focus." *BMI: The Many Worlds of Music*, winter 1976, 30-31.

Biography, awards, and excerpts from a discussion with Schwantner. The interviewer writes "Schwantner has made a new expressive music by mustering instrumental effects in the service of expression, not experimentation for its own sake."

"Fete Schwantner." *Billboard* 91 (19 May 1979): 104.

Schwantner, the 1979 Pulitzer Prize winner in music, was awarded a commendation of excellence by BMI for his "long and outstanding contribution to the world of concert music."

Kastendieck, Miles. **"Joseph Schwantner."** *BMI: The Many Worlds of Music* 2 (1979): 28-29.

Schwantner wins the Pulitzer Prize for his orchestral work *Aftertones of Infinity*. Brief biography. He considers Ives, Partch, and Crumb to be the major influences on his work. "[Music] completely engrosses me."

Kyle, Marguerite K. "AmerAllegro." *Pan Pipes* 71/2 (1979): 44.

On leave from the Eastman School of Music for 1978-79, Schwantner received a John Simon Guggenheim Memorial Foundation Fellowship in music composition and a Martha Baird Rockefeller grant.

"Names." *Music Journal* 37 (May/June 1979): 60.

Schwantner is the 1979 Pulitzer Prize winner for music.

"Schwantner Wins Pulitzer Prize." *BMI: The Many Worlds of Music* 2 (1979): 2.

Schwantner is the fifth recipient of the BMI Student Composition Award to become a Pulitzer Prize winner in music. Previous winners were George Crumb, Mario Davidovsky, Donald Martino, and Charles Wuorinen.

Stearns, David P. "Joseph Schwantner." *High Fidelity/Musical America* 29 (December 1979): MA6-7.

Schwantner wins the Pulitzer Prize, 1979. He talks about his craft: "I like to think of composing like an artisan building a fine piece of cabinetry. Somebody calls you up and wants a piece. . . . What's important is whether or not the music survives. Nothing any award or critic can do can make any difference."

Elliott Shelling Schwartz

B. New York, 19 January 1936. Studied composition with Otto Luening and Jack Beeson, Columbia University, B.A., 1957, M.A., 1958, and Ed.D., 1962. Private instruction in piano from Alton Jones, and in composition from Paul Creston; studied composition at the Bennington Composers Conference, summers 1961-66. Taught at University of Massachusetts, Amherst, 1960-64; Bowdoin College, Brunswick, Maine, where he was associate professor, 1970-75, then professor and chairman of its music department, from 1975; also held appointments as Distinguished Visiting University Professor, 1985-86, and professor of composition, 1989-91, Ohio State University. Vice president, American Music Center, 1982-88; chairman, American Society of University Composers, 1984-88; president, College Music Society, 1989-90. Author of *The Symphonies of Ralph Vaughan Williams* (Amherst: Massachusetts University Press, 1964); ed., with Barney Childs, *Contemporary Composers on Contemporary Music* (New York: Holt, Rinehart & Winston, 1967); *Electronic Music: A Listener's Guide* (New York: Praeger, 1973); and *Music: Ways of Listening* (New York: Holt, Rinehart & Winston, 1982). His 1963 dissertation is titled "The Symphonies of Ralph Vaughan Williams: An Analysis of Their Stylistic Elements" (*Dissertation Abstracts* 23 [February 1963]: 2938).

AA73, ABD, ASUC, BB78, BB92, CACA, CACJ, CC92, DCM, DN72, DN73, DN74, DN76, DN78, IWW92, KTL, NG, NGA, OL, OL95, PC71, PCM, TCH, X65, X67, X68, X69, X70, X71, X74.

Albright, William. "Fourth Festival of Contemporary Music: Hartt College." *Music* (AGO) 8 (September 1974): 23.

Elizabeth Sollenberger performs the premiere of Schwartz's *Prisms*, for organ and four-track tape, at Hartt College's Contemporary Music Festival.

Black, George. "Hartt College Annual Contemporary Organ Music Festival—A Review." *Diapason* 65 (August 1974): 2-3.

Schwartz's *Prisms* was one of five works introduced at the festival. Elizabeth Sollenberger performed the premiere of this work for organ and electronic tape. The piece is outlined.

Bowen, Meirion. "Elliott Schwartz." *Music & Musicians* 16 (March 1968): 24-27.

A thorough review of Schwartz's compositional style; composers who influenced his style are also studied.

Kyle, Marguerite K. "AmerAllegro." *Pan Pipes* 62/2 (1970): 80.

Schwartz received a Ford Foundation grant for travel and research; he was promoted to associate professor of music, Bowdoin College.

65/2 (1973): 70-71.

Schwartz will be the subject of a biographical essay in the new (sixth) edition of *Grove's Dictionary of Music and Musicians*; his book, *Electronic Music*, will be released in 1973 by Praeger, New York.

Mason, E. "Composers' Exchange." *Music & Musicians* 15 (August 1967): 35.

Schwartz takes an international exchange position at Trinity College of Music in London, 1968.

Robert E. Scoggin

B. Mercury, Texas, 30 April 1930. B.M., Midwestern College, Wichita Falls, Texas; M.Th., Southern Methodist University; studied organ with Nita Akin, Robert Baker, Anton Heiller, Jean Langlais, André Marchal, Marie-Claire Alain, Luigi Tagliavini, Piet Kee, and Gustav

Leonhardt; studied conducting with Lloyd Pfautsch; summer study at Union Theological Seminary, 1953. Organist, White Rock United Methodist Church, Dallas, 1954; organist, First United Methodist Church, Wichita Falls, Texas, 1955-56; organist-choirmaster, University Park United Methodist Church, Dallas, 1956-63; organist-choirmaster, Christ United Methodist Church, Rochester, Minn., 1963-93; president, Fellowship of United Methodist Musicians, 1973-75.

OL, OL95.

"Here and There." *Diapason* 84 (November 1993): 4.

> Scoggin retired from his position as Minister of Music at Christ United Methodist Church, Rochester, Minn., in August. Provides overview of his career.

"Rev. Robert Scoggin Goes to White Rock Church, Dallas." *Diapason* 45 (September 1954): 2.

> Scoggin is appointed minister of music and education for White Rock Methodist Church, Dallas. Education and career data are provided.

"Robert E. Scoggin." *American Organist* 44 (November 1961): 31.

> Scoggin will be on a year's sabbatical for study in Europe: church music studies at the Royal School of Church Music, England; organ study with Leonhardt in Amsterdam and Heiller in Vienna, and Langlais and Marchal in Paris.

"Robert E. Scoggin." *American Organist* 46 (August 1963): 20.

> Scoggin is appointed minister of music, First Methodist Church, Rochester, Minn., 1 June 1963. Lists his former positions, honors, and previous teachers.

"Robert E. Scoggin." *Diapason* 54 (August 1963): 25.

> Scoggin became minister of music on June 1, First Methodist Church, Rochester, Minn.

"Robert E. Scoggin, Minister of Music in Texas." *Diapason* 46 (June 1955): 19.

> Scoggin is appointed minister of music, First Methodist Church, Wichita Falls, Texas. Educational history and previous positions are provided.

"Who's Who." *Choral Guide* 9 (June-August 1956): 12. *

Rudy [Rudolph] Shackelford

B. Newport News, Va., 18 April 1944. Studied with Milton Cherry, B.M., 1966, Virginia Commonwealth University; with Gordon Binkerd at the University of Illinois, M.M., and

D.M.A., 1971. Further study with Luigi Dallapiccola, George Rochberg, and Vincent Persichetti. Fellowships at Yaddo, MacDowell Colony, and Ossabaw Island; Rockefeller Foundation; Bellagio, Italy; first prize, 1974, Spokane World Expo Composition Contest. Taught at Shenandoah Conservatory, 1972. Commissions received from the Hartt College International Contemporary Organ Music Festival. Translated and edited Luigi Dallapiccola's book entitled *Dallapiccola on Opera: Selected Writings*, vol. 1 (London: Toccata, 1988). His dissertation is titled "Problems of Editions and Transcriptions in Organ Music of the 20th Century" (*Dissertation Abstracts* 32 [February 1972]: 4652A).

ABD, CACA, DN78, KTL, OL, OL95, TCH.

"Premiered." *ASCAP*, winter 1982, 50.

> *Olive Tree, First Pilgrim*, for trumpet and organ, was introduced on March 27 at the West Side Presbyterian Church, Ridgewood, N.J.

Judith Allen Shatin

B. Boston, Mass., 21 November 1949. Studied with Robert Moevs at Douglass College, A.B., 1971; with Hall Overton and Otto Luening, M.M., 1974, Juilliard; M.F.A., 1976, and Ph.D., 1979, Princeton University, with Milton Babbitt, Peter Westergaard, and J. K. Randall. Received Julia Carlie memorial prize, Abraham Ellstein award, and Aspen Music Festival awards, 1971 and 1972. In 1978, she won a prize in the East & West Artists composition competition and several grants; scholarship to the music and dance program at the American Dance Festival, Durham, N.C., 1981; two fellowships for composition at Tanglewood; New Jersey State Council on the Arts grant; and Meet the Composer grant. On the University of Virginia faculty since 1979. Organ music listed in Cohen's book.

ABD, CACA, IWC, WCH.

"American Composer Update." *Pan Pipes* 87/2 (winter 1995): 39.

> Shatin is Associate Fellow in the University of Virginia's Institute for Advanced Computing in the Humanities, 1994-95.

Clare Shore

B. Winston-Salem, N.C., 18 December 1954. B.A., Wake Forest University, studied with Annette LeSiege and Donald Hoirup; M.M. in composition, University of Colorado, with Charles Eain and Cecil Effinger; D.Mus. in composition, 1984, Juilliard, with David

Diamond. In 1981, she received an Irving Berlin Fellowship. Further composition studies with Persichetti and Sessions at Juilliard. On music faculty, George Mason University, since 1981.

IWC, IWW92.

"Premieres." *American Organist* 20 (December 1986): 40.

> On 2 November 1986, Emma Lou Diemer presented the premiere of *Oatland Sketches* by Clare Shore in addition to other premieres, celebrating the tenth anniversary of American Women Composers Inc.

Marilyn Shrude

B. Chicago, Ill., 16 July 1946. B.M., Alverno College, 1969; M.M., Northwestern University, 1972; composition study with Alan Stout, M. William Karlins, and W. Mays. Recipient of many grants and awards. Teaches at Bowling Green State University (Ohio). Organ music listed in Cohen's book.

CACA, IWC.

No bibliographical information located.

Paul J. Sifler

B. Laibach (Ljubljana), Slovenia, 31 December 1911. Emigrated to America in 1920. Studied organ with Claire Coci, Norman Coke-Jephcott, Leo Sowerby, and Lester Groom. B.M. and M.M. from Chicago Conservatory of Music. Held positions at Temple Isaiah, Forest Hills, N.Y., and as director of the Schaefer Glee Club and Slovan Choral Society; organist-choirmaster, Cathedral of St. John the Divine, New York, 1951-54; choirmaster, First Presbyterian Church, New York, 1954-66; 1966-90, organist-choirmaster, St. Thomas Episcopal Church, Hollywood, Calif.; from 1990, organist-choirmaster, St. Barnabas Episcopal Church, Eagle Rock, Calif.

ABD, CACA, OL, OL95.

"Appointments." *American Organist* 24 (April 1990): 64.

> Sifler is named organist-choirmaster of St. Barnabas Episcopal Church, Los Angeles [Eagle Rock], Calif.

"Here and There." *Diapason* 67 (October 1976): 1.

Sifler played the premiere of his new organ work *Contemplations on the Seven Words of Christ on the Cross* and other works at the Cathedral of Ljubljana, Slovenia, 27 May 1976; the concert was given to benefit those churches ruined by earthquakes in the coastal areas of Italy and Yugoslavia.

"Here and There." *Diapason* 81 (April 1990): 4.

Sifler is appointed organist-choirmaster at St. Barnabas Episcopal Church, Eagle Rock, Calif.

"Here and There." *Diapason* 84 (February 1993): 3.

Yuletide Echos for Organ is included on a new compact disc released by Fredonia Discs.

Kyle, Marguerite K. "AmerAllegro." *Pan Pipes* 70/2 (1978): 62.

Fredonia Discs releases *Adventures in Organ Music*, featuring Sifler's works performed by John LaMontaine.

LaMontaine, John. "The Seven Last Words of Christ by Paul J. Sifler: An Analysis." *Diapason* 68 (January 1977): 4-5.

Musical examples accompany the analysis of Sifler's work. Each of the seven words is distinctly wedded to its corresponding text; the poetry gives rise to the music.

"Paul J. Sifler." *Diapason* 42 (March 1951): 26.

Sifler was recently appointed organist and choir director for the Canterbury Choir at the Cathedral of St. John the Divine, New York. Brief educational history given.

"Paul J. Sifler." *American Organist* 37 (May 1954): 161.

Sifler is appointed to Stapleton First Presbyterian Church, New York, as choirmaster. No organ exists at the church.

"Paul J. Sifler." *American Organist* 49 (October 1966): 32.

Sifler is appointed organist-choirmaster of St. Thomas Episcopal Church, Hollywood, Calif.

"Paul J. Sifler." *Diapason* 57 (September 1966): 43.

Same information as in the item above, with this addition: he will also be organist for Temple Sinai, Glendale, Calif.

"A Presbyterian Service." *American Organist* 37 (May 1954): 150-01.

Sifler's service playing is evaluated and it receives high marks for his attention to details.

Morgan F. Simmons

B. Andalusia, Ala., 6 April 1929. B.M., DePauw University, 1951, organ student of Van Denman Thompson; M.S.M., 1953, and D.S.M., 1961, Union Theological Seminary, organ with Hugh Porter and John Huston; composition study with Harold Friedell and Seth Bingham; additional organ study with Arthur Poister. Fulbright study at the Royal School of Church Music, Croydon, Surrey, and at Trinity College of Music in London. Further organ study with Berniece Mozingo and Marilyn Mason. Minister of music, Presbyterian Church, Bound Brook, N.J., 1956-62; minister of music, First Methodist Church, Evanston, Ill., 1963-68; assistant professor of church music, Garrett-Evangelical Seminary, Evanston, 1963-77; since 1968, organist-choirmaster, Fourth Presbyterian Church, Chicago. Vice president, Hymn Society of America, 1977-78; secretary-treasurer, Consultation of Ecumenical Hymnody, 1974-77.

OL, OL95.

"Here and There." *Diapason* 81 (July 1990): 3.

> John Weaver and his wife, Marianne, played the first performance of a new piece for flute and organ by Simmons, *Cecilia and Pan Do Sums and Division*, in a recital at Simmons's church, Fourth Presbyterian Church, Chicago, April 29.

"Here and There." *Diapason* 83 (December 1992): 4.

> David Schrader performed the premiere of *Cityscape*, 13 September 1992, at Fourth Presbyterian Church, Chicago. The three-movement work is inscribed to Schrader.

"Here and There." *Diapason* 84 (December 1993): 3.

> Morgan and his wife Mary were honored for 25 years of music ministry to Fourth Presbyterian Church of Chicago on September 12. The church commissioned the Simmons' friend and colleague Richard Proulx to compose an anthem in recognition of their work.

"Morgan F. Simmons." *Diapason* 46 (July 1955): 20.

> Simmons, a DePauw University graduate student, receives a Fulbright scholarship to study at the Royal School of Church Music, Croydon, England, for the academic year 1955-56. Short biography included.

"Morgan F. Simmons." *Diapason* 53 (November 1962): 3.

> Simmons is appointed minister of music at First Methodist Church, Evanston, and associate professor of church music at Garrett Theological Seminary, effective January 1.

"Morgan F. Simmons." *Diapason* 59 (October 1968): 22.

> Simmons became organist-choirmaster at Fourth Presbyterian Church, Chicago; he will continue as assistant professor and chapel organist at Garrett Theological Seminary.

"New Appointments." *American Organist* 45 (November 1962): 25.

> Simmons assumes the positions of minister of music at First Methodist Church, Evanston, Ill., and associate professor of church music, Garrett Theological Seminary. Biographical information and honors provided.

David William Smart

B. Lock Haven, Penn., 6 February 1927. B.M., 1951, and M.M., 1953, American Conservatory, Chicago. Composition student of Leo Sowerby. Since 1958, organist-choirmaster, Messiah Lutheran Church, Chicago; since 1951, professor of sacred music, Moody Bible Institute, Chicago. Organ music listed in Arnold's book.
OL, OL95.

No bibliographical information located.

Julia Frances Smith

(Vielehr is her real surname.) B. Denton, Texas, 25 January 1911; d. New York, 27 April 1989. B.A., North Texas State University, Denton, 1930; additional study in composition with Rubin Goldmark, Bernard Wagenaar, and Frederick Jacobi, and piano study with Carl Friedberg and Lonny Epstein at Juilliard; M.A., 1933, and Ph.D., 1952, New York University. Her dissertation is titled "Aaron Copland: His Work and Contribution to American Music." Composition study was with Marion Bauer, Vincent Jones, and Virgil Thomson. Pianist of the all-woman Orchestrette, New York, 1932-39; theory faculty, Juilliard, 1940-42; founder and head, department of music education, Hartt College of Music, University of Hartford, 1940-45; faculty, New Britain State Teachers' College (Conn.), 1944-46. Named one of ten leading women composers by the National Council of Women of the U.S., 1963; received two Martha Baird Rockefeller grants; National Federation of Music Clubs awards; ASCAP awards; and Ford Foundation grant. Authored *Aaron Copland: His Work and Contribution to American Music* (New York: E. P. Dutton, 1955); *Master Pianist: The Career and Teaching of Carl Friedberg* (New York: Philosophical, 1963); compiled *Directory of Women Composers* (Chicago: National Federation of Music Clubs, 1971); and, with Cecile Vashaw, *String Method*, Books 1-3.

AA73, ABD, AMH, AS66, ASC, BB78, BB92, BDA, CACA, DCM, DN72, IWC, KTL, NG, NGA, OL95, PC71, PCM, WCH, X55, X56, X64, X65, X66, X68, X69, X70, X71, X74.

Burford, Exie. "Julia Smith, Woman of Talents." *Music Clubs Magazine* 47/3 (1968): 20.
An overview of Smith's career as composer, author, recitalist, and lecturer.

Craig, M. "Composer and Ambassadress of U.S. Music." *Musical Courier* 159 (July 1959): 7. *

"Creative Work of Julia Smith Highlighted in Denton." *Pan Pipes* 65/4 (1973): 21.
The music department of the Ariel Club in Denton, Texas, honored Smith by presenting a program of her works on 6 November 1972.

"International Women's Year Ends: Decade of Women Begins." *Music Clubs Magazine* 55/3 (1976): 6+. *

Kyle, Marguerite K. "AmerAllegro." *Pan Pipes* 61/2 (1969): 75.
Prelude in D-Flat for Organ Solo was published by Mowbray Music, New York; sole distributor is Presser.

63/2 (1971): 78.
Smith compiled and edited the first *Directory of American Women Composers*, published by the National Federation of Music Clubs, Chicago.

67/2 (1975): 73.
North Texas State University, Denton, awarded Smith the First Presidential Citation and Plaque of the Floyd Graham Society "for musical achievement."

69/2 (1977): 70-71.
Smith was a recipient of the 1976 ASCAP award for her "contribution to serious music"; in addition, she was appointed to several boards for women and music groups.

"NFMC Salutes the 'Decade of Women' in a Concert of International Women Composers." *Music Clubs Magazine* 56/1 (1976): 19-20. *

[Obituary.] *Central Opera Service* 29/3 (1989): 73.
Death notice, 27 April 1989, is accompanied by career summary.

[Obituary.] *Music Clubs Magazine* 69/4 (1989): 10. *

[Obituary.] *Variety* 335 (24 May 1989): 77.
Smith's obituary notice.

Ratcliff, O. "Distinguished Composer Honored in Memoriam." *Music Clubs Magazine* 69/2 (1989): 14. *

"Town Hall Artists." *Pan Pipes* 48 (January 1956): 25. *

Lani Smith

B. Cincinnati, Ohio, 9 June 1934. Studied composition with John Larkin, Felix Labunski, and Scott Huston, University of Cincinnati College-Conservatory, B.M. and M.M. Organ study with Wayne Fisher and Katherine Loew. Joined the Lorenz Company music staff, 1967. Pseudonyms are Edward Broughton, Franklin Ritter, and David Paxton.

ABD, CACA, OL, OL95.

"Premieres." *Music Educators Journal* 65 (December 1978): 16.

Reflections was premiered in Washington, D.C., 7 May 1978.

Stuart S. Smith

B. Portland, Maine, 16 March 1948. Studied with Edward Miller and Edward Diemente, Hartt College of Music; with Salvatore Martirano, Herbert Brun, and Ben Johnston, University of Illinois, D.M.A., 1975. Received an ASCAP Merit award and a University of Maryland research grant. Taught at Hartt College of Music, 1970-73; from 1975, faculty member, University of Maryland, Baltimore County. Authored, with T. DeLio, *Words and Spaces* (Lanham, Md.: University Press of America, n.d.).

ABD, CACA, DN76, DN77, OL, OL95.

Albright, William. "Fourth Festival of Contemporary Organ Music: Hartt College." *Music* (AGO) 8 (September 1974): 23.

Stuart Smith's latest work, *Gifts*, was premiered at the festival. The work is written for organ, clarinet, and flute.

Black, George. "Hartt College Annual Contemporary Organ Music Festival—A Review." *Diapason* 65 (August 1974): 2-3.

Stuart Smith's *Gifts*, for organ and two melody instruments, was one of five new works heard at the festival. Elizabeth Sollenberger, organ, Douglas Worthen, flute, and Henry Larsen, clarinet, introduced the piece.

Smith, Stuart. "Box Scores: Notation as Visual Art." *Ear* 15 (May 1990): 36-40. *

"Various Festival Programs." *Diapason* 64 (August 1973): 17.

Two Makes Three, for organ and two percussionists, received its world premiere at the Contemporary Organ Music Workshop, Hartt College of Music, University of Hartford, Conn., June 11-15.

Randall Snyder

B. Chicago, Ill., 6 April 1944. Studied with Lavern Wagner at Quincy College; with Hilmar Luckhardt, Burt Levy, and Les Thimmig, University of Wisconsin. Faculty member, University of Wisconsin, 1973-74; from 1976 at University of Nebraska, Lincoln. First prize winner, International Double Reed Society composition contest, 1977.
ABD, CACA, OL, OL95.

Lawrence, Arthur. "The Organ and the Concert Hall." *Diapason* 73 (March 1982): 18.
> Snyder's *Chamber Concerto for Organ* is briefly portrayed as one of five substantial new works for organ and various instruments. The piece includes parts for flute, clarinet, saxophone, oboe, bassoon, trumpet, horn, and trombone.

Carl Bayard Staplin

B. Albany, N.Y., 5 December 1934. B.M. in organ, Syracuse University, 1956; M.M., Yale, 1961; Ph.D. in performance practices, Washington University, 1966. Organ teachers include Roberta Bitgood, Arthur Poister, Charles Krigbaum, Finn Viderø, Howard Kelsey, Anton Heiller, Marie-Claire Alain, and André Marchal; composition study with Ernest Bacon and Richard Donovan; musicology studies with Paul Pisk. AAGO. Faculty member, University of Evansville (Ind.), 1966-67; since 1967, minister of music, First Christian Church, and faculty member, Drake University, Des Moines, Iowa. Staplin's dissertation is entitled "Stylistic Changes in the Chorale Preludes of Johann Sebastian Bach" (*Dissertation Abstracts* 28 [August 1967]: 714A).
OL, OL95.

"Appointments." *American Organist* 50 (July 1967): 27.
> Carl Staplin is appointed associate professor of organ and church music at Drake University, effective September 1967.

"Appointments." *Diapason* 85 (December 1994): 3.
> Staplin was named Head of the Keyboard Area at Drake University. Includes overview of his career. He has recently made a CD recording of Bach's *Clavierübung III* on the Calcante label.

"Carl Bayard Staplin." *Diapason* 52 (November 1961): 38.
> Staplin is appointed to Evansville College (Ind.) as instructor of organ and advanced theory.

"Dr. Carl Staplin." *Diapason* 58 (October 1967): 2.

Staplin is appointed associate professor of organ and church music at Drake University. His educational history is provided.

Hawke, H. William. "National in the Rockies." *American Organist* 51 (August 1968): 28.

Staplin and Kathleen Thomerson perform a duo organ recital on 4 July 1968 at Mackey Auditorium, University of Colorado at Boulder, playing works of Vierne, Cherubini, Pinkham, Daquin, Guilain, and Powell, assisted by the University Summer Choir and the University Brass Ensemble.

"Honors." *Diapason* 71 (January 1980): 15.

Staplin is the recipient of an Iowa Arts Council grant for 1979-80; he will present recitals in various communities as one of several touring artists.

Owen, Barbara J. "Recitals and Concerts." *American Organist* 42 (December 1959): 435-36.

Staplin's performance at Battell Chapel, Yale University, 23 June 1959, receives kudos.

Peter Pindar Stearns

B. New York, 7 June 1931. Initial instruction in theory and composition from Leonard Stein and Miklós Rozsa; Artist Diploma, Mannes College of Music, 1952; teachers were Bohuslav Martinů in composition and Felix Salzer in theory. Composed music for educational films on the West Coast. Returned to New York, and in 1954 joined the staff of the Mannes College Library. Appointed to composition faculty there in 1957, and in 1961-73 was chairman of the composition department. Taught at Yale, 1964-65.

ABD, ASUC, CACA, OL, OL95, PCM, X56, X65, X66.

"ACA Welcomes New Members." *American Composers Alliance Bulletin* 13/1 (1965): 12.

An introduction to Peter Pindar Stearns.

Dodd, Mary Ann. "The Fifth Biennial Holtkamp-AGO Award in Organ Composition 1991-92: Observations and Reflections." *American Organist* 26 (November 1992): 54.

Invocation and Fugue on Amazing Grace is published by CPP/Belwin Mills. Indicates Stearns has over 200 works published for many combinations of instruments.

Kyle, Marguerite K. "AmerAllegro." *Pan Pipes* 50 (January 1958): 72.

Stearns is appointed to Mannes College of Music faculty as teacher of composition.

53/2 (1961): 76.

> Premiere of Stearn's *Three Chorale Preludes* is performed in Providence, R.I., by organist F. Bartlett.

"Peter Pindar Stearns." *Pan Pipes* 45 (January 1953): 67. *

Martin Stellhorn

B. 1914. Organist-director of music, Bethel Lutheran Church, University City, Mo. Ph.D., musicology, Washington University, 1964. Stellhorn's dissertation is titled "The Mid-Twentieth-Century Chorale Prelude" (*Dissertation Abstracts* 26 [July 1965]: 411). Organ music listed in Arnold's book.

OL, OL95.

No bibliographical information located.

Halsey Stevens

B. Scott, N.Y., 3 December 1908; d. Long Beach, Calif., 20 January 1989. Studied composition with William Berwald at Syracuse University, B.M., 1931 and M.M., 1937; with Ernest Bloch at the University of California-Berkeley, 1944. Taught at Syracuse University, 1935-37; Dakota Wesleyan University, 1937-41; professor and director of the College of Music, Bradley Polytechnic Institute, Peoria, Ill., 1941-46; professor, University of Redlands, 1946; and the University of Southern California, from 1946 until his retirement in 1976 as professor emeritus. Two Guggenheim fellowships, 1964-65 and 1971-72; NEA grant, 1976; Abraham Lincoln Award of the American Hungarian Foundation, 1978; numerous other awards. Authored *The Music of Béla Bartók* (New York: Oxford University Press, 1952).

AA73, ABD, ACA IV2, AMH, BB58, BB78, BB92, BBCch, BBD, BMI, CA11, CACA, CACJ, CN70, CPM, DCM, DN70, EMT, IMD, KDK, KTL, LMD, MHHH, NG, NGA, OCM, OL, OL95, PC71, PCM, PET, REM, TCAC, TCH, WI62, WI69, X50, X52, X53, X54, X55, X56, X57, X58, X59, X60, X61, X62, X64, X65, X66, X67, X68, X69, X70, X71, X74.

"Andrew Mellon Foundation Award." *Pan Pipes* 67/3 (1975): 13.

> Stevens is the first recipient of the Andrew Mellon Foundation Award in Humanities; a brief career summary is provided.

Berry, Wallace. "The Music of Halsey Stevens." *Musical Quarterly* 54/3 (1968): 287-08.

An overview of Halsey's work in various instrumental combinations; includes a brief discussion of his *Three Pieces* for organ, and an annotated list of works through 1967.

"Compositions by Halsey Stevens." *American Composers Alliance Bulletin* 4/2 (1954): 7-11.

An annotated list of compositions; quotes from reviews of his book on *Béla Bartók*.

"Halsey Stevens." *Pan Pipes* 43 (December 1950): 131. *

"Halsey Stevens." *Pan Pipes* 44 (January 1952): 45. *

"Halsey Stevens." *Pan Pipes* 45 (January 1953): 67. *

"Halsey Stevens." *Composers of the Americas* 11 (1965): 101-21.

A brief biographical sketch in Spanish and English is followed by an annotated catalog of his works.

"Halsey Stevens." *American Music Teacher* 25/2 (1975): 34.

A career summary, with honors and awards.

"Improvisation on 'Divinum mysterium.'" *American Organist* 39 (March 1956): 96.

Peer-Southern publishes Stevens's short setting on the plainsong *Divinum mysterium*.

"An Interview with Halsey Stevens." *Composer* (US) 5/1 (1973): 28-41.

Halsey Stevens discusses experimentation in composition, composition as a vocation, and electronic studios, among other topics.

Kremenliev, Boris. "Prominent Musicians of the West." *Music of the West* 7 (March 1952): 7, 19.

Stevens's views of the American idiom of composition.

Kyle, Marguerite K. "AmerAllegro." *Pan Pipes* 46 (January 1954): 61-62.

Irene Robertson premieres *Improvisation on "Divinum mysterium"* on December 14 in Los Angeles.

48 (January 1956): 73-74.

Improvisation on "Divinum mysterium" is published by Peer International.

50/2 (1958): 73.

Stevens's *3 Short Preludes* are premiered in San Marina, 14 October 1957, by organist Irene Robertson.

53/2 (1961): 76-77.

Stevens is visiting professor at Yale and also was featured at the University of Kansas Contemporary Symposium.

57/2 (1965): 80.

A revised edition of his book on Bartók is published; Guggenheim fellowship, 1964-65.

59/2 (1967): 97.

Three Pieces for Organ is premiered at Stetson University by Paul Jenkins, 8 March 1966.

62/2 (1970): 83-84.

Three Pieces for Organ is published by Westwood Press.

64/2 (1972): 79-80.

On sabbatical from USC, September 1971 to September 1972; received his second Guggenheim fellowship for composition.

66/2 (1974): 73.

Soliloquy, for organ, was published by Marko Music.

69/2 (1977): 73.

Stevens retired in June as Andrew W. Mellon professor in the humanities and professor of music after 30 years at USC; he will teach part-time in 1976-77.

70/2 (1978): 64.

The Abraham Lincoln Award of the American Hungarian Foundation for outstanding service to Hungarian culture will be presented to Stevens this year.

71/2 (1979): 46.

Announcement of the above item.

McDermott, Vincent. "Five Questions; 75 Answers." *Composer* 6/15 (1974-75): 38-52.

Discussion centers on women composers, performances, projects, recordings, and score reproduction. Fifteen composers respond to the same questions.

[Obituary.] *Tuba Journal* 16/3 (1989): 13.

Stevens's death notice cites his important work on Bartók.

[Obituary.] *Notes* 46/4 (1990): 932.

Notice of death on 20 January 1989; cites sources for Stevens's biography.

Pisk, Paul A. **"Halsey Stevens."** *American Composers Alliance Bulletin* 4/2 (1954): 2-6.

> A detailed, scholarly article on Stevens's compositional procedures, biography, and annotated list of compositions.

Stevens, Halsey. **"Today's Composer and His Audience."** *Pan Pipes* 43 (December 1950): 94-97. *

_____. **"The Composer Seeks a Style."** *Music Journal* 12 (October 1954): 35, 49-50.

> Stevens gives advice to the young composer, to "develop his abilities along traditional lines, acquiring facility to express himself in all the styles of the past and the present. . . ."

Richard Stewart

B. Cleveland, Ohio, 18 December 1942. M.S.M., Union Theological Seminary; doctorate, Michigan State University; organ study with Alec Wyton; composition study with Joseph Goodman and Jere Hutcheson. Musicology tutor, Union Theological Seminary, 1971-72; began teaching, later chairman, division of arts, Grand Rapids Baptist College, from 1972; director, Grand Rapids Symphonic Choir, 1981. Founder-director of the Baptist Choral Society. Organ music listed in Arnold's book.

ABD, OL, OL95.

No bibliographical information located.

Alan B. Stout

B. Baltimore, Md., 26 November 1932. Studied composition with Henry Cowell, Peabody Conservatory, Baltimore; courses at Johns Hopkins University, B.S., 1954; sporadic composition lessons with Wallingford Riegger, New York, 1951-56; post-graduate study, University of Copenhagen, 1954-55; lessons with John Verrall, M.A. in music and Swedish, 1958-59, University of Washington. Music department employee, Seattle Public Library, 1959-62; appointed to the music faculty, Northwestern University, 1963, full professor since 1976; visiting lecturer, Stockholm Musikhögskolan.

AA73, ABD, BB71, BB78, BB92, CACA, CACJ, DCM, IWW92, KTL, NG, NGA, OL, OL95, PC71, PCM, TCH, X62, X65, X66, X67, X68, X70, X71, X74.

"Concert Hall." *American Composer Alliance Bulletin* 10/3 (1962): 30.

Stout's *Eight Organ Chorales* receives its premiere on 14 May 1962 by organist Joseph Stephens at the Church of the Incarnation, Baltimore.

Kyle, Marguerite K. "AmerAllegro." *Pan Pipes* 60/2 (1968): 94-95.

Announcement of premiere: Stout's *Studies in Densities and Durations* is performed by James Leland, Northwestern University, Evanston, Ill.

61/2 (1969): 78.

A new set of *Three Organ Chorales* is premiered at Northwestern University by Benn Gibson.

62/2 (1970): 84.

Eight Organ Chorales is published by Augsburg.

63/2 (1971): 80.

Wilma Jensen has commissioned Stout for a work for organ and percussion.

64/2 (1972): 80-81.

The premiere of *Suite for Organ and Percussion* was played by Wilma Jensen and Dean Walker at Oklahoma City University.

65/2 (1973): 74-75.

A second, revised edition of the *Eight Organ Chorales* is released by Augsburg.

66/2 (1974): 74.

Three new Stout works using organ in solo or in combination were introduced this past year: *Arabesque for Organ*, by Karel Paukert; *Suite for Alto Saxophone and Organ*, played by Frederick Hemke and Karel Paukert; and *Triptych for Horn and Organ*, presented by Basil Tyler. Stout's organ chorales were recorded for broadcast in Norway and Finland.

Little, Jeanie R. "The Chorale Preludes of Alan Stout." *Diapason* 68 (August 1977): 8-11.

A scholarly and in-depth analysis of Stout's chorale preludes. An overview of his compositional styles is followed by the following topics: chorales with meandering counterpoints, pedal cantus firmus chorales, chorales with interludes, *Christ lag in Todesbaden*, a summary of stylistic characteristics, pedagogy and performance, and understanding the German titles, and determining which English translation of the German text is meant to better interpret the music.

————. **"Serial, Aleatoric, and Electronic Techniques in American Organ Music Published Between 1960 and 1972."** Ph.D., University of Iowa, 1975. *Dissertation Abstracts* 36 (June 1976): 7722A.

Includes Stout's organ work.

"Premieres." *BMI: The Many Worlds of Music*, February 1971, 17.

> The *Suite for Organ and Percussion* is premiered by the woman who commissioned it, Wilma Jensen. She introduced it the previous November 15 at the Bishop W. Angie Smith Chapel, Oklahoma City University.

Scanlan, Roger. "Spotlight on Contemporary American Composers: Alan Stout." *NATS Bulletin* 30/4 (May-June 1974): 27, 38.

> Short but comprehensive biographical sketch. Includes portrait and list of works.

Harold M. Stover

B. Latrobe, Penn., 26 November 1946. Graduated in organ from Juilliard. Organist-choirmaster, Second Presbyterian Church, New York, from 1968; currently organist and director of music, Woodfords Congregational Church, Portland, Maine.

ABD, CACA, OL, OL95.

"Commission." *American Organist* 28 (March 1994): 72.

> Stover is commissioned by St. Agnes Roman Catholic Church, New York City, to compose a major organ work based on the Stations of the Cross. The piece will be premiered in 1995.

Dodd, Mary Ann. "The Fifth Biennial Holtkamp-AGO Award in Organ Composition 1991-92: Observations and Reflections." *American Organist* 26 (November 1992): 52-56.

> A brief overview of his eleventh organ work *Angels*.

"Here and There." *Diapason* 69 (October 1978): 9.

> Stover's commissioned work *Ave maris stella* was written for the recently-installed Trompeta Majestatis on the Riverside Church organ in New York.

"Here and There." *Diapason* 81 (May 1990): 4.

> *Veni Redemptor*, op. 93, by the late Kenneth Leighton, was given its American premiere on February 18 at St. Bartholomew's Church, New York, by Stover.

"Here and There." *Diapason* 83 (July 1992): 3.

> Stover performed his organ work *Five Preludes on American Folk Hymns*, April 25, during the Bates College (Lewiston, Maine) Festival of New American Music. His work was the only organ music selected to be heard in the festival sponsored by the Society of Composers, Inc. and the Maine Composers Forum.

"Here and There." *Diapason* 85 (March 1994): 3.

> Stover is commissioned by St. Agnes Roman Catholic Church, New York, to compose a major work based on the Stations of the Cross. The piece will consist of one movement for each of the 14 stations, plus opening and closing movements.

"Premiered." *ASCAP Today*, winter 1987, 56.

> Leonard Raver performs the premiere of Stover's *Triptych on the Name of Bach*, for organ, at Southern College, Collegedale, Tenn., 23 April 1987.

"Premieres." *American Organist* 19 (August 1985): 32.

> Stover premieres his own organ work *Sinfonia* at the Second Presbyterian Church, New York, 6 May 1985.

"Premieres." *American Organist* 20 (July 1986): 36.

> Harold Stover receives a $1500 second prize for his *Triptych on the Name of Bach* in an international composition competition sponsored by the Southern College of Seventh-Day Adventists, Collegedale, Tenn., to mark the dedication of the new Brombaugh organ.

Newton D. Strandberg

B. River Falls, Wisc., 3 January 1921. Studied with Anthony Donato, Northwestern University; with Henry Cowell, Columbia University; and with Nadia Boulanger in Fontainebleau. Received the Faricy award; Birmingham Symphony award; Birmingham Festival of Arts award; Oregon College of Education contest, first prize. Faculty member, Denison University, 1947-49; Samford University, Birmingham, Ala., 1950-54 and 1956-67; Northwestern University, 1954-56; and from 1967, Sam Houston State University. Organ music listed in Arnold's book.

ABD, ASUC, CACA, OL, OL95, TCH, X59, X74.

No bibliographical information was located.

Conrad Susa

B. Springdale, Penn., 25 April 1935. Studied theory with Nicolai Lopatnikoff, musicology with Frederick Dorian, counterpoint with Roland Leigh, flute with Bernard Goldberg, and cello with Leonard Eisner at the Carnegie Institute of Technology, Pittsburgh, B.F.A., 1957; completed training in composition with William Bergsma and Vincent Persichetti,

Juilliard School of Music, M.S., 1961. Organ student of Charles Pearson. Won George Gershwin Memorial Scholarship; various prizes for composition. Composer-in-residence, Old Globe Theatre, San Diego, began in 1959 and was active there for over 30 years; music director, APA-Phoenix Repertory Co., New York, 1961-68; American Shakespeare Festival, Stratford, Conn., 1969-71; dramaturge, Eugene O'Neill Center, Conn., from 1986.
ABD, BB78, BB92, CACA, OL, OL95.

"Conrad Susa." *Diapason* 56 (August 1965): 10.

> A biography of Susa accompanies the announcement that he is winner of a $150 prize for the anthem he composed in the 1965 Prize Anthem Contest, sponsored by the AGO.

"Here and There." *Diapason* 78 (November 1987): 3.

> Richard and Elizabeth Chenault, duo-organists, commissioned and performed the premiere of Susa's *Canticle* at St. Stephen's Episcopal Church, Richmond, Va., 8 July 1987.

Kratzenstein, Marilou, and Bruce Gustafson. "The Minneapolis/St. Paul AGO National Convention." *Diapason* 71 (August 1980): 3.

> John Ferguson stepped in as a substitute for David Hurd and premiered Susa's *Fantasia for Organ, Brass, and Percussion*. The piece arrived a mere five days before the performance.

"Organ Recitals." *Diapason* 78 (December 1987): 19.

> Susa's commission by Elizabeth and Raymond Chenault entitled *Canticle* is premiered at St. Stephen's Episcopal Church, Richmond, Va., 8 July 1987.

"Premieres." *American Organist* 21 (November 1987): 55.

> Same information as in the item above.

"Recitals." *American Organist* 21 (December 1987): 86.

> Same information as in the item above.

Robert F. Swift

B. 1940. Ph.D., University of Rochester, Eastman School of Music, 1970. Dissertation entitled "An Analysis and Description of Three Simulation Models in Music Education." *Dissertation Abstracts* 31 (December 1970): 2963A. Organ music listed in Arnold's book.
OL, OL95.

No bibliographical information located.

William T. Sydeman

B. New York, 8 May 1928. Studied at Mannes College of Music, with Felix Salzer and Roy Travis, B.S., 1955; with Arnold Franchetti, Hartt School of Music, M.M., 1958; lessons with Roger Sessions and Goffredo Petrassi. Taught at Mannes College of Music, 1959-70, and Rudolph Steiner College, Fair Oaks, Calif., 1980-82. Received two Tanglewood fellowships; National Institute of Arts and Letters Award, 1962; State Department lectureship in Czechoslovakia, Romania, and Bulgaria, 1966.

ABD, AMH, BB65, BB71, BB78, BB92, BDA, CACA, CACJ, CRI 158, DCM, KTL, NG, NGA, OL, OL95, PC71, PCM, TCH, X60, X62, X64, X66, X67, X69, X70, X71.

"Composer-Judges: Inter-American Music Awards Competition, 1965-68." *Pan Pipes* 59/4 (1967): 3, 13.

Background, honors, awards, and major works listed.

Kyle, Marguerite K. "AmerAllegro." *Pan Pipes* 54/2 (1962): 73-74.

Sydeman wins the Pacifica Foundation Composition Competition.

55/2 (1963): 71.

Received a grant from the National Institute of Arts and Letters.

Reich, Nancy Bassen, ed. *Catalog of the Works of William Sydeman: A Machine-Readable Pilot Project in Information Retrieval.* 2nd ed. New York: Division of Music Education, New York University, 1968. *

Turok, Paul. "William Sydeman." *BMI: The Many Worlds of Music,* March 1967, 11.

Introduction to the composer: background, honors, awards, and lists several of his numerous commissions.

James H. Tallis

B. Elmira, N.Y., 1932; d. Dallas, Texas, 23 September 1969. Joined the faculty of Southern Methodist University, June 1968; D.S.M. awarded posthumously from Union Theological Seminary. Graduated Eastman School of Music, 1954, as a student of Catharine Crozier; M.S.M., *cum laude*, from Union, where he studied with Robert Baker. Fulbright grant awarded in 1963 to study in the Netherlands with Cor Kee and Gustav Leonhardt. Taught at Hastings College, Nebr.; Hope College, Holland, Mich.; served churches in New York,

New Jersey, and Michigan; organist-choirmaster of St. Luke's Episcopal Church, Dallas; assistant professor of organ and harpsichord, Southern Methodist University, at the time of his death.

A composite biography was made from OL and all of the journal articles listed below.

"James H. Tallis." *Diapason* 59 (November 1968): 4.
Tallis is appointed assistant professor of music at Southern Methodist University, Dallas, Texas, where he will teach organ, harpsichord, and improvisation.

"James Tallis." *Diapason* 51 (November 1960): 25.
Tallis joined the faculty of Hastings College (Nebr.); he will be an organ and harpsichord instructor, and will teach courses in theory, conducting, and church music.

Lodine, Robert. "National in the Rockies." *American Organist* 51 (August 1968): 27.
Tallis performs on 4 July 1968 at First Methodist Church, Boulder, Colo.; performed Joseph Goodman's new work *Fantasia for Organ*. Reviewer thought Tallis let the "music speak for itself," and did not "get in the way of the music."

[Obituary.] *Diapason* 60 (November 1969): 18.
Tallis dies from an operation for a brain tumor, 23 September 1969.

[Obituary.] *American Organist* 52 (December 1969): 22.
At age 37, Tallis dies from brain surgery complications. Highlights of his life are provided.

[Obituary.] *Music* (AGO) 4 (January 1970): 6.
Notice of Tallis's death, 23 September 1969, is given.

Louise Juliette Talma

B. Arcachon, France, 31 October 1906; d. 13 August 1996. Emigrated to the U.S. in 1922. Attended Institute of Musical Art, New York, 1922-39; Fontainebleau School of Music, summers 1926-39, composition with Nadia Boulanger; B.M., New York University, 1931; M.A., Columbia University, 1933. Piano lessons with Isidore Philipp. Numerous prizes include two Guggenheim fellowships, 1946 and 1947; Fulbright research grant, 1955-56; Stovall prize for composition, Fontainebleau, 1938 and 1939; French Government Prix d'Excellence de Composition, 1951. Taught theory and ear training, Manhattan School of Music, 1926-28; first American to teach at the Fontainebleau School of Music, summers 1936-39, 1978, 1981-82. Taught at Hunter College, New York, 1928-79, and was made professor of music there in 1952. First woman composer to be elected to the National Institute of Arts and Letters, 1974. Authored *Harmony for the College Student* (n.p., 1966); with James S. Harrison and Robert Levin, *Functional Harmony* (n.p., 1970).

ABD, AMH, AS66, BB58, BB65, BB78, BB92, BDA, CACA, CACJ, DCM, DN78, IMD, IWC, IWW92, KTL, MHHH, NG, NGA, PC71, PCM, TCAC, WCH, X50, X51, X52, X55, X62, X69, X70, X71.

Berger, Arthur. **"Stravinsky and the Younger American Composers."** *Score* (London) 12 (June 1955): 38-46.

> Berger takes different Stravinsky compositional devices and indicates how younger composers, including Talma, use those traits in their compositions.

"Contemporary Composers and Their Works." *Music & Artists* 4/2 (1971): 11. *

"A Gallery of Lifetime Achievers." *Music Educators Journal* 66 (April 1980): 49.

> The high points in Talma's career and basic influences on her compositions are mentioned.

Kyle, Marguerite K. **"AmerAllegro."** *Pan Pipes* 56/2 (1964): 82.

> Three honors to Talma: the Sibelius Medal for Composition, a citation from the National Association for American Composers and Conductors, and a National Federation of Music Clubs award "for advancing national and world culture through distinguished service to music."

59/2 (1967): 98.

> Talma receives National Endowment for the Arts grant of $7500.

67/2 (1975): 75.

> Talma is the first woman composer to be elected to the National Institute of Arts and Letters.

_____. **"With Fraternity Composers."** *Pan Pipes* 43 (December 1950): 147. *

LePage, Jane Weiner. *Women Composers, Conductors, and Musicians of the Twentieth Century: Selected Biographies.* Metuchen, N.J.: Scarecrow, 1980.

> Includes Talma's biography, discography, and list of works.

Lewinski, W. E. von. **"Komponistinen suchen Anschluss an die Avantgarde."** *Melos* 35 (January 1968): 27.

> Discusses attempts of female composers to be included in the avant-garde of modern composition. Mentions Jacqueline Tonty, Elizabeth Maconchy, and Myriam Marbe in addition to Talma, and briefly discusses highlights of their work.

"**Louise Talma.**" *Pan Pipes* 45 (January 1953): 69. *

"**Louise Talma Commissioned to Write Composition for SAI 75th Anniversary.**" *Pan Pipes* 70/2 (1978): 10.

A brief biography accompanies the announcement.

Porter, Andrew. "**Musical Events.**" *New Yorker* 62 (10 November 1986): 115-16.

"Everything Talma writes is marked by her distinction and elegance." This 80th birthday concert at Merkin Hall honors Talma with her own musical compositions.

"**Premieres.**" *Music Educators Journal* 66 (April 1980): 29.

The premiere of Talma's *Celebration* occurred in Dallas, August 1979.

Rosen, Judith, and Grace Rubin-Rabson. "**Why Haven't Women Become Great Composers?**" *High Fidelity/Musical America* 23 (February 1973): 46-52.

Talma and Radie Britain are mentioned as two of the best-known women composers to date; some historical views on reasons women haven't become great composers are presented.

"**A Salute to Women Composers.**" *Pan Pipes* 67/2 (1975): 4.

A summary of her awards.

Teicher, Susan. "**Louise Talma: Essentials of Her Style as Seen through the Piano Works.**" *Musical Woman* 1 (1983): 128-46.

Tracing the influences on Talma's keyboard music, Teicher discusses the neoclassical, tonal, and contrapuntal elements in Talma's works for piano.

Deborah Teason

B. Ossining, N.Y., 27 August 1951. B.M. in theory and composition, Arizona State University, 1980. Received Louise Kerr Award of Merit; Millay Colony for the Arts Residency. Currently resides in New Haven, Conn. *Prelude, Fugue and Passacaglia*, for organ, was written in 1989. Organ music listed in CR.

CR.

No bibliographical information located.

Paul Lindsley Thomas

B. New York, 18 March 1929. B.A., Trinity College, 1950; studied with Norman Coke-Jephcott, New York, 1950-54; with Quincy Porter and Leroy Baumgartner, Yale University, B.M., 1957, and M.M., 1958; with Samuel Adler and Merrill Ellis, North Texas State University, 1963-65, 1978, D.M.A., 1979. AAGO, 1953, FAGO, 1958. Received the Luther Noss prize in composition, Yale University, 1958; ASCAP awards, 1975-80. Organist and choirmaster, St. George's-by-the-River Episcopal Church, Rumson, N.J., 1950-55; organist-choirmaster, St. James Episcopal Church, West Hartford, Conn., 1955-60; since 1960, music director, St. Michael and All Angels Church, Dallas.

ABD, CACA, DN77, IWW92, OL, OL95.

"**Paul L. Thomas.**" *Diapason* 43 (January 1952): 24.

> Thomas's biography accompanies the announcement that he is giving a series of Sunday afternoon recitals at his church, St. George's-by-the-River, Rumson, N.J.

"**Paul L. Thomas.**" *Diapason* 50 (September 1959): 7.

> Thomas assumed the post director of music at First Presbyterian Church, LaGrange, Ill., on August 15.

Richard Toensing

B. St. Paul, Minn., 11 March 1940. Studied with Ross Lee Finney, Leslie Bassett, and George B. Wilson, University of Michigan, D.M.A., 1968. Received BMI student awards, 1963 and 1964; Joseph Bearns prize, Columbia University, 1965. Faculty member, Upsala College, 1966-73; from 1973, at the University of Colorado. For his dissertation, he composed *Requiem* (*Dissertation Abstracts* 28 [June 1968]: 5098A-99A).

ABD, CACA, OL, OL95.

"**Premieres.**" *American Organist* 21 (January 1987): 46.

> *Concerto for Organ and Orchestra* by Richard Toensing, commissioned by the 50th anniversary fund of the Denver AGO Chapter, was premiered at a gala anniversary concert, 9 July 1986, at Trinity United Methodist Church, Denver, with organist Leonard Raver and the festival orchestra conducted by Bruce Hangen.

Frederick Thomas (Fred) Tulan

B. Stockton, Calif., 5 September 1934. B.A., University of the Pacific; studied at the Universities of Maryland, Oregon, Stanford, California-Berkeley, California State University at San Francisco, Mills College, and New York. Further study in France, Germany, and England. Teachers were Seth Bingham, Charles Courboin, Hugh Giles, Jeanne Demessieux in Paris, and Helmut Winkler in Heidelberg.
OL, OL95.

Bingham, Seth. "Recital, New York." *American Organist* 53 (November 1970): 14.

Tulan performs a recital of "Magic Movies," "Serious" Music, "Different" Music, and "The Extremes" at St. John the Divine Cathedral, New York, 12 July 1970; four works received their New York premieres.

"Convention Personalities." *American Organist* 18 (April 1984): 133.

An introduction to Tulan, concert organist and author of articles on "the aliquot mutation pitches of Klais, Rieger, and Walcker organs in Germany and Austria."

"Frederick Tulan." *Diapason* 44 (April 1953): 5.

Stockton (Calif.) Symphony Orchestra's organist, Tulan, was its first organ soloist to appear in concert with them. He performed the Poulenc *Organ Concerto*; Manlio Silva conducted.

"Here and There." *Diapason* 82 (January 1991): 4.

Tulan performed organ compositions of Virgil Thomson during the concert commemorating the first anniversary of Thomson's death, which was presented 5 October 1990 by Old First Concerts, San Francisco.

"Here and There." *Diapason* 82 (June 1991): 4.

Tulan performed in Paris at Ste-Clotilde and St-Eustache on March 16 and 17. At St-Eustache, Tulan played David Carlson's *Resurrection*, composed for him to premiere at Westminster Abbey.

"Here and There." *Diapason* 84 (August 1993): 4.

Tulan performed at La Madeleine, Paris, on May 9, as guest organist at Mass. He played *Concert Etude*, which Anthony Newman composed for him to premiere at St. Paul's Cathedral, London.

"Here and There." *Diapason* 85 (February 1994): 4.

Tulan observed the 25th anniversary of French virtuoso Jeanne Demessieux by performing her music during High Mass at St. Mary's Cathedral, San Francisco, on November 14.

"Here and There." *Diapason* 85 (June 1994): 3.

> Jean Guillou composed a new concert toccata, *Chamades*, dedicated to Tulan, who premiered it February 13 at First Christian Church, Honolulu, Hawaii, during a service commemorating the 100th anniversary of the church. *Chamades* is published by FitzSimons.

"Mixtures." *American Organist* 25 (August 1991): 36.

> Tulan performs at Saint-Eustache, Paris, 16-17 March 1991. He performed David Carlson's *Resurrection*, written for him to premiere at Westminster Abbey.

"Mixtures." *American Organist* 25 (October 1991): 55.

> Tulan was organist for a concert at Old First Church Concert Series in San Francisco, to honor the memory of Virgil Thomson. Tulan performed his own work, *Portrait of Fred Tulan, An Organ Piece.*

"Premieres." *American Organist* 28 (June 1994): 51.

> Tulan premiered Jean Guillou's new toccata *Chamades* on 13 February 1994, in Honolulu, Hawaii, at First Christian Church, to commemorate the 100th anniversary of the church.

"Recital, N.Y." *American Organist* 50 (September 1967): 7-8.

> Tulan presents a brilliant recital on 6 August 1967 at the Cathedral of St. John the Divine, New York. Several works that he performed were dedicated to him: Flor Peeters's *Tune for the State Trumpet Stop* (premiere), Richard Purvis's *Lamentations of Jeremiah: The Roads to Zion Shall Mourn*, Mario Castelnuovo-Tedesco's *Preludes on the Name of Frederick Tulan (1-26 Scale)* and *Fugue on the Name of Albert Schweitzer* (premiere), and Dave Brubeck's *Organ Fantasia, Sacred Service* (premiere).

Christopher Uehlein

B. Indianapolis, Ind., 15 October 1931. Studied theory and composition at DePaul University, Chicago; graduate study in theory and composition, University of Illinois, Champaign-Urbana; composition student of Ben Johnston and Thomas Frederickson; organ student of René Desogne, Herman Pedtke, Lenough Anderson, and Leonard Palmquist. Organist-choirmaster, Blue Cloud (Benedictine) Abbey, Marvin, S.D., since 1958. Organ music listed in Arnold's book.

OL, OL95.

No bibliographical information located.

Mary Jeanne Van Appledorn

B. Holland, Mich., 2 October 1927. B.M., 1948, M.M., 1950, Ph.D., 1966, Eastman School of Music; composition with Bernard Rogers and Alan Hovhaness. Member of Texas Composers' Hall of Fame, 1973. Awards from Mu Phi Epsilon composition contests; standard ASCAP awards; named Paul Whitfield Horn Professor, 1989; and International Scholar, Phi Beta Delta, 1989. Professor and chair of graduate studies in music, 1950-82, and chair/founder of the annual symposium of contemporary music at Texas Technical University, 1950-75. Post-doctoral studies at Massachusetts Institute of Technology in computer-synthesized sound techniques, 1982. Retired, 1982. Dissertation was titled "A Stylistic Study of Claude Debussy's Opera *Pélleas et Mélisande*" (1965); authored *Functional Piano for the College Student*; *In Quest of the Roman Numeral*; *Keyboard: Singing and Dictation Manual* (1968).

ABD, BB92, CACA, CACJ, DN72, DN73, DN78, IWC, IWW92, X70.

"Composition and Publication." *Triangle* 81/4 (1987): 21.
Includes her *Missa brevis* for trumpet and organ.

"Honors and Appointments." *Instrumentalist* 43 (May 1989): 52.
Van Appledorn is named Paul Whitfield Horn Professor by Texas Technical University Board of Regents. This is the highest honor granted to a faculty member at the university. Brief biography is included.

"Van Appledorn Compositions Receive Widespread Hearings." *Triangle* 81/2 (1986-87): 15. *

"Van Appledorn Premieres." *International Trumpet Guild Journal* 12/1 (1987): 47.
Missa brevis for organ and trumpet was premiered 30 March 1987, in October Hall, Saratov State Conservatoire, Saratov, U.S.S.R. The American premiere was on May 2 in Washington, D.C., with Robert Birch, trumpet, and Carol Feather Martin, organ.

John Verrall

B. Britt, Iowa, 17 June 1908. Studied piano and composition with Donald Ferguson; then attended classes at the Royal College of Music in London with Reginald O. Morris, 1929-30; additional composition study in Budapest with Kodály and in piano with Gabriel

Zsigmondy, 1930-31. Returned to America, entered the University of Minnesota studying composition and piano again with Donald Ferguson; BB92 states that he studied at the Minneapolis College of Music and Hamline University; B.A., 1932. Further training at the Berkshire Music Center, Tanglewood, with Roy Harris, Frederick Jacobi, and Aaron Copland. Taught composition and theory at Hamline University, 1934-42; Mount Holyoke College, 1942-46; University of Washington, Seattle, 1958-73. Served as editor for G. Schirmer and Boston and Willis Music companies, 1947-48, after serving in the U.S. armed services. Guggenheim fellowship, 1947. Authored *Elements of Harmony* (n.p., 1937); with S. Moseley, *Form and Meaning in the Arts* (New York: McGraw-Hill, 1958); *Fugue and Invention in Theory and Practice* (Palo Alto, Calif.: Pacific Books, 1966); *Basic Theory of Scales, Modes and Intervals* (Palo Alto: Pacific Books, 1969); and *Basic Theory of Music: Programmed Instruction in Intervals, Scales and Modes* (Palo Alto: Pacific Books, 1971).

ABD, ACA VII4, AMH, BB58, BB78, BB92, BBCch, BDA, CACA, CACJ, DCM, DN78, KTL, LMD, MHHH, NG, NGA, OL, OL95, PC71, PCM, REM, TCAC, X50, X51, X52, X53, X56, X57, X58, X62, X64, X65, X66, X67, X68, X69, X70, X71, X74.

"AmerAllegro." *Pan Pipes* 48 (January 1956): 74-75. *

> 51 (January 1959): 87.

> The summer issue of *American Composers Alliance Bulletin* featured an article by John Beale, analyzing the works of Verrall.

Beale, John. "The Music of John Verrall." *American Composers Alliance Bulletin* 7/4 (1958): 10-15.

> A theoretical analysis of Verrall's approach to composition. Following is a biographical sketch and a list of his works.

"John Verrall." *Pan Pipes* 43 (December 1950): 132. *

"John Verrall." *Pan Pipes* 44 (January 1952): 46. *

"John Verrall." *Pan Pipes* 47 (January 1955): 69-70. *

Kyle, Marguerite K. "AmerAllegro." *Pan Pipes* 57/2 (1965): 82.

> Verrall received the D. H. Lawrence Fellowship from the University of New Mexico; in June, he took up residence at the Lawrence Ranch near Taos for the summer of 1964.

> 61/2 (1969): 80.

> *Canzona for Organ* is published by C. F. Peters.

Harold Vetter

B. Milwaukee, Wisc., 1931. Pastor, St. Paul Evangelist Lutheran, Elliotville, N.Y. Organ music listed in Arnold's book.

OL, OL95.

No bibliographical information located.

Alan D. Walker

B. Boston, Mass., 9 July 1927. B.M., Boston University, 1951; M.S.M., Union Theological Seminary, 1953; organ student of Samuel Walter, George Faxon, and Hugh Porter; composition student of Harold Friedell and Searle Wright. Organist-choirmaster, Howard Memorial Presbyterian Church, Tarboro, N.C., 1953-56; organist-choirmaster, Central Congregational Church, Worcester, Mass., 1956-66; organist-choirmaster, Central Union Church, Honolulu, Hawaii, 1966-69; organist, Calvary Lutheran Church, Honolulu, 1969-74; since 1974, organist-choirmaster, Grace Congregational United Church of Christ, Rutland, Vt.

OL, OL95.

Gardner, J. "Testing Genius by Analysis." *Composer* 24 (summer 1967): 11-14. *

Gwyneth Van Anden Walker

B. New York [CACA], Connecticut [IWC], 22 March 1947. Studied with Paul Nelson, B.A. in music, Brown University, 1968; with Arnold Franchetti, M.M., 1970, and D.M.A., 1976, Hartt College of Music, University of Hartford. Mann Music Premium award, Brown University; student awards, Hartt College; Yaddo fellowship, 1976; first place, Hartford Unitarian Church anthem contest, 1978. On faculty, Oberlin College Conservatory, from 1977; later at Hartford Conservatory. Now free-lance composer. Cohen lists her organ music.

CACA, IWC.

No bibliographical information located.

Samuel Walter

B. Cumberland, Md., 2 February 1916; d. Princeton, N.J., 4 July 1987. Degrees from Marion College, New England Conservatory of Music, Boston University, and Union Theological Seminary, where he studied with Seth Bingham. Additional study with Nadia Boulanger at Fontainebleau, France. Faculty member, Boston University, 1945-55; Union Theological Seminary, School of Sacred Music, 1957-65; Douglass College, Rutgers University, 1962-83; organist, Voorhees Chapel, Rutgers University, 1963-83; retired as professor emeritus, 1983. Also, organist-choirmaster, Church of the Resurrection, New York, 1967-83. Additional posts included St. Anne's Episcopal Church, Brooklyn, and Trinity Episcopal Church, Newton Center, Mass.; on the faculty of the Colby Church Music Institute for many years. Author of *Basic Principles of Composition and Arranging* (Nashville: Abingdon, 1965).

ABD, CACA, OL, OL95.

"Dr. Samuel Walter." *Diapason* 56 (November 1965): 2.

> Walter is appointed to teach organ at Douglass College, Rutgers University, and to serve as organist at Voorhees Chapel. Biographical information included.

[Obituary.] *American Organist* 21 (November 1987): 57.

> Walter dies 4 July 1987 in Princeton Medical Center after a lengthy illness. Includes biographical data and indicates a memorial service was held 29 August 1987 at Voorhees Chapel.

"Recitals and Concerts." *American Organist* 44 (March 1961): 26.

> Walter joined his wife Janet Wheeler, soprano, in a concert entitled "Abendmusiken" held at Christ Chapel, Riverside Church, New York, 17 October 1960. Reviewer lauds Walter for selecting "fresh, untrammeled music."

"Samuel Walter." *American Organist* 48 (November 1965): 28.

> Walter receives full-time appointment at Douglass College, Rutgers University, to teach organ and to be organist at Voorhees Chapel. Lists previous positions and recital appearances.

"Samuel Walter." *Diapason* 58 (November 1967): 7.

> Walter is appointed organist and choirmaster of the Episcopal Church of the Resurrection, New York; he continues his appointment at Douglass College.

"Samuel Walter to Direct Stamford Church Music." *Diapason* 46 (November 1955): 10.

> Walter has been appointed organist-choirmaster of St. John's Episcopal Church, Stamford, Conn.; continues on the faculty of Boston University.

Robert Eugene Ward

B. Cleveland, Ohio, 13 September 1917. Studied composition with Frederick Jacobi, Edward Royce, Aaron Copland, Bernard Rogers, and Howard Hanson, Eastman School of Music, B.M., 1939; certificate, Juilliard Graduate School, 1946; conducting studies were with Albert Stoessel and Edgar Schenkman. Taught at Columbia University, 1946-48, and Juilliard School of Music, 1946-56. Music director of the Third Street Music School Settlement, 1952-55; executive vice president and managing editor, Galaxy Music and Highgate Press, 1956-67; president, 1967-74, teacher of composition, 1967-79, North Carolina School of the Arts; Mary Duke Biddle Professor of Music, Duke University, 1979-87. Recipient of the Pulitzer Prize for music, for his opera *The Crucible*.

ABD, ACA iv.4, AMH, BB58, BB71, BB78, BB92, BDA, BMI, CA9, CACA, CACJ, DCM, EDM, EVM, GD54, HHH, IMD, IWW92, KTL, LMD, MHHH, NG, NGA, OL, OL95, PC71, PCM, REM, TCAC, WTM, X50, X51, X52, X53, X56, X57, X58, X59, X61, X62, X64, X65, X66, X67, X68, X69, X71, X74.

Belt, Byron. **"AGO/80 Twin Cities Convention Stimulating, Inspiring, Exhausting."** *American Organist* 14 (August 1980): 26.

The reviewer writes about Ward's commissioned work for the AGO convention, *Celebrations of God in Nature*: ". . . one commission did prove a real bomb—Robert Ward's *Celebrations of God in Nature*—which was injected into Robert Glasgow's otherwise glorious romantic playing. . . . My scribbled notes described it as 'wildly conservative,' and a friend noted that it was the popular opera composer's first organ commission, and hoped that it would be the last."

"Composers in Focus." *BMI: The Many Worlds of Music*, winter 1976, 32-33.

Biography of Ward includes honors and awards; many of his works were written on commission. He comments on 20th-century music and cites Debussy as the instigator of the "revolution" in music.

Daniel, Oliver. **"Saluting the American Composer, Robert Ward."** *Music Clubs Magazine* 48/3 (1969): 14-15.

Biographical information, influences on his compositional style, and quotes from critics about his work.

Kratzenstein, Marilou, and Bruce Gustafson. **"The Minneapolis/St. Paul AGO National Convention."** *Diapason* 71 (August 1980): 4.

Ward's commissioned work, *Celebrations of God in Nature*, was premiered by Robert Glasgow at the AGO convention. The work, in three movements, was Ward's first venture at writing for organ solo.

Kreitner, Kenneth. *Robert Ward: A Bio-Bibliography.* Westport, Conn.: Greenwood, 1988.

Includes biography, bibliography, works and performances, and a discography.

Kyle, Marguerite K. "AmerAllegro." *Pan Pipes* 55/2 (1963): 74.

Recipient of the 1962 Pulitzer Prize in music and the New York Music Critics Circle Citation.

59/2 (1967): 20.

Awarded a renewal of his Guggenheim fellowship; was the guest composer on the University of Kansas Contemporary Music Symposium.

Mundale, Susan. "AGO '80 National Convention, Twin Cities Minneapolis/St. Paul, June 16-20, 1980." *American Organist* 14 (February 1980): 32.

Robert Glasgow will perform Ward's new organ work *The Celebration of God in Nature*, commissioned by the Twin Cities Chapter of the American Guild of Organists, on 18 June 1980. The work is in three movements.

"Robert Ward." *Composers of the Americas* 9 (1963): 172-79.

A brief biography in Spanish and English is accompanied by an annotated catalog of his works.

"Robert Ward Is Selected as New Head of Arts School." *Diapason* 58 (April 1967): 45.

Ward succeeds Vittorio Giannini, who died in November, as president of North Carolina School of the Arts, Winston-Salem, N.C.

Stambler, Bernard. "Robert Ward." *American Composers Alliance Bulletin* 4/4 (1955): 3-6.

Ward states that, for him, the "line of tension" serves as the germinating principle of his music; an annotated list of compositions follows.

Richard Warner

B. Medina, Ohio, 1908. B.S., University of Cincinnati; M.A., Columbia University; Ph.D., Eastman School of Music. Headed music departments at Centre College and Berea College; faculty member at Kent State University and at Eastman. Organist-choirmaster, St. Paul's Episcopal Church, Rochester, N.Y. Retired.

ABD, OL, OL95.

"Dialogue on a Noel, for Organ." *Notes* 10 (September 1953): 685-86.

Published by H. W. Gray, 1952, the work is described as "a fine bit of two-part imitative writing that sparkles brightly in proper Noel style."

"Dr. Richard Warner Wins Final Psalm-Tune Award." *Diapason* 44 (October 1953): 25.

> Biographical information accompanies the announcement of Warner's success over 3,862 other composers; his setting of Psalm 150 won first prize.

"Richard Warner." *Diapason* 50 (March 1959): 6.

> Warner takes a two-month leave from Kent State University, as head of the organ department, to travel and study in England, Switzerland, Holland, Austria, and Germany.

"Richard Warner Is Named to Kent University Post." *Diapason* 46 (October 1955): 29.

> Warner is named head of the Kent State University School of Music.

Walter Robert Watson

B. Canton, Ohio, 13 October 1933. Studied with Karl Harendt, Ohio University, B.F.A., 1959, and M.F.A., 1961; with Samuel Adler, North Texas State University, Ph.D., 1967; with Darius Milhaud, Aspen Music School. ASCAP awards from 1968; Kent State University fellowships, 1968, 1970, and 1972; first prize, U.S. Navy Band contest, 1973; grants from the Rockefeller Foundation, George Gund Foundation, Boscom Little Fund, 1978. Faculty member, Stephen F. Austin State University, 1961-66; Kent State University, 1967-74; from 1974, editorial consultant, Ludwig Publishing Company; organist-choirmaster, Christ Episcopal Church, Kent, Ohio. His dissertation is titled "Symphony No. 1."

ABD, ASUC, CACA, CACJ, OL, OL95, PC71, PCM, X68, X69, X71, X74.

"News and Honors." *ASCAP* 5/2 (1971): 33.

> Watson's commissioned organ solo titled *Sanctitude* was premiered at the Ohio Valley Regional Convention Guild of Organists, 15 June 1971.

Clarence Watters

B. East Orange, N.J., 26 February 1902; d. Hartford, Conn., 26 July 1986. Early instruction in organ was with Eva Wilde and Mark Andrews. Student of Marcel Dupré at his request after hearing Watters perform. In 1932, college organist, later a member of the music faculty, professor of music, and finally head of the music department, Trinity College, Hartford, Conn. Retired as professor emeritus and honorary college organist, 1967.

Between 1968 and 1970 he was visiting professor of organ at Yale; served as organist of St. John's Episcopal Church, Hartford. Laureate in the Humanities, St. Joseph College, West Hartford, Conn., 1983.

OL, OL95.

Banta, Lorene. "Watters at Methuen." *Music* (AGO) 7 (January 1973): 59.

A review of Watters's performance at the Methuen Memorial Music Hall in Massachusetts, 25 October 1972, an all-French recital program.

Bingham, Seth. "Organ Personalities." *American Organist* 46 (December 1963): 10.

Watters is noted for his moving interpretations of the important works of his master Dupré, and also for his criticisms of AGO guild exams, which were subsequently upgraded.

"Clarence Watters." *American Organist* 20 (May 1986): inside front cover.

A salute to Clarence Watters; provides biographical information.

"Clarence Watters—In Memoriam." *The Tracker* 34/3 (1990): 10.

A brief tribute to Watters by Thomas Froehlich.

Doney, John. "Clarence Watters Farewell Recital." *American Organist* 18 (June 1984): 41.

Watters performs his final recital at Trinity College in Hartford, Conn. The recital consists of Dupré's music and is dedicated to his memory.

Faxon, George. "Watters Plays in Boston." *Diapason* 42 (June 1951): 12.

Watters performs at Trinity Church, Boston, on April 16. "An ever-tasteful banquet of music" provides a forum for fine playing.

"Here and There." *Diapason* 75 (December 1984): 4.

Charles Callahan gave the first performance of Watters's *Versets on Adoro te devote* in Trinity College Chapel, Hartford, Conn., November 4; the work was composed in memory of Marjorie Watters, who died earlier in the year.

"Letters to the Editor." *Diapason* 62 (June 1971): 15.

Watters responds to the reveiwer of his Chicago recital and discusses the question concerning an "authentic" performance of Franck's works.

[Obituary.] *American Organist* 20 (October 1986): 47.

Notice of Watters's death, 26 July 1986, in Hartford, Conn.

[Obituary.] *Diapason* 78 (January 1987): 3.

Watters died 26 July 1986 of a heart attack in Hartford, Conn. A condensed biography accompanies the notice.

Owen, Barbara. "Recital." *Diapason* 62 (July 1971): 4.

A recital at Methuen Memorial Music Hall, Methuen, Mass., was a memorial celebration for Marcel Dupré. Watters had originally billed the recital as an 85th birthday tribute, but after Dupré's death the former student announced his intention to play nothing but Dupré's works for the remainder of the year. The review was extremely favorable.

"Recitals and Concerts." *American Organist* 40 (June 1957): 195.

Watters performed at St. Thomas Church, New York, April 15. His recital "was most acceptable, in every way—to musicians. I scarcely think the same would be said by the lay listener. . . ."

"Recitals and Concerts." *American Organist* 49 (June 1966): 9.

Watters performs two recitals to honor Dupré's 80th birthday. One was played at St. Thomas Church, New York, 4 May 1966, and the other at the Church of St. Mary the Virgin, 11 May 1966. "All faultlessly played."

Terry, Mickey Thomas. "Clarence Watters: A Tribute." *American Organist* 21 (January 1987): 16, 18.

Clarence Watters's deep influence on musicians throughout the country is recalled.

————. **"Clarence Watters: The Virtuoso, the Mind, the Legend."** *American Organist* 24 (March 1990): 54-55.

An overview of Watters's life, his remarkable memory (he used no scores in over 60 years of performances), his teachers, and his positions as recitalist, composer, and teacher.

Watters, Clarence. "Improvisation." *Music* (AGO) 7 (May 1973): 27-31.

Watters's approach to improvising. Part 1 is headed by words from Marcel Dupré, recommending Watters's preliminary exercises in improvisation, followed by a discussion of the renewed interest in the skill, its history from the Renaissance to current times, and its use in hymn accompaniments, interludes, and preludes.

7 (June 1973): 24-28.

Watters concludes his detailed articles on improvisation by addressing the contrapuntal, ornate, and fugal chorale preludes, extended forms, offertory interludes, improvisation during communion, and postludes.

Wilkinson, Harry. "Clarence Watters Plays Dupré at Notre Dame." *Music* (AGO) 7 (October 1973): 30.

Watters plays an all-Dupré recital from memory in the Cathedral of Notre Dame de Paris on 17 June 1973, with nearly 3,000 people in attendance. "The total effect was one of spine-tingling magnificence."

John B. Weaver

B. Palmerton, Penn., 27 April 1937. Organ student of Richard Ross and George Markey; studied at Peabody Conservatory; organ student of Alexander McCurdy, Curtis Institute. Director of music-organist, Holy Trinity Lutheran Church, New York. M.S.M., Union Theological Seminary, with Robert Baker and Joseph Goodman. Organist-choirmaster, Madison Avenue Presbyterian Church, New York, 1970; organ teacher, Curtis Institute, 1971; taught organ at Westminster Choir College; and in 1983 appointed head of the organ department, Manhattan School of Music, New York.

ABD, CACA, OL, OL95.

"AGO Midwinter Conclave." *American Organist* 46 (February 1963): 7-8.

Reviewer reprimanded Weaver for some of his performance practice decisions such as registration on a trio sonata. Weaver's best playing was on Liszt's *Prelude and Fugue on B-A-C-H.*

"Appointments." *American Organist* 53 (August 1970): 30.

Weaver is appointed director of music at New York's Madison Avenue Presbyterian Church and conductor of the St. Andrew's Music Society Chorus and Orchestra. Gives prior job record and music studies.

"Atlanta Plays Gracious Host to Its First National." *Diapason* 57 (August 1966): 34-36.

Weaver performed his recital twice. The reviewer was "greatly gratified by the growth he is making."

Bingham, Seth. "Guilmant Organ Fest." *American Organist* 48 (April 1965): 7.

During the Organ Fest, several organists combined their talents for one exciting evening of music-making. Weaver's playing of Handel's *Concerto in F Major* was praised as "virtuosic, exciting . . . complete mastery at all times."

"'Fantasia for Organ' and 'Idem.'" *Notes* 41/4 (1985): 796-97.

Both organ works are published by Boosey & Hawkes, 1983; a description of the two works is provided by Leonard Raver. *Idem* is a passacaglia on a theme by Dunstable.

"Here and There." *Diapason* 82 (November 1991): 4.

Weaver was honored by Madison Avenue Presbyterian Church on 19 May 1991, upon completion of twenty-one years as director of music. The St. Andrew Chorale, directed by Weaver, performed a concert of music he had written within the last five years.

"Here and There." *Diapason* 84 (July 1993): 4.

Weaver is featured on a new CD recording, *John Weaver Performs*. Composers represented include Bach, Schubert, Weaver, Leighton, and others.

"John Weaver." *American Organist* 42 (July 1959): 253.

Weaver is appointed organist and choirmaster of the Lutheran Church of the Holy Trinity, New York, June 7. Previous positions listed.

"John Weaver." *Diapason* 50 (July 1959): 6.

Same information as in the item above.

"John Weaver." *American Organist* 47 (January 1964): 30.

Weaver will return to Holy Trinity Lutheran Church, New York, after two years of active duty in the U.S. Army, where he was stationed at the U.S. Military Academy, West Point, N.Y., as organist-choirmaster of the Post Chapel.

"John Weaver." *Diapason* 61 (October 1970): 2.

Weaver is appointed director of music at New York's Madison Avenue Presbyterian Church and conductor of St. Andrew's chorus and orchestra.

"John Weaver." *Diapason* 62 (April 1971): 3.

Weaver is appointed to the faculty of the Curtis Institute of Music, Philadelphia, but will continue to hold the positions listed in the item above.

"Midwinter Conclave at Oklahoma City." *Diapason* 54 (February 1963): 24-25.

Weaver performed a recital that included his own *Toccata in G*. The reviewer offered several performance suggestions to Weaver, even though he also said "There is no questioning his immediate potential as a virtuoso."

Nalle, Billy. "Recitals and Concerts." *American Organist* 44 (July 1961): 27.

Weaver's recital on 12 April 1961 at Church of the Holy Trinity, New York, receives an overall round of applause. The reviewer did not appreciate the organ at the church or Weaver's use of tremulant in the classical works.

"1966 AGO National Convention." *American Organist* 49 (August 1966): 16.

Weaver's performance at the national convention "took away the breath of many. . . ." That Weaver has begun to move away from "over-romanticising" music not of that era was applauded by the reviewer.

"A Program of Original Compositions." *American Organist* 51 (July 1968): 17.

Candidates for the degrees M.S.M. and D.S.M. composed works for a recital at James Chapel, Union Theological Seminary, 30 April 1968. Weaver's *Magnificat* and *Nunc dimittis* is premiered. A brief description of the works for organ and choir is provided.

"Recital, Washington, D.C." *American Organist* 52 (January 1969): 10-11.

Weaver's recital at the National Shrine of the Immaculate Conception, Washington, D.C., 22 November 1968, was, according to the reviewer, performed flawlessly from memory.

"Recitals and Concerts." *American Organist* 40 (May 1957): 162. *

"Recitals and Concerts." *American Organist* 43 (March 1960): 26-27.

Methuen, Massachusetts's Memorial Music Hall serves as the site for Weaver's November 18 recital. The reviewer was highly impressed with Weaver's technique and musicianship.

"Recitals and Concerts." *American Organist* 43 (April 1960): 23-24.

A stunning review of Weaver's recital at Holy Trinity Lutheran Church, New York, 2 December 1959.

"Recitals and Concerts." *American Organist* 43 (May 1960): 34.

Weaver plays a recital at St. Thomas Church, New York, 7 March 1960; the review indicates Weaver will soon come into his full potential, but has several disagreements with Weaver's interpretations.

"Recitals and Concerts." *American Organist* 45 (January 1962): 20-21.

The Lutheran Church of Holy Trinity, New York, was the setting for Weaver's recital on November 12. A varied recital program from Bach to Alain led the reviewer to write "John Weaver, already an outstanding performer, seems destined to win a place in the very top rank of American concert organists."

Sly, Allan. "Recitals and Concerts." *American Organist* 44 (October 1961): 28-29.

Weaver performs his *Toccata* at a recital in Kresge Auditorium, MIT, Cambridge, Mass., 26 July 1961, to a fine review.

Tufts, William O. **"Recitals and Concerts."** *American Organist* 48 (May 1965): 7-8.

> Weaver plays at St. Paul's Lutheran Church, Washington, D.C., 19 March 1965. The review is extremely favorable.

Wells, Frederick. **"Far West AGO Convention."** *American Organist* 50 (September 1967): 10-12.

> Weaver performs an electrifying interpretation of Messiaen's *Joie et clarté des corps glorieux.*

David August Wehr

B. Mt. Vernon, N.Y., 21 January 1934. Student of John Finley Williamson, David Stanley York, Warren Martin, Edward O. Mead, and Alexander McCurdy; B.M. and M.M., Westminster Choir College, Princeton, N.J. Organist-choirmaster, Methodist Cathedral of the Rockies, Boise, Idaho, 1958-68. Ph.D., University of Miami, 1971. Taught at the College of Idaho; University of Miami, and was university carillonneur; associate professor, director of choral activities, Eastern Kentucky University, Richmond, 1971; carillonneur, New York World's Fair, 1964. His dissertation is entitled "John Finley Williamson: His Life and Contribution to Choral Music."

ABD, CACA, CACJ, IWW92, OL, OL95.

"Appointments." *American Organist* 51 (July 1968): 20.

> Wehr receives a teaching assistantship and full-tuition grant at the University of Miami, Coral Gables, Fla., as a Ph.D. student. Gives last position and graduate school information.

"David A. Wehr." *Diapason* 50 (December 1958): 31.

> Wehr has been appointed minister of music of the First Methodist Church (Cathedral of the Rockies), Boise, Idaho. Brief biography and career summation.

"David A. Wehr." *Diapason* 59 (June 1968): 29.

> Wehr receives a teaching assistantship and a full-tuition grant at the University of Miami, Coral Gables, Fla., where he will work toward a Ph.D. degree.

"David A. Wehr." *Diapason* 62 (August 1971): 6.

> Wehr is granted the Ph.D. in conducting and choral literature at the University of Miami School of Music, Coral Gables, Fla. He is appointed assistant professor of choral music and voice, Eastern Kentucky University, Richmond, beginning in August.

Wilmer Hayden Welsh

B. 1932. B.M. and M.M., 1953, Peabody Conservatory, with Richard Ross and Paul Calloway, composition with Henry Cowell; composition with Robert Palmer at Cornell University. Organist-director of music, Mount Vernon Place Methodist Church, Baltimore, 1954-58; faculty member, Davidson College (N.C.), 1958-91.

ABD, CACA, IWW92, OL, OL95.

Deaver, John A. "The Organ Works of Wilmer Hayden Welsh." D.M.A., University of Cincinnati, 1985. *Dissertation Abstracts* 46 (December 1985): 1433A-34A.

Welsh's biography is followed by an overview of his organ music; the overview shows his stylistic development, and the formal design and compositional techniques of individual pieces. The final two chapters of the document are more detailed analyses of two large-scale organ works: *Passion Music* and *Mosaic Portrait I: Jonah*. A catalog of his complete works and a listing of his positions are included.

"Premieres." *American Organist* 24 (July 1990): 55.

Welsh was commissioned by John Pagett to write a work for narrator and organ, *Mosaic Portrait No. 3: The Sacrifice of Isaac*, which Pagett premiered on February 25 at Davidson College Presbyterian Church, Davidson, N.C.

"Retirements." *American Organist* 25 (September 1991): 50.

Welsh retires from Davidson College, where he served as professor of music, college organist, and composer in residence.

Shannon, John R. "New Organ in Charlotte." *Diapason* 70 (August 1979): 16-17.

Welsh's *Mosaic Portrait: Jonah* was commissioned for the dedication of the new Blakely organ at Steele Creek Presbyterian Church, Charlotte, N.C. David Craighead performed the premiere on 3 and 4 December 1978.

"Wilmer H. Welsh." *Diapason* 50 (November 1959): 25.

Welsh is appointed college organist and member of the faculty of Winthrop College, Rock Hill, S.C.

"Wilmer Hayden Welsh with Edmund S. Ender." *Diapason* 41 (February 1950): 24.

Welsh, 17, is photographed with his mentor Edmund S. Ender, who guided this young talent; Welsh was awarded a three-year organ scholarship to Peabody Institute, effective in September 1949.

Norma Ruth Wendelburg

B. Stafford, Kans., 26 March 1918. B.M., Bethany College, Lindsborg, Kans., 1943; M.M.Ed., University of Michigan, 1947, composition with Ross Lee Finney. Fellowship, Composers's Conference and Chamber Music Center to study with Otto Luening, 1948; M.M. and Ph.D., 1969, Eastman, with Bernard Rogers; continued study with Carlos Chavez, Berkshire Music Center, Tanglewood, 1953. Fulbright scholar to Austria, studied with Cesar Bresgen at the Mozarteum, Salzburg, and Karl Schiske, Academy of Music, Vienna, 1953-55. Assistant professor of piano, Iowa State Teachers College, Cedar Falls, 1957. Retired.

CR, IWC, OL95.

"Norma Wendelburg." *Pan Pipes* 45 (January 1953): 42 + . *

"Norma Wendelburg." *Pan Pipes* 46 (March 1954): 19-20.

> Received a Fulbright grant to study composition in Salzburg.

Kyle, Marguerite K. "AmerAllegro." *Pan Pipes* 46 (January 1954): 64.

> Same information as in the item above.

> 50 (January 1958): 76.

> Wendelburg is assistant professor of piano, Iowa State Teachers College.

> 53/2 (1961): 80.

> MacDowell Colony resident, summer 1960; also received a Huntington-Hartford Foundation grant.

> 54/2 (1962): 77.

> Wendelburg enjoyed a residence fellowship at the Hartford Foundation; included in the second edition of *Who's Who of American Women*.

"Norma Wendelburg at Huntington-Hartford." *Pan Pipes* 51 (January 1959): 41.

> Wendelburg spent the summer at the Huntington-Hartford Foundation, her second residence fellowship there; summary of major works and important career milestones included.

"Festival Director, Composer, Norma Wendelburg." *Pan Pipes* 56/2 (1964): 36-37.

> Wendelburg's achievements are presented.

Robert Paul Wetzler

B. Minneapolis, Minn., 30 January 1932. B.A., Thiel College, 1954; M.Div., Northwestern Lutheran Theological Seminary, 1957; studied with Paul Fetler and Dominick Argento at the University of Minnesota. Choirmaster, Prince of Peace Lutheran Church, St. Louis Park, 1955-63; director of publications, from 1960, and president since 1966, Art Masters Studios, Inc. (AMSI). ASCAP awards, 1967-77. Edited *Christian Hymns* (Minneapolis: AMSI, 1978).

ABD, CACA, OL, OL95.

"Awards." *American Organist* 28 (October 1994): 49.
Wetzler receives a composer award from ASCAP.

"Here and There." *Diapason* 83 (February 1992): 4.
ASCAP honors Wetzler with a composer award for the 25th year in a row.

"Here and There." *Diapason* 83 (November 1992): 4.
Wetzler was granted a composer award by ASCAP.

"Here and There." *Diapason* 84 (November 1993): 4.
Wetzler received his 27th ASCAP award.

Wood, Dale. "Contemporary Composers: Robert Wetzler." *Journal of Church Music* 15 (May 1973): 18-19.
Wetzler's background is provided; honors and awards included; not a substantial article.

Gary C. White

B. Winfield, Kans., 27 May 1937. Studied with John Pozdro, B.M.E., and M.M. (theory), 1964, University of Kansas; studied with H. Owen Reed and Paul Harder, Michigan State University, Ph.D., 1969. Appointed to the faculty in 1967, professor-director, Electronic Music Studio, University of Iowa, from 1973. Dissertation was the composition of a symphony. Arnold lists his organ music.

ABD, CACA, CACJ, IWW92, OL, OL95.

No bibliographical information was located.

Louie L. White

B. Spartanburg, S.C., 1 August 1921; d. there, 3 January 1979. B.M., Converse College, 1946; M.M., Syracuse University, 1948; composition pupil of Ernest Bacon, Edwin Gershefski, Pedro San Juan, and Nathaniel Hyatt. Originally a singer, he was a bass soloist in the New York area, a member of the Gilbert and Sullivan company, the American Savoyards, and a choral conductor. Head of music at the Brearley School in New York, 1953-69; Rutgers University music faculty, teaching composition, conducting, voice, orchestration, opera history, and choral director, since 1964; taught composition at Union Seminary School of Sacred Music, 1964-72.

ABD, CACA, CACJ, OL, OL95.

De Tar, Vernon. "Louie L. White, 1921-79." *American Organist* 13 (March 1979): 47.

> A tribute to White provides biographical information and includes a list of his compositions for choir and for organ.

"Louie White Wins 1952 Church of Ascension Award." *Diapason* 43 (June 1952): 22.

> White wins the $100 award for his solo cantata for tenor, harp, and organ, *This Son So Young*, in the fifth annual competition for the Ascension Day festival service. He won the church's first competition in 1948.

"A New Work by Louie L. White." *Diapason* 63 (May 1972): 17.

> John Rose premiered *Reflections on Southern Hymn Tunes*, April 7, at St. Matthew's Lutheran Church, Charleston, S.C. The work was composed for Rose, who had been a student at Rutgers under White.

[Obituary.] *Diapason* 70 (March 1979): 15.

> The announcement of White's death on January 3, at age 57, following a heart attack, is accompanied by a brief career summary.

"Organ." *Music & Artists* 5/3 (1972): 32.

> Includes information on *Reflections on Southern Hymn Tunes*.

Maurice C. Whitney

B. Glens Falls, N.Y., 25 March 1909; d. Sun City Center, Fla., 2 September 1984. B.S., Ithaca College, 1932; M.A., New York University, 1939; studied at Teachers College Columbia University, Westminster Choir College, Williams College, and New England

Conservatory. First prize, Composers Press contest, 1949; citation for outstanding achievement, Ithaca College, 1951; John Hay fellowship, 1961; Teacher of the Year, New York, 1966; honorary L.H.D., Elmira College, 1966. Organist-choirmaster, Christ Church, Glens Falls, N.Y., 1935; school teacher, Hudson Falls, N.Y., 1932-44; and in 1944-69 school music teacher, Glens Falls. Retired to Florida.

ABD, AS66, CACA, OL, OL95, X51, X62, X65, X69, X70, X74.

[Obituary.] *Music Educators Journal* 71 (December 1984): 25.

> Notice of Whitney's death, 2 September 1984.

[Obituary.] *American Recorder* 26/1 (1985): 34.

> Long-time reviewer for *The American Recorder*, Whitney died on September 2. He received an honorary doctorate from Elmira College in 1966 and was a member of ASCAP.

"Who Is Who." *Instrumentalist* 7 (May/June 1953): 35.

> A biography.

Richard Wienhorst

B. Seymour, Ind., 21 April 1920. Studied at Valparaiso University, B.A., 1942; with Leo Sowerby, American Conservatory, 1948; with Nadia Boulanger at Fontainebleau; musicology at Ludwige University, Germany; with Bernard Rogers and Howard Hanson, Eastman School of Music, Ph.D., 1962. Danforth Foundation award and a Lilly Foundation graduate study award. Bandleader, U.S. Army, 1942-46; from 1947, professor, Valparaiso University; now emeritus.

ABD, CACA, CACJ, DCM, OL, OL95, PC71, PCM, X56, X58, X62, X68.

Weller, George. "Composers for the Church: Richard Wienhorst." *Church Music* (St. Louis) 1 (1968): 14-24.

> An in-depth examination of Wienhorst's life, career, and music. List of works included.

David H. Williams

B. Caerphilly, Wales, 21 November 1919. Emigrated to the U.S. and became a citizen (n.d.). Studied organ with Walter Wild. Organist-choirmaster, St. John's Episcopal

Church, Flushing, N.Y.; Ft. Washington Collegiate Church, New York; Saugatuck Congregational Church, Westport, Conn.; First Congregational Church, Woodstock, Vt.; and St. Andrew's Presbyterian Church, Tucson, Ariz.

ABD, CACA, OL, OL95.

"David H. Williams." *American Organist* 36 (October 1953): 347.

Williams is named "Composer of Outstanding Merit." Brief biographical information provided.

"Prelude from the Christmas Oratorio for Organ." *Diapason* 41 (September 1950): 5.

Williams makes a simple transcription of the Saint-Saëns opus; he preserves the "pastoral note of the lyrical number." Gray publishes the work in its St. Cecilia Series.

"Prelude from the Christmas Oratorio for Organ." *Musical Courier* 142 (September 1950): 18.

Same information as in the item above.

Betty Rose Wishart

B. Lumberton, N.C., 22 September 1947. Composition study with Richard Bunger, Queens College (N.C.), B.M., 1969; composition with Roger Hanny, University of North Carolina, Chapel Hill, 1970-72, M.M., 1973; piano teachers were Evelyn Reynolds, Michael Zenge, and Wolfgang Rose, and composition with Stanley Wolf. Taught piano, theory, and composition, Kohinoor Music Company, 1972-73; on staff of Argo Classical Records, beginning 1973. Began composing in 1974. Cohen lists her organ music.

ABD, CACA, DN73, DN76, IWC, WCH.

No bibliographical information located.

Scott S. Withrow

B. Aurora, Ill., 10 September 1932; d. 11 March 1993. B.M., Oberlin College, 1953; M.M., Eastman School of Music, 1954. AAGO, 1959. Associate professor of music, George Peabody College, Nashville, Tenn., for 21 years; organist-director, St. George's Episcopal Church, Nashville; director, Nashville Symphony Chorus, and keyboardist for Nashville Symphony Orchestra; organist-choirmaster, St. Luke's Episcopal Church, Birmingham, Ala., since 1983.

OL, OL95.

"Appointments." *Diapason* 74 (January 1983): 6.

> Withrow is appointed organist-choirmaster of St. Luke's Episcopal Church, Birmingham, Ala.

"Scott S. Withrow." *Diapason* 66 (August 1975): 10.

> Withrow is appointed director of music, St. George's Church, Episcopal, Nashville, Tenn.

Darwin Wolford

B. Logan, Utah, 19 October 1936. Organ student of Alexander Schreiner and Robert Cundick; composition student of Leroy Robertson, John LaMontaine, and Ned Rorem. B.M., Utah State University, 1960; M.M., 1963, and Ph.D. in 1967, in composition and organ, with a minor in philosophy, University of Utah. Director of organ studies and professor of music, Ricks College, Rexburg, Idaho, since 1967. He wrote "Symphony No. 1" for his Ph.D. dissertation. Authored the organ method *Organ Studies for the Beginner* (Delaware Water Gap, Penn.: Flammer, 1978; and published in Japanese at Osaka, Japan: Pax Enterprises, n.d.). In a facsimile transmission to the author, Wolford comments on his musical style: "My compositional style is conservatively contemporary, rooted in the 19th century. My approach to composition is first and foremost lyric, with an economy of notes. Like Ernest Hemingway, I write on the 'iceberg principle,' with more under water than is exposed to the listener. I am not particularly impressed by composers whose music is unnecessarily difficult."

ABD, CACA, OL, OL95.

No bibliographical information located.

Dale Wood

B. Glendale, Calif., 13 February 1934. Studied at Occidental College; composition at Los Angeles Conservatory and Los Angeles City College. Since 1948, organist-choirmaster at Lutheran and Episcopal churches in Los Angeles, Hollywood, Riverside, and San Francisco; executive editor, Sacred Music Press; organist-choirmaster, Church of St. Mary the Virgin (Episcopal), San Francisco, since 1968; director of music, Cathedral School for Boys, San Francisco, 1973-74. Recipient of annual ASCAP awards, 1968-73.

ABD, CACA, OL, OL95.

"Dale Wood." *Music of the West* 10 (February 1955): 9. *

"Dale Wood." *Diapason* 59 (October 1968): 23.

Wood is appointed organist-chiormaster at the Episcopal Church of St. Mary the Virgin, San Francisco.

Kyle, Marguerite K. "AmerAllegro." *Pan Pipes* 67/2 (1975): 79.

Numerous works are published; among them, for organ, are: *Wondrous Love*, Sacred Music Press; *American Folk Hymn Suite*, for organ, harp or piano, and handbells, by Flammer; and *Pastoral on Forest Green* for organ and handbells or harp, Flammer.

"Pipings." *American Organist* 27 (July 1993): 44-45.

Wood is honored with the Exemplar Medallion Award from the Board of Regents of California Lutheran University, Thousand Oaks, for his "extraordinary contribution to the world of music."

Wetzler, Robert. "Contemporary Composers: Dale Wood." *Journal of Church Music* 14 (October 1972): 17-18.

A brief look at Wood's life, and his ideas on some aspects of contemporary church music.

Henry Lynde Woodward

B. Cincinnati, Ohio, 18 September 1908. B.A., Miami University (Ohio); B.M. and M.M., College of Music, Cincinnati; studied with Walter Piston: M.A. and Ph.D. from Harvard. Further study in Paris with Nadia Boulanger. Received a MacDowell fellowship, 1932. Editor, College Music Society's *Symposium*, 1972-73. Taught at Cincinnati College of Music, 1929-33; Western College, 1933-38, 1939-42; Vassar College, 1938-39; Carleton College, 1942-73, then professor emeritus; summers at Cornell University and Union Theological Seminary. Organist, All Saints Church, Northfield, Minn., for 15 years.

ABD, CACA, OL, OL95.

"Henry & Enid Woodward Honored in Minnesota." *Diapason* 65 (July 1974): 8.

The Woodwards were joint recipients of a 1973 Minnesota Arts Council award. The award recognizes outstanding contributions to the arts in Minnesota.

"Honors to Enid & Henry Woodward." *Music* (AGO) 7 (May 1973): 43.

After more than 25 years on the Carleton College music faculty, Dr. and Mrs. Woodward will retire in June; compositions by Henry Woodward were featured in a recent concert.

"Professors Retire." *Diapason* 64 (April 1973): 13.

    Same information as in the item above; in addition, biographical information is provided.

"Summer Plans Announced by Union Seminary School." *Diapason* 48 (May 1957): 20.

    On faculty for the summer music school session are Elaine Brown, Henry Woodward, and Hugh Porter, among others that include Claire Coci, Vernon De Tar, and Alec Wyton.

(Myron) Searle Wright

B. Susquehanna, Penn., 4 April 1918. Organ pupil of William Gomph, Joseph Bonnet, and T. Tertius Noble; studied composition with Otto Luening and Normand Lockwood, improvisation with Frederick Schlieder, conducting with Rudolf Thomas, and musicology with Paul Henry Lang and Erich Herzman at Columbia University. Organist-choirmaster, Chapel of the Incarnation, New York; director of chapel music, St. Paul's Chapel, Columbia University, 1952-71; faculty member, Union Theological Seminary; president, American Guild of Organists, 1969-71; Fellow, AGO, Trinity College of London, and Royal Canadian College of Organists; in 1971, became organist-choirmaster, Christ Church, Cincinnati, Ohio; and also that year became teacher, College-Conservatory of Music, University of Cincinnati; in 1977, became Link Professor of Music, State University of New York at Binghamton.

OL, OL95.

Angel, Clark. **"Concerto for Organ and Brasses."** *American Organist* 43 (August 1960): 22-23.

    Marilyn Mason performs the world premiere of Wright's *Introduction, Passacaglia and Fugue*, assisted by the Brass Ensemble of the University of Michigan. A description of the work is included.

"Audience of 1200 Listens to Searle Wright in Abbey." *Diapason* 45 (November 1954): 1.

    Wright is the first American-born organist to give a recital in Westminster Abbey. The crowd was one of the largest ever to attend a recital there.

Bingham, Seth. **"Ministry of Music, Riverside Church, N.Y.C."** *American Organist* 50 (May 1967): 13-14.

    A program of Searle Wright's music is performed by those in the ministry of music at Riverside. Presented on April 9, the concert includes his *Fantasy on "Wareham"* for organ, brass, and percussion, and also choral works with and without organ. Highest praise was given to his choral work *The Green Blade Riseth*, for choir, soloists, and organ.

_____. **"Organ Personalities."** *American Organist* 46 (December 1963): 11.

Largely self-taught, Wright is known for his intuitive grasp of musical problems, his technical abilities, critical judgment, and as a composer of stature.

_____. **"Searle Wright in Recital."** *Diapason* 43 (April 1952): 38.

Wright is heard in recital at the Riverside Church, New York, on March 9. "Mr. Wright rose to new heights of execution in this dazzling bravura fantasy," Bingham wrote, regarding Tournemire's *Paraphrase-Carillon* from *L'Orgue mystique.*

"M. Searle Wright Honored." *American Organist* 13 (October 1979): 31.

Searle Wright receives the Fellowship Diploma of the Royal Canadian College of Organists, *honoris causa*, for his outstanding contribution to the first International Congress of Organists, held in London in August 1957; for his devotion to the American Guild of Organists; and for his distinguished career as teacher, composer, organist, conductor, and church musician. Biographical data included.

"M. Searle Wright Takes Columbia University Post." *Diapason* 43 (November 1952): 1.

Wright has been appointed organist-choirmaster of St. Paul's Chapel at Columbia University. He continues his duties as a faculty member of the School of Sacred Music of Union Theological Seminary.

"Premieres." *American Organist* 18 (May 1984): 41.

Marlene Baver played the initial performance of *Fantasy on "St. Columba"* on 5 February 1984 at Plymouth Congregational Church, Minneapolis. Commission information provided.

Ratski, Chet, Jr. "Theater Organ Gets Culture." *American Organist* 51 (November 1968): 12-13, 32-33.

Wright performs the dedicatory recital on the Link C. Sharpe-Minor Orchestral Organ at Sears-Harkness Hall, Roberson Center, Binghamton, N.Y., 21 September 1968. The restored instrument was the same Link organ at the Capitol Theatre on which Wright played a much-acclaimed recital at the age of 12. Extensive details about the organ are provided.

"Recital." *American Organist* 48 (December 1965): 8-9.

Wright performs a program at St. Paul's Chapel, Columbia University, New York, 20 October 1965, that proves to be an "enlightening performance by an organist worthy of St. Paul's splendid instrument."

"Searle Wright." *American Organist* 33 (March 1950): 109.

The value of a good working relationship between clergy and musician are reported; sketchy details on positions and education.

"Searle Wright Is Heard a Second Time in the Abbey." *Diapason* 46 (October 1955): 25.

Wright's second performance at Westminster Abbey took place on August 11. The recital program is listed.

Spelman, Leslie P. **"How Searle Wright Gives Fine Services Amid Limitations."** *Diapason* 41 (February 1950): 32.

Wright's work at the Chapel of the Incarnation is highly praised. One of the highest tributes accorded him is at the end of the service, when not only choristers and congregation members sit and listen to the postlude, but the vicar also joins them in the pew, and greets the congregation at the conclusion of the postlude.

"Staff Notes." *Journal of Church Music* 11 (October 1969): 16.

Wright was recently elected president of the AGO; current and previous posts mentioned.

"Theatre Organ Recital." *American Organist* 43 (August 1960): 17.

Wright joins others in a theater organ recital and jam session at the Fox Theatre in Detroit, playing several standard tunes. "The guy is pretty terrific," states the reviewer.

Charles Wuorinen

B. New York, 9 June 1938. Studied with Otto Luening, Columbia University. Received many awards including the New York Philharmonic Young Composers award, 1954; Lili Boulanger award, 1960; Joseph H. Bearns prize, 1961; Brandeis Creative Arts award; honorary doctorate, Jersey City State College; American Academy of Arts and Letters award; Koussevitzky International Recording award; 1970; Pulitzer Prize in music, 1970; Guggenheim fellowship, 1972; and an NEA grant, 1976. Faculty member, Columbia University, 1946-71; also taught at Princeton University, New England Conservatory, University of Iowa, Manhattan School of Music, and the University of South Florida. Authored *Simple Composition* (New York: Longman, 1979).

AA73, ACA ix 4, ABD, ASUC, BB65, BB71, BB78, BB92, BDA, CACA, CACJ, CC92, CRI 149, DCM, DN72, DN73, IMD2, IWW92, JCN, KTL, MLSR, NG, NGA, OL, OL95, PC71, PCM, TCH, X56, X59, X60, X61, X62, X64, X65, X66, X67, X68, X69, X70, X71, X74.

"ACA Is Proud to Announce 6 New Members." *American Composers Alliance Bulletin* 9/4 (1961): 11.

Wuorinen, 23, is the youngest ACA member; recipient of several prizes already, he has been a MacDowell Colony fellow and has received numerous commissions.

"Alla Breve." *American Organist* 28 (March 1994): 72.

> *Charles Wuorinen: A Bio-Bibliography* by Richard D. Burbank is published by Greenwood Press. Includes biography, discography, interview, listing of works and performances, and annotated citations of writings about his music.

"BMI 'Genius' Winners." *BMI: The Many Worlds of Music* 2 (1986): 78. *

Bingham, Seth. "Recitals and Concerts." *American Organist* 51 (January 1968): 13.

> Leonard Raver performs *Evolutio*, composed for Raver and as a memorial to Boulanger; "only a star performer could make such music sound plausible," wrote the reviewer.

Boulanger, Richard. "Interview with Roger Reynolds, Joji Yuasas and Charles Wuorinen." *Computer Music Journal* 8/4 (1984): 45-54.

> A discussion with the composers on 9 March 1984 includes their involvement with tape music, use of space, and electronic vs. instrumental composition; Wuorinen states that "limitations are necessary to art."

Breuer, Robert. "Die Avant-Garde in den Vereinigten Staaten." *Melos* 30 (March 1963): 77-79.

> Discusses the avant-garde movement in the U.S., giving its background and influence upon American composers. Charles Wuorinen, Harvey Sollberger, Charles Whittenberger, and Ralph Shapey receive equal attention from Breuer as he illustrates the concepts, methods, and philosophies regarding their work in composing in the avant-garde idioms.

Burbank, Richard D. *Charles Wuorinen: A Bio-Bibliography.* Westport, Conn.: Greenwood, 1994.

> Includes biography, bibliography, discography, works and performances, and listing of works.

Carl, Robert. "Six Case Studies in New American Music: A Postmodern Portrait Gallery." *College Music Symposium* 30 (1990): 48-51.

> Wuorinen is recently named new music advisor for the San Francisco Symphony. Recipient of both the Pulitzer Prize and the MacArthur genius award. An overview of his style of writing indicates that Wuorinen "has not yet proven in his advocacy for an authentic American avant-garde style its superiority."

"Composers in Focus." *BMI: The Many Worlds of Music*, winter 1976, 33.

> Biography; an overview of his avant-garde style. His work is steeped in the latest, most complex techniques, "yet [are] brimming with individuality and invention."

Fleming, Shirley. **"Musician of the Month: Charles Wuorinen."** *High Fidelity/Musical America* 20 (September 1970): MA8-9.

Wuorinen wins the Pulitzer Prize for his electronic composition; discussion on what is music and his compositional style; various awards listed.

Gagne, Cole, and Tracy Caras. *Soundpieces: Interviews with American Composers.* Metuchen, N.J.: Scarecrow, 1982.

A survey of current trends in American music. Contains the interview with Wuorinen, biographical sketch, photography, and list of works through 1980.

Gann, K. **"Music: Bitter Chords (Contemporary American Composers' Lack of Recognition)."** *Village Voice* 37 (28 January 1992): 86. *

Helm, Everett. **"Experimentelle Musik in den USA."** *Melos* 31 (April 1964): 125.

The works of American composers span a broad spectrum of styles, ranging from old-style romanticism to progressive forms of experimental music. A discussion of American composers' influence upon European composition, and the difference between American and European movements. Lukas Foss and Gunther Schuller are among composers who, in common with others, do not limit themselves to or specialize in a certain system of composition or in a single theory or system of aesthetics. Devotes a paragraph to Wuorinen, who, by age 21, had composed his third symphony.

Hibbard, William. **"Charles Wuorinen: The Politics of Harmony."** *Perspectives of New Music* 7/2 (spring-summer 1969): 155-70.

Detailed analysis of the masque, which is based on a scenario drawn mainly from the writings of Ssu-ma Ch'ien (ca. 145-90 B.C.) and which traces a progression from order to disorder, from virtue to corruption.

Kastendieck, Miles. **"Charles Wuorinen."** *BMI: The Many Worlds of Music,* December 1969, 15.

Speaks of Wuorinen as a great innovator; Wuorinen comments on his electronic compositions and demands "enlightened listening" from those in his audiences.

Kresky, Jeffrey. **"The Recent Music of Charles Wuorinen."** *Perspectives of New Music* 25/1-2 (1987): 410-17.

An overview of his approach to composition, since 1956, is given. Although no organ music is cited, his evolutionary process is related through musical examples and the text. The article shows how he reconciles his 12-tone approach with the tonal past.

Kyle, Marguerite K. **"AmerAllegro."** *Pan Pipes* 55/2 (1963): 76-77.

Organist Leonard Raver first performed Wuorinen's composition *Evolutio* on April 8, for the AGO in Boston.

56/2 (1964): 87.

Winner of the BMI Award; received a Fromm Foundation commission; and was named head of the composition department of the Bennington Composers Conference for 1963.

60/2 (1968): 99.

Wuorinen receives a $2500 grant from the National Institute of Arts and Letters, New York.

61/2 (1969): 83.

Named a Guggenheim Fellow for 1968-69.

63/2 (1971): 85.

Won the Pulitzer Prize in music, 1970, the Brandeis University Creative Arts award, and a special citation of the Koussevitzky International Recording award.

64/2 (1972): 86.

Honorary doctorate received from Jersey City State College.

"Mixtures." *American Organist* 22 (February 1988): 43.

David Shuler premiered three newly-commissioned works at Park Avenue Christian Church in New York on 31 January 1988. The recital included Wuorinen's *Natural Fantasy*. Commission information provided.

"The Pulitzer Prizes." *BMI: The Many Worlds of Music* 2 (1974): 27.

Wuorinen wins a Pulitzer Prize in music for his 1970 work *Time's Encomium*, a composition for record, not intended for a live performance.

"Recitals." *American Organist* 22 (June 1988): 76.

David Shuler's recital includes the premiere of Wuorinen's *Natural Fantasy* on 31 January 1988.

Schwartz, Elliott, and Barney Childs, eds. *Contemporary Composers on Contemporary Music.* New York: Holt, Rinehart & Winston, 1967.

Essays by composers from Debussy through the present include Wuorinen. Brief biographical note included. The essays are intended for lay readers as well as musicians.

Terry, Kenneth. "Charles Wuorinen: Atonal Tonalities." *Downbeat* 48 (February 1981): 16-18.

A discussion of influences on his life and composition method, the importance of silence, and his score writing—minute details in his scores limit the interpretation; in an age when traditional styles of composition are disintegrating, Wuorinen attempts to refine a tradition using 12-tone music, and he tries to consolidate the past and the present.

Yehudi Wyner

(*Né* Weiner.) B. Calgary, Alberta, Canada, 1 June 1929. U.S. citizen at birth. Studied at Juilliard School; with Richard Donovan and Paul Hindemith, Yale University, B.A., 1950, B.M., 1951, M.M., 1953; with Randall Thompson and Walter Piston, Harvard University, M.A., 1952. Rome Prize; A. E. Hertz Memorial fellowship; Fulbright and Guggenheim fellowships; American Institute of Arts and Letters grant; Brandeis Creative Arts award; Ford Foundation grant; NEA grant; Tanglewood fellowship, 1978. Visiting lecturer, Queens College (N.Y.), 1958-59; music director, Turnau Opera Association, 1961-63; music director, Westchester Reformed Temple, 1958-68; faculty member, Yale University, 1964-77; music director, New Haven Opera Society, 1968-76; from 1968, keyboard artist, Bach Aria Group.

ABD, AMH, ASUC, BB71, BB78, BB92, CACA, CACJ, DCM, IWW92, KTL, NG, NGA, OL, OL95, REM, TCH, X58, X60, X61, X62, X64, X67, X70, X71.

Helm, Everett. "Experimentelle Musik in den USA." *Melos* 31 (April 1964): 125.

> The works of American composers span a broad spectrum of styles, ranging from old-style romanticism to progressive forms of experimental music. A discussion of American composers' influence on European composition, and the difference between American and European movements. Lukas Foss and Gunther Schuller are among composers who, in common with others, do not limit themselves to or specialize in a certain system of composition or in a single theory or system of aesthetics. Devotes a paragraph to Wyner's music.

"Music Journal's 1972 Gallery of Living Composers." *Music Journal* 30 (October 1972): 49.

> Brief biography; honors, awards, and list of major works.

Scanlan, Roger. "Spotlight on Contemporary American Composers." *National Association of Teachers of Singing Bulletin* 31/1 (1974): 46-48, 51.

> Complete biography includes awards and honors; provides Wyner's basic compositional style and focuses on his vocal music.

Alec Wyton

B. London, England, 3 August 1921. Emigrated to U.S., 1950; U.S. citizen, 1968. Studied at the Royal Academy of Music; Oxford University, B.A., 1945, M.A., 1949. Fellow, Royal College of Organists, 1942, AGO, 1950, Royal Canadian College of Organists, 1962, Royal Academy of Music, 1964, Royal School of Church Music, 1965. Substitute organist, Christ

Church Cathedral, Oxford, 1943-46; organist-choirmaster, St. Matthew's, Northampton, 1946-50; organist-choirmaster, Christ Church Cathedral, St. Louis, Mo., 1950-54, and taught at Mary Institute, St. Louis; adjunct professor, School of Sacred Music, Union Theological Seminary; and visiting professor of music, Westminster Choir College. In 1954-74, organist and choirmaster at the Cathedral of St. John the Divine, New York; president, AGO, 1964-69; 1974-87, organist and choirmaster at St. James Episcopal Church, New York. Honorary music doctorate, Susquehanna University, 1970; annual ASCAP awards from 1967.

ABD, CACA, IWW92, NGA, OL, OL95.

"Alec Wyton." *Diapason* 42 (December 1950): 7.

Wyton is appointed organist-choirmaster of Christ Episcopal Cathedral, St. Louis. A summary of his career and education history; previous schooling included chemistry and law.

"Alec Wyton." *Diapason* 54 (October 1963): 1.

Wyton premieres his own *Fanfare-Improvisation on "Azmon"* at RLDS Auditorium, Independence, Mo., 8 August 1963.

"Alec Wyton." *Diapason* 56 (March 1965): 21.

Wyton assumes the position as head of the organ department at Westminster Choir College, succeeding Alexander McCurdy, who will retire in June.

"Alec Wyton." *Musical Times* 115 (July 1974): 602.

After completing 20 years at St. John the Divine Cathedral, New York, a Festival Evensong is held to honor Wyton; he will retire on September 1.

"Alec Wyton Appointed to College Faculty." *Choral Guide* 18 (April 1965): 26. *

"Alec Wyton Is Appointed to Cathedral in New York." *Diapason* 45 (June 1954): 1.

Wyton is named organist and master of choirs at St. John the Divine, New York; he succeeds Norman Coke-Jephcott.

"Alec Wyton to St. James." *Music* (AGO) 8 (May 1974): 36.

Wyton leaves St. John the Divine to become organist and choirmaster at St. James Episcopal Church, New York. Gives biographical information.

Baglivi, Anthony. **"An Interview with Alec Wyton, Commemorating the 20th Anniversary of the *American Organist* Magazine."** *American Organist* 21 (October 1987): 64-68.

A discussion with Wyton about his life and how the magazine became a reality under his presidency in the AGO. Includes information about his Manhattan Project and the future of the Guild.

Bingham, Seth. "Organ Personalities." *American Organist* 46 (December 1963): 11.

Wyton, who came to America in 1950, has served as organist and master of the choristers at the Cathedral of St. John the Divine, New York, since 1954.

————. **"Recitals and Concerts."** *American Organist* 46 (October 1963): 9-10.

Wyton performs at the Cathedral of St. John the Divine, New York, for the Alumni School of Sacred Music, Union Theological Seminary, 24 June 1963; performs his *Fanfare* and composers' works from different times to appeal to the various palettes: Messiaen, Malcolm Williamson, and Bach, to name a few.

Drone, Jeanette, comp. "American Composer Update." *Pan Pipes* 75/2 (1983): 46.

Preludes and Fanfares and *Old Tunes in New Guises*, both for organ, are published by Sacred Music Press.

"Fanfare for Organ." *Musical Courier* 154 (1 December 1956): 37.

Published by H. W. Gray, *Fanfare* is a composition requiring a large organ and "an artist in full command of a flexible, chordal technique." Suggested for recital use.

"Here and There." *Diapason* 69 (June 1978): 15.

Wyton's *Palm Sunday*, a work composed for the dedication of the Trompeta Majestatis stop at Riverside Church, was premiered by Frederick Swann, March 19.

Kyle, Marguerite K. "AmerAllegro." *Pan Pipes* 63/2 (1971): 85-86.

Published are: *Two Chorale Hymns*, H. W. Gray; *Flourish* for organ, Presser; *Dialogue: Praise Him in the Sound of the Trumpet*, Presser; and a partita on *Christ in the Wilderness*, Gray.

66/2 (1974): 79.

Organ variants on *Earth and All Stars* was introduced by the composer at First United Methodist Church, Orlando, Fla., on August 8.

Litton, James. "Alec Wyton Honored on 20th Anniversary at Cathedral." *Diapason* 65 (July 1974): 6.

Wyton's service is recognized by a special recognition service held at the Cathedral of St. John the Divine; the service was not only one of thanksgiving but one to wish Wyton well as he leaves St. John's for work at St. James Church, New York. A list of his published compositions follows the article.

Mains, P. "Wyton in Gary." *Diapason* 58 (June 1967): 38.

The dedicatory recital Wyton played at St. Augustine's Episcopal Church in Gary, Ind., was panned. "The entire program was played with little professional finesse. . . ."

"New Organist at St. John's Cathedral." *Musical Courier* 150 (September 1954): 44.

Wyton is appointed organist and choirmaster at the Cathedral of St. John the Divine, New York, 29 August 1954; previous post listed.

"New Organs." *American Organist* 20 (June 1986): 87.

The dedication recital of St. Barnabas's Episcopal Church, Bay Village, Ohio, included the premiere performance of Wyton's *Variants on Hyfrydol*, commissioned for the occasion. Karel Paukert performed the recital, 30 October 1983.

"Premiered." *ASCAP*, winter 1987, 57.

Wyton's *Musical Setting for Psalm 136* is premiered at a Sacred Sound and Social Change Symposium, New York's Hebrew Union College, 27 October 1987.

"RSCM Personality." *Royal School of Church Music* 8 (October 1964): 5.

Wyton is highly regarded in the world of church music; the article includes an overview of his career and applauds the work that he has already accomplished in the United States.

"Two Famed Church Musicians Get New Union Posts." *Diapason* 52 (April 1961): 38.

Wyton and Vernon De Tar are named associate professors of the School of Sacred Music at Union Theological Seminary.

"Westminster Changes." *American Organist* 48 (July 1965): 20.

Wyton is appointed head of the organ department at Westminster Choir College, Princeton, N.J., succeeding Alexander McCurdy.

Gordon Young

B. McPherson, Kans., 15 October 1919. Studied at Southwestern College (Kans.), B.M., honorary S.M.D., 1973; at Curtis Institute of Music, 1944-46; organ with Alexander McCurdy, Powell Weaver, and Joseph Bonnet. Organist, First Methodist Church, Tulsa, Okla.; organist, First Presbyterian Church, Lancaster, Penn.; organist, Kansas City and Philadelphia; taught at Texas Christian University and other institutions; organist-choirmaster, First Presbyterian Church, Detroit, 1952-72. Annual ASCAP awards, from 1968. Currently resides in Chicago.

ABD, CACA, IWW92, OL, OL95.

Clark, Mary Elizabeth. "Organ Lessons on a 'Liturgical Prelude' by Gordon Young, an Easy Piece for Service Playing." *Clavier* 8/5 (1969): 33-34.

A brief lesson for the beginning organ student.

"Gordon Young Receives Honorary Doctorate." *American Organist* 47 (May 1964): 11.

Young is awarded the honorary degree doctor of music, 17 March 1964, by Southwestern University, Winfield, Kans., at a program of his music. Career and educational summary is provided.

"Here and There." *Diapason* 78 (July 1987): 2.

The First Baptist Church of Detroit presents the world premiere of two works by Gordon Young: *Trumpet Suite* and *Praise Ye the Lord*, on March 22. The program celebrated the rededication of the church's Reuter organ and the dedication of its new Festival Trumpet.

"Premieres." *American Organist* 18 (December 1984): 52.

Young's *In Praise of God* was commissioned by the First Baptist Church of Nashville, Tenn., in honor of Sharron Lyon's 20th anniversary as church organist there. The work was introduced on 3 June 1984 and is now published by Flammer.

"Premieres." *American Organist* 20 (March 1986): 46.

Prelude on "Assurance" was premiered on 8 November 1985 by Marilyn Mason at High Street United Methodist Church, Muncie, Ind. Commission information provided.

"Premieres." *American Organist* 28 (October 1994): 52.

Organist Nita Pope premiered Young's *Postlude on Thaxted* on the high-altar organ at St. Stephen's Cathedral in Vienna on 25 June 1994. "Thaxted" is based on the tune from the Jupiter section of *The Planets* by Gustav Holst. The composition will be published by Harold Flammer in 1995.

"Recitals." *Diapason* 42 (March 1959): 116.

Young plays a dedicatory recital on the Möller organ in the Evangelical Covenant Church, Detroit, October 2, and a dedicatory recital on a Casavant in First Presbyterian Church, Mt. Pleasant, Mich., October 10.

Michael E. Young

B. San Francisco, Calif., 25 June 1939 [CACA], 1942 [OL]. Studied with George F. McKay, John Verrall, and Greg Short, University of Washington, B.A. and M.A.; organ with Walter Eichinger and Edward Hansen. AAGO, 1965. Organist, Messiah Lutheran Church,

Seattle, 1961-70; associate professor of music, Whitworth College, Spokane, Wash.; since 1970, organist, Church of Saints Peter and Paul, Vancouver, British Columbia.

ABD, CACA, OL, OL95, TCH.

"Here and There." *Diapason* 71 (March 1980): 11.

Walter A. Eichinger, professor emeritus at the University of Washington, was honored on February 9 at a concert, when Young premiered his *Discoveries* (1979), dedicated to Eichinger. The recital was held at Whitworth College, Spokane, Wash.

"Pipings." *American Organist* 14 (May 1980): 31.

Same information as in the item above.

"Premieres." *American Organist* 23 (July 1989): 40.

On 21 February 1980, Michael Young performs six new works, including his own *Fanfare for Two Trumpets and Organ* and *Kiwi Images* for flute and organ. Indicates his position.

Luigi J. Zaninelli

B. Raritan, N.J., 30 March 1932. Studied with Gian-Carlo Menotti, Bohuslav Martinů, and Vittorio Giannini, Curtis Institute of Music. On faculty, Curtis Institute, 1952-58; New School of Music, Philadelphia, 1955-58; composer-conductor, RCA Italiana, Rome, 1964-66; director of music, Marymount Intonation School, Rome, 1966-68; composer-in-residence, University of Calgary, Canada, 1968-73; composer-in-residence, University of Southern Mississippi, Hattiesburg, since 1973. Received the Steinway piano composition award, 1955; annual ASCAP awards, since 1964; Alberta award.

ABD, CACA, OL, OL95, PC71, PCM, TCH, X70.

Duffie, Ora Patricia Pate. "Luigi Zaninelli: A Stylistic Analysis of 'The Battle for Vicksburg' and 'The Joseph Songs.'" D.M.A., University of Southern Mississippi, 1990.

Biographical overview of Zaninelli's life and education is included; the document explores the major influences related to his work and discerns the stylistic characteristics unique to his musical language.

Jones, Pamela Janine. "The Songs of Luigi Zaninelli." D.M.A., University of Maryland at College Park, 1992.

A biographical summary of the composer is included in this study to provide a stylistic examination of Zaninelli's songs.

Tikey A. Zes

B. Long Beach, Calif., 27 October 1927. Student of Gerald Strang, Long Beach; D.M.A., 1969, with Ingolf Dahl, University of Southern California. Received two Helen Anstead awards at USC, 1963 and 1969. Since 1964, professor of music, San Jose State University. Dissertation is entitled "Concert Liturgy for the Greek Orthodox Church, for Chorus and Orchestra" (*Dissertation Abstracts* 31 [October 1970]: 1836A). Organ music listed in Arnold's book.

ABD, CACA, OL, OL95.

No bibliographical information located.

Marilyn Jane Ziffrin

B. Moline, Ill., 7 August 1926. B.M., University of Wisconsin, Madison, 1948; M.A., Columbia University, 1949; Ph.D., University of Chicago. Private study in composition with Karl Ahrendt and Alexander Tcherepnin. Assistant professor, Northeastern Illinois State College, 1961-66; associate professor of music, New England College, Henniker, N.H., 1967-82; composition teacher, St. Paul's School, Concord, N.H., since 1972. Recipient of many awards and prizes, including two second prizes, International Society for Contemporary Music, Chicago chapter, 1955 and 1964; Delius award, 1972; Alfred Noyes scholarship; Knapp scholarship at University of Wisconsin; grant-in-aid for a biography of Carl Ruggles, from the American Council of Learned Societies, 1974; ASCAP grants recipient in 1981, 1982, and 1983; MacDowell Colony resident fellow, 1961, 1963, 1971, 1977, 1980. Authored *Ruggles' Continuous Flight for Linear Compositions: Interesting Lies and Curious Truths about Carl Ruggles* (Missoula, Mont.: College Music Society, 1979); "Carl Ruggles: Music Critic," *American Music Teacher* 32 (1983): 42.

AA73, ABD, ASUC, CACA, CACJ, IWC, IWW92, LCI, TCH, WCH, X62, X65, X68, X69, X70, X71.

Cummings, Barton. "Readers Comment: Women in Music." *Music Educators Journal* 65 (April 1979): 11.

Ziffrin is cited as an important woman composer; several of her works are mentioned.

Drone, Jeanette, comp. "American Composer Update." *Pan Pipes* 75/2 (1983): 47.

Several of Ziffrin's works were broadcast by National Public Radio on a 90-minute program entitled "A Gentle Sort of Madness," 7 April 1982.

"In Response." *Perspectives of New Music* 20/1-2 (1981-82): 328-29.

> Ziffrin responds to a survey and states she does not believe that serious music is either feminine or masculine; it is only the composer's unique voice.

Kyle, Marguerite K. "AmerAllegro." *Pan Pipes* 48 (January 1956): 77. *

> 57/2 (1965): 86.
>
> Won second prize in the 1964 Contemporary Musical Festival in Chicago.
>
> 65/2 (1973): 80.
>
> Winner of the 1972 Delius Composition Award; commissioned to write a sonata for organ and cello by Colby Junior College, New London, N.H.

Ellen Taaffe Zwilich

B. Miami, Fla., 30 April 1939. Studied composition with John Boda and Carlisle Floyd, B.M., 1956, and M.M., 1962, Florida State University; first woman to receive a doctorate in composition from Juilliard, 1975; composition with Elliott Carter and Roger Sessions. Taught at various colleges for seven years; violinist for the American Symphony Orchestra under Leopold Stokowski, 1965-72. In 1983, won the Pulitzer Prize in music for her *Symphony No. 1.* Honors: Elizabeth Sprague Coolidge Chamber Music Prize, 1974; gold medal, International Composition Competition J. B. Viotti, Vercelli, Italy, 1975; Guggenheim fellowship, 1980-81; NEA composer fellowship grant, 1976; ASCAP award, 1977; Creative Artists public service fellowship grant, 1977; Martha Baird Rockefeller Fund for Music grant, 1974; Rodgers and Hammerstein scholarship award from Juilliard; National Institute of Arts and Letters, 1984; Arturo Toscanini Music Critics Award, 1987; honorary doctorate of music, Oberlin College, 1987; and three prizes from Florida Composers' League.

ABD, BB78, BB92, CACA, CC92, IWC, IWW92, NGA, WCH.

"Bulletin Board: Pulitzer Prize in Music." *Music Educators Journal* 70 (September 1983): 19, 21.

> Zwilich, the first woman to receive her doctorate in composition from Juilliard, is the first female recipient of the Pulitzer Prize in music.

DeLorenzo, L. C. "An Interview with Ellen Taaffe Zwilich." *Music Educators Journal* 78 (March 1992): 46-47.

> Includes biography.

Drier, Ruth. "Ellen Taaffe Zwilich." *High Fidelity/Musical America* 33 (September 1983): MA4-5, MA18.

Zwilich discusses her music: "I want my music to integrate all of my past, all of my influences. I want people to hear where I came from, what was in my surroundings. That's American. That's me." Included is a description of her prize-winning symphony.

"Ellen Taaffe Zwilich Wins Pulitzer Prize." *International Musician* 82 (October 1983): 13.

Wins the Pulitzer Prize in music for her first symphony. She cites Bartók, Stravinsky, and Shostakovich as primary influences on her work for orchestra.

"International Women's Year Ends: Decade of Women Begins." *Music Clubs Magazine* 55/3 (1976): 6+. *

"Pianists' World." *Piano Quarterly* 31/122 (1983): 56.

Zwilich is named the first woman recipient of the Pulitzer Prize in music.

Terry, Ken. "Ellen Taaffe Zwilich." *BMI: The Many Worlds of Music* 2 (1983): 46-47.

An interview reveals some of her thoughts on composition: "I combine certain elements that grow out of the 12-tone adventure with older techniques, and even with newer techniques . . . however, musical techniques don't make pieces, they never do."

Waleson, Heidi. "Composer Ellen Taaffe Zwilich Living Her Dream." *Symphony Magazine* 37/2 (1986): 20-23, 67.

The desire to communicate by musical composition and receiving commissions energize Zwilich's writing because she knows that the music will be performed.

Wierzbicki, James. "FSU's New Musical Festival." *High Fidelity/Musical America* 31 (October 1981): MA18-19.

With Karel Husa, Zwilich is a guest of honor at Florida State University's festival. The two composers discuss the performers' responsibility to the composer; must they be? or are they responsible only to those with whom they share an aesthetic point of view?

Index

Authors, Performers, Compositions Not in Main Entries

Dower, Catherine, 162
Downes, Edward, 81
Drake, James M., 18
Drier, Ruth, 328
Drinkwater, David, 203-04, 248
Drone, Jeanette, 3, 32, 39, 46, 58, 87, 115, 131, 144,
    153, 160, 162, 176, 224, 241, 252, 255, 322, 326
Duff, John Andrew, 151
Duffie, Ora Patricia Pate, 325

Egan, Randall, 55
Ellinwood, Leonard, 90
Ellsasser, Richard, 82
Elmore, Robert, 60, 186
Erwin, Lee, 137
Eskey, Kathryn, 206
Evans, Peter, 67
Evett, Robert, 226

Fackrell, Mark F., 49
Fantasia for Organ (Goodman), 287
Faxon, George, 63, 120, 213, 242-43, 300
Felciano, Richard, 211
Felder, D., 101
Ferguson, John, 285
Ferré, Susan, 39
Ferris, John, 231
Ferris, Timothy, 210
Finney, John, 232, 234
Finney, Ross Lee, 24, 52, 75, 111
Fischer, Irwin, 75, 109
Fleischer, Heinrich, 12
Fleming, Shirley, 318
Folkerts, Davis Lowell, 28
Folts, Martha, 102
Foss, Lukas, 84, 263, 318, 320
Fox, Virgil, 141, 226-27
Frank, Gerald, 128
Frank, Janet, 11
Fried, Adrienne G., 6, 39
Fried, Alexander, 104
Friedell, Harold, 46, 218
Friedewald, R. E., 21
Froehlich, Thomas, 300
Fuerst-Heidtmann, Monika, 246
Fugue on the Name of Albert Schweitzer (Castelnuovo-
    Tedesco), 292

Gagne, Cole, 43, 53, 67, 75, 109, 115, 172, 318
Gann, K., 53, 204, 318
Gardner, J., 295
Gay, Harry, 23, 195
Gebauer, Victor, 196
Gehring, Philip, 243
Gena, Peter, 53
Giannini, Vittorio, 298
Gibson, Benn, 282
Ginagiulio, Richard, 127
Glandorf, Charles, 144
Glasgow, Robert, 297-98
Glass, Henry, Jr., 14
Goldman, Richard Franko, 68
Goodman, Joseph, 287
Goossen, Frederic, 109
Goss, Madeleine, 46
Gramm, Donald, 178-79
Gräter, M., 115
Gray, Peter, 159
Gress, Ed, 213
Grisham, Connie, 48
Grobe, Dalos W., 152
Grover, Neil, 243
Gruen, John, 201
Guillou, Jean, 292
Gustafson, Bruce, 43, 53, 75, 101, 137, 201, 226, 240,
    249, 285, 297

Haglund, Rolf, 39
Haines, Aubrey B., 260
Haller, William, 6, 39, 104, 115, 232
Hambro, Leonid, 176
Hamilton, Jerald, 10
Hamilton, Stephen, 61
Hancock, Gerre, 128, 186, 218
Hantz, Edwin, 7
Harbach, Barbara, 184
Harrison, Jay S., 68
Hartmann, Hans, 255
Haskins, James, 176
Hatten, Robert S., 116
Hawke, H. William, 277
Hayashi, Yuko, 264
Haydon, Glen, 221
Hayes, Laurence, Melton, 162
Heaton, Charles Huddleston, 14, 43
Heindl, Christian, 136

Index

Heintze, James R., 19
Helm, Everett, 263, 318, 320
Hemke, Frederick, 282
Henderson, Charles, 232
Henessee, Don A., 21
Hentoff, Nat, 263
Herman, H. David, 28
Herrenschwand, Franz, 238
Hertzog, Christian, 77
Hesford, Bryan, 10
Heyman, Barbara B., 21
Hibbard, William, 318
Hiemenz, Jack, 40
Higgs, David, 136, 249
Hillert, Richard, 50
Hinshaw, Donald G., 87
Hinson, Maurice, 252
Hitchcock, H. Wiley, 68, 109
Hitchens, Susan H., 109, 151
Hixon, Don, 19
Hodkinson, Sidney, 40
Hoffmann, James A., 263
Holloway, Clyde, 65
Holtz, John, 72, 85, 148, 214
Horowitz, Is, 68
Houkom, Alf S., 116
Houston, John, 120
Howell, Richard D., 10
Howerton, Beverly, 213
Hubler, Lyn Helen, 87
Huddleston, Robert, 65
Huff, Harry, 136
Hughes, Edward D., 54
Humphreys, Henry S., 139
Hunt, Eileen, 253-54
Hurd, David, 285
Husa, Karel, 328
Huston, John, 29
Hutton, Edna Raitt, 160

Jackson, Douglas, 86
Jacobson, Robert, 101
James, Richard, 52
James, Shaylor L., 162
Jensen, Wilma, 4, 248, 282-83
Johns, Daniel, 174
Johns, Donald, 242
Johns, Michele, 17

Johnson, Ellen S., 24
Johnson, Gerald, 127
Joie et clarté des corps glorieux (Messiaen), 305
Jones, Bruce, 16-17, 128, 233, 236
Jones, Martin, 73
Jones, Pamela Janine, 325
Joyce, Donald, 8, 56
Jungas, Lois, 120
Junkerman, Charles, 54

Kastendieck, Miles, 265, 318
Kay, Norman, 68
Kehl, Roy, 7
Keiser, Marilyn, 39, 65, 182-83, 247
Kelsey, Howard, 152
Kimberling, Victoria J., 83
King, Larry, 137, 168
Kirkpatrick, John, 21, 68
Knapp, Joel Davis, 207
Kneareem, Ralph, 4
Koeser, W., 255
Kohlenberg, Lee, 106
Kolodin, Irving, 172, 252
Kom, Angela, 17
Kostelanetz, Richard, 54
Koukios, Ann Marie, 153
Kratzenstein, Marilou, 7, 29, 101, 137, 226, 264, 285, 297
Kreitner, Kenneth, 297
Krellwitz, Janet, 48
Kremenliev, Boris, 279
Kremer, Rudolph, 226
Kresky, Jeffrey, 318
Kriewald, James, 72
Kupferberg, H., 116
Kushner, David Z., 154
Kyle, Marguerite K., 3, 19, 23-25, 31, 34, 38, 40, 44, 47, 57, 64-65, 68-69, 71-73, 79, 81, 84-86, 89, 91-97, 101, 106-10, 112, 116, 118, 120-21, 127-32, 144, 148, 154-55, 160-61, 163, 165-67, 176-77, 179, 185-86, 189, 192-93, 202-04, 209, 212, 229, 233, 242-44, 246-48, 252, 266-67, 271, 275, 277-80, 286, 288, 294, 298, 307, 313, 318-19, 322, 327

L'Orgue mystique (Tournemire), 315
Laidman, Janet Loretta, 78
Lamentations of Jeremiah: The Roads to Zion Shall Mourn (Purvis), 292

About the Author

SHARON L. HETTINGER (née Simons) was born in Michigan and now lives in Lawrence, Kansas, with her husband Lyle. She earned the M.M. in church music in 1989 and D.M.A. in organ in 1993, University of Kansas. She also had received the B.M. in church music at Westminster Choir College in 1978, where she won the Alexander McCurdy organ competition four years earlier. Her organ teachers include Walter R. Ginter, Donald McDonald, and James Higdon. She has been organist and choir director in Mobile, Alabama, Durham, North Carolina, and also played recitals in New Jersey, North Carolina, Alabama, Missouri, and Michigan, in addition to Kansas. She has been dean of the Topeka chapter, and now is the AGO convener for the state of Kansas. In the fall of 1995 she held a temporary position teaching organ and music theory at Bethany College, Lindsborg, Kansas. Presently she is copywriter for the concert series of the Lied Center, University of Kansas, and organist and associate director of music, Christ Episcopal Church, in the Kansas City suburb of Overland Park.